T0238808

Lecture Notes in Computer Scie

Cesare Pautasso Éric Tanter (Eds.)

Software Composition

7th International Symposium, SC 2008
Budapest, Hungary, March 29-30, 2008
Proceedings

Springer

Volume Editors

Cesare Pautasso
University of Lugano
Faculty of Informatics
via Buffi 13, 6900 Lugano, Switzerland
E-mail: c.pautasso@ieee.org

Éric Tanter
University of Chile
Computer Science Department
PLEIAD Lab, Blanco Encalada 2120, Santiago, Chile
E-mail: etanter@dcc.uchile.cl

Library of Congress Control Number: 2008923183

CR Subject Classification (1998): D.2, D.1.5, D.3, F.3

LNCS Sublibrary: SL 2 – Programming and Software Engineering

ISSN 0302-9743
ISBN-10 3-540-78788-7 Springer Berlin Heidelberg New York
ISBN-13 978-3-540-78788-4 Springer Berlin Heidelberg New York

Springer is a part of Springer Science+Business Media

springer.com

Printed in Germany

Typesetting: Camera-ready by author, data conversion by Scientific Publishing Services, Chennai, India
Printed on acid-free paper SPIN: 12244508 06/3180 5 4 3 2 1 0

Preface

The goal of the International Symposia on Software Composition is to advance the state of the research in component-based software development. We focus on the challenges related to component development, reuse, verification and, of course, composition. Software composition is becoming more and more important as innovation in software engineering shifts from the development of individual components to their reuse and recombination in novel ways.

To this end, for the 2008 edition, researchers were solicited to contribute on topics related to component adaptation techniques, composition languages, calculi and type systems, as well as emerging composition techniques such as aspect-oriented programming, service-oriented architectures, and mashups. In line with previous editions of SC, contributions were sought focusing on both theory and practice, with a particular interest in efforts relating them.

This LNCS volume contains the proceedings of the 7th International Symposium on Software Composition, which was held on March 29–30, 2008, as a satellite event of the European Joint Conferences on Theory and Practice of Software (ETAPS), in Budapest, Hungary.

We received 90 initial submissions from all over the world, out of which 70 were considered for evaluation by a Program Committee consisting of 30 international experts. Among these submissions, we selected 13 long papers and 6 short papers to be included in the proceedings and presented at the conference. Each paper went through a thorough revision process and was reviewed by three to five reviewers. This ensured the necessary quality for publishing these proceedings in time for the event, a first in the history of the symposium.

We would like to thank all the authors of submitted papers for their hard work. The ever growing number of submissions since the beginning of SC, shows that this forum is gaining importance in the area. We are very grateful to the members of the Program Committee as well as to the external reviewers for providing high-quality recommendations that enabled us to select a set of diverse and excellent papers. This has been a key point contributing to the success of SC 2008. Finally, we would like to express our gratitude to the European Network of Excellence on Aspect-Oriented Software Development (AOSD-Europe); the International Federation for Information Processing, Technical Committee on Software: Theory and Practice (IFIP, TC 2); the IBM Zurich Research Lab; and the Information and Communication Systems research group at ETH Zurich for supporting this event. Finally we would like to thank the organizers of ETAPS 2008 for hosting and providing an excellent organizational framework for SC 2008.

March 2008

Cesare Pautasso
Éric Tanter

Organization

Program Chairs

Cesare Pautasso, University of Lugano, Switzerland
Éric Tanter, University of Chile, Chile

Program Committee

Uwe Assmann, Dresden University of Technology, Germany
Alexandre Bergel, Trinity College, Dublin, Ireland
Judith Bishop, University of Pretoria, South Africa
Thierry Coupaye, France Télécom, France
Flavio De Paoli, University of Milan, Italy
Theo D'Hondt, Vrije Universiteit Brussel, Belgium
Wolfgang Emmerich, University College London, UK
Johan Fabry, University of Chile, Chile
Harald Gall, University of Zurich, Switzerland
Carlo Ghezzi, Politecnico di Milano, Italy
Thomas Gschwind, IBM Zurich Research Lab, Switzerland
Volker Gruhn, Universität Leipzig, Germany
Thomas Gschwind, IBM Zurich Research Lab, Switzerland
Robert Hirschfeld, Hasso-Plattner-Institut, University of Potsdam, Germany
Nigel Horspool, University of Victoria, Canada
Mehdi Jazayeri, University of Lugano, Switzerland
Luigi Liquori, INRIA, France
Welf Löwe, Växjö University, Sweden
Markus Lumpe, Iowa State University, USA
Jacques Noyé, École des Mines de Nantes, France
Manuel Oriol, ETH Zurich, Switzerland
Claus Pahl, Dublin City University, Ireland
Damien Pollet, Université de Savoie, France
Awais Rashid, Lancaster University, UK
Mario Südholt, École des Mines de Nantes, France
Clemens Szyperski, Microsoft, USA
Wim Vanderperren, VU Brussels, Belgium
Kurt C. Wallnau, Carnegie Mellon, USA
Roel Wuyts, IMEC and KULeuven, Belgium

Referees

Shahid Alam
Jesper Andersson
Malte Appeltauer
Domenico Bianculli
Matthias Book
Amancio Bouza
Rhodes Brown
Tobias Brueckmann
Neil Burroughs
Alberto Ciaffaglione
Marco Comerio
Rémi Douence
Morgan Ericsson
Pascal Fradet
Florence Germain
Emanuel Giger
Giacomo Ghezzi
Hervé Grall
Michael Haupt
Florian Heidenreich
Tahar Jarboui
Ugo de' Liguoro
Andrea Maurino
Marino Miculan
Joost Noppen
Marc Poulhies
Didier Parigot
Michela Pedroni
David Pereira
Marco Piccioni
Guillaume Pothier
Claudia Raibulet
Sebastian Richly
Romain Robbes
Ilie Savga
Jean-Guy Schneider
Clemens Schäfer
Mirko Seifert
Rodolfo Toledo
Carla Marina Vairetti
Alessandro Warth
Richard Wettel
Michael Wuersch
Yu Zhou

Steering Committee

Uwe Assmann, Dresden University of Technology, Germany
Judith Bishop, University of Pretoria, South Africa
Thomas Gschwind, IBM Zurich Research Lab, Switzerland
Oscar Nierstrasz, University of Berne, Switzerland
Mario Südholt, École des Mines de Nantes, France

Table of Contents

Composition Languages

Composition Middleware

Service Composition

Performance Optimization

Applications

Aspect-Oriented Programming

Growing a Language: The GLoo Perspective

Markus Lumpe

Faculty of Information & Communication Technologies
Swinburne University of Technology
P.O. Box 218
Hawthorn, VIC 3122, Australia
mlumpe@swin.edu.au

Abstract. The design of programming languages is, in general, geared towards *accumulation* rather than *composition* of features. However, by adding an ever-increasing number of built-in abstractions, any programming language is eventually at risk to reach a critical mass at which it may become increasingly difficult for designers to maintain and for developers to use an evolving language appropriately. To tackle this *language design paradox*, we have developed GLoo, a small open-ended dynamic language, whose design philosophy aims at a unified approach in which program and language evolution result directly from the definition of *extensible domain sub-languages*. Surprisingly, these extensible domain sub-languages not only provide a framework to capture domain expertise, but also give rise to a powerful compositional model for language extension. To demonstrate the effectiveness of this approach, we develop the *Language of Namespaces and Traits* in this paper. We define this extensible domain sub-language as an aggregate of various forms of object-oriented language support. Using the *Language of Namespaces and Traits* as example, we show that GLoo's extension model plays a crucial role in achieving a flexible compositional approach for the design of readily-available and extensible programming abstractions.

1 Introduction

A major contributing factor for the success or failure of a software system is not only our understanding of the underlying problem domain, but also the choices of programming languages and their support in the target environment. This poses a particular challenge for language designers, who often have to choose between the features that a language has to provide and the ones that would make the language more versatile. A well-designed programming language can yield a creative medium for making programmers write good programs easily [19]. An overloaded language, on the other hand, may increase the likelihood of occurrences of awkward or lengthy formulations as developers find it more difficult to proactively organize their solutions within the framework provided by the language.

But how do we assess language features in practice? What are the practical means to implement, test, and incorporate new language abstractions into an existing programming language? In addition, the design of industrial-strength programming languages is, in general, geared towards *accumulation* rather than *composition* of language features [12]. However, by adding an ever-increasing number of built-in abstractions any

C. Pautasso and É. Tanter (Eds.): SC 2008, LNCS 4954, pp. 1–19, 2008.

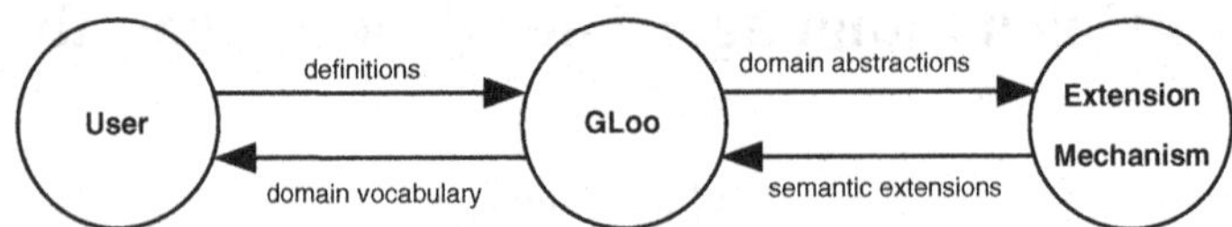

Fig. 1. The GLOO language extension model

programming language is eventually at risk to reach a critical mass at which it may become increasingly difficult to formally define, use, and maintain the language [25]. So, can we construct more effective means to "fine-tune" the level of abstraction provided by a programming language in order to avoid overwhelming both the programming language and the application programmer?

To study and experiment with different means of language support for software composition, we have developed GLOO [16, 15], a small open-ended dynamic pure functional language with a built-in extension mechanism to grow the language on demand. GLOO allows for both rapid language prototyping and the definition of readily available language abstractions. For example, we have defined the *Language of Java Services* [16] and the *Language of Traits* [15], two extensible domain sub-languages that provide an interface to incorporate existing Java software artifacts (i.e., Java classes and objects) and the concept of traits [24] into the GLOO framework. These *domain sub-languages* greatly benefit from the extension mechanism embedded in GLOO that is a key ingredient for the definition of arbitrary domain abstractions ranging from new data types to complex programming constructs in order to yield a *user-centric* view of the targeted problem domain.

The GLOO model for language extension induces two processes: *decomposition* and *abstraction*. The result of the decomposition phase is a set of *meta-level* domain abstractions that implement required core data types and their relationships in the problem domain, whereas the abstraction step yields a high-level and user-centric *domain vocabulary* to represent a desired specific aspect (or *view*) of the underlying problem domain [16]. The resulting domain sub-languages serve as fined-grained extensions to the GLOO language and can be viewed as subjects [21] or *compositional styles* [2] that encapsulate sets of first-class development artifacts to assist developers in solving problems in a given domain in a more efficient and convenient way. A schematic view of this technique is shown in Figure 1.

In this work our focus is on rapid prototyping of object- and class-based language extensions using *continuation-passing-style* (CPS). Rapid prototyping is a viable engineering technique to explore and validate desirable system characteristics of software products in a flexible and agile manner. Dynamic programming languages with their emphasis on developer productivity and software quality provide a good fit for the required programming approach. However, with the exception of Scheme or Smalltalk, languages are seldom used or designed to study programming language concepts in itself.

To explore how GLOO can be used to this purpose we define the *Language of Namespaces and Traits* in this paper. More precisely, we demonstrate how to specify the *Language of Namespaces and Traits* as aggregations of smaller domain sub-languages using the concept of *mini parsers*. Mini parsers are *guarded continuations* that mimic the parsing process of the underlying syntactic categories. The names of these guarded continuations serve as keywords in the defined sub-language, whereas their bodies define *reusable parsing automata* for the corresponding associated keywords. We use the characterization of "reusable" to denote the fact that the guards of parsing automata are defined over equivalence classes of *permissible continuations*, which allows us to recombine mini parsers to accept new syntactic forms on demand.

The benefit of defining and evaluating language extensions this way is two-fold. First, the integration of new features into an existing language may impact the underlying language processor to an extent at which language experimentation becomes not feasible anymore. GLoo does not suffer from this problem, as its fine-grained scoping mechanisms provide us with the means to control the impact and visibility of different and, in general, orthogonal language features. Second, the notion of permissible continuations enables us to compose arbitrary mini parsers by locally defining corresponding equivalence classes, a technique that yields a natural approach for language composition.

The rest of this paper is organized as follows: in Section 2, we illustrate the main features of the GLoo programming model. In the Sections 3 and 4, we discuss the details of defining language extensions in GLoo. We present a model for the *Language of Namespaces and Traits* in Section 5. We proceed with a brief review of related work in Section 6 and conclude with a summary of our main observations in Section 7.

2 Abstraction Definition in GLoo

GLoo is a statically scoped language that uses *call-by-value* as default parameter passing mode. The core language of GLoo is based on $\lambda\mathcal{F}$ [14], a variant of the λ-calculus that combines the concepts of *dynamic name resolution*, *explicit namespaces*, and *foreign code gateway* in a single formal framework. Dynamic name resolution and explicit namespaces both are crucial for a software development approach enabling a controlled admission of new functionality into an existing software base [6]. The foreign code gateway, on the other hand, allows for an easy integration of *glue code* that is required to provide operational support for new language mechanisms [15].

There is however an important aspect to the semantics of name resolution that is unique to GLoo. GLoo permits for the occurrences of *unbound* names in expressions. Unbound names are placeholders for values that may be defined in the future. Unbound names are not to confused with free names that result in open expressions. In GLoo, every expression is closed, even the ones containing unbound names. An expression with occurrences of unbound names is subject to *incremental refinement* [16] that makes it possible for programmers to alter the meaning of an expression depending on the eventual existence of suitable declarations for unbound names. This concept is similar to the way content types are handled in Web-browsers. If a Web-browser defines a specific handler for a given content type, then this handler is invoked. Otherwise, the browser triggers the default behavior or may even ignore that content type altogether. In GLoo, every expression is evaluated with respect to an actual evaluation context to assign meaning to occurrences of unbound names. If that context does not define a mapping for the occurrence of an unbound name, then that occurrence is substituted with the empty behavior.

The main programming entity in GLoo is a *specification unit*, defining a value or *component* that can be recombined with additional values or components exported by other specification units. GLoo specification units add basic data types, an import facility, term sequences, expression trees, computable binders, and a *Java gateway mechanism* to the core language. In essence, a GLoo specification unit declares a local scope for both the import of exported abstractions from other units and the definition of new abstractions that all contribute to the value exported by the current specification unit.

```
let
  load "OpenExtensibleImperativeClass.lf"
  load "LanguageOfNamespacesAndTraits.lf"
  load "System/Services.lf"

  StackNS = load "SampleNS.lf"
in
  Namespace TraceNS
    Import Stack of StackNS
       method top (\()::  println "Calling top...";
                          super.top (||))
    endImport

    apply (use TReadInt of SampleNS) to Stack
  endNamespace
end
```

Listing 1. The namespace TraceNS in GLoo

Consider Listing 1 that depicts the use of the *Language of Namespaces and Traits*. The specification in this example defines the namespace TraceNS. This namespace exports one class, Stack, that is a refinement of class Stack imported from namespace SampleNS. In namespace TraceNS the class Stack is modified twice: we (i) define method top as an extension to class Stack and (ii) apply trait TReadInt to it. As a result, in namespace TraceNS we obtain a new version of class Stack that provides all inherited members defined by class Stack in namespace SampleNS, overrides method top, and guarantees a sound composition with trait TReadInt.

The structure of TraceNS is typically for programming abstractions defined at the *application level* in GLoo. Even though GLoo offers only a few basic constructs, these language elements suffice to define high-level programming features to build domain software artifacts easily. The core elements that enable this particular application level paradigm are *functions* and *function composition*. More precisely, the structure-giving elements are all functions (e.g., Namespace, Import, of, method, or endImport), whose names serve as domain-specific keywords, whereas the function bodies implement continuations that define the semantics and the corresponding verification rules of the modeled language features. By composing related *keyword functions* we obtain a desired new language element and assign it a concrete syntax and semantics. Moreover, these language elements remain *extensible* and can, therefore, be recombined to yield support for other language abstractions.

However, GLoo is also an open-ended programming language. Therefore, rather than providing a rich set of predefined operators and statements, GLoo only defines syntactic support for them. To give operators semantics or to add new language constructs like conditionals, loops, or assignment, one has to define *language extensions* to *borrow* appropriate and matching behavior from outside the language. This approach allows for an easy integration of new domain data types into the language and to fine-tune the existing language features to specific user needs.

```
%{ // auxiliary Java runtime representation of Cell data type
   class CellValue extends LiteralValue
   {
    private Value val;

    public Value get()               { return val; }
    public void set( Value v )       { val = v; }
    public CellValue( Value v )      { val = v; }
    public String toString()         { return val.toString(); }
   }
}%

let
 // gateway functions
 makeCell= %{ return new CellValue( aArg ); }%

 get= %{ Value c = EpsilonValue.EPS;
         try { c = ((CellValue)aArg).get(); }
         catch (FormException e) { Main.error( e.getMessage() ); }
         return c;                                                  }%

 set = %{ try { CellValue c = (CellValue)aArg.select("cell");
                Value   v = aArg.select( "value" );
                c.set( v ); }
          catch (FormException e) { Main.error( e.getMessage() ); }
          return EpsilonValue.EPS;                                  }%
in
 // exported Cell data type
 (| Cell = (\val:: (| get = (\()::get this),
                      set = (\nval::set (| cell = this, value = nval |)) |)
                    [(| this = makeCell val |)]) |)
end
```

Listing 2. A mutable `Cell` abstraction

One such language extension is `Cell`, as shown in Listing 2. The unit defining the `Cell` abstraction consists of three parts: (i) the definition of the auxiliary Java code that defines the (inner) Java class `CellValue`, (ii) the local declaration of the gateway functions `makeCell`, `get`, and `set`, and (iii) the definition of the exported function `Cell`, a data type constructor for mutable storage cells.

GLoo provides an explicit means to directly incorporate Java code into the scope of a specification unit in form of *gateway code*. Gateway code is enclosed in `%{...}%` and treated as a single token by the GLoo compiler. The GLoo compiler assembles the gateway code in a corresponding Java support class and emits appropriate linkage code to bridge between the GLoo and the Java world [16, 15]. In case of the `Cell` abstraction, the gateway code comprises of the definitions for `CellValue`, a class derived from the GLoo runtime type `LiteralValue` to obtain a mutable container value type, the data type constructor `makeCell`, and the property methods `get` and `set`.

We define `Cell` as a wrapper function that returns a programming interface to `CellValue`. The body of `Cell` contains an expression of the form `a[b]`, called *context*, which denotes a term `a` whose meaning depends on the values defined in `b` if `a` contains free variables. In the case of `Cell`, the context

```
[(| this = makeCell val |)]
```

defines a binding for the variable `this`, which occurs free in the bodies of the functions bound to the exported names `get` and `set`. The effect of this context specification is that both functions share the common value `this` and since `this` is a mutable storage cell, we add *side effects* to the getter and setter.

The particular value of the `Cell` extension is that it adds a stateful programming abstraction to the GLOO language. As a pure functional language, GLOO does not possess any built-in support for assignment. However, certain approaches (e.g. object-oriented programming) are naturally *imperative* and allow or require operations to perform side effects on the state of other program entities [1]. It is one of the strengths of GLOO to accommodate *orthogonal* programming features while providing well-defined scopes within which these features are available and may impact each other. In the case of the `Cell` abstraction, the modeled assignment abstraction appears to be in fundamental conflict with GLOO's declarative programming model. However, the actual `Cell` object is implemented by means of a *read-only* literal value (i.e., an instance of class `CellValue`, a user-defined class derived from the GLOO runtime class `LiteralValue`) that hides its state-altering capability from clients of the `Cell` abstraction.

One of the rather subtle aspects in defining extensible software abstractions is *naming*. The choice of names can greatly effect our ability to recombine existing software artifacts as name clashes may occur. Also, sometimes we may not know the precise set of names to access individual features of software abstractions. For this reason, GLOO provides *computable binders*, expressions enclosed in the symbols { and }, that allow for both discovery and construction of names (i.e., labels of a namespace) at runtime.

```
let
 fix = (\F::h (| {FName} = h |))
        [(| h = (\FX::F (\Arg::(FX.{FName} FX) Arg)) |)]
in
 (\$Name:: (\FName:: (\F::fix (\{FName}::F))) (getIdString Name))
end
```

Listing 3. The recursive function builder `Rec`

A typical application of computable binders occurs in recursive functions. By design, GLOO does not provide a built-in support for the definition of recursive abstractions. We can, however, define a simple recursive function builder, as shown Listing 3. The recursive function builder `Rec` consists of two parts: (i) the local declaration of the *call-by-value* fixed-point combinator `fix` and (ii) the exported definition of `Rec`, which constructs the proper recursive image of its argument function `F`. Both parts rely on computable binders. In the case of `Rec`, the computable binder { `FName` } enables *self-application* within the body of the recursive function being defined. For example, to build a recursive image of a function `F` we write `Rec self F`, which is an expression that yields a function in which `self` is the name of `F` in the function's body.

The feature that enables this particular technique is *delayed term evaluation* that enables us to defer the evaluation of arguments to functions until their value is actually being required [15]. Hence, when using delayed term evaluation, we have to ability to explicitly define *lazy evaluation* of function arguments. The need for delayed term evaluation arises, for example, from choice functions like conditionals in which the individual branches must not be evaluated before the corresponding guard evaluates to true. We use the symbol `$` to mark an expression delayed. Prefixing an expression `e` with the symbol `$` yields the *expression tree* of `e`. An expression tree comprises of the syntax tree of the denoted value and its lifetime *evaluation context history* to maintain static scoping.

Expression trees for identifiers are of particular interest, as they enable, in combination with incremental refinement, a *macro mechanism* [23]. Incremental refinement allows for *open* sub-expressions in both function bodies and actual function arguments. The idea behind this concept is that the target environment for the evaluation of a function may provide specific local bindings for occurrences of free names. For example, `fix` contains two free occurrences of `FName`. This enables `fix` to "adapt" to any function name. The purpose of `fix` is to generate the required repetitive structure of a recursive function, but the function name is not known at point of the declaration of `fix`. By placing `fix` underneath the binder `(\FName::(\F::fix ...))`, we capture `FName` and associate it with the name of the function being constructed to achieve the desired recursive linkage. The actual value of `FName` is the string denoted by the expression tree `Name`. We can use the gateway function `getIdString` to obtain the corresponding string representation.

3 Language Composition in GLOO

The definition of new language extensions does not occur in isolation. Programming idioms supported by languages like C# [18], Haskell [5], Java [3], Python [17], Perl [28], Self [26], Scheme [12, 23], Smalltalk [10], or Tcl [22] offer already a wealth of readily available and well-explored programming abstractions. However, only a few systems provide built-in support for *syntactic* and *semantic extensions* to add or experiment with new programming concepts.

GLOO's built-in *compositional* extension mechanism enables developers to amend the language through syntactic extensions, semantic extensions, or both. The main pillar of this compositional approach is the hypothesis that a language must reveal the need for additional features by removing pertinent weaknesses and restrictions [12]. Users supply definitions to model the problem domain to the GLOO compiler. The compiler maps the corresponding domain abstractions to associated representatives in Java support classes. The extension apparatus of GLOO translates those classes into executable

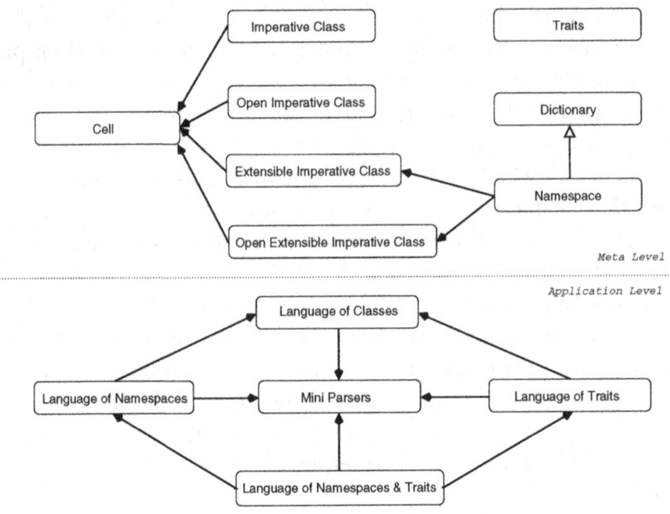

Fig. 2. A model for class-based programming features in GLOO

semantic extensions and loads them into the current GLOO runtime image [16]. Upon completion, the user-supplied definitions yield a domain vocabulary, which captures the modeled problem domain in a user-centric way and therefore facilitates program development for that domain.

Common to all GLOO domain abstractions is that they are composed from a *meta level*, a low-level layer that defines the behavior required to incorporate new domain abstractions into the GLOO runtime system, and an *application level*, a high-level layer that encapsulates the meta level and provides the application programmer with a user-centric domain vocabulary of the modeled domain. To illustrate this approach, consider Figure 2 that depicts the architecture of a set of class-based language extensions. These language extensions provide a Java-like programming model. At the meta level, we define objects, traits, classes, and dictionaries as *first-class* values. Furthermore and in order to obtain an imperative object model, all features use `Cell`. More precisely, *Imperative Class*, *Open Imperative Class*, *Extensible Imperative Class*, *Open Extensible Imperative Class*, *Dictionary*, and *Namespace* all encapsulate a `Cell` object and define an appropriate wrapper to achieve the desired corresponding imperative behavior.

The application level, on the other hand, is composed of *Mini Parsers* and the domain sub-languages *Language of Classes*, *Language of Traits*, *Language of Namespaces*, and *Language of Namespaces and Traits*. The intriguing aspect in the construction of the application level is that none of the defined sub-languages incorporates an object model directly. However, each language contains an occurrence of the unbound name `Class` that refers to a *class builder*. We bind the object model *late*, that is, rather than resolving occurrences of name `Class` within the defining scope, we use incremental refinement and provide a desired meaning in the importing scope. Consider again Listing 1. In this specification, we load the definitions for *Open Extensible Imperative Class* before we include the *Language of Namespaces and Traits* into the specification unit for

`TraceNS`. As a result, we bind `Class` within the scope of *Language of Namespaces and Traits* to the class builder defined by *Open Extensible Imperative Class* and obtain a suitable programming model for the definition of `TraceNS`.

4 Mini Parsers

For the construction of domain sub-languages at the application level we have developed the notion of *composable mini parsers*, which are first-class entities to capture the keywords of a specific syntactic category. Mini parsers provide an ambiguity-free specification format like *Parsing Expression Grammars* (PEGs) [9] to describe the syntactic structure of the underlying problem domain entities. We use continuation-passing-style to specify mini parsers. Moreover, as the mini parsers are defined in GLoo itself, we can avoid the integration of different tools and paradigms [11]. However, GLoo is not a compiler-compiler. Like Scheme [23], GLoo does presently not provide any support to alter or enrich its lexical syntax. As a consequence, we can only use identifiers as structure-giving elements when defining new language extensions.

<*Class*> ::= **'Class'** **'super'** <*Class*> (<*Member*>)* **'endClass'**

<*Member*> ::= [**'static'**] **'var'** <*VariableName*> <*InitValue*>
| [**'static'**|**'protected'**] **'method'** <*MethodName*> <*Function*>

<*Object*> ::= **'new'** <*Class*> <*Initializer*>

Fig. 3. Syntax of the *Language of Classes*

```
method =
 (\AST::
   if (canProceed method AST SUPER_SEEN)
      (\$MethodId::
          isMethodUnique (||);
          (\Body::
             let
               // build new method specification
               method_class = methodLabel (||)
               newAST = (| AST,
                          {method_class} = (| (| AST->{method_class} |),
                                               {getIdString MethodId} = Body |) |)
             in
               (\Cont:: Cont (| newAST, {MODIFIER} = DEFAULT |))
             end))
      (error "Illegal method declaration!"))
```

Listing 4. The mini parser **method** for the *Language of Classes*

Mini parsers define small parsing automata with one explicit state. This state serves as a guard for the body of the mini parser. Consider, for example, Figure 3 that shows the syntax of the *Language of Classes*. This domain sub-language requires a mini parser for the keyword **method**, as shown in Listing 4. After receiving the decorated syntax tree `AST`, a data structure that contains both attribute values and parser status information,

<*Trait*> ::= **'Trait'** <*TraitName*>
((**'method'** <*MethodName*> <*Function*> |
'requires' <*MethodName*> <*MethodName*> <*String*>)*
|
'join' <*Trait*> **'with'** <*Trait*>
|
'refine' <*Trait*> (**'alias'** <*MethodName*> <*MethodName*> |
'exclude' <*MethodName*>)*)
'endTrait'

Fig. 4. Syntax of the *Language of Traits*

we first evaluate the guard for **method**. This guard (i.e., `canProceed`) assures that the actual parser state recorded in `AST` matches `SUPER_SEEN`, which is an explicit state defined for the *Language of Classes* to indicate that we have successfully processed the super type specification for the current class. As *true*-continuation of this guard, we define a function, which consumes `MethodId`, an expression tree for the method identifier, a method body `Body`, and a class continuation `Cont`. In this function we also perform the required semantic checks and construct a new decorated syntax tree. We use *sequencing* (expressions separated by `;`) to compose the individual expressions. Please note that if the check in `isMethodUnique` fails, then the current program will terminate with an error message.

However, rather than just for one state, we define guards for mini parsers to accept an open set of *permissible continuations*. The set of permissible continuations forms an equivalence relation over parser states. By means of the predicate `canProceed`, this equivalence relation allows us to equate related explicit parser states across different domain sub-languages. More precisely, when analyzing the applicability of a mini parser, `canProceed` first compares the actual parser state recorded in `AST` with the target state defined by the mini parser. If both are the same, `canProceed` returns *true* immediately. Otherwise, `canProceed` checks whether the recorded state and the target state are considered equivalent for the current domain sub-language. If this case, `canProceed` returns *true* also, as desired. But if both tests fail, `canProceed` returns *false* and the current mini parser terminates with an error message.

The key mechanism to enable the reuse or composition of an existing mini parser for the definition of a new domain sub-language is our ability to dynamically alter the set of permissible continuations, as required for the definition of the *Language of Traits*. Traits provide a simple compositional approach to factor out common behavior and to easily integrate that behavior soundly into existing classes [24]. A possible way to capture the syntax of the *Language of Traits* is shown in Figure 4. We notice that the syntax for methods resembles closely the one used in the *Language of Classes*. Indeed, we can construct the *Language of Traits* as composition of the *Language of Classes* and trait-releated language elements. In particular, we can reuse the mini parser **method** and recover our previous development effort for the definition of the *Language of Traits*. To accomplish this, we need to declare **method** a permissible continuation for the keyword **Trait** in the *Language of Traits* using the following expression

```
addPermissibleState method IN_TRAIT
```

<Namespace> ::= **'Namespace'** *<NamespaceName>*
(*<Class>* | **'Import'** *<ClassName>* (*<Member>*)* **'endImport'**)*
'endNamespace'

<Class> ::= **'Class'** *<ClassName>* **'super'** *<Class>* (*<Member>*)* **'endClass'**

<ClassName> ::= *<PlainClassName>* **'of'** *<NamespaceName>*

<Object> ::= **'new'** *<ClassName>* *<Initializer>*

Fig. 5. Syntax of the *Language of Namespaces*

The function `addPermissibleState` and its inverse function `removePermissibleState` can be used to enlarge or shrink the set of equivalent explicit parser states for a given mini parser. By adding the explicit state `IN_TRAIT` to the set of equivalent parser states for mini parser **method**, we enable, therefore, **method** to occur within a trait specification.

We can expect that some form of additional configuration is required to make a given mini parser meet the requirements of the new context in which it is being used. The *Language of Traits* is no exception. In the case to the *Language of Traits*, this additional configuration relates to the supported trait operations. A method declaration must not occur in a context other than a *new* trait declaration (i.e., neither in a *join* nor in a *refine* specification). Furthermore, methods are always *public*. No other modifier is permitted. But these criteria can easily be satisfied, as shown in Listing 5. To guarantee that **method** only occurs within the declaration of a new trait, we add an additional guard to **method**. This guard uses the `AST` flag `TRAIT_BUILD`, which records the current trait operation. The value `DEFAULT_TRAIT` means that we are about to define a new trait, whereas `NEW_TRAIT` states that we are currently building a new trait. The exclusion of additional modifiers is standard, as we have not declared them permissible continuations for the keyword `Trait`.

```
method = (\AST::
            if (AST.{TRAIT\_BUILD} == DEFAULT\_TRAIT)
               (method (| AST, {TRAIT\_BUILD} = NEW\_TRAIT |))
               (if (AST.{TRAIT\_BUILD} == NEW_TRAIT)
                   (method AST)
                   (error "Illegal method specification!")))
```

Listing 5. The mini parser **method** for the *Language of Traits*

There is an additional and noteworthy aspect related to the composition of mini parsers and domain sub-languages. The mini parsers **Class** and **Trait** can proceed in *any* state. This is due to the fact that both mini parsers represent the *root* symbol for their corresponding domain sub-language. Root mini parsers do not depend on any explicit state. However, to guarantee composability, root mini parsers take a decorated syntax tree as argument also. But this tree is, in general, empty. When exporting the mini parsers for root symbols, we bind, therefore, `AST` to the *empty value* [14].

5 Language Composition: The *Language of Namespaces and Traits*

We construct the *Language of Namespaces and Traits* in two phases. We first define the *Language of Namespaces* as an extension of the *Language of Classes*. In the second step, we use the *Language of Namespaces* and the *Language of Traits* to build an aggregate of both domain sub-languages to form the *Language of Namespaces and Traits*.

The *Language of Namespaces* is defined in the spirit of the classbox concept [4]. A namespace defines a packaging and scoping mechanism for controlling the visibility of extensions to portions of class-based systems. In particular, (i) a namespace defines an explicitly named scope within which classes, methods, and variables are defined and (ii) namespaces support the local refinement of imported classes by adding or modifying their features without affecting the originating namespace.

The syntax of the *Language of Namespaces* is shown in Figure 5. The *Language of Namespaces* defines an extension to the *Language of Classes*. More precisely, we import the *Language of Classes* into the local scope of the specification unit of the *Language of Namespaces* to provide a default meaning for imported mini parsers and compose it with the required namespace extensions. This language composition involves three major activities:[1]

- define the keywords **Namespace**, **Import**, **of**, **endImport**, and **endNamespace**,
- add namespace-related guards to **Class**, **method**, **var**, and **endClass**, and
- define a new format for the super class specification.

Our compositional approach to language extension reduces greatly the effort required to construct the new language elements. For example, we can reuse all structure-giving elements related to member declarations defined in the *Language of Classes* for the composition of the syntactic category of *class import* in the *Language of Namespaces*. We simply have to define appropriate guards to distinguish the context within which member declarations occur. We use the `AST` flag `EXTENSION` for this purpose. `EXTENSION` is an integer to count the number of methods or variables specified in the *import* mode. In case of a class declaration, this flag is simply ignored.

```
Class = (\AST::
          if (canProceed Class AST IN_NAMESPACE)
             (\$Classname::
                 Class (| AST,
                         { EXTENSION } = (-1),
                         { QID } = buildQualifiedName (getIdString Classname) |) )
             (error "Illegal class declaration!"))
```

Listing 6. The mini parser **Class** for the *Language of Namespaces*

To adapt imported mini parsers to the new requirements, we define appropriate wrapper functions. The wrapper for **Class** is shown in Listing 6. This wrapper guarantees that a class declaration can only occur within a namespace declaration. Furthermore, it also injects the need for an occurrence of a *class name* between the keywords **Class**

[1] In this presentation, we will only highlight the steps required to reuse imported mini parsers.

and **super**. Finally, the wrapper combines the received decorated syntax tree `AST` with the attributes `EXTENSION` and `QID`. The flag `EXTENSION` is set to `-1` to denote the context *class declaration* and `QID` is set to the fully qualified class name of the class being parsed. The reader should note that the original mini parser **Class** (denoted by the name `Class` inside the wrapper) is not affected by the extra `AST` flags, as that mini parser is blind for those additions. The GLoo semantics guarantees, however, a proper forwarding of the additional information through the chain of continuations.

The wrapper for **endClass** (see Listing 7) exhibits a slightly more complex structure. It (i) checks whether the current parser state in `AST` is equivalent to `SUPER_SEEN` and (ii) verifies that **endClass** occurs within a class declaration. If both conditions are met, then we build a new class using the attribute values recorded in `AST` and add that class to the current namespace as a side effect of `buildClass`. At the end of the wrapper, we reset `AST` and return a continuation to accept further class and import declarations or **endNamespace** to close the current namespace specification.

```
endClass = (\AST::
                if ((canProceed endClass AST SUPER_SEEN) &&
                    (AST.{ EXTENSION } == (-1)))
                    (buildClass AST;
                     (\Cont:: Cont (| { STATE } = IN_NAMESPACE,
                                      { NAMESPACE } = AST->{ NAMESPACE },
                                      { THIS_NS } = AST.{ THIS_NS } |) ))
                  (error "Illegal class termination declaration!"))
```

Listing 7. The mini parser **endClass** for the *Language of Namespaces*

The wrappers for **method** and **var** implement a simple bookkeeping mechanism. If a **method** or **var** occurs within a class declaration (i.e., `EXTENSION == (-1)`), then we just forward the `AST` to the original mini parser. Otherwise, we increment the `EXTENSION` count by one and pass the updated decorated syntax tree `AST` to the original mini parser, as shown, for example, in Listing 8 for the mini parser **var**.

```
var = (\AST::
           if (AST.{ EXTENSION } == (-1))
              (var AST)
              (var (| AST, { EXTENSION } = AST.{ EXTENSION } + 1 |)))
```

Listing 8. The mini parser **var** for the *Language of Namespaces*

The final step in the construction of the *Language of Namespaces* is the aggregation of the *Language of Classes* with the newly defined namespace-related elements. This aggregation can be expressed by means of GLoo's *form extension operators* [14, 16]. Informally[2], we can write

Language of Namespaces =
Language of Classes ⊕ namespace extensions [*Language of Classes*]

[2] A detailed technical presentation of this step has been omitted in favor of readability.

<Namespace> ::= **'Namespace'** *<NamespaceName>*
(*<Class>* |
'Import' *<CassName>* (*<Member>*)* **'endImport'** |
<Trait>)*
'endNamespace'

<Class> ::= **'Class'** *<ClassName>* **'super'** *<Class>* (*<Member>*)* **'endClass'**

<ClassName> ::= *<PlainClassName>* **'of'** *<NamespaceName>*

<TraitApplication> ::= **'apply'** *<TraitSelection>* **'to'** *<ClassName>*

<TraitSelection> ::= **'use'** *<Trait>* **'of'** *<NamespaceName>*

<Object> ::= **'new'** *<ClassName>* *<Initializer>*

Fig. 6. Syntax of the *Language of Namespaces and Traits*

to denote the aggregation of the *Language of Namespaces* in which the operator $\oplus$ stands for GLOO's *form binding operator*. More precisely, this aggregation yields a new domain sub-language that is composed of the *Language of Classes* and the newly defined namespace extensions and in what the original *Language of Classes* serves as a local context to resolve occurrence of references to reused mini parsers.

We are now ready to define the *Language of Namespaces and Traits*, whose syntax is shown in Figure 6. This language provides a classbox-like programming model with explicit class extensions in form of traits. The particular value of this language is two-fold. The *Language of Namespaces and Traits*, on one hand, provides us with the means to experiment with different forms of class extensions in one single framework. For example, when using local refinement, class extensions are integrated into its associated class immediately through an import declaration, whereas the definition of traits allows us to reuse or even export extension to classes to refine multiple classes simultaneously.

On the other hand, the *Language of Namespaces and Traits* also presents us with a means to reason about a suitable semantics for extensions to classes and their effects on classes and namespaces. The ability to locally refine classes in a namespace and also to apply traits to the very same classes poses a particular challenge. Both operations are rather orthogonal. When should we perform local refinement and when should we apply traits to classes? Experiments with different semantics definitions of the *Language of Namespaces and Traits* have shown that the most reliable way for the support of both features is to require traits to be applied first to classes. Using this approach we obtain a semantic model for the *Language of Namespaces and Traits* that is backwards compatible with the *Language of Namespaces*. Backwards compatibility enables phased software evolution and, therefore, allows developers to organize their solutions within the framework of the new language gradually.

The required configuration effort to compose the *Language of Namespaces* with the *Language of Traits* is rather minimal. We need to perform the following steps:

- establish the *Language of Namespaces* as local context for the *Language of Traits*,
- define the keyword **apply**, **use**, and **to**,
- define trait-related wrappers for **Class**, **Import**, **endNamespace**, and
- define namespace-related wrappers for **Trait** and **endTrait**.

The first step involves the construction of a proper *chaining* of defined wrappers for mini parsers in the *Language of Namespaces and Traits*. Fortunately, the order in which different wrappers for the same mini parsers occur is unimportant. Each wrapper has to be executed eventually. In the case of the *Language of Namespaces and Traits*, we define that wrappers defined in the *Language of Traits* have to be executed before wrappers for the *Language of Namespaces* are visited. Informally, this behavior is established by the following local context

Language of Traits [*Language of Namespaces*]

that states that all occurrences of names referring to imported mini parsers are now resolved with respect to the *Language of Namespaces*.

The next steps are dedicated to the definition of appropriate wrappers for reused mini parsers. The wrappers for both **Class** and **Import** make the corresponding mini parsers *trait-aware* as shown, for example, for **Class** in Listing 9. Again, the original mini parsers are blind for this extra information. However, the extended state information is needed to obtain the required behavior in the trait-aware mini parser for **method**.

```
Class = (\AST:: Class (| AST, { TRAIT_BUILD } = NEW_TRAIT |))
```

Listing 9. The mini parser **Class** for the *Language of Namespaces and Traits*

The purpose of the wrapper for **endNamespace** in the *Language of Namespaces and Traits* is to *finalize* all classes defined within the current namespace. In other words, we first build a new namespace according to the specification in the *Language of Namespaces* and then update this namespace by composing all classes in the current namespaces with applicable traits.

```
endNamespace = (\AST:: finalizeClasses AST.{ THIS_NS }
                                    (endNamespace AST) AST->trait_applications)
```

Listing 10. The mini parser **endNamespace** for the *Lang. of Namespaces and Traits*

The last two wrappers establish **Trait** and **endTrait** as permissible continuations within a namespace declaration. Moreover, the wrapper for **Trait** adds the required bookkeeping mechanism for members, whereas the wrapper for **endTrait** registers the newly defined trait with the current namespace.

```
Trait = (\AST::
            if (canProceed Trait AST IN_NAMESPACE)
               (Trait (| AST, { EXTENSION } = (-1) |))
               (error "Illegal trait specification!"))
```

Listing 11. The mini parser **Trait** for the *Language of Namespaces and Traits*

```
endTrait = (\AST::
              let
                 qid = buildQualifiedName AST.traitName
              in
                AST->{ NAMESPACE }.add qid (endTrait AST)
              end;
              (\Cont:: Cont (| AST,
                               { STATE } = IN_NAMESPACE,
                               { NAMESPACE } = AST->{ NAMESPACE },
                               { THIS_NS } = AST.{ THIS_NS } |)))
```

Listing 12. The mini parser **endTrait** for the *Language of Namespaces and Traits*

In the final phase, we build the *Language of Namespaces and Traits* again as an aggregation that is captured by the following term

$$\begin{aligned}&\textit{Language of Namespaces and Traits} = \\ &\quad \textit{Language of Namespaces} \oplus \textit{Language of Traits}\ [\textit{Language of Namespaces}] \oplus \\ &\qquad \text{new language elements}\ [\textit{Language of Traits} \oplus \textit{Language of Namespaces}]\end{aligned}$$

In other words, the aggregation of the *Language of Namespaces and Traits* is a new domain sub-language composed from the *Language of Namespaces*, the *Language of Traits*, and the required new language elements whose mini parsers and wrappers start evaluation in the *Language of Traits*, pass through the *Language of Namespaces*, and terminate in the *Language of Classes*.

6 Related Work

Two systems that also provide support for language extension are Camlp5, a preprocessor and pretty-printer for OCaml [7], and Polyglot, an extensible compiler front-end for the Java programming language [20]. Camlp5 allows for the admission of new elements to and even the redefinition of the whole syntax of OCaml. Language extensions in Camlp5 are defined by means of extensible *grammar entries* that encapsulate stream parsers. Each grammar entry is associated with a corresponding scanner and grammar specification. Therefore, Camlp5 also permits the admission of new lexical elements that gives Camlp5 the flavor of a compiler-compiler. However, the scope of language extensions is restricted to the defining grammar entries. As a consequence, language extension by means of composing grammar entries is not possible.

Polyglot, on the other hand, aims at constructing extensible Java compilers. More precisely, Polyglot provides an extensible compiler for the Java base language. In the Polyglot framework, language extensions are defined as source-to-source compilers [20] that translate programs using language extensions to Java source code. For this purpose, Polyglot includes an *extensible parser generator* that enables one to specify language extensions as a set of changes to the Java base language. To assign language extensions a semantics or to alter the meaning of a given language element, Polyglot provides the AST `Node` interface and optionally allows for the refinement of existing AST node classes. Polyglot's AST rewriting mechanism guarantees a proper integration of defined language extensions in the Java base language.

Our technique of defining composable mini parsers is very similar to *parser combinators* [13], which are, in general, modeled using monads [5]. Unfortunately, not every programming feature can be modeled by monads [27]. The continuation-based approach presented here appears to not exhibit this problem even though several abstractions mimic monads. For example, `Cell` exhibits a semantics very similar to the `IO` monad, whereas the keyword continuations resemble the structure of the `STATE` monad.

Flatt et al. [8] have recently presented a comprehensive approach to incorporate object-oriented abstraction into Scheme in a purely compositional fashion. The techniques used by Flatt et al. are similar to the ones presented in this work, though the Scheme extensions are defined by means of macros [12, 23].

7 Conclusion

A major challenge in programming language design is to find the right balance between the features a new programming language has to provide and the ones that would make the new language more versatile. We advocate a compositional language design that allows for the definition of domain sub-languages, which provides support for the definition of a user-centric domain vocabulary for the underlying problem domain. This user-centric domain vocabulary can greatly simplify the comprehension, design, implementation, evolution, and reuse of readily available software artifacts. In this paper, we have illustrated how GLoo supports the compositional language design approach by defining a set of class-based language extensions. We have also demonstrated that *composable mini parsers* can be used as an enabling technology to seamlessly integrate domain sub-languages into GLoo.

Table 1. Matching object models

Domain Sub-Language	***Object Model***
Language of Classes	*Imperative Class*
Language of Traits	*Extensible Imperative Class*
Language of Namespaces	*Open Imperative Class*
Language of Namespaces and Traits	*Open Extensible Imperative Class*

In general, the most crucial ingredient in defining language support for object-oriented programming is the design of a suitable object model [1, 8, 26, 24, 4, 15]. However, the underlying object model for the language extensions presented in this work is secondary by design. We can assign each defined domain sub-language a specific object model, as shown in Table 1. But we are not required to do so, as each language is designed without targeting a particular object model. The framework provided by our object-oriented domain sub-languages is based on a compositional language design. We can, therefore, supply an appropriate and desired object model later, when all application-specific requirements are known.

GLoo provides a suitable environment for *language prototyping* in a very direct way. Unlike Scheme [23] that relies on *hygienic macros* for the definition of language extensions, we can define language extensions in GLOO naturally in terms of functions and function composition. In addition, GLOO provides a scoping mechanism that allows for a fine-grained control of the visibility of language extensions. In Scheme, for example, language extensions have to be incorporated into the system at top level, which means that language extension have global impact.

References

1. Abadi, M., Cardelli, L.: A Theory of Objects. Springer, Heidelberg (1996)
2. Achermann, F.: Forms, Agents and Channels: Defining Composition Abstraction with Style. PhD thesis, University of Bern, Institute of Computer Science and Applied Mathematics (January 2002)
3. Arnold, K., Gosling, J.: The Java Programming Language. Addison-Wesley, Reading (1996)
4. Bergel, A., Ducasse, S., Nierstrasz, O., Wuyts, R.: Classboxes: Controlling Visibility of Class Extensions. Journal of Computer Languages, Systems & Structures 31(3-4), 107–126 (2005)
5. Bird, R.: Introduction to Functional Programming using Haskell, 2nd edn. Prentice Hall, Englewood Cliffs (1998)
6. Dami, L.: A Lambda-Calculus for Dynamic Binding. Theoretical Computer Science 192, 201–231 (1998)
7. de Rauglaudre, D.: Camlp5 - Reference Manual. Institut National de Recherche en Informatique et Automatique, Rocquencourt (January 2008)
8. Flatt, M., Findler, R.B., Felleisen, M.: Scheme with Classes, Mixins, and Traits. In: Kobayashi, N. (ed.) APLAS 2006. LNCS, vol. 4279, pp. 270–289. Springer, Heidelberg (2006)
9. Ford, B.: Parsing Expression Grammars: A Recognition-Based Syntactic Foundation. In: Proceedings of POPL 2004, pp. 111–122. ACM Press, New York (2004)
10. Goldberg, A., Robson, D.: Smalltalk-80: The Language. Addison-Wesley, Reading (1989)
11. Hughes, J.: Why Functional Programming Matters. Computer Journal 32(2), 98–107 (1989)
12. Kelsey, R., Clinger, W., Rees, J. (eds.): Revised^5 Report on the Algorithmic Language Scheme. ACM SIGPLAN Notices, 33(9) (September 1998)
13. Leijen, D., Meijer, E.: Parsec: Direct Style Monadic Parser Combinators for the Real World. Technical Report UU-CS-2001-27, Department of Computer Science, Universiteit Utrecht (2001)
14. Lumpe, M.: A Lambda Calculus With Forms. In: Gschwind, T., Aßmann, U., Nierstrasz, O. (eds.) SC 2005. LNCS, vol. 3628, pp. 73–88. Springer, Heidelberg (2005)
15. Lumpe, M.: GLoo: A Framework for Modeling and Reasoning About Component-Oriented Language Abstractions. In: Gorton, I., Heineman, G.T., Crnković, I., Schmidt, H.W., Stafford, J.A., Szyperski, C.A., Wallnau, K. (eds.) CBSE 2006. LNCS, vol. 4063, pp. 17–32. Springer, Heidelberg (2006)
16. Lumpe, M.: Application = Components + GLoo. Electronic Notes in Theoretical Computer Science 182, 123–138 (2007)
17. Lutz, M.: Programming Python, 3rd edn. O'Reilly (2006)
18. Microsoft Corporation. C# Version 3.0 Specification. Microsoft Corporation, Redmond, WA (May 2006)
19. Mitchell, J.C.: Concepts in Programming Languages. Cambridge University Press, Cambridge (2003)
20. Nystrom, N., Clarkson, M.R., Myers, A.C.: Polyglot: An Extensible Compiler Framework for Java. In: Hedin, G. (ed.) CC 2003. LNCS, vol. 2622, pp. 138–152. Springer, Heidelberg (2003)

21. Ossher, H., Harrison, W., Budinsky, F., Simmonds, I.: Subject-Oriented Programming: Supporting Decentralized Development of Objects. In: Proceedings of the 7th IBM Conference on Object-Oriented Technology (July 1994)
22. Ousterhout, J.K.: Tcl and the Tk Toolkit. Addison-Wesley, Reading (1994)
23. PLT Scheme (2006), `http://www.plt-scheme.org`
24. Schärli, N., Ducasse, S., Nierstrasz, O., Black, A.: Traits: Composable Units of Behavior. In: Cardelli, L. (ed.) ECOOP 2003. LNCS, vol. 2743, pp. 248–274. Springer, Heidelberg (2003)
25. Steele, G.L.: Growing a Language. Higher-Order and Symbolic Computation 12, 221–236 (1999)
26. Ungar, D., Smith, R.B.: SELF: The Power of Simplicity. In: Proceedings OOPSLA 1987. ACM SIGPLAN Notices, vol. 22, pp. 227–242 (December 1987)
27. Wadler, P.: Monads and composable continuations. List and Symbolic Computation 7, 39–56 (1993)
28. Wall, L., Christiansen, T., Orwant, J.: Programming Perl, 3rd edn. O'Reilly & Associates (July 2000)

Superimposition: A Language-Independent Approach to Software Composition

Sven Apel and Christian Lengauer

Department of Informatics and Mathematics
University of Passau, Germany
{apel, lengauer}@uni-passau.de

Abstract. Superimposition is a composition technique that has been applied successfully in several areas of software development. In order to unify several languages and tools that rely on superimposition, we present an underlying language-independent model that is based on *feature structure trees (FSTs)*. Furthermore, we offer a tool, called FST-Composer, that composes software components represented by FSTs. Currently, the tool supports the composition of components written in Java, Jak, XML, and plain text. Three nontrivial case studies demonstrate the practicality of our approach.

1 Introduction

Software composition is the process of constructing software systems from a set of components. It aims at improving the reusability, customizability, and maintainability of large software systems.

One popular approach to software composition is superimposition. *Superimposition* is the process of composing software artifacts of different components by merging their corresponding substructures. For example, when composing two components, two internal classes with the same name, say `Foo`, are merged, and the result is called again `Foo`.

Superimposition has been applied successfully to the composition of class hierarchies in multi-team software development [1], the extension of distributed programs [2,3], the implementation of collaboration-based designs [4,5,6], feature-oriented programming [7,8], subject-oriented programming [9,10], aspect-oriented programming [11, 12], and software component adaptation [13]. All these approaches superimpose hierarchically organized program constructs by matching their levels, names, and types in the hierarchy.

It has been noted that, when composing software, not only code artifacts have to be considered but also noncode artifacts, e.g., documentation, grammar files, makefiles [8,10]. Thus, superimposition, as a composition technique, should be applicable to a wide range of software artifacts. While there are tools that implement superimposition for noncode artifacts [8,14,15,16,17,18,19], they are specific to their underlying languages.

C. Pautasso and É. Tanter (Eds.): SC 2008, LNCS 4954, pp. 20–35, 2008.

It is an irony that, while superimposition is such a general approach, up to now, it has been implemented for every distinct kind of software artifact from scratch. In our recent work, we have explored the essential properties of superimposition and developed an algebraic foundation for software composition based on superimposition [20].

We present a model of superimposition based on *feature structure trees (FSTs)*. An FST represents the abstract hierarchical structure of a software component. That is, it hides the language-specific details of a component's implementation. The nodes of an FST represent the structural elements of a component. However, an FST contains only nodes that represent the modular component structure (modules and submodules) and that are relevant for composition.

Furthermore, we have a tool, called FSTComposer, that implements composition by superimposition on the basis of FSTs. At present, FSTComposer is able to compose software components written in Java, Jak,[1] XML, and plain text. Three nontrivial case studies demonstrate the practicality and scalability of our approach and tool.

2 A Tree Representation of Software Artifacts

A software component is represented as an FST. The nodes of an FST represent a component's structural elements. Each node has a name,[2] which is also the name of the structural element that is represented by the node.

FSTs are designed to represent any kind of component with a hierarchical structure. For example, a component written in Java contains packages, classes, methods, etc., which are represented by nodes in the FST. An XML document (e.g., XHTML) may contain tags that represent the underlying document structure, e.g., chapters, sections, paragraphs. A makefile or build script consists of definitions and rules that may be nested.

An FST is a stripped-down abstract syntax tree: it contains only the information that is necessary for the specification of the structure of a component. The nature of this information depends on the degree of granularity at which software artifacts are to be composed [22], as we discuss below.

Principally, a component may contain elements written in different code and noncode languages, e.g., makefiles, design documents, performance profiles, mathematical models, diagrams, documentation, or deployment descriptors, which all can be represented as FSTs [8, 10]. While our work is not limited to code artifacts, for simplicity, we explain our ideas by means of Java.

Furthermore, type information is attached to the nodes. This is important during component composition in order to prevent the composition of incompatible nodes, e.g., the composition a field with a method.

---

[1] Jak is a Java-like language for stepwise refinement and feature-oriented programming [21]. It extends Java by the keyword `refines` in order to express subsequent class extensions.

[2] Mapped to specific component languages, a name could be a string, an identifier, a signature, etc.

The FSTs we consider are unordered trees. That is, the children of a node in an FST do not have a fixed order, much like the order of field declarations in a Java class is irrelevant. However, some languages may require a fixed order (e.g., the order of sections in a text document matters). This will be addressed in further work.

Figure 1 depicts an excerpt of the implementation of a Java component BASICSTACK and its representation in form of an FST. The FST contains nodes that represent packages, classes, interfaces, fields, and methods, etc. They do not reflect information about the internal structure of methods or the variable initializers of fields. That is, our FST only represents the *modular substructure* of a software artifact (and not more). The structure and content of modules is not always modelled completely, e.g., our FST in Figure 1 does not represent the full Java abstract syntax tree including statements, parameters, or expressions, but only the main structural elements. A different granularity would be possible [22], e.g., we could represent only packages and classes but not methods or fields as FST nodes, or we could also represent statements or expressions. However, we will demonstrate that the granularity we chose is sufficient for composition, while it simplifies the overall process. At the same time, reasoning at a finer grain is still possible, i.e., method bodies can be composed without representing their substructure, as we will show in Section 3.2.

```
package util;
class Stack {
  LinkedList data = new LinkedList();
  void push(Object obj) {
    data.addFirst(obj);
  }
  Object pop() {
    return data.removeFirst();
  }
}
```

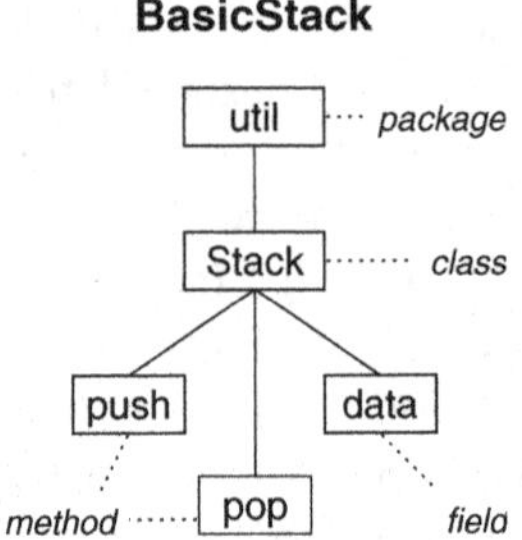

Fig. 1. Java code and FST of the component BASICSTACK

3 Component Composition by FST Superimposition

Superimposition is the process of composing trees recursively by composing nodes at the same level (counting from the root) with the same name[3] and type. Our aim is to abstract from the specifics of present tools and languages and to make superimposition available to a broader range of software artifacts. Moreover, a general model allows us to study the essence of software composition by superimposition, apart from language- and tool-specific issues. Our work is

[3] Of course, the use of aliasing techniques would allow a programmer to compose artifacts that have different names [23].

motivated by the observation that, principally, composition by superimposition is applicable to any kind of software artifact that provides a sufficient structure [8, 10], i.e., a structure that can be represented as an FST.

With superimposition, two trees are composed by composing their corresponding nodes, starting from the root and proceeding recursively. Two nodes are composed to form a result node (1) when their parents (if there are parents) have been composed, i.e., they are on the same level, and (2) when they have the same name and type. The result node receives the name and type of the nodes that have been composed. Some nodes (the leaves of an FST) have also content, which is composed as well (see Sec. 3.2). If two nodes have been composed, the process of composition proceeds with their children. If a node has no counterpart to be composed with, it is added as separate child node to the composed parent node. This recurses until all leaves have been reached.

In Figure 2, we list a Java function `compose` that implements recursive composition. In Line 2, two nodes are composed, which succeeds only when the nodes are compatible (same name and type). In the case that the two nodes are terminals, their content is composed as well. In Lines 4–9, all children of the input trees (which are in fact subtrees) are composed recursively. That is, for each node in `treeA`, `findChild` returns the corresponding node in `treeB`, if there is one. Then, in Lines 8 and 10–13, the remaining nodes that have no counterpart to be composed with are added to the new parent node.

```
1  static Tree compose(Tree treeA, Tree treeB) {
2      Node newNode = treeA.node().composeNode(treeB.node());
3      if(newNode != null) {
4          Tree newTree = new Tree(newNode);
5          for(Tree childA : treeA.children()) {
6              Tree childB = treeB.findChild(childA.name(),childA.type());
7              if(childB != null) newTree.addChild(compose(childA, childB));
8              else newTree.addChild(childA.copy());
9          }
10         for(Tree childB : treeB.children()) {
11             Tree childA = treeA.findChild(childB.name(),childB.type());
12             if(childA == null) newTree.addChild(childB.copy());
13         }
14         return newTree;
15     } else return null;
16 }
```

Fig. 2. A Java function for composing FSTs

Figure 3 illustrates the process of FST superimposition with a Java example; Figure 4 depicts the corresponding Java code. Our component BasicStack is composed with a component TopOfStack. The result is a new component, which is called CompStack$_1$, that is represented by the superimposition of the FSTs of BasicStack and TopOfStack. The nodes `util` and `Stack` are composed with their counterparts, and their subtrees (i.e., their methods and fields) are composed in turn (i.e., are merged).

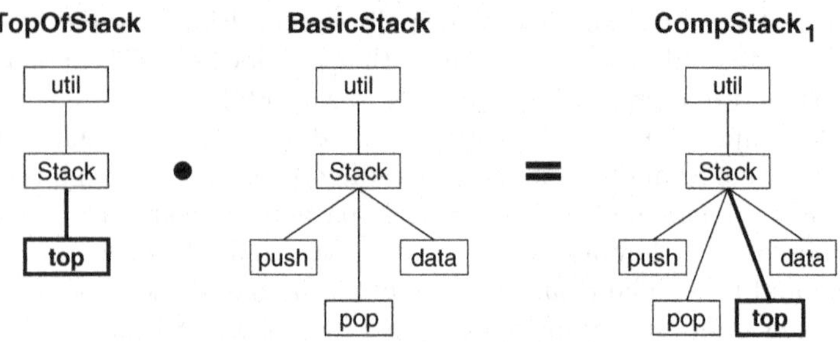

Fig. 3. FST superimposition of TopOfStack • BasicStack = CompStack$_1$

```
package util;
class Stack {
  Object top() { return data.getFirst(); }
}
```

•

```
package util;
class Stack {
  LinkedList data = new LinkedList();
  void push(Object obj) { data.addFirst(obj); }
  Object pop() { return data.removeFirst(); }
}
```

=

```
package util;
class Stack {
  LinkedList data = new LinkedList();
  void push(Object obj) { data.addFirst(obj); }
  Object pop() { return data.removeFirst(); }
  Object top() { return data.getFirst(); }
}
```

Fig. 4. Java code of TopOfStack • BasicStack = CompStack$_1$

3.1 Terminal and Nonterminal Nodes

Independently of any particular language, an FST is made up of two different kinds of nodes:

Nonterminal nodes are the inner nodes of an FST. The subtree rooted at a nonterminal node reflects the structure of some implementation artifact of a component. The artifact structure is *transparent* and subject to the recursive composition process. That is, a nonterminal node has only a name and a type, and no further content.

Terminal nodes are the leaves of an FST. Conceptually, a terminal node may also be the root of some structure, but this structure is *opaque* in our model. The substructure of a terminal does not appear in the FST. That is, a terminal node has a name, a type, and content.

While the composition of two nonterminals continues the recursive descent in the FSTs to be composed, the composition of two terminals terminates the recursion and requires a special treatment. There is a choice of whether and how to compose terminals:

Option 1: Two terminal nodes with the same name and type *cannot* be composed, i.e., their composition is considered an error.

Option 2: Two terminal nodes with the same name and type *can* be composed in some circumstances; each type has to provide its own rule for composition (see Sec. 3.2).[4]

In Java FSTs, packages, classes, and interfaces are represented by nonterminals. The implementation artifacts they contain are represented by child nodes, e.g., a package contains several classes and classes contain inner classes, methods, and fields. Two compatible nonterminals are composed by composing their child nodes, e.g., two packages with equal names are merged into one package that contains the composition of the child elements (classes, interfaces, subpackages) of the two original packages.

Java methods, fields, imports, modifier lists, and `extends`, `implements`, and `throws` clauses are represented by terminals (the leaves of an FST), at which the recursion terminates. Their inner structure or content is not considered in the FST model, e.g., the fact that a method contains a sequence of statements or that a field refers to a value or an expression.

Note that the first option of disallowing terminal composition [1] prevents method extension. But method extension is common practice in many approaches of software composition [10,24,25,26,27,28,8,6]. Therefore, we choose the second option: providing language-specific composition rules for composing terminal nodes.

3.2 Composition of Terminals

In order to compose terminals, each terminal type has to provide its own rule for composition. Here are seven examples for Java-like languages:

- Two methods are composed if it is specified how the method bodies are composed (e.g., by overriding and using the keywords `original` [27] or `Super` [8] inside a method body).
- Two fields are composed by replacing one value with the value of the other or by requiring that one has a value assigned and the other has not.

[4] Note that it would also be possible to provide specific rules for nonterminal composition, but we did not encounter this case so far.

- Two `implements` clauses are composed by concatenating their entries and removing duplicates.
- Two `extends` clauses are composed by replacing one entry with another entry (in the case of single inheritance) or by concatenating their entries and removing duplicates (in the case of multiple inheritance).
- Two `throws` clauses are composed by concatenating their entries and removing duplicates.
- Two modifier lists are composed by replacement following certain rules, e.g., `public` may replace `private`, but not vice versa.
- Two import declaration lists are composed by concatenating their entries and removing duplicates.

Overall, in Java-like languages, there are three kinds of composition rule patterns: overriding (methods), replacement (fields, `extends` clauses, modifier lists), and concatenation (imports, `implements` and `throws` clauses).

Figures 5 and 6 depict how Java methods are composed during the composition of the two features EmptyCheck and BasicStack using a *wrapping* composition rule. The methods `push` of EmptyCheck and BasicStack are composed in CompStack$_2$ by one method (`push`) wrapping the other (`push_wrappee`). The two `pop` methods are composed analogously. The keyword `original` [27],[5] provides a means to specify (without knowledge of their source code) how method bodies are merged. This composition rule is also applicable to other types and languages [8,14]. Other composition rules for composing method bodies, such as inlining would be possible.

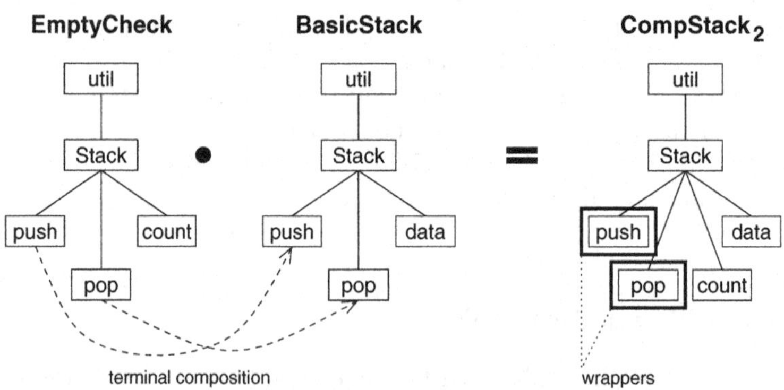

Fig. 5. Composing Java methods (FST representation)

Harrison et al. [23] propose a catalog of more sophisticated composition rules that permit a quantification over and a renaming of the structural elements of components. We argue that their rules are not specific to Java and can be reused to compose components written in other languages.

[5] In the composed variant, `original` is replaced by a call to the wrapper.

```
package util;
class Stack {
  int count = 0;
  void push(Object obj) { original(obj); count++; }
  Object pop() {
    if(count > 0) { count--; return original(); } else return null;
  }
}
```

•

```
package util;
class Stack {
  LinkedList data = new LinkedList();
  void push(Object obj) { data.addFirst(obj); }
  Object pop() { return data.removeFirst(); }
}
```

=

```
package util;
class Stack {
  int count  = 0;
  LinkedList data = new LinkedList();
  void push_wrappee(Object obj) { data.addFirst(obj); }
  void push(Object obj) { push_wrappee(obj); count++; }
  Object pop_wrappee() { return data.removeFirst(); }
  Object pop() {
    if(count > 0) { count--; return pop_wrappee(); } else return null;
  }
}
```

Fig. 6. Composing Java methods

3.3 Discussion

Superimposition of FSTs requires several properties of the language in which the elements of a component are expressed:

1. The substructure of a component must be hierarchical, i.e., an n-ary tree.
2. Every element of a component must provide a name that becomes the name of the node in the FST.
3. An element must not contain two or more direct child elements with the same name and type.
4. Elements that do not have a hierarchical substructure (terminals) must provide composition rules, or cannot be composed.

These constraints are usually satisfied by object-oriented languages. But also other (noncode) languages align well with them [8, 14]. Languages that do not satisfy these constraints do not provide sufficient structural information for a composition by superimposition. However, they may be enriched by providing an overlaying module structure [14].

4 Implementation

We have a tool, called FSTComposer, that implements superimposition based on the FST model. Currently, it supports the composition of components written in Java, Jak, XML, and plain text.

FSTComposer expects a list of software components that participate in a composition. It takes a file as input that contains a list of the component names. Then, FSTComposer looks up the locations of the components in the file system.

In FSTComposer, software components are represented by *containment hierarchies* [8]. A containment hierarchy is a file system directory that contains all artifacts (code and noncode) that belong to a component; the directory may contain subdirectories denoting Java packages, etc.

Figure 7 shows the components EmptyCheck and BasicStack containing source and nonsource code artifacts. The composition 'EmptyCheck • BasicStack = CompStack_2' composes both their containment hierarchies recursively. For example, the resulting artifact `Stack.java` is composed of its counterparts in EmptyCheck and in BasicStack, matched by name and type.

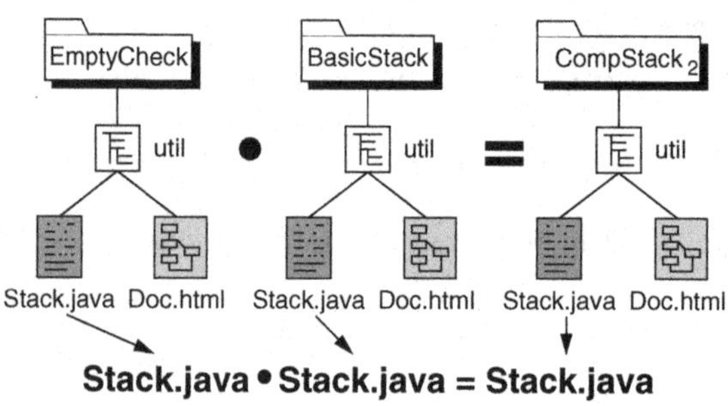

Fig. 7. Composing two containment hierarchies

Based on an input list of components (essentially, the paths of the containment hierarchies), FSTComposer generates an FST per component. There must be a distinct parser per language. That is, when composing components that contain Java and XML artifacts, two different parsers create the corresponding FSTs.

Currently, our Java and Jak parsers generate FSTs containing nodes for packages, classes, interfaces, methods, fields, imports, modifier lists, and `implements`, `extends`, and `throws` clauses. Packages, classes, and interfaces the nonterminal nodes of a Java FST. The rest are terminals. We have implemented the seven composition rules for terminal nodes, that we have explained in Section 3.2, for Java and for Jak.

Furthermore, we have an XML parser that generates, for each tag, attribute and piece of raw text content, a distinct node; tags become nonterminals; attributes and pieces of text content become terminals; attributes are composed like fields in Java (cf. Sec. 3.2) and pieces of raw text are composed by concatenating their content.

Finally, the text parser is trivial in that it creates nonterminal nodes for directories and simply stores the content of text files in a terminal node each; text nodes are composed by concatenation.

Usually, after the composition step, FSTComposer writes out the composed artifacts. But it can also write out the FSTs of the input and output components in the form of an XML document (containing all information about the Java, Jak, XML, or text artifacts). This language-independent program representation can be the input for further pre- or post-processing of components and component compositions, e.g., optimization, visualization, interaction analysis, or error checking on the basis of FSTs.

The FSTComposer tool along with some examples and case studies can be downloaded from the FSTComposer Web site.[6]

5 Case Studies

We have conducted three case studies to demonstrate the practicality of our approach. Firstly, we have composed a graphical programming tool, called *GUIDSL*, out of a set of software components, which has been implemented by Batory [29]. Secondly, we have composed a series of programs of a small library of graph algorithms, called *graph product line (GPL)*, which has implemented by Lopez-Herrejon and Batory [30]. Thirdly, we have composed several variants of a graphical UML editor, which is an open source program that has been refactored into components by a student. The source code of the three case studies can be downloaded at the FSTComposer Web site.

5.1 GUIDSL

GUIDSL is a tool for software product line configuration [29]. GUIDSL consists of 26 components. For example, there are components that implement the graphical user interface, a parser for grammars that define valid configurations, user event handling, etc. Overall, the code base of GUIDSL contains 294 classes (from which 145 result classes are being composed), implemented by 9,345 lines of Jak code.

GUIDSL was developed in a stepwise manner using components in order to foster extensibility and maintainability. Basically, there is only one valid configuration that forms a meaningful working tool. Other configurations may be valid (syntactically correct) but do not contain all necessary features to work appropriately. We generated a GUIDSL variant consisting of all 26 components, implemented by 7,684 lines of composed Java code.[7]

---

[6] `http://www.infosun.fim.uni-passau.de/cl/staff/apel/FSTComposer/`

[7] For comparability of the lines-of-code metric, we formatted the code of our case studies using a standard Java pretty printer (`http://uranus.it.swin.edu.au/~jn/java/style.htm`). Furthermore, we counted only lines that contain more than two characters (thus, ignoring lines with just a single bracket) and that are not simply comments (`http://www.csc.calpoly.edu/~jdalbey/SWE/PSP/LOChelp.html`)

We checked the correctness of the composition by testing GUIDSL manually. This was feasible since it is a graphical tool with a fixed set of functions and options that all could be tested. All parser passes and the generation of the composed Java program took less than two seconds.

5.2 Graph Product Line

GPL consists of 26 components written in Jak. For example, the basic components implement weighted, unweighted, directed, and undirected graph structures. Further components implement advanced features such as breadth-first search, depth-first search, cycle checking, the Kruskal algorithm, the Prim algorithm, etc. The overall code base of GPL contains 57 classes (from which 31 result classes are being composed), implemented by 1,308 lines of Jak code.

Beside Jak code, 9 of the 26 GPL components contain an XHTML file that documents the usage and functionality of the graph structures and algorithms. The XHTML files have been prepared by Don Batory and Salvador Trujillo in order to be ready for superimposition [31, 14]. In our case study, we have applied some minor adaptations to match the syntax of FSTComposer, i.e., we have given some XHTML tags unique name attributes in order to specify which tags superimpose other tags. Being superimposed, these XHTML files form the tailored documentation of GPL, depending on the selected components during composition. Due to the lack of space, we refer the reader to the FSTComposer Web site for XHTML examples (of the GPL case study).

Finally, GPL contains some JPEG files that are loaded by the XHTML documentation. During composition, these files are treated like text documents, but their content is not read. A composition of two JPEG files is not necessary. Nevertheless, artifacts with completely opaque content, such as images, align well with the FST model. Artifacts with the same name and type are composed by replacement (a warning is displayed).

Overall, we generated 10 different variants of graph structures along with compatible algorithms with a minimum of 8 and a maximum of 12 components. The code bases of the generated programs range from 200 to 400 lines of composed Java code and 200 to 300 lines of composed XHTML code.

We used GUIDSL to guarantee the validity of the generated configurations [29], e.g., the Kruskal algorithm requires a weighted graph. We checked the correctness of the composed graph implementation with automated tests. The entire composition process, including parsing the Jak and XHTML code, took less than a second per composed program variant.

5.3 Violet

Violet is a graphical UML diagram editor written in Java.[8] It has been refactored by a student as a class project at the University of Texas at Austin.[9] The

[8] `http://sourceforge.net/projects/violet/`

[9] The project was done in the course of the 2006 FOP class at the Department of Computer Sciences of the University of Texas at Austin.

refactored version of Violet consists of 88 components ready for superimposition. They implement support for different UML diagram types as well as drag-and-drop and look-and-feel functionality. Overall, the refactored code base of Violet contains 157 classes (from which 67 final classes are being composed), implemented by 5,220 lines of Java code.

Beside Java code, 83 of the 88 Violet component contain, in summary, 98 property files. A property file contains text-based configuration information of the Violet UML editor, e.g., `edge1.tooltip=Association`. Individual components of Violet provide individual configuration information. Property files are simply composed by text concatenation. There is no further module structure that demands a recursive descent in the FST during composition. As with GPL, Violet contains some JPEG files, but they had not to be composed.

We generated 10 different variants of Violet with a minimum of 51 and a maximum of 88 components. The code bases of the generated programs range from 3,100 to 4,100 lines of composed Java code and 160 lines of text in form of property files.

In order to guarantee their validity, we used the GUIDSL tool for selecting the components of the 10 variants. We tested the variants manually, which was feasible since they differed mainly in their options available in the graphical menus of the editor. All parser passes and the generation of the composed Java and property files took less than two seconds each.

6 Integrating Further Languages

In the previous section, we have illustrated how the FST model abstracts from implementation-specific details of programming languages, while capturing well the abstract hierarchical structure of software components. Currently, FSTComposer supports the composition of components written in Java, Jak, XML, text, and binaries. Due to the generality of the FST model, FSTComposer can be extended to compose also further kinds of artifacts.

Suppose we want to compose software components containing Bali grammar files (a declarative language and tool for processing BNF grammars) [8]. It has been demonstrated that Bali grammars are ready for composition by superimposition. That is, they can be represented as FSTs and composed by superimposition using a proprietary tool [8]. Firstly, we would need a parser that produces FSTs in a format accessible to FSTComposer. Such a parser can be built by extending an existing parser. Secondly, we would have to define the types of nodes (by providing a typically empty subclass per type) that may appear in a Bali FST, e.g., nodes for grammar production rules, axioms, etc. (analogously to nodes for classes and methods in Java). Finally, we would have to define Bali-specific composition rules for composing terminal nodes, e.g., production rules can be extended by providing additional alternatives, similarly to method overriding in Java. Section 7 lists a selection of languages that can be modeled by FSTs.

7 Related Work

Superimposition is a composition technique that has been applied successfully in different areas of software development. Superimposition was initially used for extending distributed programs in multiple places [2,3]. Subsequently, several researchers adopted this idea in order to merge class hierarchies developed by multiple teams [1], to adapt components [13], to support subject-oriented programming [9,10], feature-oriented programming [7,8], and aspect-oriented programming [11,12], and to implement collaboration-based designs [6]. Several languages support composition by superimposition, e.g., *Scala* [32], *Jiazzi* [25], *Classbox/J* [27], *ContextL* [33], *Jak* [8], and *FeatureC++* [34].

Batory et al. [8], Tarr et al. [10], and Clarke et al. [15] noted that superimposition as a composition technique is not limited to source code artifacts but applies to any kind of artifact relevant in the software development process. Several proprietary tools support the composition of nonsource code artifacts [14,8,16,17,18,19].

While it has been noted that there is a unique core of all composition mechanisms based on superimposition [8,10], researchers have not condensed the essence of superimposition into a set of general tools. We believe that our FST model captures the essence of superimposition. It is language-independent. We envision tools that operate on FSTs (or their algebraic representations) to compose, visualize, optimize, and verify software components. Thus, the FST model provides an intermediate format not only for different languages but also for different tools that aim at reasoning about components.

In a parallel line of research, we have developed an algebra and a calculus (incl. operational semantics and type system) of feature composition which is consistent with the FST model [20,35]. It will allow us to explore general properties of software composition as well as typing issues. Furthermore, it is a means to infer whether a given language fits the FST model and, more interestingly, which properties a language must have to be 'ready' for FST-based superimposition.

Beside superimposition, also other composition techniques have been proposed. For example, composition by quantification, as used in metaprogramming [36] and aspect-oriented programming [37], is a frequently discussed technique. In the context of our FST model, quantification can be modeled as a tree walk [20], in which each node is visited and a predicate specifies whether the node is modified or not. Harrison et al. [23] propose a sophisticated set of rewriting rules that are based on tree walks. Aggregation is another component composition technique. It can be modeled by FSTs that contain nodes that represent themselves components, i.e., that contain FSTs. Even aggregated components can be superimposed, since they have a hierarchical structure that can be represented as an FST. In summary, FSTs are a means to model the connection between different composition techniques and to explore their relationship; FSTs are not specific to superimposition.

So far, we do not consider inter-language interaction. That is, while FSTComposer can compose components containing artifacts written in different languages, it cannot recognize interactions between these artifacts. For example, a Java class may expect some XML document as input, which is defined in another component. Grechanik [38] et al. propose an approach based on recursive types and type reification to bridge the gap between different languages, which can be used in concert with FSTComposer.

Finally, superimposition is a specific instance of model weaving in model-driven development [39] and of graph amalgamation in model theory [40].

8 Conclusion

We model software components by tree structures and component composition by tree superimposition. The FST model abstracts from the specifics of a particular programming language or tool. Any reasonably structured software artifact that can be represented as an FST can be composed by our approach.

As a proof of concept, we have developed a tool that implements FST superimposition. Currently, we have parsers for Java, Jak, XML, text, and binaries that generate FSTs ready for composition. Beside generating code for feature composition, FSTComposer is able to generate XML documents representing the FSTs involved in a composition, ready for further processing.

Three case studies have demonstrated the applicability of our approach and our tool: FST superimposition scales to medium-sized programs (10 KLOC). Scalability to larger programs remains to be shown in further work.

We intend to plug various other languages into the tool in order to demonstrate the generality of our approach. C# and Bali have been shown to be compatible with the FST model. Furthermore, we are working on a formalization of the FST model and further tools that operate on FSTs, e.g., a tool that visualizes FSTs and a tool that analyzes interactions between components.

Acknowledgments

We thank Don Batory and Christian Kästner for helpful comments on earlier drafts of this paper, Sebastian Scharinger for implementing the Java and Jak parsers of FSTComposer, Don Batory for releasing the source code of GPL and GUIDSL, and Abhinay Kampasi for refactoring Violet into features.

References

1. Ossher, H., Harrison, W.: Combination of Inheritance Hierarchies. In: Proc. Int'l. Conf. Object-Oriented Programming, Systems, Languages, and Applications, pp. 25–40. ACM Press, New York (1992)
2. Katz, S.: A Superimposition Control Construct for Distributed Systems. ACM Trans. Programming Languages and Systems 15, 337–356 (1993)
3. Bouge, L., Francez, N.: A Compositional Approach to Superimposition. In: Proc. Int'l. Symp. Principles of Programming Languages, pp. 240–249. ACM Press, New York (1988)
4. VanHilst, M., Notkin, D.: Using Role Components in Implement Collaboration-based Designs. In: Proc. Int'l. Conf. Object-Oriented Programming, Systems, Languages, and Applications, pp. 359–369. ACM Press, New York (1996)

5. Reenskaug, T., Andersen, E., Berre, A., Hurlen, A., Landmark, A., Lehne, O., Nordhagen, E., Ness-Ulseth, E., Oftedal, G., Skaar, A., Stenslet, P.: OORASS: Seamless Support for the Creation and Maintenance of Object-Oriented Systems. Journal of Object-Oriented Programming 5, 27–41 (1992)
6. Smaragdakis, Y., Batory, D.: Mixin Layers: An Object-Oriented Implementation Technique for Refinements and Collaboration-Based Designs. ACM Trans. Software Engineering and Methodology 11, 215–255 (2002)
7. Prehofer, C.: Feature-Oriented Programming: A Fresh Look at Objects. In: Aksit, M., Matsuoka, S. (eds.) ECOOP 1997. LNCS, vol. 1241, pp. 419–443. Springer, Heidelberg (1997)
8. Batory, D., Sarvela, J., Rauschmayer, A.: Scaling Step-Wise Refinement. IEEE Trans. Software Engineering 30, 355–371 (2004)
9. Harrison, W., Ossher, H.: Subject-Oriented Programming: A Critique of Pure Objects. In: Proc. Int'l. Conf. Object-Oriented Programming, Systems, Languages, and Applications, pp. 411–428. ACM Press, New York (1993)
10. Tarr, P., Ossher, H., Harrison, W., Sutton Jr, S.: N Degrees of Separation: Multi-Dimensional Separation of Concerns. In: Proc. Int'l. Conf. Software Engineering, pp. 107–119. IEEE CS Press, Los Alamitos (1999)
11. Mezini, M., Ostermann, K.: Conquering Aspects with Caesar. In: Proc. Int'l. Conf. Aspect-Oriented Software Development, pp. 90–100. ACM Press, New York (2003)
12. McDirmid, S., Hsieh, W.: Aspect-Oriented Programming with Jiazzi. In: Proc. Int'l. Conf. Aspect-Oriented Software Development, pp. 70–79. ACM Press, New York (2003)
13. Bosch, J.: Super-Imposition: A Component Adaptation Technique. Information and Software Technology 41, 257–273 (1999)
14. Anfurrutia, F., Díaz, O., Trujillo, S.: On Refining XML Artifacts. In: Baresi, L., Fraternali, P., Houben, G.-J. (eds.) ICWE 2007. LNCS, vol. 4607, pp. 473–478. Springer, Heidelberg (2007)
15. Clarke, S., Harrison, W., Ossher, H., Tarr, P.: Subject-Oriented Design: Towards Improved Alignment of Requirements, Design, and Code. In: Proc. Int'l. Conf. Object-Oriented Programming, Systems, Languages, and Applications, pp. 325–339. ACM Press, New York (1999)
16. Alves, V., Gheyi, R., Massoni, T., Kulesza, U., Borba, P., Lucena, C.: Refactoring Product Lines. In: Proc. Int'l. Conf. Generative Programming and Component Engineering, pp. 201–210. ACM Press, New York (2006)
17. Bravenboer, M., Visser, E.: Concrete Syntax for Objects: Domain-Specific Language Embedding and Assimilation Without Restrictions. In: Proc. Int'l. Conf. Object-Oriented Programming, Systems, Languages, and Applications, pp. 365–383. ACM Press, New York (2004)
18. Czarnecki, K., Antkiewicz, M.: Mapping Features to Models: A Template Approach Based on Superimposed Variants. In: Glück, R., Lowry, M. (eds.) GPCE 2005. LNCS, vol. 3676, pp. 422–437. Springer, Heidelberg (2005)
19. Kamina, T., Tamai, T.: Lightweight Scalable Components. In: Proc. Int'l. Conf. Generative Programming and Component Engineering, pp. 145–154. ACM Press, New York (2007)
20. Apel, S., Lengauer, C., Batory, D., Möller, B., Kästner, C.: An Algebra for Feature-Oriented Software Development. Technical Report MIP-0706, Department of Informatics and Mathematics, University of Passau (2007)
21. Batory, D.: Jakarta Tool Suite (JTS). SIGSOFT Softw. Eng. Notes 25, 103–104 (2000)

22. Kästner, C., Apel, S., Kuhlemann, M.: Granularity in Software Product Lines. In: Proc. Int'l. Conf. Software Engineering, ACM Press, New York (2008)
23. Harrison, W., Ossher, H., Tarr, P.: General Composition of Software Artifacts. In: Löwe, W., Südholt, M. (eds.) SC 2006. LNCS, vol. 4089, pp. 194–210. Springer, Heidelberg (2006)
24. Hutchins, D.: Eliminating Distinctions of Class: Using Prototypes to Model Virtual Classes. In: Proc. Int'l. Conf. Object-Oriented Programming, Systems, Languages, and Applications, pp. 1–19. ACM Press, New York (2006)
25. McDirmid, S., Flatt, M., Hsieh, W.: Jiazzi: New-Age Components for Old-Fashioned Java. In: Proc. Int'l. Conf. Object-Oriented Programming, Systems, Languages, and Applications, pp. 211–222. ACM Press, New York (2001)
26. Nystrom, N., Chong, S., Myers, A.: Scalable Extensibility via Nested Inheritance. In: Proc. Int'l. Conf. Object-Oriented Programming, Systems, Languages, and Applications, pp. 99–115. ACM Press, New York (2004)
27. Bergel, A., Ducasse, S., Nierstrasz, O.: Classbox/J: Controlling the Scope of Change in Java. In: Proc. Int'l. Conf. Object-Oriented Programming, Systems, Languages, and Applications, pp. 177–189. ACM Press, New York (2005)
28. Cardone, R., Lin, C.: Comparing Frameworks and Layered Refinement. In: Proc. Int'l. Conf. Software Engineering, pp. 285–294. IEEE Computer Society Press, Los Alamitos (2001)
29. Batory, D.: Feature Models, Grammars, and Propositional Formulas. In: Obbink, H., Pohl, K. (eds.) SPLC 2005. LNCS, vol. 3714, pp. 7–20. Springer, Heidelberg (2005)
30. Lopez-Herrejon, R., Batory, D.: A Standard Problem for Evaluating Product-Line Methodologies. In: Bosch, J. (ed.) GCSE 2001. LNCS, vol. 2186, pp. 10–24. Springer, Heidelberg (2001)
31. Trujillo, S., Batory, D., Díaz, O.: Feature Refactoring a Multi-Representation Program into a Product Line. In: Proc. Int'l. Conf. Generative Programming and Component Engineering, pp. 191–200. ACM Press, New York (2006)
32. Odersky, M., Zenger, M.: Scalable Component Abstractions. In: Proc. Int'l. Conf. Object-Oriented Programming, Systems, Languages, and Applications, pp. 41–57. ACM Press, New York (2005)
33. Costanza, P., Hirschfeld, R., de Meuter, W.: Efficient Layer Activation for Switching Context-Dependent Behavior. In: Lightfoot, D.E., Szyperski, C.A. (eds.) JMLC 2006. LNCS, vol. 4228, pp. 84–103. Springer, Heidelberg (2006)
34. Apel, S., Leich, T., Rosenmüller, M., Saake, G.: FeatureC++: On the Symbiosis of Feature-Oriented and Aspect-Oriented Programming. In: Glück, R., Lowry, M. (eds.) GPCE 2005. LNCS, vol. 3676, pp. 125–140. Springer, Heidelberg (2005)
35. Apel, S., Hutchins, D.: An Overview of the gDeep Calculus. Technical Report MIP-0712, Department of Informatics and Mathematics, University of Passau (2007)
36. Kiczales, G., Des Rivieres, J.: The Art of the Metaobject Protocol. MIT Press, Cambridge (1991)
37. Masuhara, H., Kiczales, G.: Modeling Crosscutting in Aspect-Oriented Mechanisms. In: Cardelli, L. (ed.) ECOOP 2003. LNCS, vol. 2743, pp. 2–28. Springer, Heidelberg (2003)
38. Grechanik, M., Batory, D., Perry, D.: Design of Large-Scale Polylingual Systems. In: Proc. Int'l. Conf. Software Engineering, pp. 357–366. IEEE Computer Society Press, Los Alamitos (2004)
39. Bézivin, J.: On the Unification Power of Models. Software and Systems Modeling 4, 171–188 (2005)
40. Böcker, S., Bryant, D., Dress, A., Steel, M.: Algorithmic Aspects of Tree Amalgamation. J. Algorithms 37, 522–537 (2000)

Language Support for Managing Variability in Architectural Models*

Neil Loughran[1], Pablo Sánchez[2], Alessandro Garcia[1], and Lidia Fuentes[2]

[1] Computing Department, InfoLab 21
South Drive, Lancaster University, LA1 4WA, UK
{loughran,garciaa}@comp.lancs.ac.uk
[2] Dpto. de Lenguajes y Ciencias de la Computación
Universidad de Málaga, Málaga, Spain
{pablo,lff}@lcc.uma.es

Abstract. The effective management and composition of architectural variabilities has long been of importance to product line architects. Architects need to describe how conceptual variabilities are composed and realised through architectural decompositions of a product line. Architecture variabilities need to be described in terms of the chosen design decompositions, which do not often correspond naturally to feature model decompositions. Also, the fine-grained nature of certain architectural variabilities makes it difficult to represent them in a modular fashion, and describe how they are composed across different views. In order to address these issues, this paper presents a variability modelling language (VML), which supports first-class representation of heterogeneous forms of architectural variabilities. The language complements existing architectural modelling approaches for product lines by providing mechanisms to: (i) explicitly reference variation points in multiple architectural views, and (ii) support compositions involving both fine-grained and coarse-grained variabilities in an orthogonal fashion. The completeness and simplicity of VML is assessed through four case studies from different domains.

1 Introduction

A product-line architecture [1] represents a software architecture which can rapidly respond effectively to variabilities imposed by different customer requirements and changes within a well defined market segment. It is realised via core common elements and a plethora of variabilities associated with recurring architecture-wide concerns as opposed to traditional monolithic architecture designs. Hence, architectural variability modelling has been challenging to software product-line engineers over the last decade. One of the key problems is that the realisation and composition of architecturally-relevant variabilities cannot be solely expressed using conventional feature models [2] (as illustrated by [3]),

* This work has been supported by European Commission Grants IST-2-004349-NOE AOSD-Europe and the European Commission STREP Project AMPLE IST-033710.

C. Pautasso and É. Tanter (Eds.): SC 2008, LNCS 4954, pp. 36–51, 2008.

apart from its use in relatively small-scale program families. Software architects need to identify the variation points within the context of multiple architectural views. Also, the architecture-level variants are of a heterogeneous nature, ranging from optional component interfaces expressed in a component-connector model to alternative nodes hosting architecture elements in the deployment view. In addition, product-line designers also need to express how the optional or alternative architectural variants are composed with the core architecture elements.

In this context, the instantiation and evolution of product-line architectures can easily become cumbersome and error prone if the specification and composition of architectural variabilities cannot be expressed in a separate fashion. In fact, a growing number of approaches (e.g. [3,4,5,6]) are emerging to ameliorate these problems and support the systematic treatment of variabilities throughout the software lifecycle. However, many of these existing tools tend to concentrate on implementation-level variabilities, using conditional switches, templates and annotations. They are also largely unsuited to managing variability in architectural models due to the lack of underlying abstractions that are meaningful to product-line architecture stakeholders. In fact, our recent systematic analysis of existing modelling techniques concluded that they fail to fully support the orthogonal representation of architecturally-relevant variabilities [7]. Some variability modelling techniques rely exclusively on the use of feature models (e.g. [2,5]), while others (e.g. [3,6]) use advanced modelling mechanisms to relate feature models and architectural models. However, the latter approaches are restricted to only documenting variability rather than expressing its composition with the core common architecture elements.

This paper introduces a technique that facilitates architectural variability modelling using an expressive, albeit simple, description language. Before presenting the language, we discuss the motivation for our work (Section 2). Then, in Section 3, we present the *variability modelling language* (VML), which provides primitives that support: (i) references to both coarse-grained and fine-grained architectural elements, and (ii) the composition of architectural variants to variation points within classical architectural views, such as deployment, interaction, and component-connector models. In order to demonstrate the basic usage of VML, we base our descriptions using examples from the SmartHome domain [8]. We then apply and assess VML in the context of a SmartHome lock control framework (Section 4). Three other case studies were also used to support the completeness and simplicity evaluation of VML (Section 5). Finally, Section 6 concludes the paper.

2 Architectural Variability Modelling

Software variability refers to the ability of a software artefact to be changed or customised to fit a particular context [9]. Variability management refers to the holistic treatment of variability with respect to its *representation* in the problem space (e.g. feature models, domain-specific languages, etc.) through to its *realisation* in the solution space (e.g. development of architectural models, variability mechanisms in code, etc.). However, the development of product line architectures is challenging due to a number of factors:

1. Variability itself can mean something different to individual architecture stakeholders involved in the product-line development. For example, a system configurator sees variabilities in terms of domain concepts, such as rooms, floors, accounts, and so forth. The architects see variabilities in terms of how these domain concepts are realised in terms of architectural elements, i.e. components, interfaces, configurations, deployments, and component interactions. Programmers are concerned with how these architectural variabilities are realised in code using implementation mechanisms, such as conditional compilation, aspects, and partial evaluation. Additionally, these architectural variabilities may also be relevant in different ways to requirements engineers, end customers, etc.
2. With respect to the previous point, the mapping of variability decisions in the problem space (typically expressed in feature models) to variation points and variants in the early solution space (i.e. components and their interactions, interfaces, nodes, etc.) are not typically one to one (as Section 4 will illustrate), but one to many, and even occasionally many to many.
3. The way in which variability manifests itself in different kinds of artifacts cannot easily be generalised to a single unified 'one size fits all' mechanism. For instance, the treatment of variability in code-based assets (e.g. conditional compilation) will not suffice for architectural models.
4. Architectural variabilities will often have complex dependencies with core architectural elements and with other variabilities. The sole use of feature models is not enough because their composition mechanisms are not tailored to express architecture-level variabilities [3,7].

Providing effective support to alleviate these factors is crucial for product-line software architecture design. Many of the current approaches to managing variability require that architectural artifacts are specially annotated with invasive directives e.g. [5,6]. However, this strategy is not suitable for variability in architectural models as often the information that design tools produce (e.g. XMI descriptions) is complex, with variable architectural elements appearing numerous times across an XMI description. Bachmann and Pohl et al [4,3] were among the first authors to suggest the use of *orthogonal variability modelling* (OVM). OVM provides a means to describe variability separately without extending architectural models with new notations. This separation allows variability itself to be treated as a new architectural view (i.e. the *variability model*). From the literature, the OVM approach was designed to solely *document* variability. Thus, there are no explicit mechanisms to define how variable elements in architectural models are referenced and composed. Our work extends the notion of OVM to capture the referencing and composition of architectural variabilities using an innovative modelling language.

3 Variability Modelling Language

This section discusses how design of the variability modelling language for product-line architectures (Section 3.1) is conceived to address the problems discussed in Section 2. Then, it describes the key language elements (Section 3.2) and the support to express variability dependencies emerging in the product-line architecting process (Section 3.2).

3.1 Aims and Objectives of VML

The primary aim of VML is to provide a means to compose together variable elements in architectural models. In order to achieve this, the VML provides a number of primitives for referencing and invoking decisions which result in the composition of architectural elements. In effect, the VML acts as a domain specific language for architectural composition, providing the mapping from the problem space, i.e. the feature configuration model, and the solution space, i.e. architectural models, by allowing features to invoke operations which compose together variable in architectural elements (Figure 1).

A configuration is created from a feature model by a system configurator which invokes variation points pertaining to specific concerns as designated

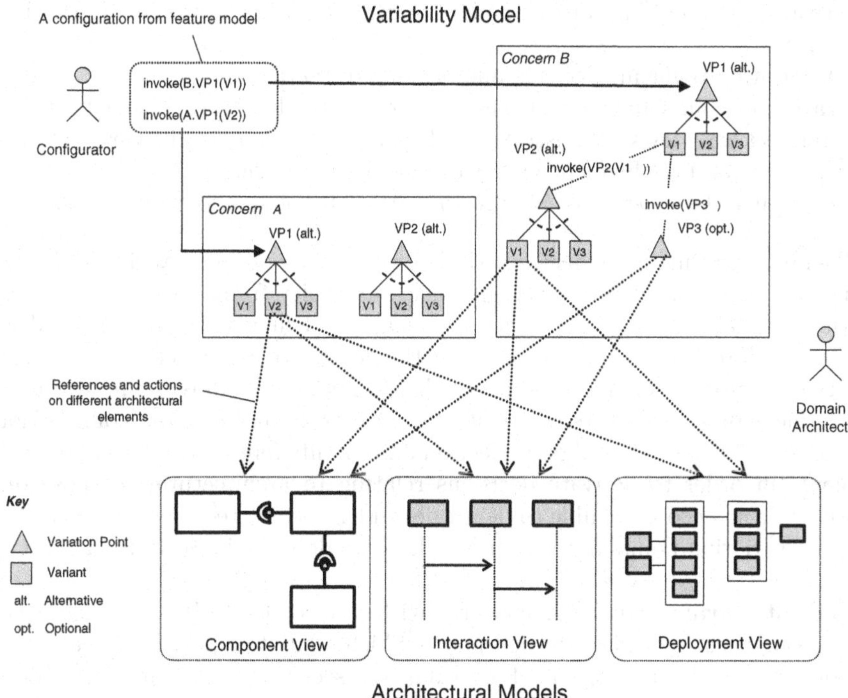

Fig. 1. High level overview of the intention of VML

by the domain architect. Then, the composition primitives (actions) contained within those variation points facilitate the composition of variable architectural elements in the different views. The approach avoids the need to include variability notations within software architecture descriptions and can be viewed as an extension to Bachmann and Pohl's OVM approach with the addition of an explicit referencing language and actions for invoking compositions. In essence, the VML can be said to complement existing variability management approaches such as [3,4,5,6] rather than replace them.

3.2 Language Elements

This section describes the different elements which make up the VML language. We focus on the presentation of the key VML abstractions; a full description of the VML meta-model and more examples can be found in [8]. Before illustrating the different elements in the variability language it is helpful to understand a number of different concepts from the perspective of a product line:

- A product line architecture contains many *concerns*;
- Each concern will have *variation points* associated with them (e.g. a security concern may have the variations in respect of encryption algorithms and so forth);
- A variation point has a name and a *variation kind* (i.e. optional, alternative, parameter);
- A variation point may offer a number of *variants*;
- Variation points and variants should *reference* architectural elements within architectural views as illustrated in Figure 1 (e.g. component view, interaction view and deployment view, etc.) using expressions;
- There may be *dependencies* between variation points and/or variants.

Therefore the main elements in the language are concerns, variation kinds, variation points and variants i.e. the basic variability framework (described in Section 3.2). The concerns might be either features defined in the feature models, or other architectural concerns arising at the design stage and relevant to different architecture stakeholders. Additionally, the domain architect will also need to be able express references to architectural elements and *actions* (composition primitives, which are described in Section 3.2) on different kinds of architectural elements in order to activate decisions relating to architectural composition. Lastly, we also need to be able to define dependencies, i.e. requires and excludes, between variation points and variants (which we describe in Section 3.2).

Variability Framework. A concern, with respect to VML, is a high-level abstraction encapsulating variation points which relate to a particular feature or any other architectural concern. For example, a security concern in VML would capture all variabilities relating to authentication, authorisation, and so forth. A variation point identifies a particular concept within a concern as being variable (e.g. choice of authentication device). A variation point has a name and a kind

```
Concern SafetyDevices {
   VariationPoint FireSprinklerType {
       Kind: alternative;
       Variant Water {… actions on arch elements}
       Variant Foam {… actions on arch elements}
   }
   VariationPoint VisualAlarm {
        Kind: optional;
        … actions
   }
}
```

Fig. 2. Partial VML description for SafetyDevices concern

i.e. option, alternative or parameter. A variant describes a particular variability decision, such as a specific choice of authentication device (e.g. card reader). A variant uses actions and expressions to invoke compositions of architectural elements. Figure 2 illustrates a simple example (with actions omitted) where variation points relating to safety devices are illustrated. The first variation point FireSprinklerType has two variants, namely Water and Foam of which one or none must be chosen. The second variation point describes an optional feature for a visual alarm.

References and Actions. In order to explain the numerous primitives in this section we will refer to Figure 3 which illustrates a number of the architectural composition primitives. A *reference* associates architectural elements with a name in order to simplify expressions when used within actions. A named reference uses expressions and designators to provide quantification power and expressiveness over architectural elements. The possible architectural elements are any of the abstractions present in component view, interaction view, and deployment view (Figure 1). For example the reference in Figure 3a would associate the FireManagement component and its required interface ISprinkler as SprinklerVP.

Actions provide the means to activate decisions which will result in architectural compositions between architectural variants and the common core elements. Actions might entail fine-grained or coarse-grained compositions of architectural elements. The key fine-grained composition mechanisms provided are connect, add, remove and deploy, which work at the level of individual elements within the models. The merge action represents a coarse-grained mechanism in that it works at the package level where these packages encapsulate multiple architectural elements rather than individual ones. The following subsections describe these individual actions in more detail.

Invoke. The invoke action activates either variation points or variants within those variation points. For example, the action in Figure 3b would invoke the variation point FireSprinklerType in the SafetyDevices concern (as originally shown in Figure 1) and select the Water variant. It may be decided that low-level details

```
Reference SprinklerVP {
  component (FireManagement.r:ISprinkler );              (a)
}
invoke (SafetyDevices.FireSprinklerType(Water )); (b)
connect (SmartHomeControl.r:IAlarm::MonitoredAlarm.p:IAlarm );(c)
add interface (r:ILight) to component (SmartHomeControl ); (d)
remove interface (r:ISprinkler ) from component (Control); (e)
deploy component (MotionSensor ) in node (CentralProcessor ); (f)
openCommsPath node (Server) to device (FireSensor ); (g)
after SmartHomeControl.soundAlarm () {
   add (send (SmartHomeControl.activateVisualAlarm ()) &&  (h)
     receive (VisualAlarm))) using (IVisualAlarm);
}
merge (FireManagement ) into (SmartHomeBase); (i)
```

Fig. 3. Composition primitives in VML

(i.e. variations in the solution space) are invoked from other higher level variation points, rather than directly from the feature model. In other words, a high-level variation point might be structured as a *composite variation point* consisting of a set of lower level variation points. Such a scenario may arise when dealing with sets of low-level variation points (e.g. algorithm choice) that map to conceptual variations in the feature models (e.g. processor type and memory size).

Connect. The connect action is a fine-grained composition mechanism for binding architectural elements in the component view. The action in Figure 3c would connect the SmartHomeControl component to the MonitoredAlarm component via their respective required and provided (as denoted by p and r) IAlarm interfaces.

Add. The add action is also a fine-grained mechanism that supports the addition of architectural elements. For example, the action in Figure 3d would add the required interface ILight to the SmartHomeControl component.

Remove. The remove action is a fine-grained mechanism for removing architectural elements in any view. It is expressed using the remove operator. For example, the action in Figure 3e would remove the required interface ISprinkler from the Control component.

Deploy. The deploy action allows architectural elements, such as components, to be assigned to a node, i.e. model elements representing computational resources (e.g. computers, sensors, etc.). The action in Figure 3f adds a MotionSensor component to the CentralProcessor node.

OpenCommsPath. Additionally architectural variabilities may also require to open communication paths to devices i.e. connect devices. This is done using the openCommsPath designator. The action in Figure 3g opens a communications path from the Server node to a FireSensor device.

Interaction view specific actions. The interaction view deals with sequences of operations between architectural elements. There are constructs specifying where, i.e. before, after, start and end, in the program flow an interaction should be added. For example, the action in Figure 3h simply states that after the soundAlarm operation in the SmartHomeControl component is called, we would like to add a new interaction from the SmartHomeControl component to the VisualAlarm component involving the operation activateVisualAlarm via the interface IVisualAlarm. The callee would represent the required part and the recipient the provided.

Merge. The merge works by composing elements of a package (a container for multiple architectural elements) with a base package. For example, the action in Figure 3i would merge the elements of the FireManagement package into the SmartHomeBase package. Merge is a new composition mechanism between packages introduced by UML 2.0. The principal reason for using merge over other actions is to allow more complex collections of architectural elements to be composed which would otherwise result in verbose VML descriptions. The merge represents a coarse-grained mechanism as the architects using VML can be agnostic to inner details of packages, i.e. all the package's internal architectural elements. However, fine-grained variabilities inside the packages can be referenced using the other actions (e.g. connect, add, etc.) and provide the architect with maximum flexibility.

Dependencies. VML allows dependencies between variabilities to be specified. Dependencies are expressed using requires and excludes designators with parameters indicating the name of the corresponding variation point or variant. The following example expression indicates that the Sprinkler variation point cannot be selected unless the Luxury variant within the Edition variation point is also selected:

VariationPoint Sprinkler **requires**(Edition.Luxury){...}

Excludes dependencies are expressed in a similar fashion using the **excludes** designator. It is also possible to express dependencies and constraints between variabilities independently of VML descriptions via a separate *dependency view*. The dependency view only contains the names of variation points and variants along with their respective dependencies. In this manner, dependencies can be viewed in their own space improving their understandability and changeability.

4 Case Study

This section details the usage of the VML in the composition of variabilities relating to the lock control framework in a SmartHome product line. The example is similar to the framework described in [3], and thus provides an ideal frame of reference for those wishing to further understand the relationship between the OVM and VML.

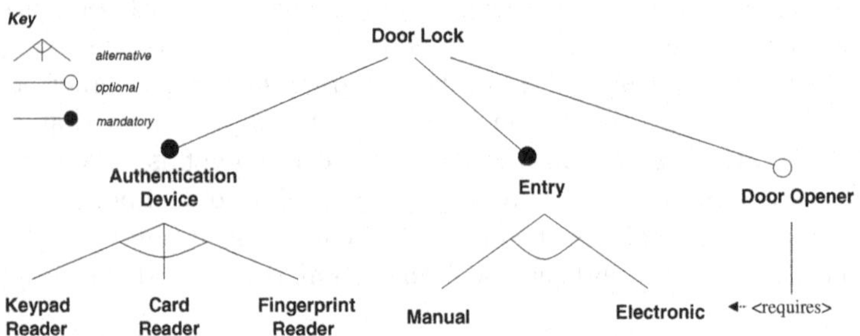

Fig. 4. Feature diagram for lock control

4.1 SmartHome Lock Control

In the SmartHome architecture there is the need to develop different products which have different compositions of features. In turn, these different feature compositions will entail changes to architectural elements in different architectural views. The lock control provides an interesting candidate for demonstrating such changes. In order to understand the variabilities in the lock control consider the feature diagram, using the classical notation from [2], in Figure 4.

The feature diagram illustrates that a lock control can be developed for use with different authentication devices, i.e. keypad, card and fingerprint readers, and provide a manual (open via a physical key) or electronic door lock alternatives (unlock via a an actuator upon authentication). Selection of the manual alternative requires that the user is authenticated once inside the house. Additionally, there is an option for the door to open using an actuator, although this is only available if the electronic alternative is chosen. A component diagram for the lock control is illustrated in Figure 5. As there is no satisfactory variability notation that describes the complete set of variabilities in a single space, we have used an ad hoc one similar to that of Clauss [10]. The figure should not be taken as a contribution of the paper as such, but more a demonstration of the problems of describing variabilities in a visual manner.

The UserControl, AuthenticationManager and LockControl components represent the core common framework. The hatched lines represent variable elements. Additionally, the diagram uses <optional> <alternative> and <requires> annotations to indicate the kinds of variabilities and dependencies between architectural elements. As can be seen from the component diagram, many of the architectural elements correspond directly with features, but many do not. For example selection of the electronic entry option would entail connecting the ElectronicLock component to the LockControl and AuthenticationManager components, and also the LockActuator component to the LockControl component.

Additionally, a new 'required' interface has to be added to the AuthenticationManager and thus a new interaction will occur between this'component and the ElectronicLock component. Additionally, each authentication device will require

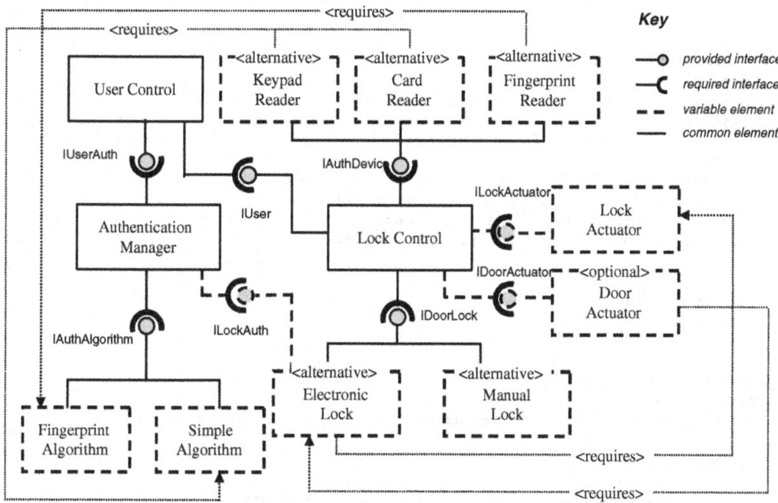

Fig. 5. Component diagram for lock control

an authentication algorithm. The KeypadReader and CardReader components require the SimpleAlgorithm component which simply confirms that the information obtained through the authentication device matches. The FingerprintReader component requires a more complex algorithm, contained within the FingerPrintAlgorithm component, which is based upon biometrics rather than simple matching. As can be ascertained from the component diagram, even a simple feature description, such as the one in Figure 4 may entail a complex set of emerging variabilities through architectural decomposition. In the following sections we will describe the variability in the lock control using the VML language constructs.

4.2 Fine-Grained VML Description

This section illustrates how architectural variability in the lock control can be described using the fine-grained primitives in the VML. Figure 6 illustrates a partial VML description indicating a number of variation points associated with the lock control framework. In the interest of brevity and clarity, we will only detail the AuthenticationDevice and Entry variation points[1]. The first variation point AuthenticationDevice provides three alternative variants namely Keypad, Card and Finger. Two references, AuthDeviceVP and AlgorithmVP, are created for the purpose of simplifying the syntax when used in the actions as they are repeated throughout the description. AuthDeviceVP references the IAuthDevice required interface on the LockControl component, while AlgorithmVP references the IAuthAlgorithm

[1] http://www.comp.lancs.ac.uk/~loughran/VML.html contains the complete description.

```
Concern LockControl {

    VariationPoint AuthenticationDevice {
      Kind: Alternative;
      Reference AuthDeviceVP {component (LockControl.r:IAuthDevice );}
      Reference AlgorithmVP {component (AuthenticationManager.r:IAuthAlgorithm );}

      Variant Keypad {
        connect (AuthDeviceVP::KeypadReader.p:IAuthDevice );
        connect (AlgorithmVP::SimpleAlgorithm.pIAuthAlgorithm );
        deploy component (KeypadReader ) in node (AuthenticationDevice );
        deploy component (SimpleAlgorithm ) in node (SmartHomeControl );
      }

      Variant Card {…}
      Variant Finger {…}
    }

    VariationPoint Entry {
      Kind: Alternative;
      Reference LockControlVP {component (LockControl.r:IDoorLock );}

      Variant Manual {
        connect (LockControlVP::ManualLock.p:IDoorLock );
        deploy component (ManualLock ) in node (SmartHomeControl );
      }

      Variant Electronic {
        connect (LockControlVP::ElectronicLock.p:IDoorLock );
        add interface (r:ILockAuth ) to component (AuthenticationManager );
        add interface (p:ILockAuth ) to component (ElectronicLock );
        connect (ElectronicLock.r:ILockAuth::AuthenticationManager.r:ILockAuth );
        add interface (r:ILockActuator ) to component (LockControl );
        connect (LockControl.r:ILockActuator::LockActuator.p:ILockActuator );

        after AuthenticationManager.authenticated () {
          add (send (AuthenticationManager.unlock ()) &&
               receive (ElectronicLock ))) using (ILockAuth );
        }
        deploy component (ElectronicLock ) in node (SmartHomeControl );
        deploy component (LockActuator ) in node (SmartHomeControl );
        …
      }
    }

    VariationPoint DoorOpener requires Entry(Electronic ) {
      Kind: Option;
      …
    }
}
```

Fig. 6. Partial fine-grained VML description of lock control

required interface on the AuthenticationManager component. A number of actions are then created for connecting components and deploying them in their respective nodes. As the descriptions for these variants are very similar we will only describe the Keypad variant. The first statement connects the LockControl to the KeypadReader component via the IAuthDevice interface.

Next, the AuthenticationManager and SimpleAlgorithm components are connected (note that in the Finger variant the FingerPrint algorithm would be connected instead) via the IAuthAlgorithm interface. Finally, the KeypadReader and SimpleAlgorithm components are deployed in the AuthenticationDevice and SmartHomeControl nodes respectively.

The Entry variation point provides the most complex and interesting set of VML primitives within the lock control description. It describes two variants, namely, Manual and Electronic. The Manual variant simply connects the ManualLock and LockControl components together via the IDoorLock interface, and then deploys the ManualLock component in the SmartHomeControl node. The Electronic variant represents a more complex VML description incorporating the composition of multiple architectural elements. First, the ElectronicLock and LockControl components are connected via the IDoorLock interface. Following this, required and provided ILockAuth interfaces are added to the AuthenticationManager and ElectronicLock components respectively, and then these components are connected. Next the required interface ILockActuator is added to the component LockControl and then the LockControl and LockActuator components are connected. The next VML description illustrates the usage of the interaction actions. The interaction simply states that after the authenticated operation within AuthenticationManager is executed, a new message should be added that sends an unlock operation (the call) from the AuthenticationManager (required) component to the ElectronicLock component (provided) via the IAuth interface . Finally, the ElectronicLock and LockActuator components are deployed in the SmartHomeControl node.

4.3 Coarse -Grained VML Description

This section reports how the lock control can be described using the coarse-grained merge composition mechanism. The merge action relies on the architect to define a core and then decompose related variabilities into separate packages using the merge decomposition mechanism. The VML merge has the same semantics as UML merge[2]. Using UML merge, an architecture can be decomposed into several packages, each one of them representing an architectural increment, delta or slice. Ideally, each package encapsulates one variant, although this might not always be the case as a variant could be encapsulated into a set of interconnected packages. The main advantage is not the one-to-one encapsulation of variants into packages, but the separation of variants from the core. Using merge, the VML descriptions then simply need to refer to the names of the packages that represents variants and specify how they should be merged with the core or other packages (variants of variants), as shown in Figure 7. As a wide range of variable elements are encapsulated into a packages, merge reduces the verbosity of VML descriptions, as all the expressions required to introduce each variable element contained in one package are replaced by a single "merge" expression.

However, there are some disadvantages with this approach:

1. Firstly, while UML package merge has a well-defined semantics for structural views or diagrams, such as component and deployment views, the semantics are not well-defined for behavioural diagrams, which can be problematic if behavioural views, such as interactions between components or state-machines representing component protocols, are to be *merged*.

[2] UML 2.0 specification,http://www.omg.org/docs/formal/05-07-04.pdf, pages 107-115.

```
Concern LockControl {
   VariationPoint AuthenticationDevice {
     Kind: Alternative;

     Variant Keypad {
       merge(Keypad) into(LockBase);
     }
     Variant Finger {
       merge(FingerPrintReader) into(LockBase);
     }
   }

   VariationPoint Entry {
     Kind: Alternative;

     Variant Manual {
       merge(ManualEntry) into(LockBase);
     }
     Variant Electronic  {
       merge(ElectronicEntry) into(LockBase);
     }
   }

   VariationPoint DoorOpener requires Entry(Electronic){
     Kind: Option;
     merge(DoorOpener) into(LockBase);
   }
}
```

Fig. 7. Complete coarse-grained VML description of lock control

2. Secondly, it is not possible to remove elements in a natural way using UML merge, so in case negative variability is required, we need to use UML merge in combination with other VML operators, i.e. the remove action.
3. Finally, when applied to single fine-grained variabilities, e.g. the presence of a single operation in the interface of a device, the UML merge would lead to the creation of packages which contain only a few elements, increasing the number of packages, and therefore leading to a complex network of interconnected packages which could be really complex to manage. Therefore, for small variabilities, the use of fine-grained VML primitives is encouraged.

This brings about a case where the need for both fine-grained and coarse-grained VML primitives may offer the balance required to attain flexibility and reduce verbosity and complexity induced by fine-grained descriptions alone.

5 Discussion and Related Work

The previous section detailed the usage of VML within the context of a Smart Home lock control framework. However, we also applied the VML to three other case studies in order to assess the completeness of the VML language itself. The other three case studies involved the development of a persistence manager framework [11], a multi-agent system framework [12], and an aspectual framework for persistence and distribution [13] which was used in a program family

Table 1. Case studies exploiting VML constructs

VML Constructs	Case Studies			
	Lock Control Framework	Persistence Manager	Multi-agent Product Line	Health Watcher Framework
invoke	Yes	Yes	Yes	Yes
connect	Yes	Yes	Yes	Yes
add	Yes	Yes	Yes	Yes
remove	No	Yes	No	Yes
merge	Yes	No	No	No
after	Yes	Yes	No	Yes
before	No	No	Yes	Yes
deploy	Yes	No	Yes	Yes
openCommsPath	Yes	No	Yes	Yes

for health management in public institutions[3]. We have selected these case studies because they are from heterogeneous domains and their architectures were documented using different modelling languages.

Table 1 summarises whether the different VML constructs were used or not in each of the four case studies. The results illustrate that the VML language was expressive enough to cope with all of the variabilities encountered within our case studies. Another interesting observation was that it was straightforward to use VML in conjunction with different architectural modelling notations. The architecture modelling of the lock control framework and the persistence manager are based on UML 2.0. The descriptions of the multi-agent product line and the Health Watcher framework use an aspect-oriented architecture modelling notation, called AOGA [14]. However, after our case studies were complete we believe that an additional primitive could be helpful in reducing the verbosity of VML descriptions. A primitive which allows the architect to create multiple architectural elements in a single place (e.g. components along with their interfaces) as opposed to the using multiple add primitives could prove to be useful. Additionally, the merge primitive has only been applied to one case study thus far (Table 1). We therefore need to investigate to what degree the usefulness of this composition operator increases in large-scale product lines. Perhaps more importantly, we would like to investigate how the addition of a visual front end to the VML can help with the specification of complex architectural descriptions.

While there are a number of variability management approaches per se, e.g. [5,6], to name but only two, there are relatively few approaches which consider variability of architectural models. Koala [15] is an example of a component based engineering approach using an ADL. Coarse-grained variabilities can be expressed in terms of different component compositions, while fine-grained variabilities are catered for using diversity interfaces (realised by conditional

[3] These case studies can be viewed at http://www.comp.lancs.ac.uk/~loughran/VML.html

compilation switches in the code). In the work of Clauss [10], UML architectural models annotated with stereotypes denoting variable elements, e.g. optional, alternative and dependencies. However, due to the embedding of variability within the model, as the number of variabilities increase it becomes increasingly difficult to understand.

Hendrickson and van der Hoek [16] use an approach to variability management using configuration management principles. In their approach product-line architectures are documented and maintained as a set of separate packages or 'slices'. In effect this is similar to the VML merge approach. However, the authors only consider the component view. MATA [17] is an approach to model composition based on graph rewriting formalisms where stereotypes denoting variability are applied to individual architectural elements. We believe that VML could provide a front end to this approach and further facilitate their composition process via higher level abstractions.

6 Conclusions

The specification of architectural variabilities and their mapping from problem space to solution space is challenging for a number of reasons. Features do not map directly to architectural models in a simple fashion, and many variability-specific decisions are dependent on the nature of design decompositions expressed in different architectural views. This paper presented a variability modelling language (VML) as a novel technique to allow for heterogeneous forms of architectural variabilities to be specified in a non-invasive manner. With VML, it is possible to modularly define all the variabilities pertaining to a particular architectural concern in a single place, thus facilitating its change and evolution. VML is a textual language that complements GUI-based tools, such as pure::variants[4], and provides a succinct yet flexible representation which can be easily understood by software product-line architects. VML also support a variety of mechanisms which facilitate variability modelling and composition, whereby individual architectural elements can be added and/or removed from a core model using a simple set of architecturally-significant actions. Our work is clearly influenced by Pohl and Bachmann's work [3,4] on OVM. However, we take their variability documentation approach and add primitives for performing composition of architectural variabilities. VML has been illustrated in this document in conjunction with architectural models. However, there is no fundamental reason why the VML, when given suitable referencing and actions for a particular context, could not be used with other kinds of software artifacts such as implementation-level code, documentation or scripts. In the future, we plan to investigate how the VML can be used in such scenarios, and assess how VML supports enhanced evolution of product-line architectures using a conventional stability metrics suite [18,19].

[4] http://www.pure-systems.com

References

1. Clements, P., Northrop, L.: Software Product Lines: Practices and Patterns, 3rd edn. Addison-Wesley, Reading (2001)
2. Czarnecki, K., Eisenecker, U.W.: Generative Programming - Methods, Tools, and Applications. Addison-Wesley, Reading (2000)
3. Pohl, K., et al.: Software Product Line Engineering: Foundations, Principles and Techniques. Springer, Heidelberg (2005)
4. Bachmann, F., et al.: A meta-model for representing variability in product family development. In: van der Linden, F.J. (ed.) PFE 2003. LNCS, vol. 3014, pp. 66–80. Springer, Heidelberg (2004)
5. Pure: variants, `http://www.pure-systems.com`
6. Gears-BigLever Software Inc, `http://www.biglever.com`
7. Loughran, N., et al.: Synthesis of state-of-the-art in spl architecture design and mdd-based architecture design. Technical Report D2.1, AMPLE Project (2007)
8. Sánchez, P., et al.: A metamodel for designing software architectures of aspect-oriented software product lines. Technical Report D2.2, AMPLE Project (2007)
9. van Gurp, J., Bosch, J.: Design erosion: problems and causes. Journal of Systems and Software 61(2), 105–119 (2002)
10. Clauß, M.: Modelling variability with uml. In: Proc. of the Young Researchers Workshop, 3rd GCSE, Erfurt (2001)
11. Rashid, A., Chitchyan, R.: Persistence as an aspect. In: Proc. of the 2nd Int. Conf. on AOSD, Boston, USA, pp. 120–129 (2003)
12. Garcia, A., et al.: Agents in object-oriented software engineering. Software Practice and Experience 34(5), 489–521 (2004)
13. Soares, S., et al.: Implementing distribution and persistence aspects with aspectj. In: Proc. of the 22nd Conf. on OO Programming, Systems, Languages and Applications (OOPSLA), Seattle, USA, pp. 174–190 (2002)
14. Kulesza, U., et al.: Towards a method for developing aspect-oriented generative approaches. In: Proc. of the Workshop on Early Aspects (EA), 24th OOPSLA, Vancouver, Canada (2004)
15. van Ommering, R., et al.: The koala component model for consumer electronics software. IEEE Computer 33(3), 78–85 (2000)
16. Hendrickson, S.A., van der Hoek, A.: Modeling product line architectures through change sets and relationships. In: Proc. of the 29th Int. Conf. on Software Engineering (ICSE), Minneapolis, USA, pp. 189–198 (2007)
17. Whittle, J., Jayaraman, P.: Mata: A tool for aspect-oriented modeling based on graph transformation. In: Proc. of the 11th Workshop on AOM, 10th MODELS, Nashville, USA (2007)
18. Greenwood, P., et al.: On the impact of aspectual decompositions on design stability: An empirical study. In: Ernst, E. (ed.) ECOOP 2007. LNCS, vol. 4609, pp. 176–200. Springer, Heidelberg (2007)
19. Molesini, A., et al.: On the quantitative analysis of architecture stability in aspectual decompositions. In: Proc. of the 7th Working IEEE/IFIP Conf. on Software Architecture (WICSA), Vancouver, Canada (2008)

Composing Components and Services Using a Planning-Based Adaptation Middleware

Romain Rouvoy[1], Frank Eliassen[1], Jacqueline Floch[2], Svein Hallsteinsen[2], and Erlend Stav[2]

[1] University of Oslo,
P.O. Box 1080 Blindern,
0316 Oslo, Norway
{rouvoy, frank}@ifi.uio.no
[2] SINTEF ICT,
7024 Trondheim, Norway
{jacqueline.floch, svein.hallsteinsen, erlend.stav}@sintef.no

Abstract. Self-adaptive component-based architectures provide methods and mechanisms to support the dynamic adaptation of their structure under evolving execution context. Dynamic adaptation is particularly relevant in the domain of ubiquitous computing, which is subject to numerous unexpected changes of the execution context. In this paper, we focus on changes in the service provider landscape: business services may dynamically come and go, and their quality of service may vary. We introduce an extension of the MADAM component-based planning framework that optimizes the overall utility of applications when such changes occur. MADAM planning is based on dynamic configuration of component frameworks. The extended planning framework supports seamless configuration of component frameworks based on both local and remote components and services. In particular, components and services can be plugged in interchangeably to provide functionalities defined by the component framework. The extended planning framework is illustrated and validated on a use case scenario.

Keywords: Adaptation planning, component-based architectures, self-adaptation, service-oriented architectures.

1 Introduction

Self-adaptive architectures provide methods and mechanisms supporting the dynamic adaptation of their structure under an evolving runtime execution context. Dynamic adaptation is particularly relevant in the domain of ubiquitous computing, where users carrying mobile devices move around in ubiquitous computing environments causing frequent and unexpected changes in the execution context of their applications. For example, a mobile device is frequently roaming, and its applications have to be dynamically adapted to remain useful under new network conditions. Such an adaptation requires the detection of context changes, but also the selection of an

C. Pautasso and É. Tanter (Eds.): SC 2008, LNCS 4954, pp. 52–67, 2008.

application configuration that maintains a satisfactory *Quality of Service* (QoS) in the new context. With the emergence of *Service-Oriented Architectures* (SOA) [1], both the availability and the QoS of the services on which the applications depend become an important part of the context. Thus, SOA is of interest for self-adaptive applications, because services are reusable and composable entities that can be dynamically exploited to improve the behavior of an application executed on a mobile device. Services in a SOA environment can be discovered and accessed without knowledge of the underlying platform implementation and hence can be exploited in the dynamic configuration of the applications. Adaptation in MADAM is generally QoS-driven. In SOA, QoS properties are part of the *Service Level Agreements* (SLAs) [2] that are negotiated between a service provider and its end-user consumers. By integrating SLA negotiation into the adaptation decision process, application adaptation exploiting SOA can still be QoS-driven.

The MUSIC planning framework introduced in this paper is an extension of the MADAM planning framework, which supports the adaptation of component-based architectures [3]. MADAM follows an architecture-centric approach where we represent architecture models at runtime to allow generic middleware components to reason about and control adaptation aims at simplifying the development of adaptive applications. In MADAM applications are modeled as component frameworks where functionality defined by a component framework can be dynamically configured with conforming component implementations. The purpose of an adaptation-planning framework is to compute and evaluate the utility of alternative configurations in response to context changes, and to select a good one for the current context. The extension we propose supports self-adaptation of ubiquitous applications to changes in the service provider landscape. The planning middleware evaluates discovered remote services as alternative configurations for the functionalities required by an application. This means that the extended planning framework, when triggering an adaptation, can support seamless configuration of component frameworks based on both local and remote components and services. In particular, components and services can be plugged in interchangeably to provide implementation of functionalities defined by the component framework. In the case of services, the planning framework deals directly with SLA protocols supported by the service providers to negotiate the appropriate QoS for the user.

In this paper, we first introduce a motivating scenario for the support of remote services in mobile applications (cf. Section 2). After presenting the various foundations of this work (cf. Section 3), we introduce our planning framework capable of supporting SOA when adapting applications (cf. Section 4). This planning framework is illustrated and validated on a use case extracted from the motivating scenario (cf. Section 5). Finally, related work is discussed (cf. Section 6) before concluding and presenting our perspectives (cf. Section 7).

2 Motivating Scenario

To further motivate the need for adaptation in service-oriented computing environments, let us consider the following scenario. A sales agent spends much of his time visiting customers. To assist him in his work, he is using an extended

Customer Relationship Management (CRM) system. The system offers traditional CRM functionality, such as keeping track of and sharing customer- and business-related information. In addition, it assists the agent with route planning, detection of traveling delays and notifying customers affected by such delays.

Scene 1. The scenario starts with the sales agent meeting a customer, and using the CRM system on his laptop to record agreements with the customer. Before the meeting terminates, he is notified about an upcoming meeting at another customer site and decides to prepare for this new meeting. He picks up his smartphone and launches the mobile CRM application to find the best route and estimate the travel time. For this, the application uses a location service, a map service, and a route planning service. There are several providers both for the map service and the route planning service, and the CRM application has to select providers facilitating a quick and precise answer to the agent. In this case the location service provided by the WLAN at the customer site and a route planning service available through the Internet are the best alternatives.

Scene 2. The agent ends the current meeting, and walks out to his car to go to his next meeting. As he drives away from the customer's building, the smartphone looses connection to the customer WLAN, and the Internet connection is switched seamlessly to GPRS by the mobile IP software installed on the smartphone. The connection to the location service, which the CRM application needs to monitor progress, is lost. The GPRS provider also offers a location service, but with a lower accuracy. However, the car has a navigation system based on GPS, which provides a more accurate location service via a Bluetooth connection. The car navigation system also offers a navigation aid service. The CRM application reconfigures itself to use these services, since this solution provides a better accuracy, and a increased visibility to the user because of the larger display of the car navigation system. It also saves battery life on the smartphone since the navigation aid component of the CRM application has been replaced by an external service.

Scene 3. Half way to the meeting, the agent runs into a traffic jam caused by an accident partly blocking the road, resulting in a temporary slowdown of his progress towards his next destination. The CRM application detects this situation, alerts the agent that he will be late, estimates the delay using data obtained from the route planning service and offers the agent to notify affected customers. The agent accepts this proposal and the CRM application sends text messages to the customers using the available smartphone interface. The CRM application monitors progress and re-estimates the arrival time regularly in order to be able to alert the meeting about changes. Meanwhile the selected route planning service becomes congested, leading to slow response and out-of-date information. The application detects this and reconfigures to an alternative service that costs more to use but which provides more up-to-date information.

3 Foundations

This section introduces the basis of the proposed approach by presenting concepts related to planning-based middleware (cf. Section 3.1), and service-oriented architectures (cf. Section 3.2). The section concludes by identifying the assumptions that are considered in our contribution (cf. Section 3.3).

3.1 Planning-Based Middleware

Planning-based middleware refers to the capability of adapting an application to changing operating conditions by exploiting knowledge about its composition and *Quality of Service* (QoS) metadata associated to the application components [4]. We therefore consider applications that are developed with a QoS-aware component model. The QoS model associated with a ubiquitous application defines all the reasoning dimensions used by the planning-based middleware to select and deploy the component implementations that contribute to provide the best utility. The utility of an application grows when its constituting components better fulfill user preferences while optimizing device resource consumption.

Planning refers to the process of selecting components that make up an application variant that provides the best possible utility to the end user. This process can be triggered during several steps of the application life cycle, such as during the deployment of the application or at runtime if the execution context suddenly changes. The parts of the application that are considered during planning are called *variation points*. These correspond to functionalities (type of behavior) defined in the component frameworks modeling the application. Thus, each variation point identifies a functionality of the application that can be implemented differently. In addition, each component implementation suitable for a variation point is reified as a *plan* by the planning-based middleware. A plan mainly consists of a structure that reflects the type of the component implementation and the QoS properties associated to the services it provides. In particular, the plan exhibits both *requested properties* (*e.g.*, memory consumption, network bandwidth, network connectivity) and *offered properties* (*e.g.*, request throughput, response time, result accuracy) referring to the QoS model of the application. To estimate the offered properties of a plan, the planning-based middleware relies on *property predictors*. The property predictors are used to predict the offered properties of a component implementation as a function using the required properties and the current execution context as parameters. The predictors can also take into account the state of the component implementation associated to the plan—*i.e.*, described, deployed, or running—to refine the prediction. The QoS model used by the planning framework can be customized to handle new QoS dimensions (*e.g.*, monetary cost), while the property predictors can be configured to support complex heuristics (*e.g.*, QoS negotiation protocols). The predicted properties are input to a normalized *utility function* that computes the expected utility of a composition of plans making up an alternative application configuration. The planning-based middleware compares the expected utility of all alternate application configurations, and finally selects the one that provides the highest value.

Fig. 1 illustrates the architecture of the MADAM adaptation middleware. The component Adaptation Manager supports the *planning procedure* by operating a generic reasoning heuristics that exploits metadata included in the available plans. In particular, the plans are composed based on their type compatibility to describe alternative application configurations. Then, the heuristics ranks the application configurations by evaluating their utility with regards to the application objectives.

This evaluation is achieved by computing the offered properties using the property predictors associated to each plan contained in the selected application configuration and retrieved from the component Plan Repository.

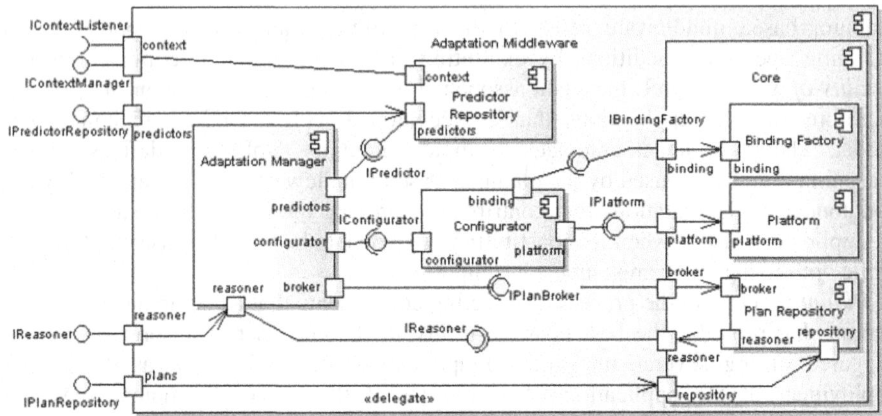

Fig. 1. The Architecture of the MADAM planning-based adaptation middleware

The component Plan Repository provides an interface IPlanBroker for the Adaptation Manager to retrieve plans associated with a given component type during planning. The Adaptation Manager may request plans that are compatible with a given variation point, at which point the Plan Repository will search for matching component types. Any additional metadata on the required component type will help the Plan Repository to exclude plans and filter the search space [5]. Plans are typically published to (and discarded from) the Plan Repository by applications and component development tools using the interface IPlanRepository, and can thus trigger the Adaptation Manager for re-planning of the application if needed (*e.g.*, the discarded plan was associated to a running component).

The *reconfiguration* process is handled by the component Configurator and consists of taking the set of plans selected by the component Adaptation Manager and reconfiguring the application. Before deploying the application configuration selected by the reasoning engine, the component Configurator brings the current application into a stable state, by suspending the execution of its contained components. Then, if the component described by a plan is in the running or deployed state, the associated component instance is configured for the variation point and connected to other components using the component Binding Factory. If the component is in the described state, then the component should be preliminary instantiated and deployed by the component Platform using the component implementation description associated to the plan. The result of the reconfiguration (*e.g.*, reference of the deployed instance) is automatically reflected into the selected plans.

Thus, the MADAM planning-based middleware offers a modular and extensible approach for adapting applications built with various types of component models. In particular, the concept of *plan* can be derived to support heterogeneous artifacts and their associated states. Furthermore, the components Platform and Binding Factory provide sufficient abstractions for supporting different middleware platforms (*e.g.*, CORBA, J2EE, and Web Services).

3.2 Service-Oriented Architectures

When studying the SOA domain, we observe that there is no standard, universally accepted definition of *Service-Oriented Architectures*. Erl [1] proposes to characterize SOA by a set of fundamental design principles for service-orientation, such as abstraction, reusability, composition, and loose coupling. SOA can also be considered as an evolution of component-based architectures. In component-based software engineering, applications are assembled from components that can be used without any knowledge of either their implementation or their underlying platform. SOA goes a step further by introducing an abstract business model defining the concepts of *functionality* as a product or an enterprise resource, *service provider*, *service consumer*, and *service contract*. While the owner of a component-based application is responsible for the instantiation of components, the service provider is responsible for the creation and the management of services. The most fundamental principle of service-orientation is the standardized service contract [6]. In particular, services express their semantics and capabilities via a service contract. Although SOA was initially proposed to organize business software, service-orientation provides facilities that are applicable beyond that scope. For example, support has been developed for interface type and semantics descriptions, QoS descriptions, service discovery protocols, and binding factories. Nowadays, the SOA concepts are more and more exploited in a large set of producer/consumer systems, such as ubiquitous systems.

Service QoS properties are normally negotiated between the service provider and the service consumer, and are described as part of the service contract as a *Service Level Agreement* (SLA). A service level is used to describe the expected performance behavior, such as response time and availability, or other properties such as billing, termination terms and penalties in the case of violation of the SLA [1]. An SLA can simply be created after selection of a fixed service level offer among several pre-defined offers or, in more complex cases, after customization via a negotiation process. An SLA may be valid for a limited period, or may be terminated explicitly. During service provisioning, the provider should monitor the service quality, and adapt the resources to avoid a violation of an SLA. The consumer may also perform monitoring as well to avoid blindly trusting the provider.

In our work, support for services is motivated by the possibility to control the usability, usefulness, and reliability of a ubiquitous application by adapting it to changes in the service landscape. The following changes are relevant:

1. The service providers add (resp. remove) services in (resp. from) the environment,
2. New services become accessible depending on changes in the ubiquitous execution context, such as network conditions or locations,
3. The quality of service becomes better or worse due to context changes,
4. The violation of an SLA (by the user or the provider) leads to the termination of the SLA.

Mechanisms for discovering changes in the service landscape and contract violations are not discussed in this paper. The planning process is triggered when changes occur. Planning requires the ability to reason on service properties (including QoS) and dependencies between service properties and context.

3.3 Assumptions

Although it is also relevant to investigate our planning-based middleware to support the planning of service compositions, this paper concentrates on the adaptation of component-based applications operating in service-oriented environments. In particular, our middleware does not explicitly control the resources in the provider domain. Thus, we assume that the description and the deployment of SLA contracts, made available to customers, are realized by the service providers. We assume that service discovery and service levels identification are performed prior to planning. Whether a SLA contract or a set of potential SLA contracts are negotiated during discovery or during planning depends on the flexibility of provider offers and on the consumer needs. Thus, we aim at providing flexible solutions and foresee that a service level offered during service discovery may no longer be valid when requested after selection during planning. Our solution must therefore cope with the possible denial of the requested service level by the service provider.

4 Service Planning with SOA

Based on the above foundations, the SOA concepts can be integrated in our planning framework by supporting a common and uniform representation of the different forms of services—*i.e.,* component descriptions, component instances, and remote services. This common representation provides all the meta-information that is required to evaluate the utility of a service for a given application. Thus, when a service is discovered by the platform, its meta-information needs to be made available to the planning framework in a suitable form (cf. Section 4.1). And, if selected by the planning heuristic (cf. Section 4.2), a remote service should be connected to the ubiquitous application by using a proper binding framework that provides interoperability between the user- and provider-sides and that contributes to SLA monitoring (cf. Section 4.3).

4.1 Plan Discovery and Brokering

According to Fig. 2, we propose to extend the component Adaptation Middleware introduced in Fig. 1 to support the integration of remote services and service level agreements. In particular, we have introduced new components (the darkest ones in the figure) to support different types of remote services. To do so, the component Adaptation Middleware integrates a composite component SOA that isolates the integration of a given SOA technology (*e.g.*, Web Service, CORBA, or UPnP). This separation of concerns allows also the adaptation middleware to combine several SOA technologies using different implementations of the component SOA. This combination is achieved by extending the component Plan Repository with a component Plan Broker that federates the local Plan Repository with the components Service Discovery used to generate plans describing discovered remote services. In particular, the component Service Discovery encloses the service discovery protocols integrated in the middleware to advertise any newly discovered services to the Plan Repository [7]. Plans for these remote services are generated based on contracts negotiated by the component SLA Negotiation when discovered so that they are available when the Adaptation Manager initiates an adaptation at a later time. Plans are automatically discarded and removed from the Plan Repository when remote services disappear or for some reason become unavailable to the middleware.

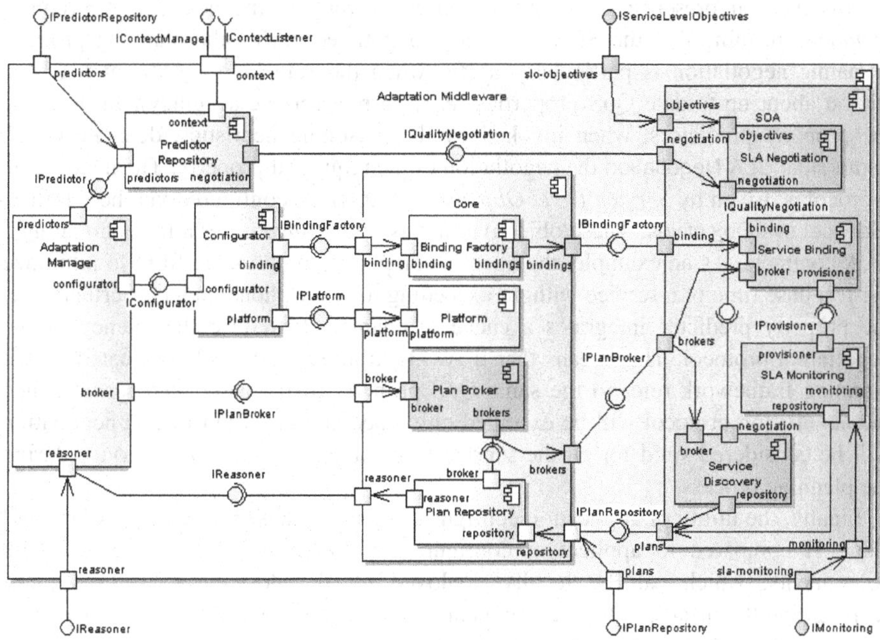

Fig. 2. The Architecture of the MUSIC planning-based adaptation middleware

SLA contracts can be either static or allow for some dynamic negotiation [2]. One example is a service level described by the service provider as QoS properties that are available at either static or negotiable cost. Furthermore, a service may offer a predefined set of service levels. When such a service is detected by the component Service Discovery, it generates a new service plan enclosing structural and behavioral metadata related to the service (*e.g.*, interface type description and contracts). Then, for each service level associated to this service, the component Service Discovery publishes an extended version of the service plan into the Plan Repository to reflect the alternative service levels available. This service level plan inherits from the metadata of the service plan and completes it with the additional QoS properties described by the service level (*e.g.*, service accuracy and cost).

4.2 Plan Reasoning

The component Adaptation Manager is then able to take into account each set of service levels when applying the reasoning heuristics. For planning to be efficient, service negotiation is a time critical factor that should be resolved as soon as possible. In our middleware, the negotiation is generally *static*, meaning that the negotiation is performed during service discovery for static QoS properties (*e.g.*, service cost) described by the service levels. The resulting static QoS property values are included into the service plan so that the property predictors can automatically report them at a later time.

However, in presence of a flexible service level [1], the negotiation becomes *dynamic*, meaning that the SLA contract is negotiated during the planning process. Dynamic negotiation is particularly useful when the Adaptation Manager needs to reason about up-to-date QoS properties (*e.g.*, current service accuracy). In this case the property predictors, when invoked by the reasoning heuristics, delegate to the component SLA Negotiation the negotiation of the requested property. The negotiation protocol is driven by *Service Level Objectives* (SLOs) [8] configured via the interface IServiceLevelObjectives. These objectives act as pre-defined criteria for negotiating a SLA contracts. As an example, the agent's company can define an SLO to minimize the response time of a service without exceeding its daily phone budget. Furthermore, the property predictor integrates a cache mechanism to reduce the latency of the negotiation protocol. This means that if two flexible service levels evaluated by the planning framework refer to the same QoS property of the associated service, then the negotiation protocol will be executed only once and the result of this negotiation will be considered valid for all the service levels associated with this service during the planning process.

Finally, the utility of application configurations using these service level plans will also get compared to application configurations based on plans associated with components, which can be locally deployed on the device, as well as plans representing the instance of the component or service already used by the application. The reasoning heuristics will therefore provide a uniform ranking of alternative application configurations, and the Adaptation Manager will select and deploy the configuration predicting the highest utility.

4.3 Plan Deployment and Configuration

As mentioned in Section 3.1, the component Configurator generally iterates over the plans composing the new application configuration to reconfigure the application. The support of remote services implies that it can now face three different situations. If the plan refers to an instance of a component, which is already used by the current application, the Configurator reuses this instance in the new configuration. If the plan refers to a component for which no instance is currently available, the Configurator uses the component Platform, to create and deploy a new instance of the component. Finally, if the plan refers to a remote service available in the environment, the Configurator uses the component Service Binding to generate a specific component that will act as a *service proxy*[1]. A service proxy is a local representative of the remote service accessed by the application. In particular, it implements the service type described by the application components and encapsulates the communication protocol used to access the remote service. During this binding phase, the SLA contract associated with the selected plan is provisioned and enforced by the involved parties. This includes the reservation of computing resources by the provider and the deployment of SLA monitoring facilities [8]. This means that the SLA contract associated to the selected service is transferred to the component SLA Monitoring.

The service proxy implements also a *disconnection detection algorithm* due to the ubiquitous aspect of the application. This disconnection support is inspired from the principles of Ambient programming [9]. When loosing the connection to a remote service, the proxy stores the incoming service requests in a queue and returns a *non-blocking future object* to the application. The future object includes a block of code that is triggered when the service connection is resolved to process the result of the request. If the connection is lost for a long period, the service proxy breaks the SLA contract via the component SLA Negotiation. This notification triggers an adaptation of the application, and transfers the request queue to the new component (or service proxy) that will be planned and deployed.

Finally, the service proxy is also responsible for *monitoring the dynamic QoS properties associated to the SLA contract* agreed with the service [10]. To do so, the service proxy collects metrics at runtime (*e.g.*, the service response time) and reports the observed values to the component SLA Monitoring. This component is responsible for breaking the SLA contract if the observed value violates the value agreed. An example of violation of this contract can be a response time observed by the service proxy above the threshold agreed in the SLA. In practice, the component SLA Monitoring removes the associated service level plan from the Plan Repository to trigger a new adaptation of the application.

5 Case Study

As a preliminary validation of our approach, in this section we present a case study based on the scenario described in Section 2.

The architecture of the CRM application is introduced in Fig. 3. It basically supports two alternative compositions. Both contain a component GUI that presents a graphical user interface on the smartphone and a component Main that embeds the application logic and binds the different functionalities together. Main interacts with the CRM service to retrieve calendar and customer information, and with a Route Planning service to find the shortest route to reach a meeting location as well as the estimated travel time. It also uses a Navigation service to provide navigation aid to the user and a messaging service to alert affected customers about delays. In composition *a)* the navigation service is provided by a component Navigation deployed on the smartphone, which displays a map, the recommended route, and the current location on the smartphone display using the GUI. This component Navigation depends on a Map service and a Location service provided by a third party service provider. In

[1] Service proxy component bytecode is generated at runtime using the ASM bytecode manipulation framework (cf. http://asm.objectweb.org). The implementation details are out of the scope of this paper.

composition *b)* the Navigation service is provided by a third party service provider, supposed to use the provider's display to show the same information to the user. The QoS properties and service types relevant for the case study are specified in Table 1 and 2. Property predictors for the application, specified as functions of the properties of the services the application depends on, are associated with the compositions in Fig. 3.

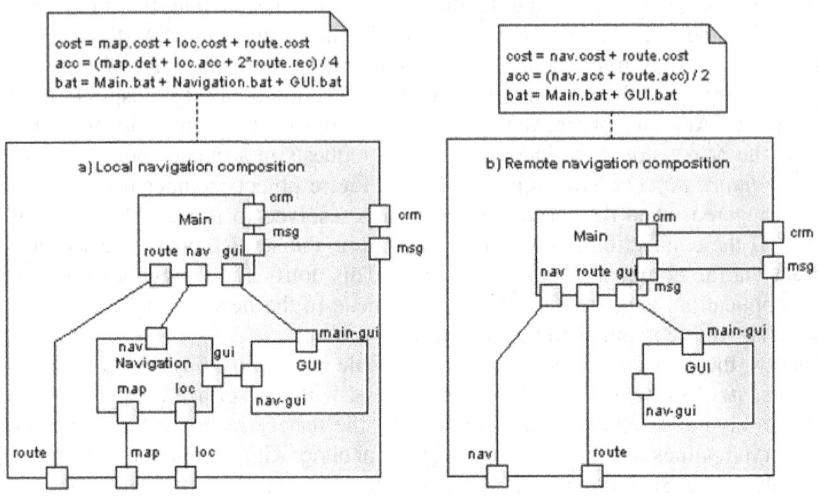

Fig. 3. The architecture model of the CRM client application

Table 1. The relevant QoS properties defined in the CRM client application

Property Name	Description	Value range
cost	Cost of using the service	0-?
acc	Accuracy, for example of a location	1-10
det	Level of detail of a map	1-10
rec	Recency of traffic info	1-10
bat	Battery units consumed by a component	1-100

Table 2. The service types defined in the CRM client application

Service Name	Description	Requested properties
loc	Locates the device geographically	cost, acc
map	Provides a map of a limited area	cost, det
route	Establish the fastest route between two locations and estimates the travel time	cost, rec
nav	Provides navigation aid	cost, acc

The landscape of remote services and how it evolves through the scenario is described in Fig. 4. The services are described by QoS properties that, together with the resources needed for communicating with them, determine the adaptation of the application.

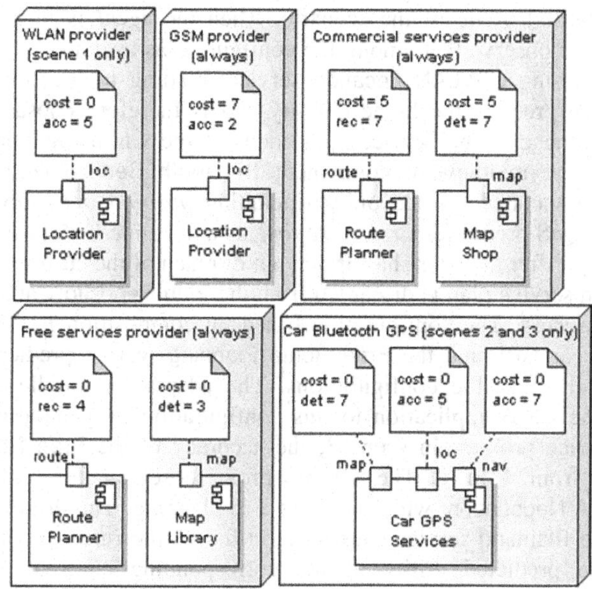

Fig. 4. The service landscape for the CRM client application

We did a simulation of the adaptation reasoning on this use case. In the simulation we also took into account estimation of the power consumption of the different alternatives, based on predictors for usage of memory, CPU, and network bandwidth. For the sake of simplicity[2], we used a simplified utility function assuming that the user prefers low cost (*i.e.*, to minimise cost), high accuracy (*i.e.*, to maximise acc), and needs to save battery (*i.e.*, to minimise bat). Thus, we define the function evaluating the utility of a CRM application configuration as the weighted sum of the normalised QoS properties (using the function *norm(…)*):

$$utility = \frac{user_{cost}}{norm(cost)} + user_{acc} \times norm(acc) + \frac{user_{bat}}{norm(bat)}$$

Table 3 summarizes the computed utility of the best configurations in different situations during the scenario.

Table 3. The CRM alternative configurations with their associated normalized utilities

Configuration				Utility	
Composition	loc	map	route	Scene 1&2	Scene 3
Local navigation	WLAN	Commercial	Commercial	**0,42**	0,42
Local navigation	WLAN	Free	Free	0,40	0,35
Remote navigation	Bluetooth	Free	Free	**0,66**	0,54
Remote navigation	Bluetooth	Free	Commercial	0,58	**0,58**

[2] In this scenario, we do not demonstrate the direct impact of memory, CPU, or network bandwidth variations on the computed utility values.

During the initial scene of the scenario, when the agent is in a meeting at a customer site, we observe that among the configurations available in this situation, composition *i)* using a WLAN Location service, binding to the commercial route planning service predicts the highest utility and is therefore chosen. In scene 2, when entering the car, the services provided by the car navigation system are discovered by the middleware component Bluetooth Service Discovery, which publishes the associated service plans (including *position accuracy* and *battery usage* as static QoS properties / *response time* as a dynamic QoS property) into the Plan Repository. After the agent has driven out of reach of the customer WLAN, the WLAN Location service plan is discarded from the Plan Repository and thus triggers the planning process. The configuration based on composition *ii)*, the Navigation service of the car GPS and the Free Route Planning service predicts the highest utility among the possible configurations. The adaptation middleware therefore reconfigures the CRM application to this configuration by generating Navigation and Route service proxies. In scene 3, the accuracy of the Free Route Planning service drops from 4 to 1. The service proxy observes this and notifies the component SLA Negotiation, which triggers a re-planning. The drop in accuracy of the Free Route Planning service causes the utility of the running configuration to fall below the predicted utility of the corresponding configuration with the Commercial Route Planning service. Therefore the Adaptation Manager selects this configuration and asks the Configurator to perform the reconfiguration of the service binding of the application.

6 Related Work

Adaptive Service Grids (ASG) is an open initiative that enables dynamic composition and binding of services, which is used for provisioning adaptive services [11]. In particular, ASG proposes a sophisticated and adaptive delivery service composed of three sub-cycles: *Planning*, *binding*, and *enactment*. The entry point of this delivery lifecycle is a *semantic service request*, which consists of a description of what will be achieved and not which concrete service has to be executed. Compared to our planning-based middleware, ASG focuses only on the planning per request of service workflows with regards to the properties defined in the semantic service request. Thus, ASG does not support a uniform planning of both components and services as our planning-based framework for ubiquitous applications does. However, we think that our planning-based middleware can be extended to integrate ASG adaptive services and seamlessly support dynamic enactment of service workflows that can provide the services required by a ubiquitous application.

Menasce and Dubey [12] propose an approach to QoS brokering in SOA. Consumers request services from a QoS broker, which selects a service provider that maximizes the consumer's utility function subject to its cost constraint. Utility functions express the usefulness of a system as a function of several attributes, such as response time, throughput, and availability. The approach assumes that service providers register with the broker by providing service demands for each of the resources used by the services provided as well as cost functions for each of the services. The QoS broker uses analytic queuing models to predict the QoS values of the various services that could be selected under varying workload conditions. This approach is of interest from both the viewpoint of a consumer and a provider. While the client is relieved from performing service discovery and negotiation, the provider is given support for QoS management. The approach, however, requires the client device to be able to access the broker, but this might not be possible in mobile environments. It also assumes that the consumer is able to determine the expected service properties. Our approach differs in that it considers the offered properties as alternatives to determine the best application configuration.

CARISMA is a mobile computing peer-to-peer middleware exploiting the principle of reflection to support the construction of context-aware adaptive applications [13]. Services and adaptation policies are installed and uninstalled on the fly. CARISMA can automatically trigger the adaptation of the deployed applications by detecting execution context changes. CARISMA uses utility functions to select application profiles, which is used to select the appropriate action for a particular context event. If there are conflicting application profiles, then CARISMA proceeds to an auction-like procedure to resolve (both local and distributed) conflicts. Contrary to MUSIC, CARISMA does not deal with the discovery of remote services that can trigger application reconfigurations. However, the auction-like procedure used by CARISMA could be integrated in the MUSIC middleware as a particular implementation of the component SLA Negotiation.

ReMMoC is a dynamic middleware that supports interoperability between mobile clients and ubiquitous services [14]. During run-time, the ReMMoC service discovery component reconfigures itself and the remote service binding to match the protocols of the discovered ubiquitous services. Like MUSIC, ReMMoC uses architecture specifications for both the initial configuration and reconfigurations. However, ReMMoC does not support anything like service planning or discovery of service implementation alternatives, but applies rule-based policies that are limited to a fixed set of static component compositions.

7 Conclusion and Perspectives

In this paper we have introduced the design of a QoS-driven generic planning framework for self-adaptive mobile applications, which seamlessly supports and mixes component-based and service-based configurations. In particular, we have shown that the framework is able to adapt to changes in a landscape of ubiquitous remote services that may dynamically come and go, and where the offered service quality may vary. The framework exploits these changes to maximize the overall utility of applications. To that aim, the paper has shown how the planning middleware evaluates discovered remote services as alternative configurations for the functionalities required by a mobile application. The planning framework deals directly with SLA protocols supported by the services to negotiate the best quality of service for the user.

As a preliminary validation of our approach, the paper also explained how the planning framework handles a use case scenario in which a CRM application of sales agents exploits ubiquitous services, such as a location service, map service and traffic information service to improve the utility of the CRM application whenever such services are available.

In our future work, the presented planning framework will be realized as part of the MUSIC project. The framework will be validated using real world pilot applications of the industrial partners of the MUSIC project (http://www.ist-music.eu).

Acknowledgements

Thanks to partners of the MUSIC project and reviewers of the SC symposium for valuable comments. This work was partly funded by the European Commission through the project MUSIC (EU IST 035166). The scenario was inspired by a demonstrator application developed in the OSIRIS project (ITEA 04040 – http://www.itea-osiris.org) to evaluate the OSIRIS service platform.

References

1. Erl, T.: Service-Oriented Architecture: Concepts, Technology, and Design. Prentice-Hall, Englewood Cliffs (2006)
2. Dan, A., Ludwig, H., Pacifici, G.: Web service differentiation with service level agreements. IBM White Paper. pages 24 (May 2003)
3. Alia, M., Eide, V.S.W., Paspallis, N., Eliassen, F., Hallsteinsen, S., Papadopoulos, G.A.: A Utility-based Adaptivity Model for Mobile Applications. In: Proceedings of the 21st International Conference on Advanced Information Networking and Applications Workshops (AINAW), pp. 556–563. IEEE, Niagara Falls, Ontario, Canada (2007)
4. Floch, J., Hallsteinsen, S., Stav, E., Eliassen, E., Lund, K., Gjørven, E.: Using architecture models for runtime adaptability. IEEE Software 23(2), 62–70 (2006)
5. Brataas, G., Hallsteinsen, S., Rouvoy, R., Eliassen, F.: Scalability of Decision Models for Dynamic Product Lines. In: International SPLC Workshop on Dynamic Software Product Line (DSPL). Kyoto, Japan, pages 10 (September 2007)
6. Erl, T.: SOA: Principles of Service Design. Prentice-Hall, Englewood Cliffs (2007)
7. Flores-Cortés, C.A., Blair, G.S., Grace, P.: An Adaptive Middleware to Overcome Service Discovery Heterogeneity in Mobile Ad Hoc Environments. IEEE Distributed Systems Online 8(7), 1 (2007)
8. Keller, A., Ludwig, H.: The WSLA Framework: Specifying and Monitoring Service Level Agreements for Web Services. Journal of Network and Systems Management 11(1), 53–81 (2003)
9. Dedecker, J., Van Cutsem, T., Mostinckx, S., D'Hondt, T., De Meuter, W.: Ambient-Oriented Programming. In: Companion of the 20th annual ACM SIGPLAN Conference on Object-Oriented Programming, Systems, Languages, and Applications (OOPSLA) (2005)
10. Morgan, G., Parkin, S., Molina-Jimenez, C., Skene, J.: Monitoring Middleware for Service Level Agreements in Heterogeneous Environments. In: Proceedings of the 5th IFIP conference on e-Commerce, e-Business, and e-Government (I3E), Poznan, Poland, October 26-28, 2005, vol. 189, pp. 79–93 (2005)

11. Fahringer, T., et al.: Adaptive Service Grids, White Paper. Deliverable (March 2007), http://asg-platform.org
12. Menasce, D., Dubey, V.: Utility-based QoS Brokering in Service Oriented Architectures. In: Proceedings of the International Conference on Web Services (ICWS), Salt Lake City, Utah (July 9-13, 2007)
13. Capra, L., Emmerich, W., Mascolo, C.: CARISMA: Context-Aware Reflective Middleware System for Mobile Applications. IEEE Transactions on Software Engineering 29(10), 929–945 (2003)
14. Grace, P., Blair, G., Samuel, S.: ReMMoC: A Reflective Middleware to Support Mobile Client Interoperability. In: Meersman, R., Tari, Z., Schmidt, D.C. (eds.) CoopIS 2003, DOA 2003, and ODBASE 2003. LNCS, vol. 2888, pp. 1170–1187. Springer, Heidelberg (2003)

Component-Based Access Control: Secure Software Composition through Static Analysis*

Pierre Parrend and Stéphane Frénot

INRIA ARES / CITI, INSA-Lyon, F-69621, France
Tel.: +334 72 43 71 29; Fax.: +334 72 43 62 27
{pierre.parrend, stephane.frenot}@insa-lyon.fr

Abstract. Extensible Component Platforms support the discovery, installation, starting, uninstallation of components at runtime. Since they are often targeted at mobile resource-constrained devices, they have both strong performance and security requirements. The current security model for Java systems – Permissions – is based on call stack analysis. This is very time-consuming, which makes it difficult to use in production environments.

We therefore define the Component-Based Access Control (CBAC) Security Model, which emulates Java Permissions through static analysis at the installation phase of the components. CBAC is based on a fully declarative approach that makes it possible to tag arbitrary methods as sensitive. A formal model is defined to guarantee that a given component have sufficient access rights, and that dependencies between components are taken into account.

A first implementation of the model is provided for the OSGi Platform, using the ASM library for code analysis. Performance tests show that the cost of CBAC at install time is negligible, since it is executed together with digital signature verification which is much more costly. Moreover, unlike Java Permissions, the CBAC security model does not have any runtime overhead.

1 Introduction

Extensible Component Platforms enable the composition of components which are provided by several issuers and that can be loaded, installed and uninstalled at runtime. In the Java world, such platforms can be Java Cards [17], MIDP [12], or the OSGi platform [14]. The functional composition is supported for instance, in the case of the OSGi Platform, through efficient support of dependency resolution. Composition of non-functional properties, such as security, are so far not supported in such systems.

To support the composition of access rights of components, we propose the Component-based Access Control (CBAC) Security Model. The objective is to

* This work is partially funded by MUSE II IST FP6 Project n026442.

C. Pautasso and É. Tanter (Eds.): SC 2008, LNCS 4954, pp. 68–83, 2008.

replace Java Permissions through validation of the access rights via static code analysis. Permissions prove to be difficult to use in production environments due to the excessive overhead they imply at runtime[1]. To reduce this, we take advantage of the installation phase of the bundles to perform suitable checks to free the runtime phase from costly checks. The advantages of this approach based on static-analysis are numerous. The main ones are the gain of performance at runtime, the absence of program interruption, and the flexibility of policy expression. The latter is fully declarative, which makes it possible to protect additional JVM methods (Threads, ClassLoader) and component methods.

This paper is organized as follows. Section 2 presents the existing security models for Java Component Platforms. Section 3 presents the CBAC Security Model. Section 4 presents the validation of our approach. Section 5 concludes this work.

2 Security Models for Java Component Platforms

Since it has been designed with security in mind and since it has been subjected to extensive testing by the community after its initial releases, the Java Virtual Machine [13] is usually considered a very secure execution platform.

Various security mechanisms have been proposed to build secure Java Platforms. In this section, we review them to identify whether they provide suitable solutions for Component Platforms. First, the J2SE security mechanisms are presented. Then, optimizations for access control through static analysis, which limit verification overhead at runtime, are discussed. Lastly, security mechanisms for Component Systems are presented.

2.1 Java Security

The security properties of the Java Component Platform are supported by the Virtual Machine itself, which provides a platform that is able to fully isolates the applications from their environment. These mechanisms build a sound basis to support a specific Access Control mechanism based on method calls stack inspection: *Stack-based Access Control* (SBAC).

The Java Virtual Machine is characterized by following built-in security features that makes it safe: type safety, automatic memory management, Bytecode validation and secure class loading.

Type Safety ensures that programs cannot contain type mismatches, and cannot execute elements that are not functions [21]. It prevents the use of pointers to execute arbitrary code and to prevent buffer overflows.

Automatic memory management is performed through Garbage Collection. It prevents memory leaks and thereby relieves the developer from memory management, which is error prone.

Bytecode validation consists of checking the compliance of the executable code to the JVM specification before it is loaded for execution. In particular,

[1] Our tests show that the performance loss amounts between 55% and 144% for specific calls.

this prevents the delivery of malicious code in an untrusted component that could be contrived to abuse the platform.

Secure class-loading provides a sound namespace isolation between different ClassLoaders. The namespace isolation ensures that no conflict occurs when independent components provides classes with the same name and that no access is possible to objects and classes that are not purposely made publicly available. Some platforms have been developed that allow to re-establish and control the access between ClassLoaders: the OSGi platform is an example [14]. Secure class-loading therefore allows the concurrent execution of applications that should not interact with each others.

Thanks to these language-level security properties, access control models can be defined in Java-based System. The initial paradigm is Sandboxing, which prevents an untrusted application (such as an Applet) to access the host system [9]. This restrictive view of security has been extended to allow secure execution of partially trusted code [10]: an application could need to access the file system, but may not be trusted to perform network communications to avoid backdoors. In this case, granted permissions would encompass 'FilePermission', but not 'SocketPermission', for instance.

To support such a security model, Stack-based Access Control (SBAC) is used. Whenever a sensitive call is reached, the whole call stack is re-built, and the different Protection Domains of the code are identified. A Protection Domain matches a code signer (*i.e.* code provider) or a specific code location on the local file system. For each Protection Domain access is granted to a certain number of actions. If all Protection Domains are associated with sufficient grants to execute the whole call stack, the sensitive call is executed. Otherwise, the call is aborted and an Exception is launched.

SBAC provides a fine-grained security model that is tightly integrated in the JVM and in the application. However, it has also several limitations. First, the permissions are defined programmatically and cannot be extended for additional methods. Secondly, the program aborts if no sufficient permissions are available, which can cause significant user trouble. Thirdly, the runtime performance overhead is excessive, and often causes the security features to be neglected in production systems. Significant optimization efforts have been done [11], but performance overhead in unavoidable when the whole call stack is to be rebuilt at each check.

2.2 Static Analysis for Optimization of Runtime Checks

The performance overhead at runtime that is implied by the SBAC paradigm urges the optimization of the verification process. Two main solutions exist: optimization of runtime analysis, and identification and removal of redundant checks.

The first approach to SBAC optimization is to perform optimization of runtime analysis through static analysis before the execution. This approach avoids rebuilding the call stack at each security check.

The process is the following: an abstract model of the code is built out of the program code. This model is exploited at the check point instead of the actual call stack. One method used to perform validation and to make this abstract model available throughout the code is Security Passing Style (SPS) [19,20]. SPS consists in rewriting method calls to add an additional parameter which is a pointer to the abstract model. This method can be used to enforce arbitrary security model. Its application to SBAC is presented by [19,20].

Optimization can be done through two different strategies: eager [5,4] and lazy [8] computation of the program state. The eager approach avoids numerous re-computation when the number of security checks is high. The lazy approach provides usually better performances since security checks are usually scarce in the code. Both strategies are proved to be formally equivalent [3].

The main limitation of static analysis is that the abstract model of the program builds a slightly bigger set than the actual call stack. This causes a (limited) number of false positive.

The second approach to SBAC optimization is the identification and removal of redundant checks. Actually, when a given piece of code has the right to access a given file, this right will not be withdrawn if the same code - with the same call stack - have a renewed access to the file.

Removal of redundant checks and of dead code is defined in an abstract way by [6]. Algorithmic example of such removal is given by [3]. The implementation of these models can be done with call graphs [8].

Removal of redundant checks is performed as a complement to optimization of call stack computation and uses the same techniques of code rewriting. It implies an additional overhead during code analysis but provides only limited performance gain at runtime.

Such optimizations do not solve all drawbacks of the SBAC model. The runtime overhead is still non negligible, and the conservation of runtime checks preserves program interruption which is not compatible with a satisfactory user experience.

2.3 Securing Java Components

The strong security features that are provided by the JVM and the sound modular support enables Component Platforms to be defined that enable the realization of complex applications through software composition. Securing these component platforms is done in two steps. First, the deployment must be secured. For more information related to this aspect, see [15] and [16]. It will not be considered further here. Secondly, access control must be adapted to support the dynamic life-cycle of the components.

Dynamic Permissions. In single application Java systems, permissions to access sensitive methods are set statically in the `java.policy` file. In extensible component platforms, where components are installed, started, stopped and uninstalled at runtime, these permissions must be set at runtime. Dynamic permissions are therefore defined: for each issuer, a specific permission set is given. When components from new issuers are installed, a suitable permission set is introduced.

Dynamic permissions are defined both in MIDP [1], and in OSGi [14]. However, few implementations seem to be actually available, which let think that the specified solutions do not match widespread use cases with a satisfactory usability level. The main restriction is the following: dynamic permissions are often set by the user when required. This causes an uncomfortable alternative: either the program crashes in the middle of a computation, or the user is disturbed every now and then to add new permissions which consequences she does not understand. Moreover, software composition and the interdependence between components is not taken into account. Dynamic permissions also have the same drawbacks as standard permission: runtime performance overhead, and the impossibility of defining new permissions types, which could be necessary in highly dynamic environments. Due to a lack of maturity, the current dynamic permissions for software component platforms do not seem to be well suited for their target applications.

Taking Composition into Account for building secure Systems. The specific programming paradigm that is implied by software composition provides new anchors to build secure software: the component life-cycle management support, and the interaction between the components. However, none of them are so far exploited in security specifications, which are directly derived from monolithic security mechanisms.

The life-cycle support provides a suitable check point for security control that enable disturbance free execution: the install phase. Currently, only digital signature validation is performed at this moment. More control, such as static analysis, could be introduced to free the runtime from performance overhead and impaired user experience that is caused by standard execution permissions.

The interaction between the components can be exploited at this install time check point. Actually, dependency resolution is performed during this phase. Extending the performed computation with security checks would prevent a later analysis of the program state and call stack, and makes it possible to validate the security properties of the applications before they are launched. Consequently, runtime checks would be greatly limited, which would prevent unpleasant program interruption - or dangerous user intervention.

3 The CBAC Security Model

The CBAC - Component-based Access Control - Security Model aims at taking advantages of the specific properties of software composition to propose a security model that is both more performant and more suitable to the use cases of Java Component Platforms.

3.1 Principles

The principle of the CBAC Security Model is to perform an install time analysis of the installed components, while taking the emerging compositional properties into account.

The access rights for a component that is to be installed are checked immediately before its installation. If the rights are sufficient, the component is installed. It they are not, the component is rejected. The access rights must be computed in two complementary fashions: first, the component must not perform forbidden actions itself; secondly, the component must not depend on components that perform actions that it is not allowed to perform. This interdiction must consider two specific cases: privileged components that can perform sensitive actions on behalf of others with less rights (for instance a log service must access the file system, but the logged component need not to have itself the access right to the log file); services, which build runtime dependencies, and are used in Service-Oriented Programming [7] environments.

3.2 Hypotheses

The CBAC Security Model is valid when the two following hypotheses are valid:

- the component platform itself is not modified *i.e.* the process of access right verification cannot be tampered with. This can be obtained through the use of a Trusted Computing Base [2].
- each component contains a valid digital signature, which guarantees that no modification has been done to the component archive and that the component signer name is unique and known by the platform[2].

The CBAC Security Model is defined to fully support secure OSGi applications. Since it considers fundamental properties of software composition, it should be easily adaptable to other specifications of component platforms. However, it may be that specific options or features are not defined.

3.3 Modelization

The definition of CBAC is performed in two steps.

First, CBAC is defined for one component. When a single component is installed, does it own the rights to execute all the method calls it performs ? The dependencies to other bundles are not considered, and sensitive methods from the platform API only are considered.

Secondly, CBAC is defined for N components, taking into account the protection of component methods. When a component is installed that has dependencies to other, does it have sufficient rights to execute the method calls it performs both directly and indirectly via the dependencies ? Suitable grants are to be available for the whole call stack. The methods provided by the platform can be tagged as 'sensitive', as well as the ones provided by bundles. This means that if a given bundle has a method that triggers a malicious action, such as *e.g.* sending private data over the network, its access can be restricted.

[2] In particular, this implies that default Java Archive signature verification tools should not be used [16].

Static Permissions for one Component. **Hypotheses** Following parameters are defined to describe security policy-related entities in a dynamic extensible component platform:

b: a given bundle,
pf: the Component Platform,
C: the set of calls made by a bundle,
S: the set of all sensitive method calls in the Platform API,
I: the set of all innocuous method calls in the Platform API,
$C_S = C \bigcap S$: the set of all sensitive method calls made by a bundle,
$C_I = C \bigcap I$: the set of all innocuous method calls made by a bundle,
$\{p\}$: the set of bundle providers,
A_p: the set of authorized sensitive calls for the provider $p \in \{p\}$, *i.e.* the policy for the provider p.

Theorem. CBAC permissions for one component ($CBAC\_1C$) are valid if:

$$p, pf, b \vdash C_S \wedge A_p, C_I \quad (1)$$
$$with\ PSC_{pf,b} = C_S$$

Which means that for a given platform (pf) with a given bundle (b) and a given bundle provider (p), calls are either innocuous (C_I) or sensitive and authorized for this provider ($C_S \wedge A_p$). $PSC_{pf,b}$ is the set of Performed Sensitive Calls by the bundle b on the Platform pf. This means that the set of Performed Sensitive Calls by the bundle b on the Platform pf is the set of sensitive calls that are identified in the bundle. Otherwise, that is to say if some sensitive calls that b may perform is not allowed by the policy, the bundle is rejected. This mechanism supports robust coarse-grained access control policies.

Proof. A bundle b is associated with the calls C it performs on the platform. A platform pf is associated with the set of sensitive calls S, and the set of innocuous calls i it makes available. C is a part of S and I. Thus, the platform pf and the bundle b are associated to C, and consequently to the set of sensitive calls it performs C_S, which is a subset of C.

The bundle provider p is associated with the policy A_p, which is defined at the platform level. If the permission is given, the performed sensitive calls C_S build a subset of the policy for p. Consequently, C_S and A_p build a coherent policy for the bundle b provided by p on the platform pf. b can thus be installed. If the permission is denied, C_S is not a subset of p, and C_S and A_p do not build a coherent policy. b cannot be installed.

A demonstration with Sequent Calculus is given in appendix A[3].

Static Permissions for N Components - with Protection of Platform and Bundle Calls. The computation of the component validation status for a new component must consider two types of bundles in the dependency tree:

[3] http://www.rzo.free.fr/publis/parrend08cbac_appendix.pdf

- Leaves L: the components that have dependencies to platform-provided packages only (simple applications, or libraries),
- Nodes N: the components that have dependencies both to the Platform and to other components (complex applications, GUI ...).

The Figure 1 shows an example of a dependency tree for a default configuration of the Apache Felix platform (version 1.0), which is an implementation of the OSGi R4 Specifications.

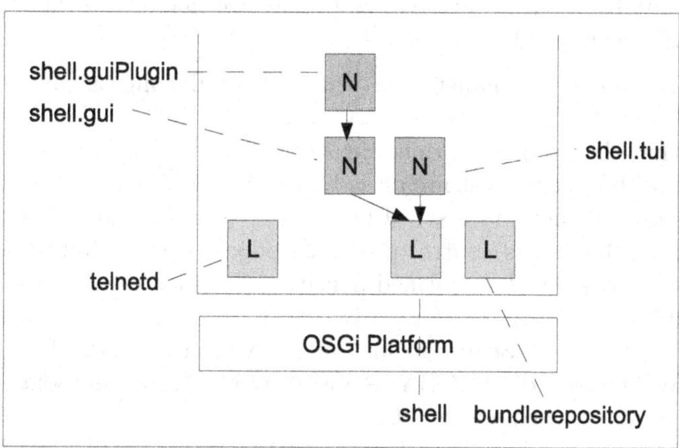

Fig. 1. The Dependency Tree for a default Configuration of the Apache Felix Platform

Hypotheses. Following parameters are defined to describe security policy-related entities in a dynamic extensible component platform for N components:

b_i**:** the ID of the considered bundle,
$\{b\}_i$**:** the list of bundles on which the bundle i depends,
$C_{S_{pf,b_i}}$**:** the sensitive calls performed by the bundle i directly to the platform, or directly to the bundles on which it depends,
A_{p_i}**:** the set of authorized sensitive calls for the provider p of the bundle i,
PSC_{b_i}**:** the set of Performed Sensitive Calls by the bundle i, directly to the Platform or via method calls to other bundles,
PSC_{pf,b_i}**:** the set of Performed Sensitive Calls by the bundle i that are made directly to the Platform, or directly to the bundles on which it depends,
$PSC_{\{b\}_i}$**:** the set of Performed Sensitive Calls by the bundles on which the bundle i depends. $PSC_{\{b\}_i} = \sum_{b_j \ in \ \{b\}_i} PSC_{b_j}$.

Theorem. The computation of the validation status of a component can be made recursively.

- A leaf component $b_i \in L$ is valid if:

$$b_i, p_i, pf \vdash A_{p_i} \wedge C_{S_{pf,b_i}}, C_{I_{pf,b_i}} \quad (2)$$
$$with \ PSC_{pf,b_i} = C_{S_{pf,b_i}}$$

Which matches the case for one single component.

- A node component N is valid if:

$$b_i, p_i, pf \vdash A_{p_i} \wedge PSC_{\{b\}_i}, \neg PSC_{\{b\}_i} \tag{3}$$

$$with\ PSC_{b_i} = Cs_{S_{pf,b_i}} \vee PSC_{\{b\}_j} \tag{4}$$

PSC_{b_i} is the set of Performed Sensitive Calls by the bundle b_i b on the Platform pf or on the bundles on which it depends. This means that a bundle can be installed when the sensitive calls that are made directly to the platform or to other bundles and all sensitive calls that are made via other bundles are allowed by the current policy.

Proof. This can be demonstrated with the following argument through recursion.

Suppose that the set of Performed Sensitive Calls for the bundle k, PSC_{b_k}, is available for all bundles k that are already installed on the gateway. The bundle i, which has dependencies to a set of bundle b_j, can be installed if its execution does not break the access control policy through direct or indirect calls. The value of PSC_{b_i}, the set of Performed Sensitive Calls for the bundle i, can then be extracted.

A demonstration with Sequent Calculus is given in appendix B[4].

The implementation of the CBAC security model for N components requires two complementary mechanisms: checking at install time for the calls that are made directly from the bundle to be installed to the platform, and building of the dependency tree to verify that the required permissions are granted. The bundle b_i can only be installed if a valid dependency tree can be identified.

The mechanism presented so far provides a minimal enforcement process for execution permissions that can yet be used to protect real applications. As for the CBAC model for one component, the benefits are the absence of run-time overhead, and the declarative - and thus extensible - policy declaration mechanism.

The limitations are the following. First, the validation is performed at a quite coarse-grain level. For instance, the installation of an application can be denied since it relies on a library that contains forbidden sensitive methods, even though these methods are never called. This can occurs for instance in the case of conditional instructions. Secondly, it is not possible to define sensitive method calls that would be provided by the components themselves.

The mechanism of protection of bundle calls shows both the flexibility and limitation of component-grained static access control. The advantage is that permissions can be set in a declarative manner, that is to say that unlike default Java Permissions, any call can be considered as 'sensible' - for instance for a particular application type, or in case a vulnerability is discovered. The limitation is that component-grained access control does not provide the policy designer with context-dependent behavior: if a given sensitive method is used only in rare cases or is never used, but forbidden by the policy, the bundle cannot be installed.

---

[4] http://www.rzo.free.fr/publis/parrend08cbac_appendix.pdf

Advanced Features. To as to provide a proper protection of OSGi-based applications, several advanced features have to be defined.

The first feature is *Privileged Method Calls.* Privilege calls means that a given component can execute sensitive calls, even though the initial caller of the method does not own sufficient rights. This is for instance the case of logging mechanisms. An component from a less trusted provider can log its action on a file through the platform logger without having access rights to the file system.

The second advanced feature which is provided by the CBAC model thanks to its declarative nature is the support of both *Positive and Negative Permissions.* Negative permissions are set by identifying a given method call as 'sensitive'. Positive Permissions are set by allowing a given signer to execute some methods. A more flexible expression could be introduced in the future, in particular to support negative permissions without impacting the policies for other providers.

The last required feature is to support *Access Control for Service Calls.* The OSGi Platform support Service Oriented Programming (SOP) [7], and thus calls through services that are published inside the platform. Since the services are resolved at runtime, a runtime mechanism is to be defined that enforces the CBAC policy for these service. Otherwise, package level access control can be by-passed through service calls.

4 Validation

The validation of the Component-Based Access Control model is performed through its implementation, performance analysis and identification of the advantages and drawbacks of the current prototype.

The principle of CBAC is the following. When an OSGi bundle is to be installed on an OSGi Platform, its digital signature is checked. If this latter is valid, the CBAC Engine verifies whether the bundle signers have sufficient rights to execute all the code that is contained in the archive. If enforced policies do allow it, the bundle is installed, and then executed without further constraints. Otherwise, it is rejected.

The innovation of the approach is to take advantage of the installation phase of the OSGi bundles to perform access right verification.

4.1 Implementation

The implementation of the CBAC security model is presented in this section. Development choices are justified, and the integration with the *Secure Felix*[5] platform is explained. Expression of CBAC policies are then given, along with an example.

The implementation of the CBAC Model is performed on the Felix[6] implementation of the OSGi framework. Static Bytecode analysis is performed with

[5] http://sfelix.gforge.inria.fr

[6] http://felix.apache.org/

Table 1. Example of the cbac.policy File

```
sensitiveMethods {
 java.io.ObjectInputStream.defaultReadObject;
 java.io.ObjectInputStream.writeInt;
 java.security.*;
 java.security.KeyStore.*;
 java.io.FileOutputStream.<init>;
};

sensitiveManifestAttributes {
  Fragment-Host;
}

grant Signer:bob {
  Fragment-Host;
  java.io.ObjectInputStream.defaultReadObject;
  java.io.ObjectInputStream.writeInt;
  java.io.FileOutputStream.<init>;
  java.security.Security.addProvider;
  java.security.NoSuchAlgorithmException.<init>;
  java.security.KeyStore.getInstance;
  ...
};
```

the ASM[7] library, which is much smaller than other libraries for Bytecode manipulation, such as BCEL [8] or SERP[9]. An earlier prototype has also been built using the Findbugs framework, which often implies an overhead of more than 100% in performance.

The CBAC model is part of a research project conducted at the Amazones Team of the INRIA (CITI Laboratory, INSA-Lyon, France) that aims at defining a secure OSGi platform. It is therefore integrated with SFelix, which support a proper verification of the digital signature of OSGi bundles [16]. SFelix is modified to make the list of valid signers available for the CBAC Engine. This latter can then check whether the signers have suitable rights to execute all the methods that it contains.

An example of CBAC policy is given in the listing 1: a policy file cbac.policy, defines sensitive methods and required grants for a given signer. The syntax is similar to Java Permissions 'java.policy' files.

CBAC policy is defined as follows. A list of sensitive methods, and one of sensitive OSGi-related meta-data are defined. If a bundle contains sensitive methods or meta-data, its provider must be granted the right to execute them all. Otherwise, it is rejected at install time. The policies are defined according to a

[7] http://asm.objectweb.org/
[8] http://jakarta.apache.org/bcel/
[9] http://serp.sourceforge.net/

declarative approach: it is possible to mark any method call as being sensitive. This makes it possible to protect the framework against vulnerabilities that are discovered after the release of the platform. On the contrary, Java Permissions mechanisms that are coded in the framework itself freeze the set of sensitive methods when the platforms (or any application) is released.

4.2 Performances

The main objective of the CBAC model is to relieve the OSGi platforms which are often executed in resource-constrained environments from the overhead that is implied by Java Permissions at runtime. It is therefore important to control that the performances of the system are not too much impacted by this new mechanism.

Tests have been performed with the implementation of the CBAC security model for one component. Figure 2 shows the duration of the CBAC check only, and Figure 3 shows the performance of Digital Signature validation and CBAC Check, which are to be performed together to ensure the validity of the analysis. It highlights the fact that for a limited number of sensitive methods (which is usually the case), the overhead implied by CBAC is negligible when compared to the duration of digital signature check. Note that the abscissa is not linear, but represents the size of the various bundles that are available in the Felix distribution of the OSGi Platform.

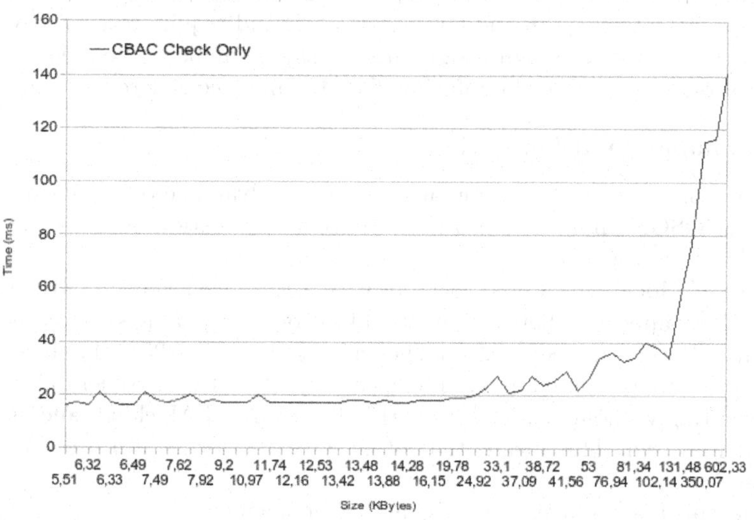

Fig. 2. Performances of OSGi Security: CBAC Check only

The test are conducted for all the bundles that are provided together with the Apache Felix distribution, utility bundles and tests bundles. The performance

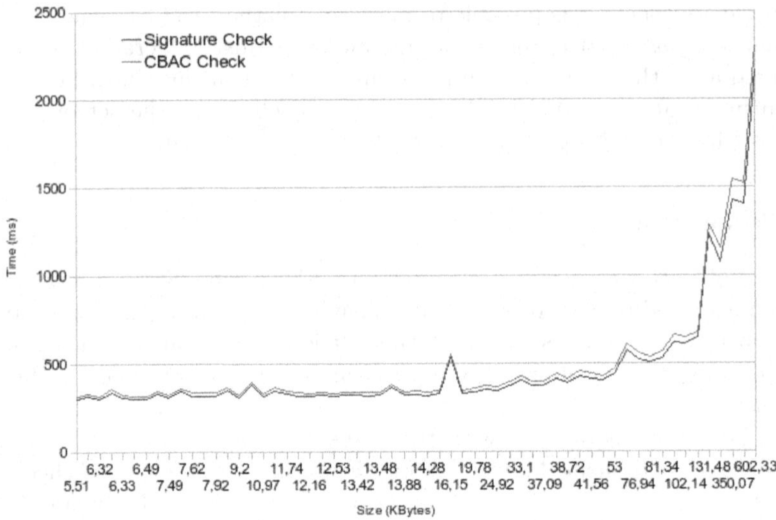

Fig. 3. Performances of OSGi Security: Signature and CBAC Check

overhead for small bundles (less that 25 KBytes) is less than 20 ms (between 3,2% and 6,7% of the total validation process). For bigger ones (up to 130 KBytes), less than 40 ms are required (less than 7,7% of the total validation process). Out of the 59 test bundles, only five have a longer verification time. The bigger bundles are 350 KBytes, 356 and 602 KBytes big, and require respectively 115, 116 and 141 ms. Since the digital signature for these bundles is checked in more that one second, the overhead implied by CBAC can be considered as negligible.

4.3 Advantages and Limitations

The innovation of the CBAC approach is to take advantage of the installation phase of the OSGi bundles to perform access right verification. Identified advantages and known drawbacks are now presented.

The CBAC Model, when used together with a Hardened Version of the OSGi Platform [15], supports a better protection that other available security mechanism such as Java Permissions. This is shown in Figure 4. The 25% of unprotected vulnerabilities are presented in our Technical Report on OSGi vulnerability [15], and, interestingly enough, are due to the Java Virtual Machine, and not to the OSGi Platform. This means that other Java Platforms also present these weaknesses.

The identified advantages of CBAC are the following:

- no runtime overhead (unlike Java Permissions),
- no application interruption due to unsufficient execution rights (unlike Java Permissions),
- no unsecure behavior of the users, which are driven with classical permissions into allowing the execution of all untrusted code [18],

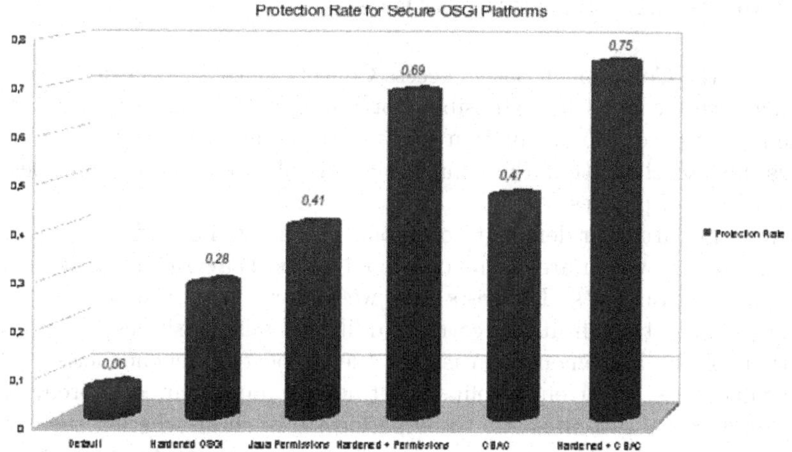

Fig. 4. Protection Rate of existing OSGi Security Mechanisms: CBAC and others

- possibility of defining arbitrary sensitive methods and meta-data, which makes it possible to protect the system from vulnerabilities that are discovered after the platform release.

Moreover, the expression of policies is simpler that in the case of Java Permission, since it is declarative rather that programmative. Since the syntax is very similar, they can very easily be learned by Java developers.

The known drawback of the CBAC approach are the following:

- false positives are to be expected when compared to Java Permission. This may not be a problem if the configuration (*e.g.* the trusted signers, the applicative bundles) of the target platforms is known beforehand, as is currently the case in most OSGi-based systems: sufficient permissions can be set at design time. However, it can be a restriction for pervasive systems, which require an important interoperability of mutually unknown code.
- install time overhead (negligible, as shown in Figures 2 and 3),
- disk space consumption (333 KBytes, 319 KBytes of which are built by the - unmodified - ASM library). Our current prototype is much smaller than the original implementation as Findbugs Plugin (2,026 MBytes, mostly because of the Findbugs and BCEL libraries that amounts to 2,003 MByte), and much more performant (between 40 and 60 % of benefits for the various archives). To be used in embedded systems, the unused code of the library is to be pruned.

The formalization of CBAC is given in this study, and a first validation is given based both on qualitative and quantitative criteria, which show that the CBAC model is a performant and useful approach to Access Control for Extensible Component Platforms, such as the OSGi Platform.

5 Conclusions and Perspectives

We propose the Component-Based Access ControL (CBAC) Security Model for enforcing access control in Extensible Component Platforms. The principle is to take advantage of the installation phase of the components to perform static analysis, and to check that the composition of software components does not break the defined policies.

CBAC is in particular defined to overcome the known limitation of standards Java Permissions, which are often considered as too heavyweight to be used in production environments. The tests that we perform show that this objective is achieved, even though at the cost of additional false positives. The current limitations of our implementation is that the support of dependencies (CBAC for N components) is currently defined, but not yet implemented. Moreover, the validation in a real system is still to be performed to check whether the defined policy language is flexible enough. So far, there is no reason to think that this is not the case.

Two directions of future works are to be considered. First, the CBAC security model is to be tested for other specifications of component platforms, for instance Java MIDP Profile, or non-Java environments. Our prototype has been tested over the OSGi Platform, but only a limited set of OSGi-specific features have been introduced, and adaptation should not introduce major issues.

Secondly, the prototype is to be validated in resource-constrained environments, to ensure that the process is lightweight enough to be used in PDA or set-top boxes.

References

1. Porting Guide - Sun Javatrademark Wireless Client Software 2.0 - Java Platform, Micro Edition. Sun Microsystem (May 2007)
2. Arbaugh, W.A., Farber, D.J., Smith, J.: A secure and reliable bootstrap architecture. IEEE Symposium on Security and Privacy, 65–71 (1997)
3. Banerjee, A., Naumann, D.A.: A simple semantics and static analysis for java security. Technical Report 2001-1, Stevens Institute of Technology (2001)
4. Bartoletti, M.: Language-based security: access control and static analysis. PhD thesis, Universita degli Studi di Pisa (2005)
5. Bartoletti, M., Degano, P., Ferrari, G.L.: Static analysis for eager stack inspection. In: Workshop on Formal Techniques for Java-like Programs (FTfJP 2003) (2003)
6. Bartoletti, M., Degano, P., Ferrari, G.L.: Stack inspection and secure program transformations. International Journal of Information Security 2, 187–217 (2004)
7. Bieber, G., Carpenter, J.: Introduction to service-oriented programming (rev 2.1). OpenWings Whitepaper (April 2001)
8. Chang, B.-M.: Static check analysis for java stack inspection. ACM SIGPLAN Notices 41(3), 40–48 (2006)
9. Dean, D., Felten, E.W., Wallach, D.S.: Java security: From hotjava to netscape and beyond. In: SP 1996: Proceedings of the 1996 IEEE Symposium on Security and Privacy, p. 190. IEEE Computer Society Press, Washington, DC, USA (1996)

10. Gong, L., Mueller, M., Prafullchandra, H., Schemers, R.: Going beyond the sandbox: An overview of the new security architecture in the java development kit 1.2. In: Proceedings of the USENIX Symposium on Internet Technologies and Systems (1997)
11. Gong, L., Schemers, R.: Implementing protection domains in the java development kit 1.2. In: Network and Distributed System Security Symposium (1998)
12. JSR 118 Expert Group. Midp 2.0. Sun Specification (November 2002)
13. Lindholm, T., Yellin, F.: The Java(TM) Virtual Machine Specification, 2nd edn. Prentice-Hall, Englewood Cliffs (1999)
14. OSGI Alliance. Osgi service platform, core specification release 4. Draft, 07 (2005)
15. Parrend, P., Frenot, S.: Java components vulnerabilities - an experimental classification targeted at the osgi platform. Research Report RR-6231, INRIA, 06 (2007)
16. Parrend, P., Frenot, S.: Supporting the secure deployment of osgi bundles. In: First IEEE WoWMoM Workshop on Adaptive and DependAble Mission- and bUsiness-critical mobile Systems (ADAMUS 2007), Helsinki, Finland (June 2007)
17. Sun Inc. Java card platform specification 2.2.2 (March 2006)
18. Takesue, M.: A scheme for protecting the information leakage via portable devices. In: International Conference on Emerging Security Information, Systems and Technologies, IARIA SecurWare (2007)
19. Wallach, D.S.: A New Approach to Mobile Code Security. PhD thesis, Department of Computer Science, Princeton University (1999)
20. Wallach, D.S., Appel, A.W., Felten, E.W.: Safkasi: A security mechanism for language-based systems. ACM Transactions on Software Engineering and Methodology (TOSEM) 9(4), 341–378 (2000)
21. Wright, A.K., Felleisen, M.: A syntactic approach to type soundness. Information and Computation 115(1), 38–94 (1994)

Adding Support for Dynamics Patterns to Static Business Process Management Systems

René Wörzberger, Nicolas Ehses, and Thomas Heer

Department of Computer Science 3 - Software Engineering
RWTH Aachen, Germany
{woerzberger,ehses,heer}@i3.informatik.rwth-aachen.de

Abstract. Many companies use business process management systems (BPMS) for modeling and execution support of their business processes. Many processes are highly dynamic and require changes even during execution. Common commercial BPMS fail to support such processes appropriately since they work in a rather static manner, i.e. they demand that the structure of a process is fixed before execution.

Our research group cooperates with an industry partner who uses a static BPMS. This paper describes an approach that posteriorly extends this static BPMS inasmuch as dynamic changes of processes during execution are supported. The benefit of this approach is that our partner in industry gains support of dynamic processes but still use the existing BPMS and save investments related to it.

1 Introduction

The organization of most modern companies is aligned to their business processes. *Business process management systems (BPMS)* provide means to define, control and monitor business processes, which are often called *workflows* in this context.

Common BPMS distinguish between *build time* and *run time* with regard to processes. During build time *workflow definitions* are specified, which model a certain *process type*, e.g. "adjustment of a claim" in an insurance company. At *run time*, for each actual *process case* a *workflow instance* is created and executed according to a certain workflow definition.

Although companies strive for automation of their business processes, most processes are at least partly conducted by humans. These processes are often *dynamic*, i.e. the structure of such processes evolves during process execution. Most commercial BPMS support rapid adaptions of workflow definitions but prohibit dynamic changes in workflow instances, like adding missing activities. Thus, they cannot optimally support dynamic processes. This problem gave rise to a new research field [1,2,3].

Within the collaborative research center IMPROVE [4] our research group has realized the prototype AHEAD [5], which aims at the management of highly dynamic development processes and interdigitates build time and run time. In an ongoing research project we transfer our concepts to industry in cooperation

C. Pautasso and É. Tanter (Eds.): SC 2008, LNCS 4954, pp. 84–91, 2008.

with our partner AMB Generali Informatik Services (AMB-Informatik). Our partner is the information technology service provider for the Generali Group, which is a combine of insurance companies.

AMB-Informatik uses the *WebSphere BPMS* consisting of the workflow definition tool *WebSphere Integration Developer (WID)* and the run time environment *WebSphere Process Server (WPS)*[1] as solution basis for their customers. WebSphere BPMS is rather oriented towards highly automated and predictable processes. The support for dynamic processes is not in its focus. However, these dynamic processes occur and must also be handled by insurance companies. Thus, we transfer the concepts of the prototype AHEAD by *extending* WebSphere BPMS. Thereby, we gain support for dynamic processes while investments of our partner in the WebSphere-based infrastructure can be saved.

The paper is structured as follows: Section 2 clarifies terms related to flexibility and dynamics of BPMS. Dynamics can be categorized according to patterns, which are described in Section 3. Section 4 explains our approach with regard to the patterns and the extended WebSphere BPMS. Connections to other research approaches are illustrated in Section 5. Section 6 concludes this paper with an outlook on future work.

2 Flexibility and Dynamics of Workflows

Most workflow definition languages provide construct types like decision or iteration to define at build time execution sequences of activities, which are valid at run time. These construct types allow for some *build time flexibility*, that is, one workflow definition specifies a (possibly infinite) set of valid execution sequences. The workflow definition depicted in Figure 1(a), a simple review process, allows for two execution sequences: one with Add Corrections and one without.

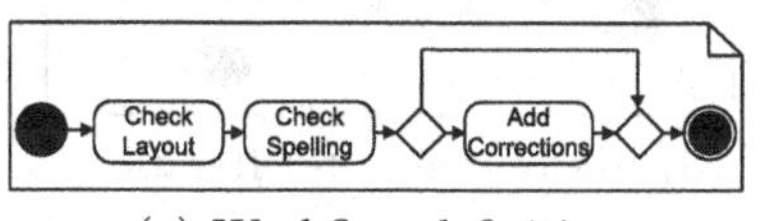

(a) Workflow definition

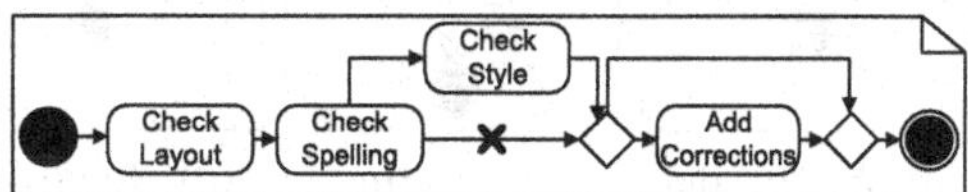

(b) Definition with additional Check Style

Fig. 1. Example for run time dynamics

According to our industry partner, for a non-trivial process type it is neither possible due to limited anticipatability nor desired because of lower maintainability to build a workflow definition that covers all reasonable execution sequences. For instance, it might turn out during execution of Check Spelling that the particular document is written in a bad style. Then, there is a need for an additional activity Check Style before Add Corrections in the respective workflow instance. In this case, it would be appropriate to dynamically change the running

[1] All WebSphere trademarks are in possession of IBM Corp. (http://www.ibm.com).

workflow instance (*run time dynamics*) such that the instance would conform to the hypothetical workflow definition of Figure 1(b).

3 Dynamics Patterns

In most cases, the necessity to modify a workflow instance is recognized by *workflow participants* of the respective workflow instance and should therefore be conducted by them.

A *workflow modeler* normally needs the full set of constructs types at build time to cover all reasonable execution sequences he is able to envisage. In contrast, at run time a workflow participant just uses a small subset of the available construct types. That is because he does not consider workflow modeling as his primary task but rather wants to satisfy current or oncoming exigencies for a single workflow instance by a dynamic modification. Furthermore, we think that most dynamic modifications follow certain patterns, which we exemplify in the following by a simplified process type of a medical practice (cf. Fig. 2(a)).

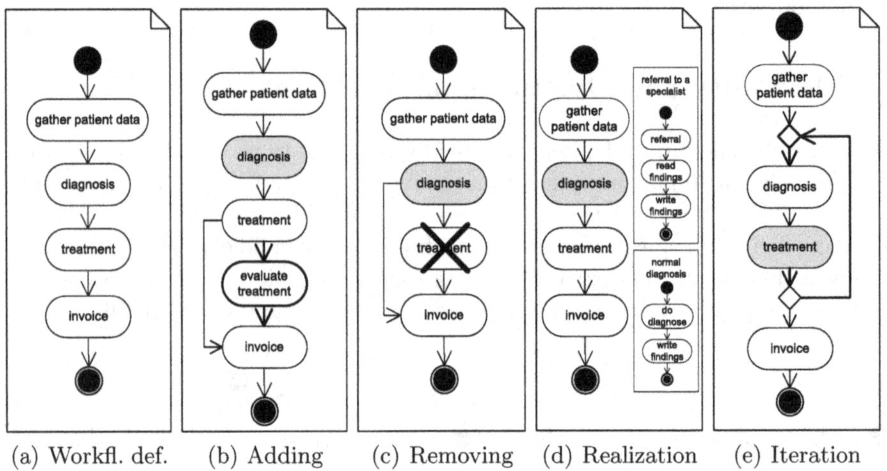

(a) Workfl. def. (b) Adding (c) Removing (d) Realization (e) Iteration

Fig. 2. Examples for dynamics patterns

Dynamic Adding. During the enactment of diagnosis in a certain workflow instance the doctor might recall a research project concerning the effectiveness of certain treatments. Since the patient is willing to partake, the doctor has to assure that the evaluation of the treatment will be executed after the treatment itself. The best way to do this is to dynamically add an additional activity evaluate treatment between the existing activities treatment and invoice (cf. Fig. 2(b)).

Dynamic Removing. In the process of the medical practice it is possible that there are no findings resulting from diagnosis because the patient just suffers from a slight indisposition. Consequently, the doctor dynamically removes the activity treatment from the respective workflow instance (cf. Fig. 2(c)).

Dynamic Realization. In a hierarchically defined workflow, where activities are actually realized via sub-workflows, the best realization can often not be identified before run time. E.g., the doctor might dynamically realize diagnosis by normal diagnosis conducted by himself or by a referral to a specialist (cf. Fig. 2(d)). This decision is specific to each particular workflow instance.

Dynamic Iteration. In the medical process, errors might occur in each activity. For instance, a severe mistake is a wrong finding resulting from a faulty diagnosis. Such an error might be recognized during execution of treatment. Then, the affected activities of the workflow instance, namely, diagnosis and its successor activity treatment have to be dynamically re-iterated, i.e., they are carried out again such that the data they produce can be corrected (cf. Fig. 2(e)).

4 Approach: Simulate Dynamics on a Static BPMS

In this section we describe our approach to provide support for the dynamics patterns described in Section 3. The distinctive feature of this approach is that our prototype is not implemented from scratch. Instead, we rather add another layer on top of an existing BPMS by which we simulate a dynamic BPMS (cf. Fig. 3). The fact that the underlying BPMS is static is hidden from both the workflow modeler at build time and from the workflow participant at run time. Although we have implemented a prototype on top of the concrete system WebSphere BPMS in order to verify our approach, we think that it can be easily adapted to other BPMS.

4.1 Approach Overview

At *build time* a WS-BPEL transformer augments workflow definitions modeled in the language WS-BPEL[2] via WID by additional WS-BPEL activities (e.g. `<invoke>`, `<switch>`, `<while>`) yielding an augmented workflow definition Xa. The transformer requires no user interaction. Hence, the additional dynamics layer is opaque to the workflow modeler.

The *run time* counterpart of the WS-BPEL transformer is the dynamics component. This component is accessed through two interfaces that serve different purposes: (1) The dynamics component stores instance specific run time information, e.g. actual variable values and routing informations for sub-workflow calls. This run time information is accessed by the WPS through the WPS interface. WPS uses this information for those WS-BPEL activities that have been added at build time by the WS-BPEL transformer. (2) Likewise the WS-BPEL transformer hides the dynamic aspect at build time, the dynamics component hides the additional WS-BPEL activities from a workflow participant at run time. Instead, it provides a participant interface which is used by a participant GUI to render a graphical view of dynamic workflow instances. Furthermore, the

[2] http://www.oasis-open.org/committees/wsbpel/

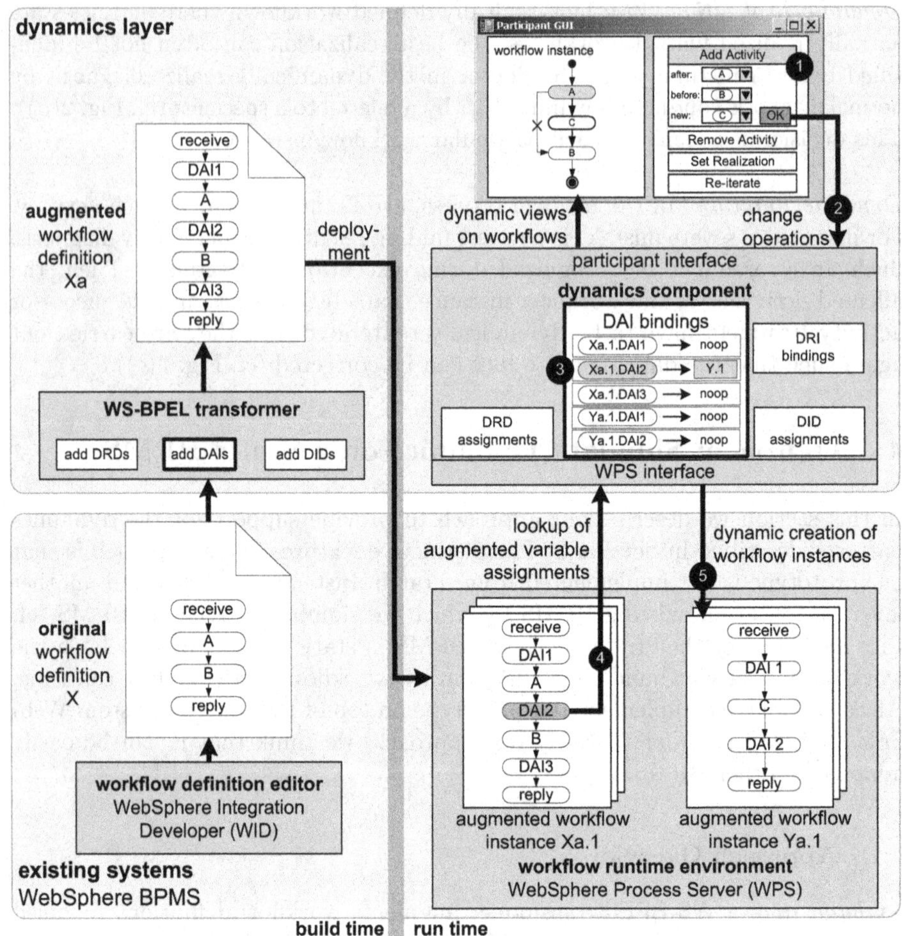

Fig. 3. System overview and example for Dynamic Adding support

participant interface of the dynamics component offers operations that can be invoked by a workflow participant via the participant GUI to perform a dynamic change in the graphical view.

4.2 Realization of Dynamic Adding

The approach is aligned to the dynamics patterns explained in Section 3. In order to keep our explanation brief, we just exemplify our approach with Dynamic Adding in a rather small workflow.

Build Time. Enabling a workflow definition to support Dynamic Adding (s. Sec. 3) requires the addition of `<invoke>` activities which we call *Dynamic*

Adding Invocations (DAI) in the following. DAIs serve as placeholders for possible additional activities. Since Dynamic Adding might take place in arbitrary positions, the WS-BPEL transformer inserts a DAI before and after each activity.

The left hand side of Figure 3 exemplifies the transformation of a simple workflow X definition, which just consists of the sequential `<invoke>` activities A and B, depicted as rounded rectangles. The transformation yields an augmented workflow definition Xa[3] with three more `<invoke>` activities DAI1 to DAI3.

Run Time. A Dynamic Adding edit operation is initiated by a workflow participant via his participant GUI (1). He specifies *which activity* is to be inserted at *which position* in the control flow. In this case, during the execution of activity A, the participant inserts a new activity C right after the existing activity A and before B. The participant GUI notifies the dynamics component about this edit operation (2). Consequently, the dynamics component replaces the default noop-binding[4] of DAI2 in workflow instance Xa.1 by a sub-workflow call to a workflow instance Ya.1 (3). When the control flow reaches DAI2, this activity calls the dynamics component (4) which creates a new workflow instance Ya.1 (5). After Ya.1 is completed, the control flow returns to Xa.1, which proceeds with activity B.

The other dynamics patterns can similarly be realized (in combination with each other), e.g. by means of so called *Dynamic Removing Decisions (DRD)* and *Dynamic Iteration Decisions (DID)*. Both require additional transformation steps in the WS-BPEL transformer and additional run time data in the dynamics component (cf. Fig. 3). *Dynamic Realization Invocations (DRI)* are similar to DAIs but refer to activities, which are already part of the original workflow definition like A or B in Figure 3.

5 Related Work

Flexibility and Dynamics. Our distinction between build time flexibility and run time dynamics is clearly aligned with the common distinction between build time and run time in workflow management systems. A similar distinction between "a-priori flexibility" versus "a-posteriori flexibility" and "offline changes" versus "online changes" is made by Joeris [6] and Bandinelli et al. [7], respectively.

Dynamic WfMS. There are several workflow and process management systems, which support run time dynamics to some extend. A comparison of some academic prototypes like ADEPT [8] or WIDE [9] and commercial systems is given by Weber et al. [10]. There is no approach known to us that posteriorly extends an existing workflow management system with a given workflow definition language by support for run time dynamics.

---

[3] In the figure we use a restricted subset of the notation for UML activity diagrams since there is no official graphical notation for WS-BPEL.

[4] "Noop" stands for "no operation".

Patterns. Aalst et al. [11] introduced a classification for workflow languages based on patterns which concentrates on build time flexibility. Voorhoeve [12] et al. make an implicit classification for run time dynamics with regard to preservation of certain consistency properties of petri nets. Weber et al. [10] also range run time dynamics but not with regard to a concrete technical implementation basis.

6 Conclusion

Summary. In this paper we described how support for run time dynamics, e.g. dynamic modifications of workflows, can be realized by an additional dynamics layer based on a static workflow management system. Our approach is motivated by requirements of our industrial partners at AMB-Informatik who want to support dynamic processes but also keep the existing static WebSphere BPMS. We classified dynamic changes according to dynamics patterns. In our twofold architecture, consisting of a WS-BPEL transformer for build time and a dynamics component for run time, there is dedicated support for each dynamics pattern.

State of Implementation. Presently, we are implementing the dynamics layer and the graphical participant GUI only using common and publicly available technologies. The WS-BPEL transformer is realized with XSL Transformations whereas the dynamics component is written in plain Java. The graphical participant GUI is implemented using the Graphical Editing Framework (GEF) of the Eclipse Foundation. Though the implementation is still in an early phase, first results already substantiated the suitability of our approach.

Current Limitations and Future Work. In the original workflow definition X in Figure 3 we only used a small subset of all WS-BPEL construct types. Actually, occurrences of *complex construct types* like decisions and iterations but not yet compensation and fault handlers. We will also deal with problems arising from the *concurrency* and *distribution* of workflows. Here, we can continue work that has been done in a preceding project of our group [13]. *Generalization* of the approach is another important goal beginning with the adaption of other WS-BPEL-based workflow management systems and proceeding with workflow management system of other kinds. *Optimizations* will be applied particularly to the WS-BPEL transformer in order to reduce the size of the augmented workflow definitions. Besides the work presented in this paper there are *other related parts* in our cooperation with our partner AMB-Informatik again carrying on preceding work. Dynamic changes made by workflow participants have to be checked against certain constraints in order to guarantee technical consistency, e.g. data dependencies between activities. Furthermore, professional constraints have to be enforced, e.g. non-deletability of strictly mandatory activities. Both will be supported by a *consistency checker*. We will also build a tool that provides a *condensed view* of completed workflow instances with dynamic changes to the workflow modeler. By using this tool, the modeler can identify similar dynamic changes among the workflow instances and copy them to the workflow definition where appropriate.

References

1. Ellis, C.A., Keddara, K., Rozenberg, G.: Dynamic change within workflow systems. In: COOCS, pp. 10–21. ACM Press, New York (1995)
2. van der Aalst, W.M.P., Jablonski, S.: Dealing with workflow change: identification of issues and solutions. International Journal of Computer Systems Science and Engineering 15(5), 267–276 (2000)
3. Bernstein, A., Dellarocas, C., Klein, M.: Towards adaptive workflow systems: CSCW-98 workshop report. SIGGROUP Bull. 20(2), pp. 54–56 (1999)
4. Nagl, M., Marquardt, W. (eds.): Collaborative and Distributed Chemical Engineering Design Processes / From Understanding to Substantial Support. Springer, Heidelberg (2008)
5. Westfechtel, B.: Ein graphbasiertes Managementsystem für dynamische Entwicklungsprozesse. Informatik Forschung und Entwicklung 16(3), 125–144 (2001)
6. Joeris, G.: Flexibles und adaptives Workflowmanagement für verteilte und dynamische Prozesse. PhD thesis, University of Bremen (2000)
7. Bandinelli, S., Di Nitto, E., Fuggetta, A.: Policies and Mechanisms to Support Process Evolution in PSEEs. In: Proceedings of the 3rd International Conference on the Software Process, pp. 9–20. IEEE Computer Society Press, Los Alamitos (1994)
8. Reichert, M., Dadam, P.: ADEPTflex-Supporting Dynamic Changes of Workflows Without Losing Control. Journal of Intelligent Information Systems 10(2), 93–129 (1998)
9. Casati, F.: Models, Semantics, and Formal Methods for the Design of Workflows and their Exceptions. PhD thesis, Politecnico di Milano (1998)
10. Weber, B., Rinderle, S.B., Reichert, M.U.: Change patterns and change support features in process-aware information systems. In: Krogstie, J., Opdahl, A., Sindre, G. (eds.) CAiSE 2007. LNCS, vol. 4495, pp. 574–588. Springer, Heidelberg (2007)
11. Van Der Aalst, W.M.P., Ter Hofstede, A.H.M., Kiepuszewski, B., Barros, A.P.: Workflow Patterns. Distrib. Parallel Databases 14(1), 5–51 (2003)
12. Voorhoeve, M., Van der Aalst, W.: Ad-hoc Workflow: Problems and Solutions. In: Tjoa, A.M. (ed.) DEXA 1997. LNCS, vol. 1308, p. 36. Springer, Heidelberg (1997)
13. Heller, M., Wörzberger, R.: A Management System Supporting Interorganizational Cooperative Development Processes in Chemical Engineering. Journal of Integrated Design and Process Science: Transactions of the SDPS 10(2), 57–78 (2007)

Interface Composition for Web Service Intermediaries

Sara Forghanizadeh and Eric Wohlstadter

University of British Columbia

Abstract. The use of XML as a format for message exchange makes Web services well suited for composition of heterogeneous components. However, since clients must manage differences in message schemas between services, interoperability is still a significant problem. Interoperability currently can be supported through the use of transformations provided by a Web service intermediary. However, intermediary technologies do not provide a way for clients to reason about the composition of services and intermediaries. We propose an approach to provide clients with an interface composed of schema information from a Web service and an intermediary. Composition is performed by applying rewriting rules, defined by the intermediary, to the server interface schema. This new interface takes into account what transformations are available at an intermediary. The advantage of the approach is that clients can continue to benefit from code-generation and static type-checking offered by interface definition languages such as WSDL; while still making use of the flexibility offered by intermediary transformations. We provide the algorithmic details of composition, including a proof of correctness and an upper bound on complexity. We demonstrate the approach in the context of a Web service composition of three publicly available Web services.

1 Introduction

Web services are flourishing on the Web as an important part of the information technology infrastructure. They provide building blocks for clients who can compose new applications or services out existing reusable services. Here, a client could also be a service itself, made up of a "mash-up" of existing services. The use of XML as a message exchange format makes Web services well suited for composition of heterogeneous components. The schemas [1] of these messages define the service's interface and are often described by an interface definition language such as the Web Services Definition Language (WSDL) [2]. However, since clients must manage differences in schemas between services, interoperability is still a significant problem. There is often some level of semantic overlap between schemas even when there is no syntactic match.

Since distinct services will naturally have certain distinct semantics, we cannot realistically hope to completely shield clients from differences in schemas. So, we are investigating support for interoperability through the use of *element-wise type-based adaptation*. This partial approach to adaptation is motivated by the desire to keep client applications simple. Complexity is reduced because clients only have to understand one particular schema for those XML elements where the types of multiple schemas semantically overlap (i.e. intersect).

Previous work on type-based adaptation [3,4] has solved problems related to the reuse of components in contexts that were not originally anticipated. The core problem

C. Pautasso and É. Tanter (Eds.): SC 2008, LNCS 4954, pp. 92–108, 2008.

is to take a typed interface provided by a component, a typed interface required by a client, and to help produce or locate a type adaptor which adapts between the required and provided interface. This helps a developer who takes components "off-the-shelf" and needs a way to connect them, as illustrated in Figure 1.a.

We seek to extend this line of work to an element-wise approach, for use in a Web services setting. Using Web service middleware, clients can make use of adaptive message transformations provided by a Web service *intermediary* [5]. Transformations can be implemented using *handlers* (described in Section 3) which can be applied to individual elements of XML messages. In our setting, an intermediary could either be a network proxy (e.g. Enterprise Service Bus [6]) or a local middleware layer. The important property of an intermediary is that it can be managed separately from the client business logic.

Consider a company that uses Web services to schedule shipments with companies such as FedEx and UPS. Naturally, FedEx and UPS share many semantic elements in common. In this case, the intermediary for the company could be programmed to transform to and from the company schema to FedEx and UPS. Here is how our approach would apply: when a developer at the company starts to write client code to communicate with FedEx or UPS, they can see what the FedEx and UPS interfaces (WSDL) look like, after the semantically overlapping elements have been replaced with their internal schema. This way they can reason about the composition of their intermediary with either the FedEx or UPS service. We call this a *composite schema*.

So we extend previous work in the following way: given a target Web service schema, $\mathcal{TS}$, and an intermediary, we generate a composite schema, $\mathcal{CS}$. Once this composite interface is provided to the client, it can then use it to generate stub code and perform type-checking. In our research the adaptations are known variables and the interface the client can use is an unknown variable, as opposed to the interfaces being the known variable and calculating the adaptors for the conversion between them. Our setup is then shown in Figure 1.b.

Our contribution is to demonstrate an architecture and algorithm for intermediary interface composition. We provide the algorithmic details including a proof of correctness and an upper bound on complexity. We demonstrate the approach in the context of a mash-up of three publicly available Web services.

The rest of the paper is as follows: Section 2 presents a motivating scenario, Section 3 describes background material, Section 4 presents an architectural overview, Section 5

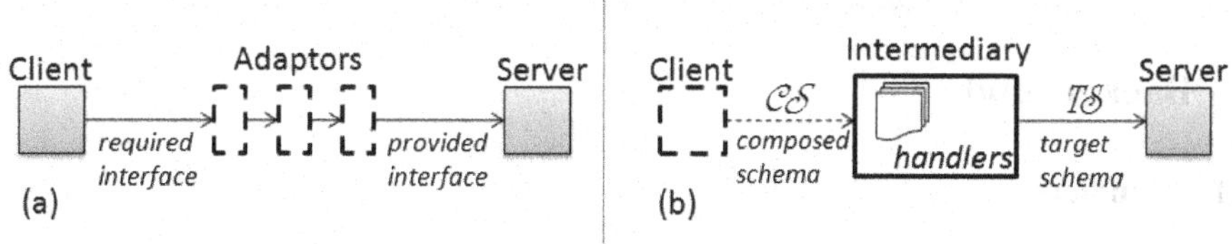

Fig. 1. (a) Interface adaptation, and (b) Intermediary interface composition. Dotted lines represent the unknown variable and solid lines show known variable.

presents technical details, Section 6 presents the example scenario in more detail, Section 7 presents related work and Section 8 concludes the paper.

2 Motivating Scenario

We consider a typical mash-up scenario where a Web service is built by composing services from eBay, FedEx, and UPS. Let's examine a typical business process flow for the mash-up.

First, a request is made to the `GetSellerTransactions` operation for eBay. This provides information regarding auctions managed by a particular user. The response contains transaction information, including a shipping address and a choice of shipping options for auction winners. Here we assume FedEx was chosen by some auction winner.

Second, the mash-up company wants to verify the address of the buyer before scheduling a shipment with FedEx. Unfortunately, the FedEx service does not include a separate operation for validating address information, but UPS does. So, the mash-up sends an `AVRequest` (address validation) to UPS. A part of the information in this message is specific to UPS, such as the UPS account number. On the other hand the address to be validated can be extracted from the response message received from eBay and simply routed to UPS.

Finally, after address validation, the mash-up must additionally transform address information to FedEx before sending a final `FDXShipRequest` request. This motivates transformation of the address information between eBay, UPS, and FedEx formats, but complicates things for the programmer without additional support.

Motivated by this scenario, a separate transformation layer deployed on a intermediary could be implemented which imports and exports address information in a common format. This has the benefit of factoring the entire transformation concern out of the core mash-up business logic. This could simplify the mash-up implementation since the address format will be a common element in many operations for all three services. However, without additional support, this would break the sound engineering process of writing software against statically defined interfaces. The WSDL of the three services does not take into account the intermediary transformations so their presence is implicit and not explicitly accounted for in a typed interface. The client could not generate stub-code from the WSDL that accounts for the transformations or type-check against these stubs.

3 Background

3.1 Handlers

Intermediaries are often a repository of message handlers (i.e. interceptors [7]) which read and write elements of XML-based messages. For example, a handler might be responsible for just the translation of elements representing shipping addresses in two schemas with disparate formats. Traditional handlers could be modeled as a function with a type `Document→Document`, since they accept any XML document type and do not place any guarantees on the output document type.

This type does not provide useful information for reasoning about the composition of document handlers. On the other hand, if handlers specified specific types at the granularity of entire documents, for example `PlaceEBayOrder→PlaceAmazon-Order`, the types could be too specific. This is because document handlers might apply specific element-wise transformations. For example, they might transform just the address information in an eBay or Amazon order. These problems help motivate a different approach based on element-wise type information.

3.2 XML Schema

WSDL [2] is based on the standard W3C XML Schema [1] grammar for defining types of XML documents. Web service developers use this grammar to specify sets of XML documents that are accepted or provided by service operations. A document instance that is a member of the set, defined by a type, is said to be *valid* for the type. Figure 2 provides the grammar and notation of a mini-schema language that we use throughout the paper to model salient properties of XML Schema.

Here a schema consists of a root `ElementType` which defines an XML element tag name and the `ContentModel`. The types of elements can also be declared through reference to existing definitions by use of an `ElementRef`. The content model defines the valid structure of nested children. The content model[1] is either a `Primitive` type or a regular expression of element types. The use of recursion to other `ElementTypes` in an expression is what gives XML Schema its power to express tree structures; as opposed to flat strings which are normally described by regular expressions.

Web services middleware can perform *validation* to ensure messages match the types defined in their WSDL. Our approach combines the mechanism of message validation with a message transformation mechanism. Here we describe some technical details of standard message validation mechanisms so we can build on this background to describe details of our approach.

Message validation can be performed by middleware at runtime using a parser. An important property of the W3C XML Schema specification is that many aspects of the specification are motivated by the requirement to keep this parsing process simple. In particular, the schema language is designed to prevent parsers from needing to *back-track* at runtime[2]. This is achieved by restricting the regular expressions describing a `ContentModel` to those that are unambiguous.

This property allows XML Schema parsers to be implemented using only small extensions to standard deterministic finite automaton (DFAs). As usual, a DFA is a mechanism for parsing sequences of strings which consists of: a set of states and a set of transitions between states. One state is distinguished to be the initial state and some subset of states are final (accepting) states. Each transition is associated with a symbol

[1] For simplicity, we do not currently deal with some features of XML Schema, such as numeric occurence indicators or the `all` content model. These features could be added using the approach in [8].

[2] This is called Unique Particle Attribution in W3C parlance.

ElementType ::=	*name*[ContentModel]	//Named element with child content
	ElementRef	//Reference to a named element
ContentModel ::=	*Primitive*	//primitive type
	ContentModel, ContentModel	//sequence
	ContentModel || ContentModel	//choice
	ContentModel*	//unbounded occurences
	ContentModel?	//optional occurence
	ElementType	//recursive nesting of elements

Fig. 2. Mini XML schema language BNF. Note: This figure defines a grammar language, Mini-Schema, in terms of another grammar language, BNF. We avoid using any symbols from the BNF language except for the non-terminal assignment (::=). Non-terminal alternatives are separated by newlines. All other symbols are part of the defined Mini-Schema language. Terminals are shown in italics. Java-style comments are used.

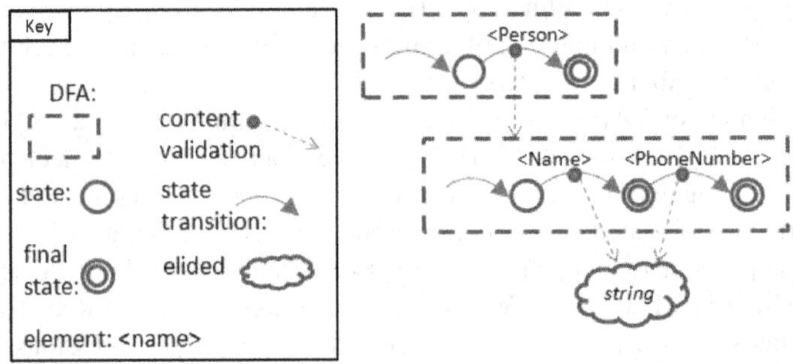

Fig. 3. A parser for the ElementType: Person[Name[*string*], PhoneNumber[*string*]?]. Parsing begins at the root (top-most) DFA and its final state is the final state for validating a complete document. Final states of internal DFAs are used to determine if transitions in a parent DFA are successful.

from some alphabet. Parsing begins at the initial state and is driven by reading symbols of an input string from left to right. As each symbol is read, the current state is changed by following a transition labelled with that symbol. If the sequence is consumed and the automaton is in a final state then the string is accepted.

But XML documents consist of trees instead of strings! Still, Thompson shows how XML Schema is parsed using a set of cooperating DFAs [9]. Intuitively, each level of sibling elements in the hierarchy of the XML tree is considered as a separate string. When an element is consumed, the parser processes the content of the element using a different DFA, before allowing the transition to occur. Parsing of XML trees is thus handled through this nesting of operations on separate DFAs. This process is illustrated in Figure 3.

Our approach to composition involves integrating this parsing process with the process of message transformation. This is achieved by building automata that are aware of the transformations that handlers can make.

3.3 Regular Expression Types

We use the paradigm of regular expression types [10] for added flexibility during the process of creating a composite schema. Unlike popular OO languages, under this discipline a sub-type relationship holds for two types if the set of instances described by one type completely contains (i.e. subsumes) the set of instances described by another type. This is different from typing in standard OO languages where a sub-type relationship needs to be explicitly declared.

So under regular expression typing, `person` (below) would be a sub-type of `personExtra` because the set of documents validated by `personExtra` includes all of the those validated by `person`. Here new types are declared using an `element` keyword in the obvious way. Intuitively, a `person` can be used wherever a `personExtra` is expected. This is commonly notated using the sub-type operator (`<:`), as in, `person <: personExtra`.

element person = Person[Name[$string$]]
element personExtra = Person[Name[$string$], PhoneNumber[$string$]?]

We will especially take advantage of these two axioms of regex typing:
Axiom 1. `(a <: b)` implies `(a <: (b || c))`, for all types `a`, `b`, and `c`.
Axiom 2. `(a || a)` = `a`, for all types `a`.

Axiom 1 is clear since `(b || c)` accepts a larger set of documents than `b` alone. Axiom 2 simply says that a choice between a type and itself is idempotent.

4 Overview of the Approach

Our approach is divided into two stages: interface composition and handler composition. We describe how these stages work from a high-level architectural viewpoint before going into low-level details in Section 5.

4.1 Interface Composition

One technical challenge is to return a new composed schema, $\mathcal{CS}$, to the client. This is an extended version of some target schema, $\mathcal{TS}$. This requires that programmers assign a typed interface to each handler on an intermediary (Section 5.1). This interface composition process (Section 5.2) occurs off-line at development-time, not during the actual execution of a deployed system. Our middleware uses our algorithm described in Section 5.3 to compose handler type information with a Web service's type information.

The data-flow of this process is shown in Figure 4. First (1), a client chooses some $\mathcal{TS}$ that it wants to compose with an intermediary. It submits $\mathcal{TS}$ to any intermediary that makes use of our prototype middleware. Second (2), the intermediary runs an algorithm using $\mathcal{TS}$ and *handlers* deployed on the intermediary, to compose their type information. Certain information about the algorithm execution is stored in a *composition trace*. This information will serve as handler dispatching instructions at run-time (Section 5.4). Finally (3), the client receives the composed interface, $\mathcal{CS}$ from the intermediary. The client can now use $\mathcal{CS}$ to generate stub code and type-check against.

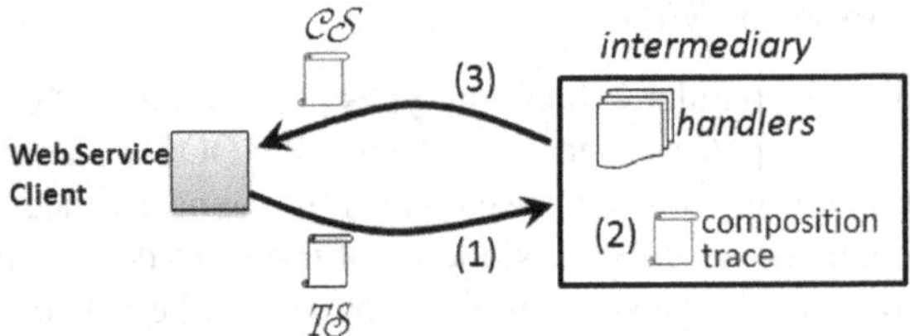

Fig. 4. Data-flow in Interface Composition. The composition service produces a composite schema, given the set of handlers and some server interface chosen by the client. A digest of this process is saved by the intermediary for use at run-time. We place certain terms in italics; these terms will be referred to as Java objects in the algorithm of Figure 7.

4.2 Handler Composition

At run-time, our middleware dispatches the handlers to execute transformations. This occurs when the intermediary receives a message from a client (or server reply). The data-flow of this process is illustrated in Figure 5. In this paper, we focus only on the algorithmic details and complexity of our approach. In an online technical report [11], we have provided some initial benchmarks of our prototype performance.

First (1), a client sends a message valid for $\mathcal{CS}$, which is intercepted by the intermediary. Second (2), client messages are validated and transformed by the intermediary. Our prototype middleware decides which handlers should be executed, on which message elements, and in what order. These decisions are guided by the composition trace derived off-line, so no complex processing is required at this time. Finally (3), a message valid for the $\mathcal{TS}$ is forwarded by the intermediary. This process is described in more detail in Section 5.4. The reverse process for server replies is similar so we do not show this data-flow in the figure or discuss the details specifically.

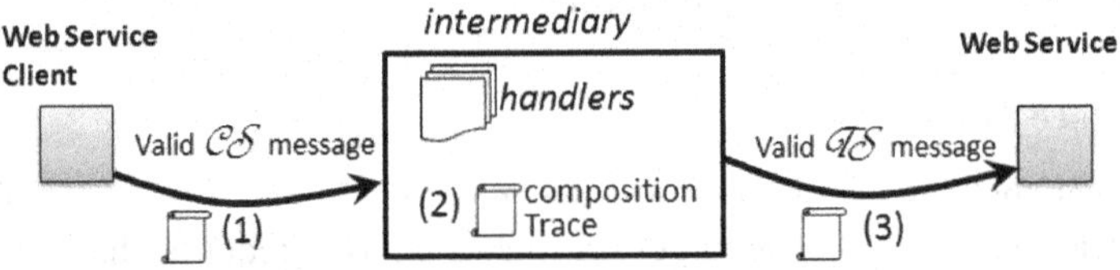

Fig. 5. The intermediary dispatches the handlers at run-time to make the message compatible with the Web service, using the digest derived at development-time

5 Technical Details

5.1 Handler Interfaces

Our composition mechanism requires a formal representation of the input and output types of handler components. We provide support for programmers to describe *element-wise interfaces* using XML Schema.

Definition 1. *Element-Wise Interface.* An element-wise interface is a pair of `ElementTypes`, (*input*, *output*). The contract for a handler which implements the interface specifies that the handler can transform any element of type *input* in a document to some element of type *output*.

The implementation of the handler can be written as either Java or XSLT and can perform arbitrarily complicated computation to make a transformation. The implementation could be as simple as the logic required to convert between postal code formats or as complicated as contacting an external service to perform a currency conversion. Our tool uses the element-wise interfaces as input to schema composition and associates an identifier with some implementation component which will be used as a call-back by our intermediary middleware. In our algorithm we assume each handler has a unique identifier, denoted as $handler.id$. The input and output element types are denoted $handler.input$ and $handler.output$ respectively.

To motivate how element-wise interfaces are used, consider the simple example of Figure 6. Here there are three type definitions for some user contact information in different formats i.e. contact1-3. Following there are two element-wise interfaces for some handlers listed: hander1-2. Notice that from the type information, we can infer that a message of type contact1 can be transformed into a message of type contact2 by applying handler1 to the `Number` element embedded within a contact1 message. From there we can now apply handler2 on the whole message to obtain a message of type contact3.

Composition in this case is not achievable by a traditional composition of function types. Here, the output type of handler1 does not match the input type of handler2. Still, composition is achievable if we consider element-wise composition. So we need a new approach for composition in this setting.

```
element contact1 = Contact[Person[string], Number[string]]
element contact2 = Contact[Person[string], Phone[string]]
element contact3 = Person[Name[string], PhoneNumber[string]?]

element numberType = Number[string]
element phoneType = Phone[string]
handler1: numberType ↪ phoneType

handler2: contact2 ↪ contact3
```

Fig. 6. If we apply handler1 to an instance of contact1 (element-wise) and then handler2 to that result, we are guaranteed an instance of contact3

5.2 Interface Composition

At development-time an intermediary can be composed with the interface of a server. Our middleware prototype exposes a Web service operation to accept WSDL schemas from clients. The schema is processed into a composite schema and returned. Here we explain how our middleware can reason over the composition of element-wise transformations in an efficient way.

Using a naive approach, determining the correct composition of handlers could take exponential time in the number of handlers, because all permutations may need to be examined. Also, if handlers are allowed to execute multiple times (for example to perform element-wise operations) the problem is even more complicated. Here, we limit our approach to handlers providing *optional transformation*. This enables us to implement a tractable solution. This is exactly the case we have motivated: intermediaries provide transformations as an optional convenience for clients. These optional handlers are in contrast to handlers which enforce policies such as security. Our work does not address that kind of mandatory interposition of intermediaries.

Using the interfaces of handlers deployed on an intermediary, an inference algorithm is performed to determine the composed interface exposed to the client. This process makes use of a *rewrite rule* which is a transformation to the server schema itself; as opposed to the transformations made by handlers at run-time on a message instance. We use the term "rewrite" here, rather than "transform", to keep it clear when changes are being applied to schema types versus message instances.

Definition 2. *Rewrite Rule.* Assume there exists a handler with the element-wise interface, (*input*, *output*), and also there exists an element type, `t` somewhere in the target server schema. If `output` is a sub-type of `t`, then any reference to `t` should be rewritten to the choice type: `t || input`.

Notice that we are matching *output*s and then adding *input*s to the schema. Intuitively, this process infers, in reverse, the transformations that handlers will be capable of making at run-time.

In our algorithm, we repeatedly apply the rewrite rule until it is no longer useful. Notice that since rewriting only causes the schema to grow, we do not need to worry about what order we apply the rewrite rules. This is because some application of the rewrite rule using one handler interface will never prevent the application of another rewrite rule, at any later point in time (by Axiom 1). In other words, the types of the schema only get wider.

However, we do need information to know at what point to terminate the algorithm. Termination occurs when only idempotent rewrites can be made (as in Axiom 2). For this purpose we introduce annotations on the composed schema that we call a composition trace. The trace also records the "backwards" type inference so that the trace can be followed in the forwards direction at run-time to actually transform message instances.

Definition 3. *Composition Trace.* Whenever a rewrite rule for the handler, h, with interface, (*input*, *output*), is applied at an element type t, we add an annotation on the reference to *input* that is created. The annotation is a sequence of handler identifiers, consisting of the identifier for h appended to the beginning of any existing sequence which annotates t. If t has no such annotation already, then the annotation is simply the single handler identifier.

As a convenience for clients, our intermediary supports an additional post-processing step to filter large composite schemas. Clients can provide preferences in the form of a partial-ordering on XML Schema namespaces. If a choice exists between two element types, `a` and `b`, and the namespace of `a` is preferred over `b`, then `b` will be removed as a choice. An example of this is demonstrated in Section 6.

With these definitions in place, we can define an algorithm that computes a composed schema. The question we need to answer is: given an intermediary and a server schema, what is the schema which describes all documents that can be transformed into a document valid for the server schema, using any combination of the element-wise handlers?

5.3 Interface Composition Algorithm

The composite schema begins as a copy of the target schema, in Figure 7 line 1. The algorithm is structured as a comparison between all element types in the schema and all handler outputs. This is implemented as a double nested-loop, as in lines 3-4. Whenever the schema is changed by a rewrite, the entire process begins again, because references to new element types are added through the rewriting. This "restart" can be seen by the `break` statement on line 10, which breaks out to line 2. This is certainly not the most efficient implementation but it simplifies presentation of the algorithm and worst-case analysis.

Now, we can see that the algorithm will continue to execute until one of the `if` statements on line 5-6 fails for all iterations. The first `if` statement (line 5) implements part of the rewrite rule that checks whether the handler output type (as in Definition 1) is a subtype of some schema element type. The second `if` statement (line 6) checks the trace annotation (as in Definition 3) on the existing schema type to ensure this rewrite would not be idempotent. If both of these checks succeed then a new reference to the handler input type is created (line 7). The trace annotation on the new reference is updated (line 8), according to Definition 3. Finally, the schema is rewritten (line 9), according to Definition 2.

Before proving the correctness and complexity of the algorithm. We walk through a specific example where a target schema is composed with handler information. The example makes use of the previous type definitions and handlers of Figure 6. In Figure 8, we see four schema files which consist of type definitions enclosed in curly braces. The first file, $\mathcal{TS}$, is the original schema chosen by the client. The next three files are versions of the composite schema as it is rewritten. We use a subscript to denote the number of rewriting steps.

$\mathcal{CS}_0$ starts out as a copy of $\mathcal{TS}$. Then, in $\mathcal{CS}_1$, handler2.output is matched, so handler2.input is added to the schema and added as a new choice. Next, in $\mathcal{CS}_2$, handler1.output is matched (element-wise), so handler1.input is added to the schema and added as a new choice. At that point no new matches can be made so the algorithm terminates. The superscripts on types are the composition trace and will be discussed in Section 5.4.

Termination Proof: Termination is guaranteed because each rewrite does not actually copy the type information for some *handler.input* type into a new location in the composite schema. Instead, a reference to that type is used as an alternative in the additional choice.

We know that the algorithm starts out with a fixed number of named types available as input at the beginning of execution. During execution, no new named types are created. Since the algorithm will not add any idempotent choices, it must eventually run out of rewrites that can be made and line 6 in the algorithm must fail for an entire iteration of both loops.

```
1. CS = TS;
2. loop:
3.   forall(element in CS.elements)
4.         forall(handler in intermediary)
5.               if(handler.output.isSubTypeOf(element))
6.                     if(!element.trace.idempotent(handler.id))) {
7.                           ref = new ElementRef(handler.input);
8.                           ref.trace = concat(handler.id, element.trace);
9.                           CS.rewrite(element, new Choice(element, ref));
10.                          break loop;
11.                    }
```

Fig. 7. Composition Algorithm, shown in Java pseudo-code. Local variable declarations are elided. Local variables shown in italics. We assume a method `Schema.rewrite(SchemaElement, SchemaElement)` which replaces the occurence of the first argument with the second argument by mutating the target schema. The constructors `Choice` and `ElementRef` simply model the construction of new schema productions as given in Figure 2.

Correctness Proof: We need to show that a message, msg, is a $\mathcal{CS}$ message if and only if there is a sequence of element-wise transformations that can be performed on msg to create a $\mathcal{TS}$ message. This can be shown in two directions. First, we show that (1) if msg is a $\mathcal{CS}$ message, then it can be transformed into a $\mathcal{TS}$ message. Second, we show that (2) if msg can be transformed into a $\mathcal{TS}$ message, then it is a $\mathcal{CS}$ message.

1. This is shown by induction on the sequence of rewrites (line 9) performed during algorithm execution.

Base Case: When the algorithm begins, $\mathcal{CS}$ equals $\mathcal{TS}$. So, if msg is valid for $\mathcal{CS}$, it is already a valid $\mathcal{TS}$ message.

Induction: We assume that all valid $\mathcal{CS}_{k-1}$ messages can be transformed into $\mathcal{TS}$ messages. Now, we show, that $\mathcal{CS}_k$ messages can be transformed into $\mathcal{TS}$ messages. We know on the kth rewrite, one additional choice is added by some handler's interface to $\mathcal{CS}_{k-1}$. So assume there is some message that is valid for $\mathcal{CS}_k$ but not for $\mathcal{CS}_{k-1}$. We know the message can only differ from a $\mathcal{CS}_{k-1}$ message by use of this additional alternative. However, we also know we can transform the alternative type back to one accepted by $\mathcal{CS}_{k-1}$ using the same handler. By the assumption, all $\mathcal{CS}_{k-1}$ messages are $\mathcal{CS}_k$ messages. Therefore, by induction, after the termination of the algorithm, all $\mathcal{CS}_i$ messages can be transformed to $\mathcal{TS}$ messages for any integer i.

```
TS  =  { element contact3 = Person[..]; }

CS0 =  { element contact3 = Person[..]; }

CS1 =  { element contact3 = Person[..] || contact2^(h2);
         element contact2 = Contact[Person[string], Phone[string]];
       }

CS2 =  { element contact3 = Person[..] || contact2^(h2);
         element contact2 = Contact[PersonName[string],
                                    Phone[string] || numberType^(h1) ];
         element numberType = Number[string];
       }
```

Fig. 8. Composing a schema. The example makes use of the previous type definitions and handlers of Figure 6. We use a subscript on CS to denote the number of rewriting steps. The superscripts on types are the composition trace and will be discussed in Section 5.4.

2. This direction is straightforward. msg is valid for $\mathcal{TS}$, and $\mathcal{TS}$ is a sub-type of $\mathcal{CS}$ by Axiom 1 and Definition 2. Therefore, msg is valid for $\mathcal{CS}$.

Complexity: We show that our offline algorithm runs in polynomial-time with respect to the input size. This suffices to show that the algorithm is tractable. In other words, execution will not suffer from "exponential explosion". In the future we plan to give a tighter upper-bound.

As was described, the input to the algorithm consists of n handlers and $\mathcal{TS}$. Let the sum of the sizes of all handler inputs and outputs be denoted $|H|$. Let the size of $\mathcal{TS}$ be denoted $|TS|$. These sizes are in terms of the length of the respective type definitions.

In the pathological case, the *output* of all handlers could match every element type in $\mathcal{TS}$, and also every element type in the *input* of all handlers. Recall that handler.input types become referenced by the schema as the algorithm progresses, so they become fair game for matching. So the schema could have a maximum of $(|H|+|TS|)$ element types. Each element type could be a choice between all types, giving a size of $(|H|+|TS|)^2$. To simplify analysis we assume that each match might require $n*(|H|+|TS|)$ iterations of the double loop. In other words, we conservatively assume that matching fails all the way up to the last evaluation of the loop body. Also, for clarity we assume $(|H|+|TS|)$ is much larger than n. Therefore we have $\mathcal{O}(|H|+|TS|)^3$ total evaluations of the loop body.

The only step of the loop body which cannot be implemented in constant time is the check for sub-types (line 5). This check can be performed in polynomial-time [9] with respect to the size of the input types[3]. So, then the total complexity is this polynomial sub-typing cost times the number of loop body evaluations, which is clearly polynomial.

As in the case of all XML Schemas, the composite schema should be unambiguous as in Section 3.2. We can check that this is the case using the algorithm from [9] in polynomial time.

[3] As described in [9], this is because the regular expression types are restricted to be unambiguous.

5.4 Handler Composition

When an intermediary receives a particular XML message, the intermediary needs to determine: for this message exactly which handlers should be used, on which message elements, and in what order? We use the trace information from the interface composition to construct a transformation-aware automata. This allows handlers to be dispatched as part of the standard message validation process.

Revisiting Figure 8 we now see how annotations were added during rewriting. These annotations are shown as superscripts on types: (h1) and (h2) for handler1-2. When a message is received by our intermediary, we validate that message according to the algorithm published by Thompson [9]. When some element validates to a type with a trace we know that type is not actually valid according to the target server schema. However, the trace annotation tells us the series of handlers which can be applied to create a valid message element. So, we dispatch the sub-tree rooted at that element to the sequence of handlers specified in the trace.

Finally, a transformation-aware automata is now illustrated by the example in Figure 9. Certain transitions introduced by rewriting are attached to handlers. When these transitions are followed, the handler is fed the XML message element for transformation.

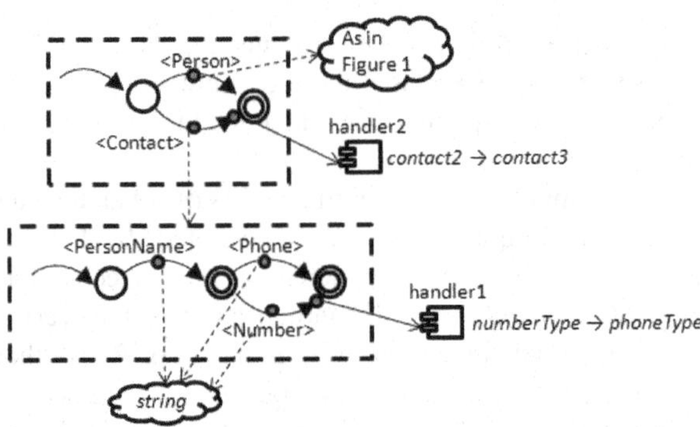

Fig. 9. Transformation-aware automata for the type constructed in Figure 8: `Person[..]` || `Contact[PersonName[..], Phone[..]` || `Number[..]]`.

6 Example Revisited

Recall the example client implements a mash-up of three services: eBay, FedEx, and UPS. This client prefers to use data formatted according to FedEx standards. So, they develop several transformation handlers, two of which are listed in Figure 10. Next, they compose these handlers with both the eBay and UPS schemas. Now we consider each of these in turn. We qualify elements with namespaces using a (:) to avoid confusion.

In Figure 11, on the left, we see part of the original type definition for the eBay `GetSellerTransactions` operation response. This is the first operation called by the client in our example workflow. On the right, is the composed type definition after being processed by the intermediary. Notice that the operation can now return addresses

eBay to FedEx	eBay:address[*Address*] ↪ FDX:destination[*Destination*]
FedEx to UPS Validator Address	FDX:destination[*Destination*] ↪ UPS:address[*AVContent*]

Fig. 10. eBay, FedEx, UPS handlers

```
element SellTxResponseT =
  eBay:getSellerTxResponse[
    transaction[
      buyer[..,
        address[..]
      ],
  ..],
..]
```

```
element SellTxResponseT =
  eBay:getSellerTxResponse[
    transaction[
      buyer[..,
        address[..] ||
        UPS:address[..] ||
        FDX:destination[..]
      ],
  ..],
..]
```

Fig. 11. Original and composite eBay GetSellerTransactions response using transformations from Figure 10

```
element AVType =
   UPS:AVRequest[
      RequestElement,
      address[AVContent]
   ]
```

```
element AVType =
   UPS:AVRequest[
      RequestElement,
      address[AVContent] ||
      eBay:address[Address] ||
      FDX:destination[Destination]
   ]
```

Fig. 12. Original and composite UPS Address Validation message using transformations from Figure 10. Elements in italics are references to schema elements not shown.

in either one of three formats. If the client needs to pass this returned information to another service as part of the mash-up, the client may no longer need to embed data formatting conversion as part of the mash-up business logic. This can be seen by considering the next operation in the example workflow.

Recall the second operation in the workflow was to validate the address returned from eBay. This is done through the UPS `AVRequest` operation, as shown on the left of Figure 12. Some of this information is specific to UPS, such as the `RequestElement` which carries UPS account information. We could not hope to provide any conversion from eBay account information to UPS. Still, we can see in the composite on the right of Figure 12, that at least the address information can be made uniform. Finally, in Figure 13 we see both the composite types after being filtered for a preference to FedEx, using the described post-processing step. Now, when the client receives an eBay response it will already include an address in FedEx format. That address can be taken and passed

```
element SellTxResponseT =
  eBay:GetSellerTxResponse[
    transaction[
      buyer[..,
        FDX:destination[..]
      ],
  ..],
..]
```

```
element AVType =
   UPS:AVRequest[
      RequestElement,
      FDX:destination[Destination]
   ]
```

Fig. 13. Composite types for both eBay and UPS after being post-processed with a preference for FedEx

directly to the UPS address validation operation. So we can see how the implementation of the client might be simplified by making use of only the FedEx format whenever possible.

7 Related Work

7.1 Web Services

The standard language for XML transformation is the eXtensible Stylesheet Language Transformation (XSLT). XSLT does not support any kind of inference for reasoning about the composition of templates. We see our work, not as an alternative to such languages but as complementary. Our approach applies at the level of interface definition languages. So, it is agnostic to the implementation language that is used.

Several tools [12] have been developed to type check an XSLT program given an input and output type, but this does not address the motivation described in this paper where a composite type definition should be provided given a particular target output type.

In previous work [13] we proposed an AOP approach to programming transformation using the familiar advice-pointcut style. However that work did not address the generation of a composite schema or automatic middleware dispatching and shares very little in terms of technical details to the research here.

Work on the semantic web [14] including standards for semantic web services (WSDL-S) could help to ease the task of manually programming transformations for interoperability. However, since many enterprises still do not have semantic standards, we have focused on helping automate handler composition where the transformation handlers are programmed manually by developers using common languages such as Java and XSLT.

Ponnekanti [15] presented a taxonomy of Web service interface mismatches that can occur when interfaces are allowed to evolve independently as well as a static and dynamic analysis tool to discover mismatches in WSDL. We think their taxonomy provides a good overview to the kinds of problems where an intermediary can be useful.

7.2 Adapters for Components

Purtilo et al. [16] show how external adaptation can be valuable to reduce the non-functional constraints affecting application code. They provide a new language called Nimble that is used to generate adaptation code. In some cases, the generation of adapters can be automated [17] using type-based inference.

Gschwind et al. [3] provide a solution for the problem of composing software component interfaces and software built on different component models. That work was done under the paradigm of OO typing where sub-type relationships are explicitly declared. So an element-wise transformation approach was not applicable. To address element-wise transformation in a Web service environment, we have provided a new composition algorithm.

Other works [18] concentrate on mismatches between components at the behavioural level (i.e., the protocol between components). We have not addressed this issue in our research.

8 Conclusion

The transformation of an entire schema can be broken down into handlers responsible for only specific pieces. This comes at a price to service clients who are then unable to reason about the composition of an intermediary and a service. Our approach is to provide the flexibility of transformation without sacrificing an explicit interface contract for clients.

Currently we are planning an empirical study of the performance of our prototype implementation. We expect the performance overhead should not be prohibitive because the complex processing in our approach occurs mainly offline. We expect that at run-time the actual message transformations will dominate the time for handler dispatching. Thus far this has been the case in our initial studies [11]. In addition to standard validation mechanisms, our approach only adds constant-time hashtable lookups to dispatch handlers at run-time. For high-performance applications, additional consideration will be needed to determine how the buffers which hold message streams should be allocated and copied. We have not yet considered these fine-grained performance characteristics.

This paper described an architecture and algorithm for composition of Web service interfaces with intermediaries. We provided a proof of algorithm correctness and showed that it executes in polynomial-time. Finally, we motivated and demonstrated a realistic mash-up scenario as an illustration of our approach.

References

1. Thompson, H.S., Beech, D., Maloney, M., Mendelsohn, N.: XML Schema Part 1: Structures. W3C Recommendation (2004)
2. Chinnici, R., Moreau, J.J., Ryman, A., Weerawarana, S.: Web Services Description Language 2.0 Part 1: Core Language. W3C Recommendation (2007)
3. Gschwind, T.: Type based adaptation: An adaptation approach for dynamic distributed systems. In: Proc. of the International Workshop on Software Engineering and Middleware (2002)

4. Oberleitner, J., Gschwind, T., Jazayeri, M.: The Vienna component framework enabling composition across component models. In: International Conference on Software Engineering (2003)
5. Fielding, R.T., Taylor, R.N.: Principled design of the modern web architecture. ACM Transactions on Internet Technology 2(2), 115–150 (2002)
6. Chappell, D.A.: Enterprise Service Bus. O'Reilly, Sebastopol (2004)
7. Wang, N., Parameswaran, K., Schmidt, D.: The design and performance of meta-programming mechanisms for object request broker middleware. In: Proc. of the COOTS, pp. 677–694 (2000)
8. Thompson, H.S.: Efficient implementation of content models with numerical occurrence constraints. In: Proc. of the European XML Conference (XTech) (2006)
9. Thompson, H.S.: Using finite state automata to implement W3C XML Schema content model validation and restriction checking. In: Proc. of the European XML Conference (2003)
10. Hosoya, H., Pierce, B.: Xduce: A statically typed xml processing language (2002)
11. Forghanizadeh, S., Minevskiy, I., Wohlstadter, E.: Interfaces for web services intermediaries (Tech Report), `http://www.cs.ubc.ca/~wohlstad/extended.pdf`
12. Kirkegaard, C., Moller, A., Schwartzbach, M.I.: Static analysis of XML transformations in Java. IEEE Trans. on Software Engineering (2004)
13. Wohlstadter, E., Volder, K.D.: Doxpects: aspects supporting xml transformation interfaces. In: Aspect-Oriented Software Development (2006)
14. Halpin, H., Thompson, H.: One document to bind them: Combining xml, web services, and the semantic web. In: World Wide Web Conference (2003)
15. Ponnekanti, S., Fox, A.: Interoperability among independently evolving web services. In: Jacobsen, H.-A. (ed.) Middleware 2004. LNCS, vol. 3231, pp. 331–351. Springer, Heidelberg (2004)
16. Purtilo, J.M., Atlee, J.M.: Module reuse by interface adaptation. Software Practice and Experience 21(6) (1991)
17. Thatte, S.R.: Automated synthesis of interface adapters for reusable classes. In: Proc. of Symposium on Principles of programming languages (1994)
18. DeLine, R.: Avoiding packaging mismatch with Flexible Packaging. In: Proceedings of the 21st International Conference on Software Engineering (1999)

Goal-Oriented Composition of Services

Sebastian Nanz and Terkel K. Tolstrup

Informatics and Mathematical Modelling
Technical University of Denmark
{nanz,tkt}@imm.dtu.dk

Abstract. One fundamental issue in service-oriented computing concerns the question whether services can be composed in a manner that allows them to achieve their individual goals. In this paper we use a variant of interface automata as an abstraction of the input/output behaviour of services, which are themselves represented as terms in the π-calculus extended with an action for expressing service collaboration. In this setting, the question whether two or more services can meaningfully compose is then reduced to checking a simple property of the product automaton of the involved interfaces.

1 Introduction

Service-oriented computing [17] has evolved from component-based software development as an effective approach to building distributed applications. A service can be described as a process that can be addressed and used by other services on a network, based on its published interface that identifies the capability it provides. Two of the main research problems arising from this approach are thus concerned with the design of this interface: in order for it to enable the *discovery* of services that may achieve a certain computational task; and, to facilitate the *composition* of services.

Web Services [1] are the example of the services paradigm that is currently developed furthest. Here, the static interface of a service can be described in the *Web Services Description Language (WSDL)* [4], an XML-based format which contains a definition of the messages and ports that are involved in a communication with a service. This description limits severely the behavioural complexity the service can implement, since interactions can only be described with a limited variety of message exchange patterns. In an advanced service model, services could offer complex functionality that likewise may result in more complex interactions with other services. For such a model to be successful, it has to be supported by interface descriptions that allow to check the compatibility of services with respect to their communication behaviour, e.g. to ensure that services do not deadlock waiting for each other's input.

In this paper we suggest a variant of interface automata [5] as a means to provide this interface information. Transitions in an automaton are labelled with the types of ports and message formats or internal actions, and describe the input/output behaviour of the service. We view these automata as abstractions

C. Pautasso and É. Tanter (Eds.): SC 2008, LNCS 4954, pp. 109–124, 2008.

Table 1. Syntax of the polyadic π-calculus with service collaborations

$P ::=$	0	nil process	$\pi ::=$	$x\tilde{y}$	reception
$\mid$	$\sum_{i \in I} \pi_i.P_i$	guarded sum	$\mid$	$\overline{x}\tilde{y}$	sending
$\mid$	$P_1 \mid P_2$	parallel composition	$\mid$	$\mathsf{com}\ x$	collaboration initiation
$\mid$	$(\mathsf{new}\ x)\ P$	restriction	$\mid$	τ	unobservable action
$\mid$	$!P$	process replication			

of processes which implement the actual service. Such processes are written in a variant of the polyadic π-calculus [15] that enriches the usual syntax with an action to express the initiation of a service collaboration. We define a type system to statically describe the conformance of the abstract interface with its implementing process. We prove for typed processes whose interface automata compose *optimistically* [5] (i.e. there is *some* sequence of interactions to lead to a final state) that the process composition also evolves in a way that the goals of the collaboration can be achieved.

The remainder of this paper is structured as follows. In Section 2 we describe our extension of the π-calculus syntax and semantics that allows us to describe service collaborations, and we introduce the running example of the paper. Section 3 presents interface automata and their use as process abstractions. Also, a non-standard semantics is introduced which describes the execution of interface-conformant processes. In Section 4 we complement this dynamic view of conformance with static type checking, and in Section 5 we discuss goal-oriented compositions of interface automata. We present related work in Section 6 and conclude in Section 7.

2 Modelling of Service Composition

The π-calculus [15] is a fundamental process algebraic approach to describing concurrent systems whose configuration may change during the computation. We use the π-calculus in its polyadic form as a basis for the description of services with complex interactive behaviour, adding an action which explicitly describes the agreement of two processes to collaborate.

2.1 A Process Model for Services

The polyadic π-calculus models two entities: *processes* and *names*. Processes interact by synchronising on channels where they exchange a sequence of data values; both channels and data are uniformly described by names. Names are (unstructured) values drawn from the infinite set $\mathcal{N}$.

The syntax of processes is shown in Table 1 and its entities can be informally described as follows. The terminated process is represented by 0. The term $\sum_{i \in I} \pi_i.P_i$ models an external choice, that allows one action π_i to be executed

Table 2. Structural congruence of the π-calculus

$$\begin{array}{rl} P \mid 0 \equiv P & (\mathsf{new}\ x)\ (P \mid Q) \equiv P \mid (\mathsf{new}\ x)\ Q \text{ if } x \notin fn(P) \\ P \mid Q \equiv Q \mid P & (\mathsf{new}\ x)\ 0 \equiv 0 \\ P \mid (Q \mid R) \equiv (P \mid Q) \mid R & (\mathsf{new}\ x)\ (\mathsf{new}\ y)\ P \equiv (\mathsf{new}\ y)\ (\mathsf{new}\ x)\ P \\ !P \equiv\ !P \mid P & \end{array}$$

Table 3. Reaction rules of the π-calculus with service collaborations

$$\tau.P + M \to P \qquad \frac{|\tilde{y}| = |\tilde{z}|}{(x\tilde{y}.P + M) \mid (\overline{x}\tilde{z}.Q + N) \to P[\tilde{z}/\tilde{y}] \mid Q}$$

$$\frac{\Gamma(x) = \Gamma(y) \qquad z \text{ fresh}}{(\mathsf{com}\, x.P + M) \mid (\mathsf{com}\, y.Q + N) \to (\mathsf{new}\ z)\ (P[z/x] \mid Q[z/y])}$$

$$\frac{P \to P'}{P \mid Q \to P' \mid Q} \qquad \frac{Q \equiv P \quad P \to P' \quad P' \equiv Q'}{Q \to Q'} \qquad \frac{P \to P'}{(\mathsf{new}\ x)\ P \to (\mathsf{new}\ x)\ P'}$$

and to continue with P_i. In our syntax variant, there are the four types of actions; we describe first the three classical ones: an input process $x\tilde{y}.P$ receives a sequence of names along channel x and substitutes it for $\tilde{y}$ in P; an output process $\overline{x}\tilde{y}.P$ sends $\tilde{y}$ along channel x; and an internal action τ executes without interaction.

As an extension of the standard syntax, we add an action $\mathsf{com}\, x$ which describes the readiness of a process to compose with some other process on channel x; in the term $\mathsf{com}\, x.P$, the action $\mathsf{com}\, x$ binds x in P. Two processes running in parallel $\mathsf{com}\, x.P \mid \mathsf{com}\, y.Q$, which are both ready to compose, can then evolve to $(\mathsf{new}\ z)\ (P[z/x] \mid Q[z/y])$, i.e. collaborate using a fresh name z as a common channel. The intuition is that executing a com-action describes a handshake taking place between two processes. While this could be expressed also with standard syntax, having an explicit syntax element available enables us to identify the starting points of a collaboration, which is important for our analysis.

Processes are composed in parallel by $P_1 \mid P_2$, and replication $!P$ represents an infinite number of copies of P. The expression $(\mathsf{new}\ x)\ P$ creates a new name with scope P.

As in the original π-calculus, we present a formal semantics based on a structural congruence and a reaction relation. The structural congruence is the least equivalence relation that is generated by the rules in Table 2, and is standard.

Also the reaction rules of Table 3 are standard, with the exception of the rule for composition which implements the semantics explained informally above. In addition, we introduce a typing environment Γ that maps names into a finite set of *channel types*, and require that collaborations can only take place if both collaboration partners expect the same channel type. We omit to associate Γ explicitly with the reaction rules, as Γ is defined globally.

2.2 Example: Web Auctions

In order to illustrate our π-calculus extension as a formalism to describe service interactions, we present an example from the area of web-based auctions.

$$
\begin{aligned}
\mathit{Buyer} \triangleq\ & !\mathsf{com}\ \mathit{buyer}. \\
& \quad (\mathsf{new}\ \mathit{bid})\ (\mathsf{new}\ \mathit{item})\ \overline{\mathit{buyer}}(\mathit{bid}, \mathit{item}, \mathit{buyer}). \\
& \qquad (\mathit{buyer}(\mathit{lost}, \mathit{item}).0 + \mathit{buyer}(\mathit{won}, \mathit{item}, \mathit{product}).0)
\end{aligned}
$$

A buyer can place a bid on a certain item, using a channel *buyer* that will be determined by a new collaboration. We imagine that the buyer might both try to directly collaborate with the web auction or through an auction agent, both of which are services as well. The buyer immediately places his maximum bid. As the result of the auction, the buyer expects to receive either the message to have lost the auction, or to have won, and then get the product.

$$
\begin{aligned}
\mathit{Auction} \triangleq\ & !\mathsf{com}\ \mathit{auction}. \\
& \quad \mathit{auction}(\mathit{bid}, \mathit{item}, \mathit{buyer}). \\
& \qquad !(\overline{\mathit{auction}}(\mathit{higherbid}, \mathit{item}). \\
& \qquad\quad (\mathit{auction}(\mathit{bid}, \mathit{item}, \mathit{buyer}).0 + \tau.0) \\
& \qquad + \\
& \qquad \overline{\mathit{auction}}(\mathit{won}, \mathit{item}, \mathit{product}).0)
\end{aligned}
$$

The auction service waits for bids on items it receives via the *auction* channel which is also determined by a new collaboration. On this channel, it can announce two outcomes. First, it can send a message to the bidder that it has received a higher bid than the current bid. It will then give the bidder the possibility to raise its bid by sending another bid message on the same channel, or it terminates after executing τ, meaning that the auction is over and lost by the bidder. Second, it can output the message that the bidder has won the item, and send along the product.

Note that throughout the examples we resolve $+$ with external choice, which would be problematic for example in the case of a buyer missing the $\mathit{buyer}(\mathit{lost}, \mathit{item}).0$ branch: the buyer could then always force the winning branch of the auction. In this case we could however modify our examples by using internal choice, i.e. by prefixing the actions in sums with τ.

Finally, the auction agent can collaborate with two other services in order to bid on behalf of a service in a certain auction. With its first collaborator, it expects a bidding instruction via the *client* channel. On reception it will start a second collaboration on the *bidding* channel, in order to pass on this bidding instruction. The agent then expects either to be outbid and receive the *higherbid* message, or to win the item and receive the product. In the first case, it will decide according to its bidding algorithm either to place another bid (and restart, using replication), or communicate on the *client* channel that this item is considered lost. In the second case, it will send the product on to the service that placed the original bidding instruction.

$$
\begin{aligned}
Agent \triangleq\ & !\mathsf{com}\ client. \\
& \quad client(bid, item, client). \\
& \quad\ \mathsf{com}\ bidding. \\
& \quad\quad (\mathsf{new}\ bid')\ \overline{bidding}(bid', item, client). \\
& \quad\quad\ !(bidding(higherbid, item). \\
& \quad\quad\quad (\overline{client}(higherbid, item).0 \\
& \quad\quad\quad + \\
& \quad\quad\quad (\mathsf{new}\ bid')\ \overline{bidding}(bid', item, client).0) \\
& \quad\quad\ + \\
& \quad\quad\ bidding(won, item, product). \\
& \quad\quad\quad \overline{client}(won, item, product).0)
\end{aligned}
$$

In terms of composition, we may confirm by inspection that it should be possible for *Buyer* to use *Agent* in order to bid conveniently on a certain item offered by *Auction*. However, it is hard to establish this compatibility automatically when working directly with process descriptions. We therefore propose in the following section interface automata as a process abstraction, that enables the automatic inference of this result.

Furthermore, if we assume that all collaboration channels exhibit the same channel type, i.e. $\Gamma(buyer) = \Gamma(auction) = \Gamma(client) = \Gamma(bidding)$, collaborations turn out to be completely promiscuous: in addition to the already described collaborations, *Buyer* might potentially bid directly using the *Auction* service, or – as depicted below – auction agents might rely on other auction agents (maybe with advanced algorithms for specific types of auctions) in order to do the bidding.

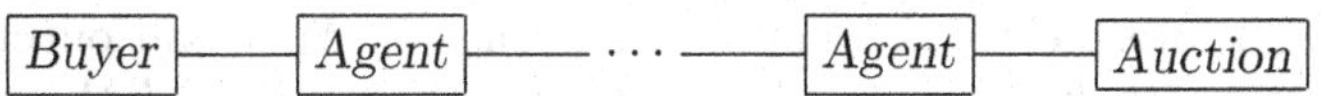

As a matter of fact, entities may also try to compose with themselves, for example *Buyer* with *Buyer*. Not all these compositions would lead to successful computations (clearly, *Buyer* with *Buyer* would not), but using our approach, we will be able to select the meaningful ones.

3 Automata-Based Abstractions of Processes

Interface theory provides an approach to describing the interfaces of components, where each component is represented by its input and output behaviour, and interface composition is the key operator. One is usually interested to have two properties on interfaces, namely that a component conforms to its interface, and that composed components have compatible interfaces. In the following we shall use a variant of a popular interface theory, *interface automata* [5], as an abstraction that describes the behaviour of services.

3.1 Interface Automata

Interface automata [5] are finite state transition systems in a concurrent setting. An interface automaton describes a computational component by its input, output, collaboration, and internal actions. The automata synchronise on communications and are interleaved on internal actions.

Definition 1 (Interface Automaton). *An* interface automaton *A is a 5-tuple $(S, \Sigma, \delta, s_0, F)$ where S is a finite set of states, $\Sigma = \Sigma^O \cup \Sigma^I \cup \Sigma^C \cup \{\tau\}$ an alphabet with output actions Σ^O, input actions Σ^I, collaboration actions Σ^C, and the internal action τ, $\delta : S \times \Sigma \to S$ a transition function, $s_0 \in S$ an initial state, and F a set of final states.*

Note that interface automata are deterministic, and that we can thus use equations like $\delta(s, \sigma) = s'$ to describe the transition function; given an interface automaton A with transition function δ, we may then also write $A(s, \sigma) = s'$.

Interface automata distinguish themselves from I/O automata [13,14] by not being *input-enabled*, i.e. it is not required that the transition function δ is defined on all combinations of states and input actions. Instead one takes an *optimistic* approach by assuming that the environment never generates unmatched inputs. Interface automata come with a theory for interface conformance and the composition of components. In our variant approach, we redefine these terms in order to have interface automata serve as abstractions for π-processes, and to describe their goal-oriented composition. For this reason we have added in Definition 1 a notion of final states (that correspond to goals), which is not present in the original approach. In the following, we describe informally how processes are abstracted by automata, and elaborate on this using our running example; Section 3.2 establishes the formal connection.

The main idea of the abstraction is to have the actions of a process matched by transitions in the interface automata. The alphabet Σ of the interface automaton is defined and interpreted as follows: in the case of input and output actions, we take $\alpha\langle k\rangle$ and $\overline{\alpha}\langle k\rangle$, respectively, where α is the type and k the arity of the channel; in the case of collaboration actions, we take $\alpha\langle \mathsf{c}\rangle$; and for τ actions simply τ. For example, an output process $\overline{x}\tilde{y}.P$ with $\Gamma(x) = \alpha$ and $|\tilde{y}| = 3$ can be described by the following automaton, where the behaviour of P is described starting with state 2:

$$\to (1) \xrightarrow{\overline{\alpha}\langle 3\rangle} (2) \xrightarrow{\cdots}$$

We use the meta-variable σ to range over the elements of Σ, and may sometimes write $\overline{\sigma}$ to denote $\overline{\alpha}\langle k\rangle$ when σ is given by $\alpha\langle k\rangle$.

We shall abstract each parallel process and each process in a sum by its own interface automaton. If a process splits into several processes, e.g. in the case of $\tau.(xy.P \mid uv.Q)$ or $\tau.(xy.P + uv.Q)$, we abstract this by having a branch for each process in the automaton:

$$\to (1) \xrightarrow{\tau} (2),\quad (2) \xrightarrow{\Gamma(x)\langle 1\rangle} (3) \xrightarrow{\cdots},\quad (2) \xrightarrow{\Gamma(u)\langle 1\rangle} (4) \xrightarrow{\cdots}$$

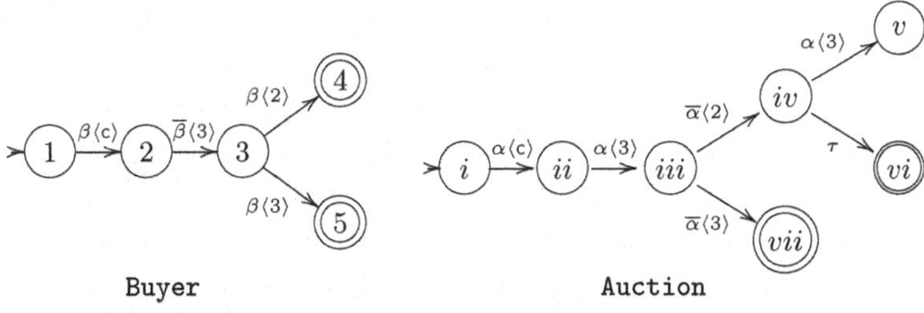

Fig. 1. Interface automata for the processes *Buyer* and *Auction*

An automaton abstracting process replication $!P$ is given by the automaton abstracting P. The introduction of new names is likewise ignored in the abstraction.

We take a state in the abstraction to be a final state if the corresponding process has reached a termination point 0, and if in addition the goal of the interaction has been reached. Such goals should match the identified *functional* goals [11] of the service. Final states are thus annotations that depend on the intended process semantics. We could however generate them automatically from a process by having an additional syntax element 0_g for terminated goal states that otherwise behaves like 0.

Example. We illustrate the abstraction of processes by interface automata by considering our running example. The buyer process is ready to collaborate in the start state and, after the handshake, accepts communication over the channel *buyer* on which it outputs a bid message (arity 2) and accepts input that is either win (arity 3) or lose (arity 2). Assuming β as type of the buyer channel, the abstracting automaton `Buyer` is given in Figure 1. Note that both the win and the lose situation determine goals of the buyer's collaboration, and are thus represented by final states. The process abstraction of *Auction* can be argued for similarly, where α is the type of the *auction* channel.

The interface automaton for *Agent* is depicted in Figure 2. The automaton communicates with the client, i.e. the *Buyer* or another *Agent*, on the channel *client* with type γ_1, and bids on an *Auction* (possibly through another *Agent*) using the channel *bidding* with type γ_2. The intuition behind these automata is that they can compose by connecting all channels of a given type, thus one way of composing the example automata would be connecting $\beta \leftrightarrow \alpha$, this correspond to connecting the *Buyer* and *Auction* directly. Another composition would result from connecting $\beta \leftrightarrow \gamma_1$ and $\gamma_2 \leftrightarrow \alpha$, here the *Buyer* is connected to the *Agent*, which in turn is connected to the *Auction*.

3.2 Interface Semantics

In order to formalise the conformance of an interface automaton with a process in our π-calculus variant, we propose a non-standard semantics, called *interface semantics*, that describes the behaviour of tagged processes. A *tagged process*

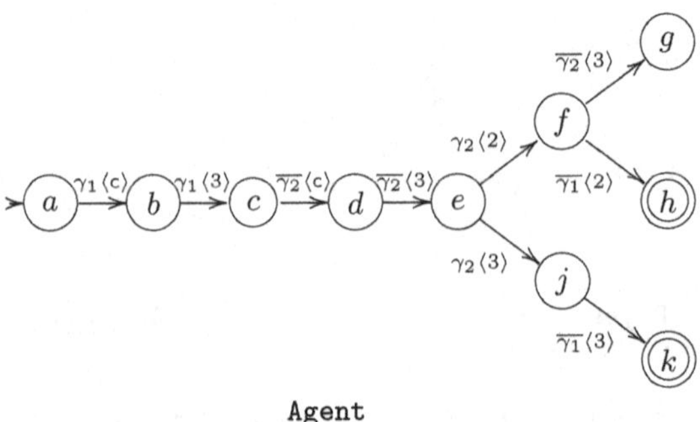

Fig. 2. Interface automaton for the process *Agent*

$[P]_{A,s}$ relates the process behaviour P with the interface automaton A abstracting it, together with the state s the automaton is currently in. For example, we have argued earlier that the `Buyer` automaton of Figure 1 describes the behaviour of the process *Buyer* in Section 2.2. This means we can use the tagging $[Buyer]_{\texttt{Buyer},1}$. Once *Buyer* has agreed to a collaboration and sent its first bid, the tagging corresponds to

$$[buyer(lost, item).0 + buyer(won, item, product).0]_{\texttt{Buyer},3},$$

meaning that we are now in state 3 of the describing automaton.

The interface semantics checks this agreement of processes and their tags explicitly. We first present in Table 4 a structural congruence $\equiv_{\mathsf{t}}$ for tagged processes. The creation of new names is abstracted away by our automaton model and therefore the new name construct can leave the tagged process. We explicitly require a scope extrusion rule in the tagged semantics since it cannot be inferred from the standard congruence in all cases. Parallel processes using the same tag are equivalent to a tagging of their composition. And if processes are equivalent using the standard congruence $\equiv$, they are equivalent under the same tag.

The equivalence rule for new name creation shows that we can have both tagged and untagged elements in this semantics. We use calligraphic lettering to express this situation:

$$\mathcal{Q} ::= [P]_{A,s} \mid \mathcal{Q}_1 \mid \mathcal{Q}_2 \mid (\mathsf{new}\ x)\ \mathcal{Q}$$

Using this syntactic convention, we can now describe the reaction rules in the interface semantics (Table 5). The rule for τ expresses that a process, tagged with automaton A at state s, can only execute a τ-action if the automaton has a corresponding τ-transition from s to a state s'; the resulting process is $[P]_{A,s'}$. Likewise, in the case of an interaction where the input process is tagged with (A, s) and the output process with (B, t), we require that these automata contain transitions labelled with the channel type $\Gamma(x)$, the communication direction,

Table 4. Structural congruence for tagged processes

$$
\begin{aligned}
[(\mathsf{new}\ x)\ P]_{A,s} &\equiv_{\mathrm{t}} (\mathsf{new}\ x)\ [P]_{A,s} \\
(\mathsf{new}\ x)\ ([P]_{A,s} \mid [Q]_{B,t}) &\equiv_{\mathrm{t}} [P]_{A,s} \mid (\mathsf{new}\ x)\ [Q]_{B,t} \text{ if } x \notin \mathit{fn}(P) \\
[(P \mid Q)]_{A,s} &\equiv_{\mathrm{t}} [P]_{A,s} \mid [Q]_{A,s} \\
[P]_{A,s} &\equiv_{\mathrm{t}} [Q]_{A,s} \text{ if } P \equiv Q
\end{aligned}
$$

and the arity $|\tilde{z}|$ of the corresponding message. As an example, the buyer and auction processes

$$[\overline{buyer}(bid, item, buyer).P]_{\mathtt{Buyer},2} \mid [buyer(bid, item, buyer).Q]_{\mathtt{Agent},b}$$

could interact by connecting the channels β and γ_1, because $\Gamma(buyer) = \beta$ and in automaton `Buyer` there is a transition labelled $\overline{\beta}\langle 3\rangle$ from state 2 and in the `Agent` automaton there is a matching transition $\gamma_1\langle 3\rangle$ from state b.

In the collaboration rule note that we require collaboration channels to be of the same type. The remaining rules for parallelism, structural congruence, and name creation are straightforward.

The following result for the interface semantics is straightforward: if processes can be executed under some tagging, they can be executed in the standard semantics. In order to formulate the theorem we introduce the notation $\lfloor \mathcal{P} \rfloor$ which strips all tags off the processes of $\mathcal{P}$:

$$
\begin{aligned}
\lfloor [P]_{A,s} \rfloor &= P \\
\lfloor \mathcal{Q}_1 \mid \mathcal{Q}_2 \rfloor &= \lfloor \mathcal{Q}_1 \rfloor \mid \lfloor \mathcal{Q}_2 \rfloor \\
\lfloor (\mathsf{new}\ x)\ \mathcal{Q} \rfloor &= (\mathsf{new}\ x)\ \lfloor \mathcal{Q} \rfloor
\end{aligned}
$$

Then the theorem can be presented in the following concise form:

Theorem 1. *If* $\mathcal{P} \rightarrow_{\mathrm{t}} \mathcal{P}'$ *then* $\lfloor \mathcal{P} \rfloor \rightarrow \lfloor \mathcal{P}' \rfloor$.

Proof. The result is proved by induction over the inference of $\mathcal{P} \rightarrow_{\mathrm{t}} \mathcal{P}'$, using Table 5 and Table 3. □

4 Interface Conformance

In this section we present an approach for checking conformance between processes and their abstractions, which are given as interface automata. We use a type system for specifying whether an abstraction conforms to a process. The judgements are of the following form:

$$\Gamma, s \vdash P : A$$

Here Γ is a typing environment (see Section 2.1), s is the state in which the conformance check starts, and A is the smallest interface automaton that conforms to the process P. The typing rules for processes are given in Table 6 and for actions in Table 7.

Table 5. Reaction rules with interface semantics

$$\frac{A(s,\tau) = s'}{[\tau.P + M]_{A,s} \rightarrow_{\mathrm{t}} [P]_{A,s'}}$$

$$\frac{A(s,\Gamma(x)\langle|\tilde{y}|\rangle) = s' \qquad B(t,\overline{\Gamma(x)}\langle|\tilde{z}|\rangle) = t' \qquad |\tilde{y}| = |\tilde{z}|}{[x\tilde{y}.P + M]_{A,s} \mid [\overline{x}\tilde{z}.Q + N]_{B,t} \rightarrow_{\mathrm{t}} [P[\tilde{z}/\tilde{y}]]_{A,s'} \mid [Q]_{B,t'}}$$

$$\frac{A(s,\Gamma(x)\langle \mathsf{c}\rangle) = s' \qquad B(t,\Gamma(y)\langle \mathsf{c}\rangle) = t' \qquad \Gamma(x) = \Gamma(y) \qquad z \text{ fresh}}{[\mathsf{com}\ x.P + M]_{A,s} \mid [\mathsf{com}\ y.Q + N]_{B,t} \rightarrow_{\mathrm{t}} (\mathsf{new}\ z)\ ([P[z/x]]_{A,s'} \mid [Q[z/y]]_{B,t'})}$$

$$\frac{\mathcal{P} \rightarrow_{\mathrm{t}} \mathcal{P}'}{\mathcal{P} \mid \mathcal{Q} \rightarrow_{\mathrm{t}} \mathcal{P}' \mid \mathcal{Q}} \qquad \frac{\mathcal{Q} \equiv_{\mathrm{t}} \mathcal{P} \qquad \mathcal{P} \rightarrow_{\mathrm{t}} \mathcal{P}' \qquad \mathcal{P}' \equiv_{\mathrm{t}} \mathcal{Q}'}{\mathcal{Q} \rightarrow_{\mathrm{t}} \mathcal{Q}'}$$

$$\frac{\mathcal{P} \rightarrow_{\mathrm{t}} \mathcal{P}'}{(\mathsf{new}\ x)\ \mathcal{P} \rightarrow_{\mathrm{t}} (\mathsf{new}\ x)\ \mathcal{P}'}$$

Table 6. Type checking of processes

$$\Gamma, s \vdash 0 : s \qquad \frac{\Gamma, s \vdash \pi_i : \{s \xrightarrow{\sigma} s_i\} \qquad \Gamma, s_i \vdash P_i : A_i}{\Gamma, s \vdash \sum_{i\in I} \pi_i.P_i : \bigcup_i(\{s \xrightarrow{\sigma} s_i\} \cup A_i)}$$

$$\frac{\Gamma, s \vdash P : A}{\Gamma, s \vdash !P : A} \qquad \frac{\Gamma, s \vdash P_1 : A \qquad \Gamma, s \vdash P_2 : B}{\Gamma, s \vdash P_1 \mid P_2 : A \cup B} \qquad \frac{\Gamma, s \vdash P : A}{\Gamma, s \vdash (\mathsf{new}\ x)\ P : A}$$

The rules match the intuition behind the abstractions we have introduced informally in Section 3.1. A nil-process can be abstracted by a single state s. In the rule for replication, we only require the conformance of the replicated process and the automaton. The conformance of the automaton associated with parallel processes follows from the union of the automata that conform to each process. The introduction of new names is abstracted away.

The rule for summation makes use of the auxiliary judgement for actions, and requires that for every occurring action π_i, we can find an outgoing edge abstracting it and leading to some state s_i, and a conformance check taken from s_i will take care of the continuation process P_i. The judgements for actions simply ensure that actions are directly matched by transitions in the automaton.

Type soundness. Before stating the soundness of the type system we first introduce a convention. Note that if we have two typings $\Gamma, s \vdash P : A$ and $\Gamma, s \vdash P : B$, the automata A and B have isomorphic structure but may differ in the names of the states they contain. When relating two automata, we will therefore assume in the following that their states are already renamed in the proper manner.

The following two simple properties express that conformance is preserved under substitution and structural congruence.

Lemma 1. *If* $\Gamma, s \vdash P : A$ *and* $\Gamma(x) = \Gamma(y)$ *then* $\Gamma, s \vdash P[y/x] : A$.

Table 7. Type checking of actions

$$\Gamma, s \vdash x\tilde{y} : \{s \xrightarrow{\Gamma(x)\langle|\tilde{y}|\rangle} s'\} \qquad \Gamma, s \vdash \overline{x}\tilde{y} : \{s \xrightarrow{\overline{\Gamma(x)}\langle|\tilde{y}|\rangle} s'\}$$

$$\Gamma, s \vdash \mathsf{com}\, x : \{s \xrightarrow{\Gamma(x)\langle \mathsf{c}\rangle} s'\} \qquad \Gamma, s \vdash \tau : \{s \xrightarrow{\tau} s'\}$$

Lemma 2. *If $\Gamma, s \vdash P : A$ and $P \equiv Q$ then $\Gamma, s \vdash Q : A$.*

In order to formulate the theorem we introduce the notation $\mathsf{E}(\mathcal{Q})$ for the set of tagged processes in $\mathcal{Q}$:

$$\begin{aligned} \mathsf{E}([P]_{A,s}) &= \{[P]_{A,s}\} \\ \mathsf{E}(\mathcal{Q}_1 \mid \mathcal{Q}_2) &= \mathsf{E}(\mathcal{Q}_1) \cup \mathsf{E}(\mathcal{Q}_2) \\ \mathsf{E}((\mathsf{new}\ x)\ \mathcal{Q}) &= \mathsf{E}(\mathcal{Q}) \end{aligned}$$

Furthermore we write $A \simeq_s B$ whenever the same states are reachable from a state s in both A and B, i.e. if the following holds

$$A \simeq_s B \text{ iff } \forall\, \omega.\ A^*(s,\omega) = B^*(s,\omega)$$

where as usual $\delta^*(s, \sigma\omega) = \delta^*(\delta(s,\sigma),\omega)$.

The subject reduction result states that conformance of processes to the associated automata is preserved under the operational semantics.

Theorem 2 (Subject Reduction). *If $[P_i]_{A_i,s_i} \in \mathsf{E}(\mathcal{P})$ and $\Gamma, s_i \vdash P_i : B_i$ such that $A_i \simeq_{s_i} B_i$ and $\lfloor \mathcal{P} \rfloor \to P'$ then there exists a $\mathcal{P}'$ and indices k and j such that $P' = \lfloor \mathcal{P}' \rfloor$ and $[Q_j]_{A_j,t_k} \in \mathsf{E}(\mathcal{P}')$ and $\Gamma, t_k \vdash Q_j : B_j$ and $A_k \simeq_{t_k} B_j$.*

Proof. The result follows from induction in the shape of $\mathcal{P}$, matching the conditions from the type system to those of the interface semantics while applying Lemmas 1 and 2. □

5 Goal-Oriented Compositions

In the previous sections we have seen how interface automata can be used as abstractions for processes. The aim of this development is to obtain a strong compositionality result for processes from the composition of interface automata, which we define in this section. We define the composition of interface automata as the following product automaton:

Definition 2 (Composition of Interface Automata). *The composition $A_1 \otimes_{\alpha_1 \leftrightarrow \alpha_2} A_2$ of two interface automata $A_1 = (S_1, \Sigma_1, \delta_1, s_1, F_1)$ and $A_2 = (S_2, \Sigma_2, \delta_2, s_2, F_2)$ with $\sigma_1 = \alpha_1\langle k\rangle \in \Sigma_1^I$ and $\sigma_2 = \alpha_2\langle k\rangle \in \Sigma_2^I$ is defined by*

$$A_1 \otimes_{\alpha_1 \leftrightarrow \alpha_2} A_2 = (S_1 \times S_2, (\Sigma_1 \cup \Sigma_2) \setminus \{\sigma_1, \overline{\sigma_1}, \sigma_2, \overline{\sigma_2}\}, \delta, (s_1, s_2), F_1 \times F_2)$$

where δ is given by:

1. *If $\delta_1(s_1, \sigma_1) = s_1'$ and $\delta_2(s_2, \overline{\sigma_2}) = s_2'$ then $\delta((s_1, s_2), \tau) = (s_1', s_2')$*
2. *A symmetrical rule to 1.*

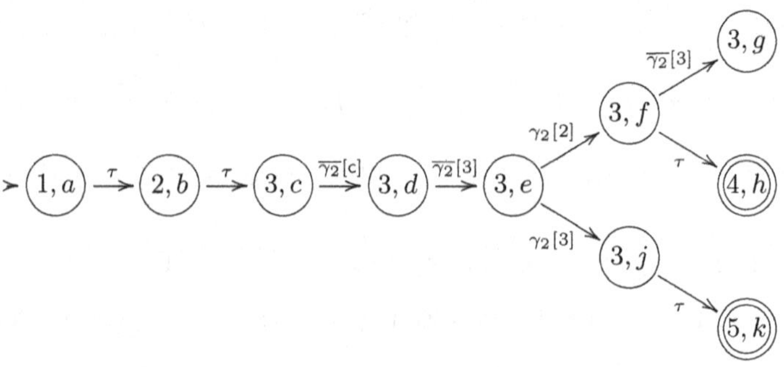

Fig. 3. Composed Automaton: `Buyer` $\otimes_{\beta\leftrightarrow\gamma_1}$ `Agent`

3. *If* $\delta_1(s_1, \sigma) = s_1'$ *and* $\sigma \notin \{\sigma_1, \overline{\sigma_1}, \sigma_2, \overline{\sigma_2}\}$ *then* $\delta((s_1, s_2), \sigma) = (s_1', s_2)$ *for all* $s_2 \in S_2$
4. *A symmetrical rule to 3.*
5. *If* $\delta_1(s_1, \alpha_1\langle\mathsf{c}\rangle) = s_1'$ *and* $\delta_2(s_2, \alpha_2\langle\mathsf{c}\rangle) = s_2'$ *then* $\delta((s_1, s_2), \tau) = (s_1', s_2')$

Note that although $\otimes_{\alpha_1\leftrightarrow\alpha_2}$ is a binary operator, we can of course compose arbitrarily many automata together by composing them in sequence, i.e. $A_1 \otimes_{\alpha_1\leftrightarrow\beta_1} A_2 \otimes_{\alpha_2\leftrightarrow\beta_2} \cdots \otimes_{\alpha_n\leftrightarrow\beta_n} A_n$, where we assume left-associativity of the composition operator.

In contrast to the approach of [5] where all shared channels are used for composition, we explicitly parametrise the composition operator $\otimes_{\alpha_1\leftrightarrow\alpha_2}$ with the channels α_1 and α_2 that get connected in the resulting system. These channels are subsequently removed from the alphabet of the resulting automaton, and this automaton contains a τ-transition instead (rules 1 and 2). Channels that are not mentioned in the composition parameter are kept in the result automaton (rules 3 and 4). Also matching collaborations are replaced by a single τ-transition (rule 5). The product thus coincides with the composition of input-enabled automata, such as I/O-automata [14], however, some steps present in A or B may not be present in the product, as not all inputs have to be matched by outputs.

As shown in Definition 2, we also extend the common notion of composition to take the final states of the automata into account by saying that a composition is *goal-oriented* or meaningful if a final state is reachable, and hence the individual goals of the services are preserved.

Definition 3 (Goal-oriented Composition). *A composition* $A_1 \otimes_{\alpha_1\leftrightarrow\alpha_2} A_2$ *is said to be* goal-oriented *if it contains a reachable final state.*

A composition is said to be *closed* whenever all the necessary interactions are available in the composed processes (and hence no interaction from the environment is needed) and furthermore a final state is reachable in the product automaton.

Definition 4 (Closedness). (A, s) *is said to be* closed *if, starting from* s, *there is a final state reachable following only* τ *transitions.*

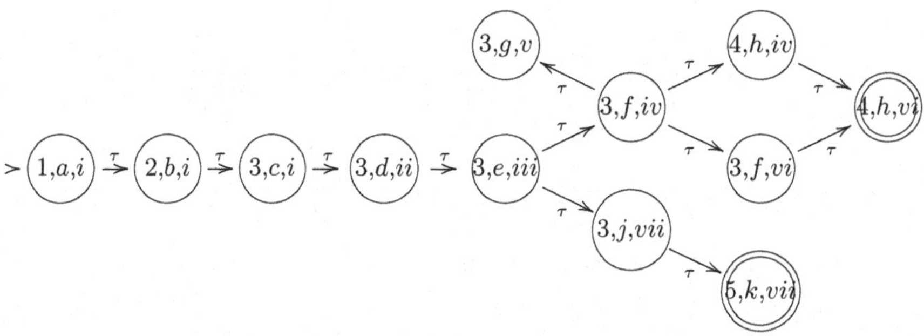

Fig. 4. Composed Automaton: **Buyer** $\otimes_{\beta\leftrightarrow\gamma_1}$ **Agent** $\otimes_{\gamma_2\leftrightarrow\alpha}$ **Auction**

Observe that the traditional definition of closedness is more restrictive than ours, as we only require the *existence* of one path consisting of internal actions, and not every transition to be internal. This allows us to be more flexible because a service may have more than one option to achieve some acceptable goal, and we require that only one is reachable. As an example, consider a scenario where a service acting on behalf of a traveller wishes to compose with either a train ticket service or a plane ticket service. Here it is the case that although the traveller has goals representing both successful train and plane ticket reservations, the agencies provide only one kind of tickets.

Example. As an example of goal-oriented composition, Figure 3 shows the product automaton `Buyer` $\otimes_{\beta\leftrightarrow\gamma_1}$ `Agent`. The automata is connected on the channels β and γ_1, resulting in τ-transitions replacing these in the product automaton. The γ_2 channel present in the `Agent` remains unconnected, hence making further composition possible. Indeed, the automaton can be composed further with `Auction`, as shown in Figure 4. Observe that the resulting composition is closed, as there exists paths containing only τ-transitions that reach final states.

The composition of the buyer and auction automaton, illustrated in Figure 5, shows how transitions might be lost during composition. Here the buyer places his maximum bid immediately and, when outbid, accepts defeat. The auction however is willing to take another bid from the buyer after the first one is outbid. The composition succeeds because there are still goal states present in the composed automaton; in fact the resulting automaton is closed.

Properties. The main result we establish in this section tells us under which conditions the composition of services leads to a situation where common goals are achieved. More precisely it expresses the following: if the product automaton of process-conformant automaton is closed, then there exists an execution of the processes such that they reach their common goal as specified in the automaton.

Theorem 3. *For* $i = 1, \ldots, n$, *let* $[P_i]_{A_i,s_i} \in \mathsf{E}(\mathcal{P})$ *and* $\Gamma, s_i \vdash P_i : A_i$ *be a typing, and let* $A = A_1 \otimes_{\alpha_1\leftrightarrow\beta_1} A_2 \otimes_{\alpha_2\leftrightarrow\beta_2} \cdots \otimes_{\alpha_n\leftrightarrow\beta_n} A_n$ *be the composition of*

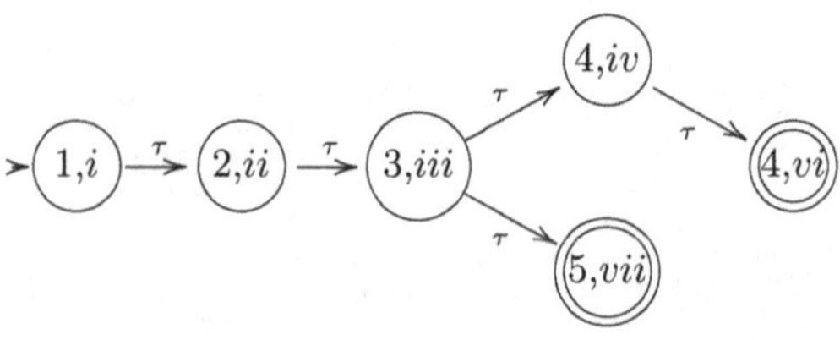

Fig. 5. Composed Automaton: `Buyer` $\otimes_{\beta\leftrightarrow\alpha}$ `Auction`

all A_i. *If* $(A,(s_1,\ldots,s_n))$ *is closed, then* $\mathcal{P} \mid \mathcal{Q} \rightarrow^*_{\mathsf{t}} \mathcal{P}' \mid \mathcal{Q}'$ *and* $[P'_i]_{A_i,s'_i} \in \mathsf{E}(\mathcal{P}')$ *and* $(s'_1,\ldots,s'_n)$ *is a final state in* A.

Note that the property expressed in this theorem can be seen as a relaxation of the common notion of liveness by exploiting the optimistic approach: we ensure that from the state we compose in we can always choose a right path to end up in a desired state (i.e. such a path will always exist).

6 Related Work

Previous work on service oriented computing has primarily focused on web services, for which the *Web Services Description Language (WSDL)* [4] has been influential in describing the static interfaces of services. Another line of work has focused on the choreography of web services, for which the *Web Services Choreography Description Language (WS-CDL)* [10] is a recent attempt at a standard. In this paper we deal with the orthogonal topic of composing services. Several approaches to composing systems based on process algebras and automata have been proposed. However, many of these [16,20,19] have limitations that do not allow them to describe systems in a modular manner, and checking compatibility cannot be performed with a feasible complexity. Canal et al. [3,2] use roles to define protocol specifications, making them modular, yet the computational complexity of composing systems remains NP-hard. One main benefit of choosing interface automata over other alternatives such as process algebras or input-enabled automata is that the compatibility of services can be checked in linear time [5].

Another approach that deals with these issues is session types. The use of session types [8,9] was introduced to describe structured communication. Gay and Hole [6,7] introduced subtypes for compatibility and conformance testing of processes. Vallecillo et al. [18] continued the investigation of composition of compatibility of session types, applying their approach in the commercial environment CORBA. The present work differs from session types in a core point, namely the fact that goal-oriented composition allows us to express when composition is meaningful. Another novel feature is the ability to compose services component-wise, allowing arbitrarily large dynamic composition scenarios, rather than focusing on two sessions being dual or complementary.

Recently, Larsen et al. [12] have presented an interface theory, *modal I/O automata*, that adds modalities to interface automata such that requirements of the system can be directly modelled. As modal I/O automata are more general than the interface automata, it would be interesting to see what benefits can be gained by lifting our abstractions to this approach.

Goal-orientation is an important term in requirements engineering [11]. In this field the term is used to describe techniques to identify and refine requirements guided by goals. In our work we use goals to guide the composition of services. Hence our work is orthogonal to these techniques.

7 Conclusion

We have extended the π-calculus with an explicit action for service collaborations, and have presented an interface automata-based abstraction of these processes in order to reason about the meaningfulness of the arising process compositions. A type checking algorithm has been provided for ensuring the conformance between a process and its abstracting automaton, and we have extended the theory of composition of interface automata by introducing goal conditions. The notion of closedness of compositions could then be relaxed in a way that only the required interactions needed to be part of a composition, thus establishing a very flexible notion of compositionality.

In future work we would like to investigate the flexibility of having optional as well as required goal states, resulting in an even more fine grained specification of meaningful service composition. Furthermore, we could strengthen the semantics of the collaboration action by transforming it from a mere annotation of the start of a collaboration to an action which checks compositionality before executing, allowing us to express statically when a process is safe with respect to goal-oriented composition.

Acknowledgements. This work has been partially sponsored by the project SENSORIA, IST-2005-016004, and by Deloitte Business Consulting, Denmark.

References

1. Alonso, G., Casati, F., Kuno, H., Machiraju, V.: Web Services: Concepts, Architecture and Applications. Springer, Heidelberg (2004)
2. Canal, C., Fuentes, L., Pimentel, E., Troya, J.M., Vallecillo, A.: Adding roles to CORBA objects. IEEE Transactions on Software Engineering 29(3), 242–260 (2003)
3. Canal, C., Pimentel, E., Troya, J.M.: Compatibility and inheritance in software architectures. Science of Computer Programming 41(2), 105–138 (2001)
4. Christensen, E., Curbera, F., Meredith, G., Weerawarana, S.: Web services description language (WSDL) (March 2001), `http://www.w3.org/TR/wsdl`
5. de Alfaro, L., Henzinger, T.A.: Interface automata. In: Matsui, M. (ed.) FSE 2001. LNCS, vol. 2355, pp. 109–120. Springer, Heidelberg (2002)

6. Gay, S.J., Hole, M.: Types and subtypes for client-server interactions. In: Swierstra, S.D. (ed.) ESOP 1999. LNCS, vol. 1576, pp. 74–90. Springer, Heidelberg (1999)
7. Gay, S.J., Hole, M.: Subtyping for session types in the pi-calculus. Acta Informatica 42(2-3), 191–225 (2005)
8. Honda, K.: Types for dynamic interaction. In: Best, E. (ed.) CONCUR 1993. LNCS, vol. 715, pp. 509–523. Springer, Heidelberg (1993)
9. Honda, K., Vasconcelos, V.T., Kubo, M.: Language primitives and type discipline for structured communication-based programming. In: Hankin, C. (ed.) ESOP 1998. LNCS, vol. 1381, pp. 122–138. Springer, Heidelberg (1998)
10. Kavantzas, N., Burdett, D., Ritzinger, G., Fletcher, T., Lafon, Y., Barreto, C.: Web services choreography description language (WS-CDL) (November 2005), `http://www.w3.org/TR/ws-cdl-10/`
11. van Lamsweerde, A.: Goal-oriented requirements engineering: A guided tour. In: 5th IEEE Intl. Symposium on Requirements Engineering (RE 2001), pp. 249–262. IEEE Computer Society Press, Los Alamitos (2001)
12. Larsen, K.G., Nyman, U., Wasowski, A.: Modal I/O automata for interface and product line theories. In: De Nicola, R. (ed.) ESOP 2007. LNCS, vol. 4421, pp. 64–79. Springer, Heidelberg (2007)
13. Lynch, N., Tuttle, M.: Hierarchical correctness proofs for distributed algorithms. In: 6th Annual Symposium on Principles of Distributed Computing (PODC 1987), pp. 137–151 (1987)
14. Lynch, N., Tuttle, M.: An introduction to input/output automata. CWI-Quarterly 2(3), 219–246 (1989)
15. Milner, R., Parrow, J., Walker, D.: A calculus of mobile processes, Parts I and II. Information and Computation 100(1), 1–77 (1992)
16. Nierstrasz, O.: Regular types for active objects. In: 8th Annual Conference Conference on Object-Oriented Programming Systems, Languages, and Applications (OOPSLA 1993), pp. 1–15. ACM Press, New York (1993)
17. Singh, M.P., Huhns, M.N.: Service-oriented Computing: Semantics, Processes, Agents. John Wiley & Sons, Chichester (2005)
18. Vallecillo, A., Vasconcelos, V.T., Ravara, A.: Typing the behavior of software components using session types. Fundamenta Informaticae 73(4), 583–598 (2006)
19. Wehrheim, H.: Behavioral subtyping relations for active objects. Formal Methods in System Design 23(2), 143–170 (2003)
20. Yellin, D.M., Strom, R.E.: Protocol specifications and component adaptors. ACM Transactions on Programming Languages and Systems 19(2), 292–333 (1997)

Composing Components with Shared Services in the Kmelia Model

Pascal André, Gilles Ardourel, and Christian Attiogbé

LINA - UMR CNRS 6241 - University of Nantes
F-44322 Nantes Cedex, France
{Pascal.Andre,Gilles.Ardourel,Christian.Attiogbe}@univ-nantes.fr

Abstract. The Kmelia abstract component model is extended to allow the description of component compositions with multipart interactions leading to simultaneous communications between more than two services. Shared services are defined to explicitly control multipart interactions. Accordingly the communication actions of Kmelia are extended. The formal definitions of the Kmelia model, the composition of components via their services and their analysis are revisited to integrate the extension of the model. An example illustrates the need and the usage of shared services.

Keywords: Component, Composition, Shared services, Multipart Communication.

1 Introduction

The Kmelia component model [3] was introduced as an abstract formal component model dedicated to the specification and development of correct components. The model is equipped with a language which is evolving together with the expressive power of the model. In [3] we have distinguished two semantics for the link between component services. Only one, *monadic semantics*, was treated in this previous article. The second one, *polyadic semantics*, was not treated. The hypothesis for the *monadic semantics* is: only one provided service may be associated to a required service; a component is both a component type and the unique instance of it; a required service may be linked to at most one provided service; only one instantiation of a service exists at any time.

In the current article we consider the *polyadic semantics*: a provided service may be linked with various required services (allowing broadcast communications); as an example, a chat system provides an interaction service for multiple clients. In the same way a required service may be linked to various provided services. We present the new features of our Kmelia model, the language aspects that support these features and how these improvements are integrated with the previous works on Kmelia.

Motivations. The modelling of various real life systems such as auction systems, chat systems, distributed brokers, etc requires the use of several components of the same type or several services with identical functionalities but coming

C. Pautasso and É. Tanter (Eds.): SC 2008, LNCS 4954, pp. 125–140, 2008.

from different components. This leads to the need of interaction means to support the assembly and the composition w.r.t to the multiplicity of services that may be connected. The current Kmelia model and language provide a one to one service/component interaction even if several components participate in the assembly. This does not cover the kind of systems listed above.

Contribution. The contribution of this article is the improvement of the expressivity of the Kmelia component model with shared services, multipart interaction based on synchronous n-ary communications. We extend Kmelia to support multiple connections between services. Also, we explicitly distinguish between *component types* and *components (as elements)*, hence we may use several components of the same type in an assembly. Accordingly, the interaction between Kmelia services is updated.

The article is structured as follows. In Section 2 we give an overview of the Kmelia abstract model and we mention some new features introduced in this article. Section 3 is devoted to multiple links on the same service and the impact on the interaction between services. In Section 4 we deal with shared services and their impact on the assembly description. Section 5 shows an example of a component-based system with shared services and related interactions; Formal analysis issue is treated. The article is concluded in Section 6 where we discuss related works and give some perspectives to this work.

2 Overview of the Kmelia Model and New Features

2.1 Overview of the Kmelia Component Model

In [3,2] we have presented various aspects of our abstract component model called Kmelia. Here we recall the main elements of this component model and we build on them in order to improve the model according to the new communication features.

A Kmelia abstract component is a mathematical model of an open multiservice system that supports synchronous communication with its environment.

The main specification of a component [3] is preserved and referred to as the specification of a *component type*. The interface of a component is still made of required services and provided services. The core specification of a service is not changed. We recall the definition of a component; it stands now explicitly for a *component type*.

Component Type Specification. A component type (C) is a 8-tuple $\langle \mathcal{W}, Init, \mathcal{A}, \mathcal{N}, I, \mathcal{D}_S, \nu, \mathcal{C}_S \rangle$ with:

- $\mathcal{W} = \langle T, V, V_T, Inv \rangle$ the state space where T is a set of types, V a set of variables, $V_T \subseteq V \times T$ a set of typed variables, and Inv is the state invariant;
- $Init$ the initialisation of the V_T variables;
- $\mathcal{A}$ a finite set of elementary actions;
- $\mathcal{N}$ a finite set of service names;
- I the component interface which is the union of two disjoints finite sets: I_p the set of names of the provided services that are visible in the component environment and I_r the names of required services. We have $I \subseteq \mathcal{N}$.

- $\mathcal{D}_S$ is the set of service descriptions which is partitioned into the provided services ($\mathcal{D}_{S_p}$) and the required services ($\mathcal{D}_{S_r}$).
- $\nu : \mathcal{N} \rightarrow \mathcal{D}_S$ is the function that maps service names to service descriptions. Moreover there is a projection of the I partition on its image by ν: $n \in I_p \Rightarrow \nu(n) \in \mathcal{D}_{S_p} \wedge n \in I_r \Rightarrow \nu(n) \in \mathcal{D}_{S_r}$
- $\mathcal{C}_S$ is a constraint related to the services of the interface of $\mathcal{C}$ in order to control the usage of the services.

The behaviour of the component relies on the behaviours of its services. A service is *activated* by a call; It may activate other services during its evolution. Only one action of an activated service may be observed at time. Due to dependencies between services and interaction between components, the actions of several activated services may interleave or synchronise. The constraint $\mathcal{C}_S$ describes general conditions on the service usage: it can be an ordering of services or a predicate (safety properties, ...). Specific Kmelia provided services (called protocols) can *implement* a *Component Behaviour Protocol* in the sense of [9,13]. Kmelia allows the use of several protocols for the same component.

A service of a Kmelia component is defined with an interface and a behaviour. The interface is made of a signature, a pre-condition, a post-condition, a service dependency which gives the services on which the current one depends (*subs*: the subprovided services, *cals*: the service required from the caller, *reqs*: the services required from any component, *ints*: the internal services). The behaviour of a service is described with an extended labelled transition system. The labels may be either elementary actions (assignments, function call, ...) or communication actions which support the interaction between Kmelia services. Therefore a Kmelia service is not reduced to a single running stream from its start to its termination, when a service is called, it may have interaction with the caller or with other services.

A communication action is either a *service call/response* or a *message send/receive*. The Kmelia syntax of a communication action (inspired by the Hoare's CSP) is: `channel(!|?|!!|??) message(param*)`. Therefore communication actions are matching pairs:

send message(!) - *receive message*(?),
call service(!!) - *wait service start*(??),
emit service result(!!) - *wait service result*(??)

We use the channel identifier `_CALLER` to denote the channel associated to a service for a call.

A Kmelia service s has callers (the services that call s) and callees (the required services that are called by s). When a service *reqServ* is required by a service s, the latter uses the channel named `_reqServ` to communicate with the service linked with *reqServ* in assemblies.

Assembly. An assembly is a set of components that are linked (composed) through their services; they interact via their activated services which communicate through the abstract channels that support the links established between the services. Graphically, a component is depicted as a box (See Fig. 1). On the frontier of the component box, required services are depicted as empty small boxes included in the component box (like `rs1`). Provided services are depicted as empty small boxes outside the component box (like `ps1`).

2.2 New Features of the Kmelia Model

Component. A component is one element of a component type (see above Sect. 2.1). A component is referred to with a variable typed using the component type; for example `c1: CT` where `c1` is a variable and `CT` a component type. Several components of the same type will be denoted with `c[n]:CT` where `n` is a natural number. In the same way an assembly is one element of an **Assembly Type**.

Shared Service. Sharing is concerned with services and at low level with communication actions: several services may be involved in a communication, like in the broadcast messages.

A *shared provided service* is a provided service that can simultaneously interact with several services from other components. Therefore a subset I_{sp} of the interface I (where $I = I_p \cup I_r$) of a component constitutes the shared provided services of the component. Accordingly, $I_{sp} \subseteq I_p$.

As far as required services are concerned, we now allow that a (provided) service performs a simultaneous communication with the (provided) services that are linked to its required services. Therefore *required services may also be shared.* Sharing a required service forces the synchronisation of the linked services. A subset I_{sr} of the interface I of a component constitutes the shared required services of the component: $I_{sr} \subseteq I_r$.

Multipart communication. Within an assembly, a service may be linked to several other services, leading to a multipart communication between the involved services. For instance a provided service may send a message simultaneously to several callers or wait for a message coming from several callers. In the same way a service may simultaneously call all the services linked to its required service (*reqServ*) using the channel named `_reqServ`. A shared provided service may wait using `??` (resp. `?`) for a call (resp. a message emission) from several other services linked with it. Consequently the shared provided service sends a response (resp. a message) with `!!` (resp. `!`) to all its callers.

We also introduce the **role** concept to qualify some links and the related interactions.

In the following we give the details, the constraints of these kinds of interaction and the associated communication actions.

3 Shared Services: Impact on Service Interactions

The context here is multipart interaction between components via their services. The actions performed by the interacting services are interleaved but the services synchronise on communication actions. In our previous work, pairwise interactions are considered between components; only one-to-one linked services are involved, and only one provided service may be linked to a required one. We consider now the cases where the interactions between several components are not restricted to one-to-one links between the services.

In the following we examine the various interaction cases with multiple services with respect to the expressivity of the Kmelia model. First we consider several provided services linked to one required, and one provided related to several required services. Then we generalise to a service interacting, even with synchronising communications, with several callers or several callees.

3.1 Linking Several Provided Services with one Required Service

A service rs required by a component may be fulfilled by one or several other services ps from one or several components (see Fig. 1). Each one of the ps services should be compatible with the requirement. Thus, at the specification level all the provided services linked with rs should be compatible with rs. The compatibility between services is already defined in [3].

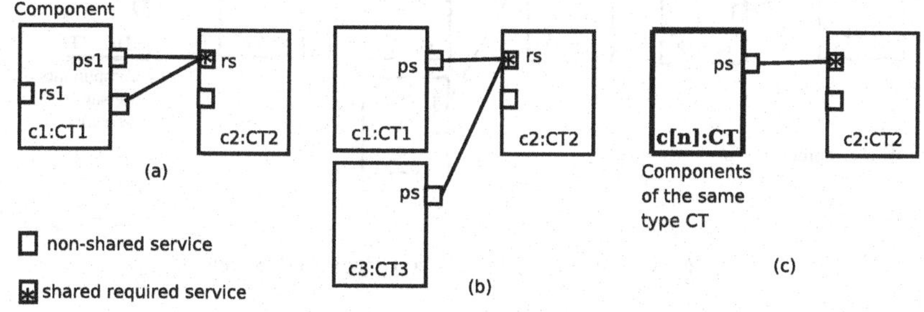

Fig. 1. Assemblies with Shared Required Services

If the provided services are from the same component (Fig. 1 (a)) or from different components (Fig. 1 (b)), the interaction may result in a synchronous multipart communication between, on the one hand, the provided services and on the other hand, the service that uses the required one (which should then be shared).

If the provided services are from components of the same component type (Fig. 1 (c)), the interaction may be specifically done with one component (provided that there is only one at time) or with several (or all) components if the caller service (associated to the required one) is designed to behave like this.

The expressive power of the Kmelia model had to be extended to cover the case depicted in Fig. 1 (a) and Fig. 1 (b) by considering simultaneous calls, message sending, call response, or message receiving from the provided services via the shared required service.

To handle the case represented by Fig. 1 (c), a service may call simultaneously *all* the provided services linked with it[1]; the called services may respond to

[1] There are other hypothesis that do not involve *all* the provided services; they are not considered here.

their common caller. Specific communication actions are needed to handle this kind of interaction which should be distinguished from those already existing in the Kmelia model (they are binary). From the semantic point of view, the called services evolve simultaneously and send their results back to the caller. We maintain here the use of a synchronous communication. The needed communication actions are introduced later in this section.

3.2 Linking one Provided Service with Several Required Services

In an assembly of components, several components may use one component and its provided services. In this case a given provided service may be linked with several required services (see Fig. 2). Practically, several services may call their shared provided either in exclusion with the other callers or simultaneously.

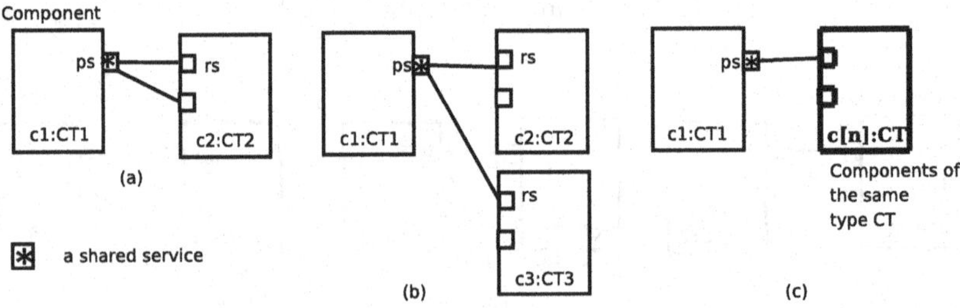

Fig. 2. Assemblies with Shared Provided Services

If we assume the exclusion between the running of the actions of the interacting services, the cases depicted with Fig. 2 (a) and Fig. 2 (b) will be correct interactions with respect to the current Kmelia model; but in this case the provided service (not shared) does not use multipart synchronous communication actions. However, sharing the provided service may force to multipart synchronous communication using a *wait for all.* Thus we consider simultaneous calls to the shared provided service (this also includes the case depicted in Fig. 2 (c), where several services of components of the same type are interacting with the same provided service), then the interaction between the provided service and the linked required services is not straightforward. We have a one-provided to n-required relationship. In this case the provided service should be shared: its communications are shared among the n callers which either belong to different components types (Fig. 2 (b)) or are components of the same type (Fig. 2 (c)). It does not matter to link a non-shared provided service to several callers, because each caller will interact separately in its call context. It is the provided service designer which should consider the ability to interact with several callers, otherwise there is no sharing.

To sum up we have to deal with the composition of a shared provided service with several services. The new feature to be treated is the composition of one shared provided service with several required ones. From the caller side, there is no new requirement for the interaction. From the callee side, the interaction may be performed either with one specific caller, or with any caller, or with all the callers; it depends on the designer.

In the following we present the proposals to improve the communication actions of Kmelia in order to encompass the new communication needs.

3.3 Interaction with Shared Services

In this section we extend the communication actions of the Kmelia model to deal with the new kinds of interaction due to shared services.

Consider *sp* as a shared provided service; it may be called by several other services (the callers). The service *sp* may communicate with one specific caller, all the callers, or one among the callers. The interaction between the linked services is explicitly achieved from the shared provided service using different identifiers for the caller services. The communication actions (see Sect. 2.1) are now extended as multipart communication actions using a channel selector:

```
channel[<selector>](!|?|!!|??)message(param*)
```

The values of `<selector>` are: `ALL`, `i` and `:i`. For instance, `CALLER[ALL]` identifies all the callers; `CALLER[i]` identifies precisely the caller i where i is a natural number; `CALLER[:i]` will identify one of the callers, the identifier of which is then bound to i. These two last cases of communication are not detailed in this article. `ALL` stands for all the callers that are currently linked to a channel end. We introduce in Kmelia, additional communication actions (Tab. 1) to support the interaction between a shared provided service and its callers.

Table 1. Communication actions from a shared provided service to its callers

`CALLER[i]!msg(val)`	Emission of `msg(val)` to the caller `i`
`CALLER[ALL]!msg(val)`	Broadcast of `msg(val)` to all the callers
`CALLER[i]?msg(x: x_Type)`	Reception of a value from the caller `i`
`CALLER[:i]?msg(x: x_Type)`	Reception of a value from any caller `i`; the other received values are not taken into account.
`tab_x := CALLER[ALL]?msg(x: x_Type)`	Reception of values from all the callers, the received values are collected in a structure `tab_x` indexed with the identifiers i of the callers
`CALLER[i]!!subServ(val)`	Call of a sub-service of the caller `i`
`CALLER[ALL]!!subSerb(val)`	Broadcast of a sub-service call to the callers
`CALLER[i]??subServ(x: x_Type)`	Wait the return of a sub-service from the caller `i`
`CALLER[ALL]??subServ(x:x_Type)`	Wait the return of all sub-services from all the callers

In the current case, the communications are all synchronous. The case of `CALLER[:i]?msg(x: x_Type)` may be asynchronously treated but this is not the concern of the current article; only the synchronous semantics is considered.

As far as a shared required service *sr* is concerned, the services linked to *sr* are referred to using the default channel `_sr`. The extensions of communication actions are similar to those in the Tab. 1 replacing the channel `CALLER` with `_sr`.

3.4 Adding Roles to Interactions

When several services call a shared provided service, they may play different roles in the interaction. For example in a chat system where several members achieve a connection to a server and participate in discussions, one member may play the role of moderator. Distinguishing between several callers' roles gives more flexibility in the assemblies. Roles can be shared or not: for instance, moderator could be a non-shared role. A shared provided service can support multiple roles by suffixing the channel by the role identifier in communications that only concern a specific role. From the syntactic point of view we use the following form for the communication actions.

`channel:<RoleId>[<selector>](!|?|!!|??)message(param*)`

`<RoleId>` is a role identifier that qualifies the communication channel.

All the roles supported by a service *ps* should be fulfilled and every caller of the service should assume a role. Therefore considering a role of *ps* from a service *cs* can be done in two ways: either in the behaviour of *cs* by using a `<RoleId>` suffix in all its communication actions with *ps* or in the assembly by assigning `<RoleId>` to the link.

4 Shared Services and Component Assembly

4.1 Specification of Shared Services in Kmelia

It is the role of the specifier to qualify a provided or required service as *shared*. In the behaviour of a shared service, some transitions are labelled with the multipart communication actions described in Sect. 3.3. But a service may be declared to be *shared* without using the specific communication actions; it does not matter.

In the same way as it was done for the use of protocols in our model [2], we propose the use of qualifier. Therefore the interface of a shared provided service has the following forms (the same holds for shared required services):

```
shared provided serviceName(parameters)
        {... specification of the service ...}
```

or equivalently

```
provided serviceName(parameters)
        properties = {shared, ... }
        {... specification of the service ...}
```

An analysis of a service behaviour may lead to determine that it is shared or not. Formally we check that a provided service is effectively shared by checking the type of communication actions used in its behaviour. In the same way, we formally check that a required service is effectively shared, by examining the communication labels of the services that use it.

A shared service (or subservice) may be used by a non-shared service (sub-service).

4.2 Composition: Component Assembly

The new communication means do not impact the definition of the assembly of components but they do impact the assembly correctness.

We recall that the composition of services is based on the links that support the interaction between the services. According to the use of component types, components and shared services, the following points are revisited:

- Assembly of components (explicitly the elements of given component types). An assembly as it is defined until now [3], is specified by considering components; therefore there is no changes to the assembly specification.
- Assembly of component types. It is an assembly defined from component types; it results in an assembly type and should be instantiated by specific components in place of the component types used in the assembly. A component type may appear more than once in an assembly.
- Component Composition. A component composition (via their services) is defined until now by considering the links and sublinks established via an assembly of components, by linking required and provided services. Now, we also permit the link of one provided service with several required ones. But, as *shared* provided/required services are provided/required services (inclusion property), the link and sublink definitions are still correct; they include shared provided services.
- Interaction and simultaneous evolving. The services in different components may evolve simultaneously with interleaving; an activated service may interact with another activated one which is linked to it. With the current improvement of the Kmelia model, a service may synchronise with several activated services from different components via the introduced communication actions (see Sect. 3.3).

In the following formal definitions, we use a set theory notation close to that of the Z or B languages where $X \leftrightarrow Y$ denotes the relation from X to Y (a set of pairs); dom and ran denote respectively the domain and the range of a relation; $a \mapsto b$ denotes the pair (a, b).

In the remainder let $\mathcal{C}$ be a set of C_k components with $k \in 1..n$ and $C_k = \langle\langle T_k, V_k, V_{Tk}, Inv_k\rangle, Init_k, \mathcal{A}_k, \mathcal{N}_k, I_k, \mathcal{D}_{Sk}, \nu_k, \mathcal{C}_{Sk}\rangle$ as defined in Sect. 2. Let $\mathcal{N}$ be the set of service names of $\mathcal{C}$ ($\mathcal{N} = \bigcup_{k \in 1..n} \mathcal{N}_k$).

The formalisation of an assembly [3] remains mainly unchanged (for component and assembly) when we integrate the new communication actions of the Kmelia model. However we now distinguish explicitly components and component types; therefore we update here the involved parts of the existing formlisation.

Component Assembly Type. An assembly of components (recall from [3]) results in an Assembly Type; it is a composition of components described by a tuple $A = (\mathcal{C},\ links,\ subs)$ where $\mathcal{C}$ is a set of components, $links$ is a set of links between the component services and $subs$ is a relation from links to sublinks. It may be abstracted as $(\mathcal{C}_T,\ links,\ subs)$ by considering in $\mathcal{C}_T$ the types of the components C:

$$
\begin{array}{l}
links \subseteq Link\ \wedge \\
(1)\ (\forall (C_i, sn_1, C_j, sn_2) : links \bullet C_i \in \mathcal{C} \wedge C_j \in \mathcal{C}\ \wedge \\
\qquad\qquad ((sn_1 \in I_{p_i} \wedge sn_2 \in I_{rj}) \vee (sn_1 \in I_{ri} \wedge sn_2 \in I_{pj}))) \\
subs : Link \leftrightarrow SubLink\ \wedge \\
(2)\ \mathrm{dom}\, subs = links\ \wedge \\
(3)\ (\forall ((C_i, sn_1, C_j, sn_2) \mapsto (C_k, sn_3, C_l, sn_4)) \in subs \bullet C_i = C_k \wedge C_j = C_l)\ \wedge \\
(4)\ (\forall (C_i, sn_1, C_j, sn_2) : \mathrm{ran}\, subs \bullet ((\nu_i(sn_1) \in \mathcal{D}_{S_{P_i}})\ \mathrm{xor}\ (\nu_j(sn_2) \in \mathcal{D}_{S_{P_j}})))
\end{array}
$$

The linked components are the components of the assembly (1). The sublinks are related to links (2) that concern the same components (3). Provided services are linked to required services (1 and 4).

The links ($Link$) and sublinks ($SubLink$) between component services are specified as follows. The links are 4-tuple of component and service names with the following properties: (1) the service names are those of their owner components, (2) any component service is not linked to itself (not recursive).

$$
\begin{array}{ll}
BaseLink : \mathbb{P}\ (\mathcal{C} \times \mathcal{N} \times \mathcal{C} \times \mathcal{N}) & \\
(1) \quad \forall (C_i, sn_1, C_j, sn_2) : BaseLink \bullet sn_1 \in \mathcal{N}_i \wedge sn_2 \in \mathcal{N}_j & \\
(2) \quad \forall C_i : \mathcal{C},\ sn_1 : \mathcal{N}_i \bullet (C_i, sn_1, C_i, sn_1) \notin BaseLink &
\end{array}
$$

A link connects two services of the interfaces of their owner components.

$$Link \subseteq BaseLink \wedge \forall (C_i, sn_1, C_j, sn_2) : Link \bullet sn_1 \in I_i \wedge sn_2 \in I_j$$

Assembly of Components. In the same way as a component is an element of a component type, a component assembly is one element of a component assembly type (viewed as a set of possible values of the defined assembly type and related properties, see above). A component assembly is referred to with a variable typed using the component assembly type; for example `ca: CAT` where `ca` is a variable and `CAT` a component assembly type.

Well-Formed Assembly Revisited. The well-formedness is modified as follows. A component *assembly* described by the triple $A = (\mathcal{C},\ links,\ subs)$ is a *well-formed component assembly* if the following properties hold:

- all the members of $\mathcal{C}$ are components;
- the services in the sublinks are not in the involved component interfaces, but they are in the dependencies of the involved services (w.r.t $sublinks$).

$$
\begin{array}{ll}
(5) \quad \forall (l, sl) \in subs \mid l = (C_i, sn_1, C_j, sn_2) \wedge sl = (C_k, sn_3, C_l, sn_4)\ \bullet \\
\qquad\qquad ((sn_3, sn_1) \in depends_i{}^{*} \vee (sn_4, sn_2) \in depends_j{}^{*})
\end{array}
$$

where $depends_i{}^*$ is the transitive closure of $depends_i$. The relation $depends_k$ between component services is defined as a part of the service dependency in a component C_k where $sm = \nu_k(m)$:

$$depends_k : \mathcal{N}_k \leftrightarrow \mathcal{N}_k$$
$$\forall (n, m) : depends_k \bullet (n \in cal_{sm}) \vee (n \in req_{sm}) \vee (n \in sub_{sm})$$

Practically a *link* establishes an implicit communication channel between the involved services. This channel is shared with the sub-services.

- when a service with a dependency (*subs*: the subprovided services, *cals*: the service required from the caller, *reqs*: the services required from any component, *ints*: the internal services) is shared, its dependencies *subs* are also shared.
- shared provided services are linked with one or several required services from one or several components. But non-shared provided services may also be linked with several required service. Therefore there is no specific assembly constraints. Correctness is checked w.r.t behaviours.
- only shared required services may be linked with several provided services. Let $linkedWithC(C, sn)$ be the set of links with the service sn of the component C; we have to check for the services linked to several other services (hence the use of card, the cardinal of a set).

  $$linkedWithC(C, sn) = \{(C_i, sn_i, C_k, sn_k) \in link \mid C_i = C \wedge sn_i = sn\}$$

  Let $sharedRequired(C)$ be a function that denotes the set of the shared required services of the component C. They are the services of Ir (the required services of C) which have the property `shared`.

  $$(6) \quad \forall (C,\ sn) \mid C \in \mathcal{C} \wedge sn \in \mathcal{N} \wedge sn \in I_r \bullet$$
  $$\mathsf{card}(linkedWithC(C,\ sn)) > 1 \Rightarrow sn \in sharedRequired(C)$$

From the practical point of view, the parser-compilers of Kmelia specifications should be updated in order to raise some errors when the added well-formedness rules are not respected.

4.3 Composition: Composite Component

An encapsulation of a well-formed component assembly within a component type results in a composite component type. We have defined an operator named compose that builds a new component type by combining one or several components (see [3]). Inner component services are promoted at the interface of the composite component; the properties of the services are preserved by the promotion (for instance a shared service remains shared). In this paper, we do not emphasize other aspects of composition such as the access rules to inner components.

A well-formed assembly type cannot be used to build a composite component. It should be first instantiated with components. Informally, the instantiation of an assembly type $A_T = (\mathcal{C}_T,\ links,\ subs)$ consists in replacing each component type CT of $\mathcal{C}_T$ by a component with the type CT.

4.4 Revisiting Behavioural Compatibility Analysis

The behavioural compatibility of an assembly of components with multipart communication actions follows the general principle already formalised in the previous version of Kmelia [3], where we defined composability and behavioural compatibility analysis. The principle is: first, to consider a service s_i of a component C_i, one required service *req* of s_i, and one service s_j (of a component C_j) that is linked to *req*; the triple (s_i, *req*, s_j) constitutes the analysis context to check each service of C_i. Second, considering the labelled transitions B_i and B_j, that describe the behaviours of s_i and s_j, after checking the composability at service and component level, one should ensure $compatible(B_i, B_j)$ which is the interleaving of elementary actions and the matching of communication actions.

Now, the matching of communication actions is extended to multipart communications. To capture this aspect, we proceed as follows. The context of a service analysis, previously defined as a triple, is extended to: one service s_i, one required service *req* of s_i, and S_J the services linked to *req*. The third element of the triple may now be a set of services. Therefore checking the behavioural compatibility of (s_i, *req*, S_J), with B_i the behaviour of s_i and $\mathcal{B}_J$ the set of behaviours of the services s_j in S_J, results in:
i) checking (s_i, *req*, s_j) for each $s_j \in S_J$; that is denoted with:

$$\mathsf{compatible\_gen}(s_i, S_J) \Leftrightarrow \forall s_j \in S_J \mid compatible(B_i, B_j)$$

with B_i the behaviour of s_i and B_j the behaviour of s_j

ii) checking *one-to-n matching* between s_i and S_J. They match if at each communication point we have the following matching conditions:
when s_i performs `_req[ALL]?msg(...)` each s_j in S_J performs `CALLER!msg(...)`;
when s_i performs `_req[ALL]!msg(...)` each s_j in S_J performs `CALLER?msg(...)`;
when s_i performs `_req[ALL]??srv(...)` each s_j in S_J performs `CALLER!!srv(...)`;
when s_i performs `_req[ALL]!!srv(...)` each s_j in S_J performs `CALLER??srv(...)`.

Formally this results in a synchronous communication between n communicating entities, where one of the entities synchronise with the other entities considered together. Recall the specification of the extended labelled transition system of a service s_i (from [3]): $s_i \mathrel{\widehat{=}} \langle S_{s_i}, L_{s_i}, \delta_{s_i}, \Phi_{s_i}, S0_{s_i}, S_{F_{s_i}} \rangle$. The set $S0_{s_i}$ contains the initial state of s_i; it may be used as the current state of s_i. Thus if $S0_{s_i}$ is $\{cst_i\}$ then $((cst_i, \texttt{ll}), nst_i) \in \delta_{s_i}$ means that there is a transition labelled with `ll` from the current state cst_i to the state nst_i.

Using the previous matching conditions, we specify $\mathsf{one\text{-}to\text{-}n\_matching}(s_i, S_J)$ as follows (only the first condition is expressed, the other ones are similar):

$$\frac{\begin{array}{c} s_i \mathrel{\widehat{=}} \langle S_{s_i}, L_{s_i}, \delta_{s_i}, \Phi_{s_i}, \{cst_i\}, S_{F_{s_i}} \rangle \ \wedge \ ((cst_i,\ \texttt{\_req[ALL]?msg(...)}),\ nst_i) \in \delta_{s_i} \ \wedge \\ \forall s_j \in S_J \mid s_j \mathrel{\widehat{=}} \langle S_{s_j}, L_{s_j}, \delta_{s_j}, \Phi_{s_j}, \{cst_j\}, S_{F_{s_j}} \rangle \ \wedge \\ ((cst_j,\ \texttt{CALLER!msg(...)}),\ nst_j) \in \delta_{s_j} \end{array}}{\mathsf{one\text{-}to\text{-}n\_matching}(s_i, S_J)}$$

Consequently behavioural compatibility is generalised to (s_i, req, S_J) with:

$$\frac{\mathsf{compatible\_gen}(s_i, S_J) \wedge \mathsf{one\text{-}to\text{-}n\_matching}(s_i, S_J)}{\mathsf{beh\_compatible\_gen}(s_i, S_J)}$$

From now on, the Kmelia model includes multipart interactions, synchronous synchronisation of several interacting services, and an up-to-date behavioural compatibility checking.

5 Experimentations and Formal Analysis

5.1 A Chat System with Shared Services

Consider a chat system made of a server component with the type CHAT_SRV and several client components with the type CHAT_CLT, see Fig. 3.

```
COMPONENT CHAT_SRV
INTERFACE
 provided: {connection,interaction}
 required: {}
SERVICES
provided  connection()
  {...}
shared    provided  interaction()
  //  sends 'news'
  //  receives 'msg', 'close'
  {...}
news ()
  {...}
END_SERVICES
```

```
COMPONENT CHAT_CLT
INTERFACE
 provided: {chat_session}
 required: {interaction}
SERVICES

required interaction()
  // receives 'news'
  // sends  'msg', 'close'
  {...}

provided chat_session()
  {...}
END_SERVICES
```

Fig. 3. The components CHAT_SRV and CHAT_CLT

In this system the server provides the services: `connection` to wait for connection from clients and `interaction` to exchange with the clients. Several clients may simultaneously interact with the server (the service `interaction` of the server is then shared). The actions performed during the interaction are: `msg` to receive/send messages from/to clients, `news` to broadcast messages to clients, etc. At any time a client may connect to the server, close the connection, send a message to the server, receive (and display) a message received from the server. Consider an assembly with one server (`srv1`) and three clients (`clt[3]`). The assembly is specified in Kmelia as depicted in Fig. 4. The behaviour of the main service (`chat_session`) of a chat client is depicted in Fig. 5.

```
COMPOSITION
{  srv1: CHAT_SERV
   clt[3]: CHAT_CLT  }
{  (p-r srv1.interaction, clt[3].interaction) }
```

Fig. 4. An assembly with one chat server and three clients

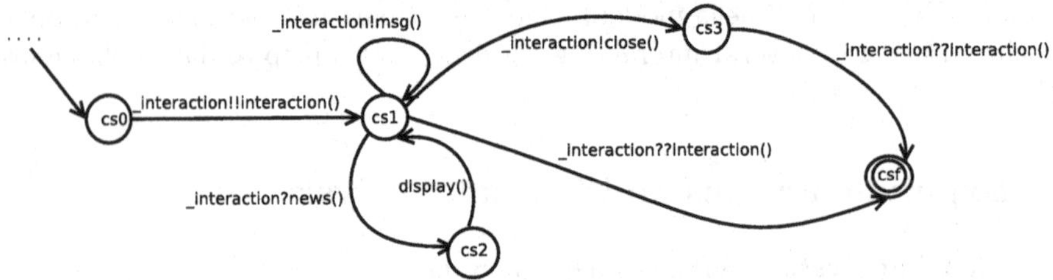

Fig. 5. A part of the behaviour of the `chat_session` service of the chat client

The behaviour of the service `interaction`, provided by the server component (CHAT_SRV), is depicted in Fig. 6.

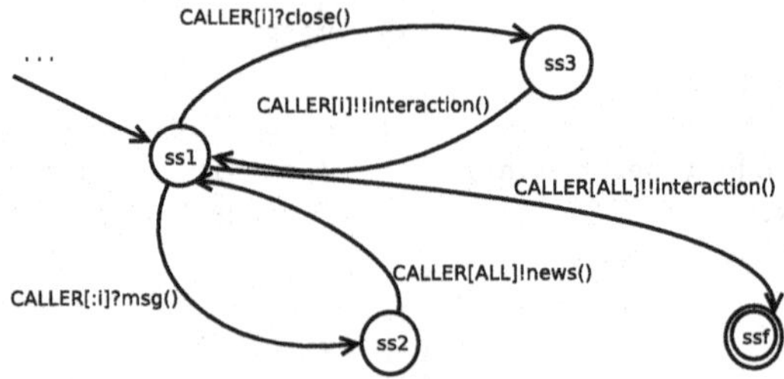

Fig. 6. A part of the behaviour of the `interaction` service of the chat server

5.2 Formal Analysis

Since the beginning we have designed the Kmelia model with the sake of pragmatism. For that purpose the COSTO toolbox [1] is being built.

The toolbox already enables us to parse Kmelia specifications, and to check behavioural compatibility using external tools such as LOTOS [10]. We defined bridges that translate Kmelia service specifications into LOTOS processes and we use the LOTOS/CADP[2][6] toolbox to check service properties including behavioural compatibility. Now, we have extended the expressive power of the Kmelia model; we have to provide or extend the tools to analyse Kmelia specifications. As far as behavioural compatibility is concerned we have to deal with multipart interactions involving synchronous n-ary communications.

N-ary communication supports are not generally provided by formal analysis frameworks. However LOTOS offers the negotiated multiway rendez-vous [10,7] that can be used for instance to model broadcast. We target this n-ary communication mechanism to partially analyse Kmelia multiway communications. Indeed several LOTOS processes may synchronise on the same gate G to exchange values. Thus the following communication actions from four LOTOS processes

[2] www.inrialpes.fr/vasy/

synchronise: `G!val`, `G?var1:T`, `G?var2:T` and `G?var3:T`. After the synchronisation the variables `var1`, `var2`, `var3` receive the value `val` sent by one of the processes on the gate `G`.

Processes may use negotiation to wait for a specific value; this is expressed with a guard (a predicate) following the wait action (`G?var:T [guard]`). The negotiated value is the one that satisfies the predicate of all the involved guards. It is also possible to synchronise with more than one emitted values (but they should be the same).

The new multipart communication actions may be performed using LOTOS processes. It is the case with `CALLER[ALL]!msg(...)` and `CALLER[ALL]!!srv(...)` which are broadcast. They are translated as a multiway communication between the processes associated to the caller services and the current process. The case of `CALLER[ALL]?msg(...)` is not straightforward; we have to collect all the values proposed by the environment; therefore we have to generate matching actions w.r.t the involved processes.

The current work in this direction is the extension of our translation modules of the COSTO tool in order to generate the LOTOS processes with the communication actions appropriate to the new features.

6 Discussion and Conclusion

Summary. In this paper we have presented some extensions to the Kmelia abstract component model: multipart interaction with synchronous communication; shared services; composition of component with shared services and multiway communication. The formal specification and analysis of the model are revisited accordingly.

Related works. In [12], a survey of component-based specification and architecturing languages is presented. The distinction between component types and their elements is widely used, it is the case for example with Wright[8], SOFA[13] and Fractal[4]. But some architecture description languages use a specific language to deal with type (Rapide[11] for instance). To our knowledge, component models do not support simultaneous interaction at the service level, but they allow multiple components connection (via connectors). SOFA and CCM[3] permits a connection from one to many components but no multipart communication between the services. Sharing is treated at component level in Fractal, in Kmelia we deal with communication and sharing at service level. More generally, the multiway communication among component services is not well-studied; one reason for that is the fact that several component models consider programming level instead of specification level. Component models based on the CSP process algebra may benefit from the synchronising n-ary rendez-vous to handle multipart synchronising interactions. Component models relying on programming levels (EJB, .NET) implicitely base synchonisation on execution threads. The current

[3] www.cca-forum.org

work engages a long-term investigation on this challenging subject through different abstraction levels.

Perspectives. Many aspects remain to deal with regarding sharing and the related properties, composition and correctness of component assemblies. We plan to investigate further the issues on multipart communication by considering the cases on selecting specific entities for a given communication. Another challenging point is the support for interoperability with other component models. The ideas under investigation are the structuring of the component interface (which should be more expressive) and the adaptation of the models with respect to the structuring of the information coming from other component model interfaces.

References

1. André, P., Ardourel, G., Attiogbé, C.: A Formal Analysis Toolbox for the Kmelia Component Model. In: Proceedings of ProVeCS'07 (TOOLS Europe), Technical Report. ETH Zurich, 567 (2007)
2. André, P., Ardourel, G., Attiogbé, C.: Defining Component Protocols with Service Composition: Illustration with the Kmelia Model. In: 6th International Symposium on Software Composition, SC 2007. LNCS, vol. 4829. Springer, Heidelberg (2007)
3. Attiogbé, C., André, P., Ardourel, G.: Checking Component Composability. In: Löwe, W., Südholt, M. (eds.) SC 2006. LNCS, vol. 4089. Springer, Heidelberg (2006)
4. Bruneton, E., Coupaye, T., Leclercq, M., Quéma, V., Stefani, J.-B.: The Fractal Component Model and Its Support in Java. Software Practice and Experience 36(11-12) (2006)
5. Bruneton, E., Coupaye, T., Stefani, J.: Recursive and Dynamic Software Composition with Sharing. In: Proceedings of the 7th ECOOP International Workshop on Component-Oriented Programming (WCOP 2002) (2002)
6. Fernandez, J.-C., Garavel, H., Kerbrat, A., Mateescu, R., Mounier, L., Sighireanu, M.: CADP: A Protocol Validation and Verification Toolbox. In: Alur, R., Henzinger, T.A. (eds.) CAV 1996. LNCS, vol. 1102, pp. 437–440. Springer, Heidelberg (1996)
7. Garavel, H., Hermanns, H.: On Combining Functional Verification and Performance Evaluation Using CADP. In: Eriksson, L.-H., Lindsay, P.A. (eds.) FME 2002. LNCS, vol. 2391, pp. 410–429. Springer, Heidelberg (2002)
8. Garlan, D., Allen, R.: Formalizing Architectural Connection. In: Proceedings of the 16th ICSE, pp. 71–80. IEEE Computer Society Press, Los Alamitos (1994)
9. Giannakopoulou, D., Kramer, J., Cheung, S.-C.: Behaviour Analysis of Distributed Systems Using the Tracta Approach. ASE 6(1), 7–35 (1999)
10. ISO LOTOS. A Formal Description Technique Based on The Temporal Ordering of Observational Behaviour. International Organisation for Standardization - Information Processing Systems - Open Systems Interconnection, Geneva (1988)
11. Luckham, D.C., et al.: Specification and Analysis of System Architecture Using Rapide. IEEE Transactions on Software Engineering 21(6), 336–355 (1995)
12. Medvidovic, N., Taylor, R.N.: A Classification and Comparison Framework for Software Architecture Description Languages. IEEE Transactions on Software Engineering 26(1), 70–93 (2000)
13. Plasil, F., Visnovsky, S.: Behavior Protocols for Software Components, 2002. IEEE Transactions on SW Engineering, 28(9) (2002)

OptBPEL: A Tool for Performance Optimization of BPEL Process

Sheng Chen, Liang Bao, and Ping Chen

Software Engineering Institute, Xidian University.
Xi'an, 710071, China
chensheng_cs@yahoo.com, baoliang@mail.xidian.edu.cn,
chenping@sei.xidian.edu.cn

Abstract. The Business Process Execution Language (BPEL) is now a de facto standard for specifying and executing business process for web service composition and orchestration. As more and more web services are composed using BPEL, tuning these compositions and gain better performance becomes increasingly important. This paper presents our approach for optimizing the BPEL process and introduces *OptBPEL*, a tool for performance optimization of BPEL process. The approach starts from the optimization of synchronization structure concerning *link* in BPEL. After that, some concurrency analysis techniques are applied to obtain further performance improvement. Finally, we give some experiments and prove the efficiency of these optimization algorithms used in *OptBPEL*.

Keywords: Performance Optimization, *OptBPEL*, Synchronization Analysis, Concurrency Analysis, Optimization Algorithms.

1 Introduction

Service-Oriented Architecture (SOA) is now a prevalent architectural style for creating an enterprise IT architecture that exploits the principles of service-orientation computing to achieve a tighter relationship between the business and the information systems that support the business [1].

With the growing adoption of service oriented computing, Web services composition is an emerging paradigm for enabling application integration within and across organizational boundaries. Business Process Execution Language (BPEL) [2] is now a promising and de facto language describing the Web services composition in form of business process.

BPEL supports concurrency and synchronization, hence BPEL processes may suffer from deadlocks and time-dependent data races [3] due to the erroneous use of *flow* and *link* like any other multi-threaded programs. For these reasons, while orchestrating processes, business modelers may hesitate to use concurrent paradigm, they prefer to invoke services sequentially even they could be executed concurrently. In this paper, we propose OptBPEL, a tuning tool for performance optimization of BPEL process. It first reads a BPEL process and performs some

C. Pautasso and É. Tanter (Eds.): SC 2008, LNCS 4954, pp. 141–148, 2008.

synchronization analysis on the *link* structure in process, generates a refined BPEL process. After that, the refined process is transformed by applying some concurrency analysis techniques and gains further optimization promotion.

2 Tool Description

Fig. 1 depicts the role of OptBPEL in the design and execution of BPEL process. The BPEL process may be manually written or generated by a BPEL design tool, e.g. ActiveBPEL Designer [4]. OptBPEL takes the BPEL code as input and performs some synchronization related optimization (in synchronization optimizer), generates the refined BPEL process. After that, concurrency related optimization (in concurrency optimizer) is applied to this refined BPEL process and gives the final optimized BPEL process. In section 3 and 4, we describe these two types of optimization that currently supported by OptBPEL.

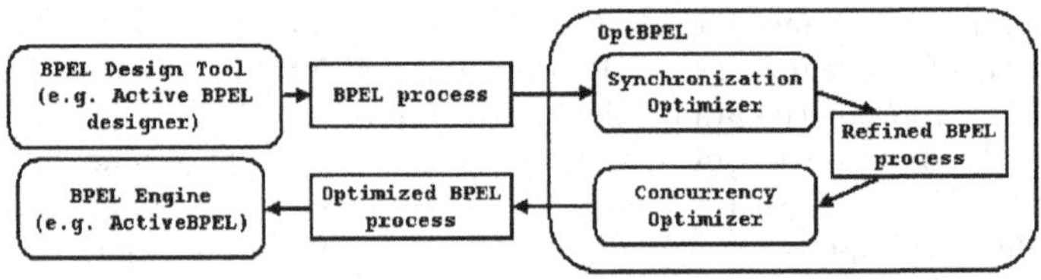

Fig. 1. The architecture of OptBPEL

3 Synchronization Optimization

In this section, we focus on the optimization opportunities with respect to the *link* construct in BPEL. These opportunities can categorized into three types: namely refining synchronization granularity, removing unnecessary *link* and augmenting concurrency.

When optimizing a process, it is critical to guarantee that the original process and its optimized version have equivalent semantics. Since this issue may take pages to describe formally, in this paper, we concentrate on the data race and deadlock aspect. If optimization operations that are related to *link* only don't induce data race and deadlock, then we can safely say that the optimized process is equivalent to the original one.

3.1 Transform BPEL Process to BSG

The approach we exploited focuses on activity segment [5] rather than activity itself, in order to reduce complexity and thus enhance efficiency. BPEL uses *flow* and *link* to express concurrency and synchronization respectively. While the *flow* could be modeled as *fork* and *join*, the *link* could be modeled as *wait* and *notify*, as the semantics of them stated in BPEL specification [2]. To concentrate on how we tune the process, we intentionally omit the details as how to handle the *transition condition* of the *link* and the *join condition* of activity.

The activity segments and their relation are captured by abstract graph model, which we call BPEL Segment Graph (BSG), is a directed graph $G =< S, E >$. Where the non-empty set of segments S contains all the segments in G, the edges set E expresses the relation among them. We classify the edges into two types: the first is sequential edge represented by SEQ used to express sequential relation; the second, and more important type is the synchronization edge represented by SYN used to express synchronization dependencies.

The BSG of a BPEL process can be established statically by the virtue of BPEL synchronization semantics and that BPEL can not create thread dynamically [2]. Koenraad [6] provided great details about how to construct series-parallel tack graph for parallel program, the construction of BSG for a BPEL process is kind of similar to that.

3.2 Optimization Algorithm

A deadlock can not arise during the optimizing process due to the fact that any type of the three optimization operations that impairs the synchronization of the process may in turn incur data races. If any two segments in the BSG will not conflict in variable access, then the process is free from data race.

Two legs of the race detection between two segments are their concurrency and variable sharing. Whether two segments are concurrent or not can be obtained by deciding they are reachability in BSG. Given two segments, if there exist a path from one segment to the other, then they are ordered. Otherwise, they are concurrent. When two concurrent segments access the same variable, and, at least one access is write, then the race occurs. Since BPEL can not create variable dynamically, the read/write variables set of a segment can calculated statically [2].

The "Link Optimizing" algorithm, which takes BSG as its parameter and optimizes it, sketches the optimizing process. The algorithm terminates when no optimizing can be done any more. During each iteration of **while**, we inspect each SYN edge in *bsg* for optimizing opportunities. In the part marked (1), we survey the edge if it can be removed, if we get it, then no further optimizing is need. Otherwise, in part (2), we try to refine it. We keep on refining a SYN edge until it can be removed or it can not be refined any more. In part (3), we deal with the augmenting of concurrency.

4 Concurrency Optimization

4.1 Process Modeling and PDGs

In order to apply static analysis to a BPEL process, we must first convert the BPEL process into its equivalent representation of TCFG. As described in [7], the transformation is straightforward. Note we distinguish the *interaction nodes* (representation of *reply*, *receive* and *invoke* activities) and *calculation nodes* (representation

Input: BSG *bsg*
Output: Optimized *bsg*
while *1* **do**
  foreach *SYN edge se in bsg* **do**
    let t and h be the tail and head node of se respectively;
    if *exist a path from t to h besides se* **then** // (1)
      remove *se* from *bsg*;
    else if *no node in bsg conflict with h* **then** // (2)
      $heads = (s) \mid (h, s) \in E \ in \ bsg$;
      add a SYN edge from t to each node in *heads*, remove *se*; **continue**;
    end
    seq_nodes=the set of nodes that are reachable from h by sequential edges merely and are not reachable from t, excluding h;
    if *no node in bsg conflicts with none of seq_nodes* **then** // (3)
      delete the sequential edges entering and leaving h;
  end
  if *no optimizing operation is done during this iteration* **then** **break**;
end

Algorithm 1. Link Optimizing

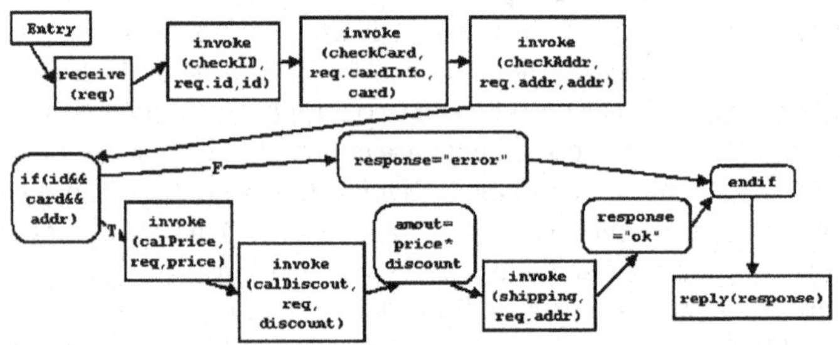

Fig. 2. The TCFG representation of BPEL process

of other activities). This distinction is meaningful because the experiment result in [8] shows that the time cost of execution of *interaction nodes* is at least 5–10 times higher than that of *calculation nodes*. Fig. 2 shows an example of TCFG, the *interaction nodes* are represented by rectangular boxes and the *calculation nodes* by rounded boxes.

To obtain a program dependence graph (PDG) representation of this process, we need to insert control and data dependency that model the partial ordering on activities in the BPEL process that must be followed to preserve the semantic of the original process, [8] gives a detailed description.

4.2 Node Partitioning and Merging

In this section, we describe a simple algorithm called *merge-reorder* partitioning algorithm. The aim of this algorithm is to determine the best partition at which

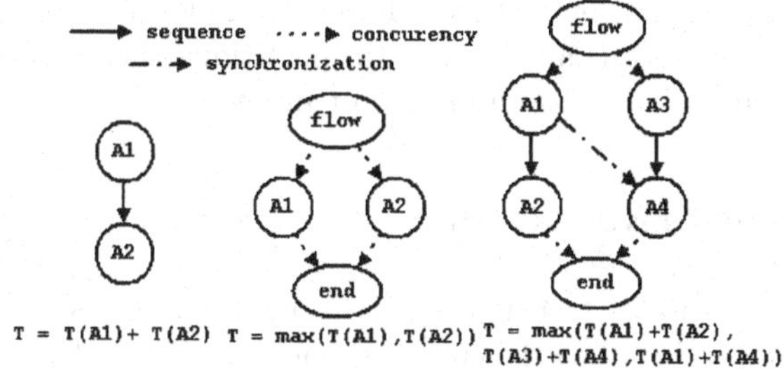

Fig. 3. Time cost model

each *calculation node* must be executed in some *interaction nodes* in order to minimize the total execution time of the BPEL process.

Before giving the description of the algorithm, we first define the time cost model of the execution. Fig. 3 shows the time cost under different (basic) situation (Note T(A_i) represents the time cost of the execution of activity A_i).

***Merge-reorder* algorithm.** An informal description of the merging and reordering algorithm is as follows:

1. Locate a control node, in the PDG whose child nodes are all leaf nodes. For all nodes that have the same control dependence condition on, repeat steps 2 through 6. Continue till all control nodes have been processed.
2. **Merging:** identify the set of dependence edges E, that pertain to a dependence between siblings with the control dependence condition chosen in step 1, such that at least one of the sibling is a *calculation node.* Pick an edge in E and merge the source and destination nodes of the edge. The resultant dependence of the merged task is the union of the component nodes.
3. When a *calculation node* gets merged with an *interaction node*, the combined node is an *interaction node.* When a *calculation node* gets merged with another *calculation node*, the combined node is also marked as a *calculation node.*
4. **Reordering:** for all configurations generated in step 4, using the time cost model to choose the merging configuration that likely to yield the minimum time cost value. For all partitions that only have one single *calculation node*, merge them into other different partitions averagely.
5. Exhaustively consider all merging configurations of siblings that can be generated by merging some subset of the dependence edges in E. Since the size of E for a single region is usually small, this exhaustive search is usually feasible in practice.
6. Once a region (subgraph) has been merged, we treat the whole subgraph as a single node for the purpose of merging at the next higher level. The dependence of the merge is a union of all dependence.

This algorithm is revised from the one in [8], the main difference between them is that in [8], author finds the partitions to maximize throughput, whereas the objective function we used here is to minimize completion time, another difference is that the our algorithm must create partitions such that each partition has exactly one *interaction node* and zero or more *calculation nodes.*

5 Performance Evaluation

Our experimental setup for testing optimized orchestration is as follows. We use a cluster of Intel Pentium based Windows machines (2.8G, 512MB RAM) connected by a 100 Mb/s LAN. Each test case we use runs on ActiveBPEL+Axis2 and RCbpel+RCWS respectively. RCbpel is a portable engine which is BPEL specification compliant developed by our research center implemented in C++, and RCWS is a web service container implemented by means of hybrid programming in C++ and Python. The reason why we use two settings is to demonstrate that performance enhance brought by OptBPEL is generic and not BPEL engine dependent, rather to compare execution duration and resource consumption between them.

Since BPEL is a relatively new language, there are currently no standardized BPEL benchmarks that we could use in our performance evaluation. However, we have tested many BPEL process including these taken from real-world, such as banking system. Fig. 4(a) presents the result of the optimization of travel reserve process (note the letter R represents the RCbpel engine and A represents the ActiveBPEL engine in these figures), Fig. 4(b) shows the optimization result of online book purchase process. The gain is minor when average service response time is relatively short, this is because the gain is offset by lengthy and frequent network connecting to some extent. However, when average service response time is long, as is the most case of real services, and the network connecting impact is negligible, we see drastic performance enhancement.

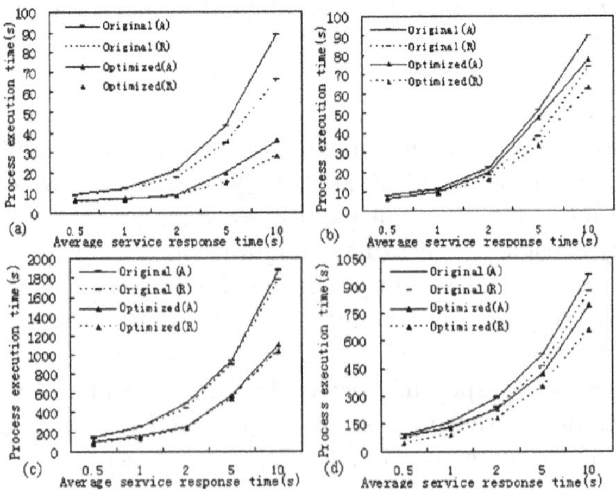

Fig. 4. Experimental results

Fig. 4(c),(d) show the optimization result by OptBPEL of two complex BPEL processes, the left one is a banking process and the other is a real-life train ticket purchase process, both them consist of hundreds of *invoke* and *receive* activities and twisted control flow. We once more see a significant performance improvement after the optimization by OptBPEL. The performance gain, which is average service response time correlated, ranges from 15% to 57%. When the process is complicated, there is always, as can be seen in banking process and ticket purchase process, bundles of performance optimization opportunities. OptBPEL taps and exploits all these opportunities, and thus speeding up the process dramatically.

6 Related Works

There has been considerable research effort paid to BPEL. WofBPEL [9] translates BPEL processes to Petri nets and imposes existing Petri nets analysis techniques to perform static analysis on processes, [10] modifies the CWB to support BPE-calculus by means of PAC to ensure that each *link* has one source and target activity exactly, and to guarantee that the process is free of deadlocks. Mads [11] describes some region-based memory techniques for programs that perform dynamic memory allocation and de-allocation, which is similar with our *merge-reorder* algorithm.

A mathematical performance model of BPEL process is addressed in [12], thus we may capture a deeper understanding of the performance of a process; on the other hand, it does not mention how to optimize a process.

Much work has been done on automatic parallelization of sequential programs based on PDGs, e.g. [13]. In contrast, this paper focuses on the use of PDGs in partitioning of composite web service applications for reducing execution time of BPEL process. Although the IBM Symphony project [8] employs a similar way of partitioning composite web services, its final goal is to implement the decentralized orchestration, which is a totally different problem.

7 Conclusions and Future Work

This paper presents our approach for tuning and optimizing the BPEL process and introduces OptBPEL, a tool for performance optimization of BPEL process. The approach starts from the architecture of OptBPEL, which contains two optimizers, namely synchronization optimizer and concurrency optimizer respectively. Then two important analysis methods, synchronization analysis and concurrency analysis, are introduced. We argue the efficiency of these algorithms used in OptBPEL and give some experiments to prove it.

Our further work will focus on the following three issues: 1) in some specific situations(e.g. grid computing), the resources, particularly computing resources, may be restricted. While optimizing under these circumstances, we will take the constraints into account. 2) the approach imposed in synchronization optimizer will emphasize on activity level rather than activity segment level since the current algorithm misses some optimizing opportunities; and 3) the elaborate time cost model of BPEL execution is needed and more efficient *merge-reorder* algorithm deserves a deeper observation.

References

1. Papazoglou, M.P.: Service-oriented computing: Concepts, characteristics and directions. In: 4th International Conference on Web Information Systems Engineering (WISE), pp. 3–12. IEEE Press, New York (2003)
2. Jordan, D.: Web services business process execution language version 2.0. OASIS Specification (2007)
3. Savage, S., Burrows, M., Sobalvarro, P., Anderson, T.: Eraser: A dynamic data race detector for multi-threaded programs. ACM Transactions on Computer Systems 15, 391–411 (1997)
4. Active-Endpoints: Active Endpoints Corp. (2007), `http://www.active-endpoints.com/active-bpel-designer.htm`
5. Christiaens, M., Bosschere, K.: Trade: a topological approach to on-the-fly race detection in java programs. In: Java Virtual Machine Research and Technology Symposium (JVM), Usenix Association (2001)
6. Audenaert, K., Levrouw, L.: Space efficient data race detection for parallel programs with series-parallel task graphs. In: 3rd Euromicro Workshop on Parallel and Distributed Processing, pp. 508–515. IEEE Press, New York (1995)
7. Yuan, Y., Li, Z.J., Sun, W.: A graph-search based approach to bpel4ws test generation. In: International Conference on Software Engineering Advance (ICSEA), pp. 16–22. IEEE Computer Society Press, Los Alamitos (2006)
8. Nanda, M., Chandra, S., Sarkar, V.: Decentralizeing execution of compostite web services. In: 19th Object-Oriented Programming, System, Languages, and Applications (OOPSLA), pp. 170–187. ACM Press, New York (2004)
9. Ouyang, C., Wil, M.P., van der Aalst, Breutel, S.: Wofbpel: A tool for automated analysis of bpel processes. In: Benatallah, B., Casati, F., Traverso, P. (eds.) ICSOC 2005. LNCS, vol. 3826, pp. 484–489. Springer, Heidelberg (2005)
10. Koshkina, M., Breugel, F.: Modelling and verifying web service orchestration by means of the concurrency workbench. TAV-WEB Proceedings/ACM SIGSOFT 29–5 (2004)
11. Tofte, M., Talpin, J.-P.: Region-based memory management. Information and Computation 132, 109–197 (1997)
12. Rud, D., Schmietendorf, A., Dumke, R.: Performance modeling of ws-bpel-based web service compositions. In: IEEE Services Computing Workshops (SCW), pp. 140–147. IEEE Computer Society Press, Los Alamitos (2006)
13. Ferrante, J., Ottenstein, K.J., Warren, J.D.: The program dependence graph and its use in optimization. ACM Transactions on Programming Languages and Systems 9 (1987)

Controlling the Performance Overhead of Component-Based Systems*

Olivier Lobry[1] and Juraj Polakovic[2,**]

[1] France Telecom R&D, Issy-les-Moulineaux, France
olivier.lobry@orange-ftgroup.com
[2] STMicroelectronic, Grenoble, France
juraj.polakovic@st.com

Abstract. Flexibility can significantly impact performance. Some component-based frameworks come with a near to zero overhead but provide only build-time configurability. Other solutions provide a high degree of flexibility but with an uncontrollable and a possibly unacceptable impact on performance. We believe that no flexible systems give programmers a means to control the inherent overhead introduced by flexibility. This prevents from reaching acceptable tradeoffs between performance and flexibility, according to the applications needs or hardware targets. This paper presents an ongoing work that aims to redesign the existing THINK component framework. Once revisited, the framework makes possible to finely adjust the flexibility to the actually desired needs and thus better control the induced performance overhead. A categorization of the dimensions of flexibility is also introduced in order to articulate our proposition.

1 Introduction

In the domain of embedded devices, Component-Based Software Engineering (CBSE) enables programmers to build operating systems tailored to specific platforms or application needs. Systems like OSKIT [8], ECOS [3] or TINYOS [9] provide tools, languages and compilers to construct, out of components, customized kernels of embedded operating systems. Programmers generate binary images of a system by specifying the desired modules through some configuration file or architecture description. Such solutions are able to produce efficient systems but with however no reconfiguration capabilities (that is, flexibility at runtime).

On the opposite, some other component-based solutions like MMLITE [13], SPIN [4], SYNTHETIX [11], CONTIKI [6] or lately K42 [12] implement various mechanisms that achieve run-time flexibility. In such systems, components are runtime entities that constitute as many *points of flexibility* in the architecture. They expose some kind of *control interfaces* in order to change its architecture or behavior. While they provide efficient mechanisms that bring flexibility, this

* This work has been partially supported by the ANR/RNTL project Flex-eWare.
** This work was done while the author was a PhD student at France Telecom R&D.

C. Pautasso and É. Tanter (Eds.): SC 2008, LNCS 4954, pp. 149–156, 2008.

provided flexibility is however tied to the architecture of the system to build. More precisely, such systems lack the possibility to finely choose where, when and how to pay for it: given a *same* architecture, it is not possible to produce different binaries having different number of flexible points, associated control interfaces or implementation directives, and thus, providing different tradeoffs between flexibility and performance.

This paper presents an ongoing work that intends to redesign the THINK component framework, that already provides flexibility [7,10] but in a rather fixed manner, in order to reach our goals. Section 2 proposes a categorization of the ability to tune the provided flexibility. Section 3 gives an overview of the flexibility provided by the THINK component while section 4 details the necessary design changes to be made and how we did them. Section 5 concludes the paper.

2 Dimensions of Flexibility

The ability of a component framework to adapt the injected flexibility to actual application needs can be characterized along the following dimensions[1].

Where. Component-based systems provide flexibility points at component boundaries. Unfortunately, the presence of a component often *imposes* a point of flexibility. This may lead to a prohibitive overhead, thus preventing from encapsulating small services into components. This unfortunately results in loosing other benefits of CBSE that go far beyond the ability to generate flexible systems [14].

What. The nature of flexibility is generally defined by the provided control interfaces. A system may simply provide introspection interfaces to query the architectural state of a component or it may provide more advanced interfaces to change a binding between two components, replace a component with another, add a stub before, etc. As all possible kinds of flexibility are not necessarily *always* wanted for *any* component, a component-based system should not impose a set of control interface.

How. Flexibility may be implemented in different ways with different impacts on performance. For example, one implementation of a control interface may optimize memory footprint whereas another may reduce CPU or power consumption. Also, implementations that take advantage of hardware specificities may not have the same overhead on all platforms. Therefore, programmers should be able to choose between different implementations so as to match the constraints imposed by the targeted platforms and application needs.

When. The requirement for flexibility may evolves over the release timeline of the system software. Consider the case of semaphores. Conceptually, implementing semaphores with (very small) components makes sense since they participate to

[1] These dimensions characterize *control* over the specification and implementation of flexibility, not flexibility itself for which a classification can be found in [2].

the architecture of the system. Code for monitoring their state may help during debugging phases but may however be removed in production releases because of memory constraints. Programmers should then be able to specify *when* flexibility is actually required and not pay for it when it is not.

3 Flexibility in Think

THINK is an open-source implementation of the FRACTAL model, a hierarchical and reflective component model intended to implement, deploy and manage software systems [5]. A FRACTAL component is both a design and a runtime entity that constitutes a unit of encapsulation, composition and configuration. Components provide *server interfaces* as access points to the services that they implement while functional requirements are expressed by *client interfaces*. Components interact through *bindings* between client and server interfaces. Finally, a component may have attributes that represent primitive properties.

The model is hierarchical since components may contain functional code and/or sub-components. The FRACTAL model also defines standard control interfaces to observe and manipulate the internal structure of a component at runtime. In particular, a component may implement the `ComponentIdentity` interface to give access to its server interfaces, the `BindingController` interface to rebind its client interfaces, the `AttributeController` interface to query and change attribute values and/or the `ContentController` interface to list, add or remove subcomponents.

The THINK compiler (written in Java) takes as input the description of an architecture — written in a textual Architecture Description Language (ADL) — and a component repository. The *HelloWorld* example shown below gives an overview of the THINK ADL[2].

```
component helloworld {
  contains main = hwMain
  contains termConsole = terminalConsole
  binds main.console to termConsole.console
}
component hwMain {
  provides activity.api.Main as main
  requires video.api.Console as console
  attribute int position = 10
  content hwMain
}
```

The *helloworld* component contains two components *main* and *termConsole* bound to each other through their *console* interface. The *hwMain* component provides a server interface *main*, requires a client interface *console* and an attribute *position* of type *int* with an initial value of 10. Finally, the file *hwMain.c* that contains the functional code is listed bellow:

[2] To simplify, the component definition *terminalConsole* is not given here.

```
1  struct hwMaindata {
2    Rvideo_api_Console *console;
3    int    position;
4  };
5  static void mainentry(struct hwMaindata* self,
6                        int argc,
7                        char** argv) {
8    self->console->putcxys->proc(
9         self->console->selfdata,
10        0, self->position, "Hello World !");
11 }
12 struct Mactivity_api_Main hwMain_mainmeth={main: mainentry};
```

Beyond the difficulty of writing such a functional code, this simple example shows that the programming approach is strongly tied to the glue implementation choices. For example interface calls are implemented using as indirect function calls (lines 8), the *self* of component is systematically declared in method declarations (line 5) and passed when called (line 9), attributes are implemented as struct fields (line 3), etc. Should we change the structure of the produced meta-data, the the compiler would no longer accept the above code. This unfortunately prevents for doing any optimization or providing a way to choose among glue implementation alternatives.

As an implementation of the FRACTAL model, THINK allows developers to produce highly flexible systems. The framework however imposes, for a given architecture, what, where, when and how to implement this flexibility. Indeed, flexibility points are imposed by the architecture description (*where* dimension) since bindings are always dynamic, attributes are always variable, etc., Moreover, the control interfaces are imposed (*what* dimension) and there is no possibility to choose between alternative implementations (*how* dimension). Discussing the *when* dimension is pointless since there is no degree of freedom on the other ones.

Consequently, one can *never* adjust the performance vs. flexibility tradeoff of a given application according to its needs and the targeted platforms. Our proposition is then to redesign the framework so that it produces code and meta-data *only* where flexibility is desired (in a given release), with the ability to choose among several implementations. Once redesigned, THINK will still be able to produce highly flexible systems as before. But it will also better address the embedded world with the ability to produce different binary images of a same system with varying degrees of flexibility and varying implementation choices of flexibility, according to the constraints of targeted platforms.

4 Redesigning the Think Framework

This section first discusses the necessary design requirements to reach our objective before we show what we have been developing to satisfy these requirements.

4.1 Requirements

Specification of Flexibility. THINK provides flexibility points to any component, binding or attribute. To make them optional the framework must permits programmers to selectively specify that a binding is static, an attribute is constant, etc. Also, programmers must be able to specify which control interfaces must be added and how to implement the different instances of the model entities.

Separation of concerns. As the flexibility requirements may change over the development cycle of a system, the above-mentioned specification must be separated from the description of the architecture itself. With such a separation, an architecture description will be reusable in different moments of the system release timeline, according to different flexibility requirements.

Glue-agnostic programming. Based on this specification, the compiler must be able to produce meta-data and code that add flexibility (and hence overhead) only where desired without having to change the functional code. A necessary condition is that the provided programming language does not make any assumption on the organization of the produced meta-data and code.

AST-based code generation. While independent in terms of decisions, builders need to exchange information concerning the produced code and the meta-data. They produce types and variables that may depend on types and variables produced by other builders. This implies the need for a tool to produce and represent an abstraction of produced code.

4.2 Implementation

Specification of Flexibility. We extended the THINK ADL so that entities can be tagged with textual properties that can be used to express flexibility as shown with the following annotated *HelloWorld* example:

```
component helloworld {
  contains main = hwMain [single=true]
  contains console = terminalConsole [single=true]
  binds main.console to console.console [static=true]
}
component hwMain {
  provides activity.api.Main as main
  requires video.api.Console as console
  attribute int position = 10 [const=true]
  content hwMain
}
```

Here, the components are specified as single instances of their respective component types, the binding is set as static and the attribute *position* is constant. We choose to extend the ADL instead of defining a new language to limit the number of languages to learn to program THINK components.

Separation of concerns. To specify flexibility separately from the description of the architecture, we adopt an approach close to aspect-oriented programming (AOP) applied to architectural description. This is done through the notion of *global extensions*. A mechanism is introduced in the compiler in order to automatically extend component definitions. For example, the following global extension makes static any binding of any component (*where dimension*):

```
component * {
  binds * to * [static=true]
}
```

In a similar manner, one can also specify to add an attribute controller to any component that has at least one attribute (*what dimension*):

```
component * {
  provides AttributeController as ac if hasAttribute
  content att-controller if hasAttribute
}
```

Global extensions can be seen as the equivalent of *pointcuts* in AOP[3], where the set of points is essentially expressed using regular expressions on the name of flexibility points (component, interfaces, attributes, ...) and predicates over component definitions (like the *hasAttribute* predicate in the above global extension).

Finally, programmers can use global extensions to specify the builders to be called during compilation:

```
component * [builder=MyCompBuilder] {
  attribute * *   [builder=MyAttributeBuilder]
  provides * as *   [builder=MyServerItfBuilder]
  requires * as *   [builder=MyClientItfBuilder]
  implementation *  [builder=MyImplementationBuilder]
}
```

This time the mechanism is used to tweak the build process, and hence, to produce glue code and data that suit the platform constraints or application requirements (*how* dimension). For that reason, this approach provides some kind of compile-time meta-programming facility.

Using global extensions, it is now possible to specify what, where and how flexibility should be implemented. Besides, this specification can be completely separated from the architecture description, thus enabling different flexibility capabilities given a same architecture (*when* dimension).

[3] However quite simpler that the usual pointcut meaning since there is no notion of workflow here.

AST-based code generation. In order to help the collaboration of builders in the process of generating code and meta-data, we developed the CodeGen Java package. CodeGen aims to represent, manipulate and produce C code. The package provides a collection of classes to abstract semantic entities of the C language (types, variables, expressions, declarations, etc.) and functions to gradually produce C Abstract Syntax Trees (AST).

The CodeGen package includes a C parser that can transform a C translation unit into an AST. The parser notifies parsing events through a listener interface when it encounters interesting statements: new type and variable declarations, undefined symbols, etc. The parser also handles and notifies annotations found in comments.

Functional code is parsed by the CodeGen parser which notifies Think of annotations and code parsing events. For example, when parsing the *pos* symbol of the example bellow, Think is notified that this symbol is undefined. An attribute builder is called to return the right expression as a CodeGen AST: access to the corresponding variable if the attribute is modifiable or its initial value if it is constant. Other optimizations like removing the $self$ parameter in calls to single components, produce direct calls for static bindings can be perform in a similar way.

Glue-agnostic programming. Using CodeGen we can propose a new component programming language, called NuptC, to program functional code, exclusively based on annotations:

```
1 // @@ Attribute(position, pos) @@
2 // @@ ClientMethod(console, putxycs, putxycs) @@
3 // @@ ServerMethod(main, main, mainentry) @@
4 void mainentry(int argc, char** argv) {
5   putxycs(0, pos, "Hello World !");
6 }
```

Annotations are here used to express the mapping between architectural entities and C symbols: attribute *position* is represented by symbol *pos* (line 1), *putxycs* method of interface *console* is represented by symbol *putxycs* (line 2) and server method *main* of interface *main* is represented by symbol *mainentry* (line 3). These symbols can then be used in the functional code to define server methods (lines 4-6), call client methods (line 5) or access the attributes (line 5).

This new programming approach does not make assumption on the produced meta-data. For instance, it does not impose to pass a $self$ parameter when calling interfaces, implement interface calls as indirect function calls, or implement an attribute as a variable.

5 Conclusion

This paper showed a work-in-progress that consists in redesigning the Think framework to make it able to generate, given a same architecture description, different system images having different flexibility versus performance tradeoffs. The new version, called NUPTSE, exploits the possibility provided by the CODEGEN Java package designed to transform and produce C code in a collaborative way[4]. We also propose NUPTC, a component programming language based on annotations that does not make assumption on the generated meta-data, hence enabling optimizations and implementation alternatives. The ADL has been extended to enable the specification of flexibility properties and a global extension mechanism based on pattern-matching is introduced in order to separate, if desired, this specification from the architectural description.

As a work-in-progress, our proposition needs better evaluation. At the conceptual level, we need to better formalize the approach, identify its limitations and compare it to aspect-oriented programming and compile-time meta-programming [1]. At the technical level, we need to evaluate the performance gain that we can actually obtain on a real case-study.

References

1. Assmann, U.: Invasive Software Composition. Springer, New York (2003)
2. Denys, G., Piessens, F., Matthijs, F.: A survey of customizability in operating systems research. ACM Comput. Surv. 34(4), 450–468 (2002)
3. eCos, `http://sources.redhat.com/ecos`
4. Bershad, et al.: Extensibility safety and performance in the SPIN operating system. In: Proc. of the 15th ACM Symposium on Operating Systems Principles (1995)
5. Bruneton, et al.: The Fractal Component Model and its Support in Java. Software - Practice and Experience, special issue on Experiences with Auto-adaptive and Reconfigurable Systems (2006)
6. Dunkels, et al.: Contiki - A Lightweight and Flexible Operating System for Tiny Networked Sensors. In: LCN 2004: Proc. of the 29th Annual IEEE Intl. Conf. on Local Computer Networks (LCN 2004) (2004)
7. Fassino, et al.: Think: a software framework for component-based operating system kernels. In: Proc. of the 2002 USENIX Annual Technical Conference (June 2002)
8. Ford, et al.: The Flux OS Toolkit: Reusable Components for OS Implementation. In: Proc. of the 6th Workshop on Hot Topics in Operating Systems (1997)
9. Hill, et al.: System architecture directions for networked sensors. In: Proc. of the ninth Intl. Conf. on Architectural support for programming languages and operating systems (ASPLOS) (2000)
10. Polakovic, et al.: Building reconfigurable component-based OS with THINK. In: 32nd Euromicro Conf. on Software Engeneering and Advanced Applications (2006)
11. Pu, C., et al.: Optimistic incremental specialization: Streamlining a commercial operating system. In: Proc. of the 15th Symp. on Operating System Principles (1995)
12. Soules, et al.: System support for online reconfiguration. In: Proc. of the 2003 USENIX Annual Technical Conference (June 2003)
13. Helander, J., Forin, A.: MMLite: a highly componentized system architecture. In: EW 8: Proc. of the 8th ACM SIGOPS European workshop on Support for composing distributed applications (1998)
14. Szyperski, C.: Component Software, 2nd edn. Addison-Wesley, Reading (2002)

[4] THINK and CODEGEN are freely available at `http://think.objectweb.org`

Profile-Guided Composition

Jesper Andersson[1], Morgan Ericsson[1], Christoph Kessler[2], and Welf Löwe[1]

[1] Software Technology Group, MSI, Växjö University, Sweden
{jesan,mogge,wlo}@msi.vxu.se
[2] Programming Environments Laboratory, IDA, Linköping University, Sweden
chrke@ida.liu.se

Abstract. We present an approach that generates context-aware, optimized libraries of algorithms and data structures. The search space contains all combinations of implementation variants of algorithms and data structures including dynamically switching and converting between them. Based on profiling, the best implementation for a certain context is precomputed at deployment time and selected at runtime. In our experiments, the profile-guided composition outperforms the individual variants in almost all cases.

1 Introduction

Libraries of predefined and reusable algorithms and data structures, e.g. the Java class libraries, LEDA [10] and the Standard Template Library (STL) for C++, and the .NET foundation classes, have improved the productivity of software developers. However, by making a library reusable in as many contexts as possible, the library cannot be tailored to any particular platform. Therefore, many libraries provide a wide range of different algorithms and data structures, or even several implementation variants thereof, and leave it to the developer to pick the best.

A library that allows to change algorithm and data structure implementations can be designed using well-known design patterns. The change of algorithm implementation variant is enabled by the *Strategy* pattern [5]. In the library design, the abstract data structure constitutes a context, each abstract algorithm a strategy, and each implementation variant a concrete strategy. Changing the data representation variant is possible as long as all algorithm implementations access the data via the interface provided. However, efficient algorithms often require refined implementations of the data representations and, moreover, the data structure itself may be in a refinement hierarchy orthogonal to the refinement towards different data representations. This problem is solved using the *Bridge* pattern [5]. Similar designs have been suggested earlier [4,9].

However, many of the algorithms and data structures in the library internally use other library components. So, even if a developer may pick the best-fitting variants at the shallow, they may refer to others deep down in the library that do not fit at all. Especially, algorithms and data structures may recursively depend on themselves, and it is well known that often different implementation variants

C. Pautasso and É. Tanter (Eds.): SC 2008, LNCS 4954, pp. 157–164, 2008.

are optimal for different problem sizes. We suggest a solution that better separates the roles of library designer and library user and reduces the effort of both roles. The *library designer* defines interfaces for algorithms and data structures in a straightforward way, ignoring performance aspects. Additionally, the library designer provides interface functions in the data structures probing performance-relevant properties of the data. Finally, the library designer provides a sample input data generator interface and a default implementation thereof for generating data varying over the performance-relevant properties. The *library user* selects the subset of performance-relevant properties of the data that actually may occur in the application context. The library user starts a training phase, after which an optimization algorithm determines the algorithm variants and data structures that are expected optimal with respect to the properties selected and the data generated. The results are stored in look-up tables that are finally used in automated composition of algorithm and data representation implementations at runtime.

2 Profile-Guided Composition

This section introduces our profile-guided composition approach for the dynamic selection of algorithm implementation variants based on *training* at deployment time and *dynamic composition* at runtime. This is described in Sections 2.2 and 2.1, respectively. Section 2.3 generalizes the approach to also select the implementations of the data representations in a profile-guided way.

2.1 Dynamic Composition

The dynamic composition is based on the design presented earlier [6]. Each call to the adaptive library represents a variation point encoded by a dispatch mechanism. Whenever a call to a variation point is executed, it triggers a lookup in the dispatch table and an invocation of the implementation returned by the lookup.

We assume that all implementation variants $Algo_{impl}$ of an abstract algorithm $Algo$ implement the same signature $Algo_{impl} : Arg_0 \times Arg_1 \times \ldots \times Arg_m \rightarrow Res$. In order to define a call context, we assume a set of property functions, i.e. $property_1 : Arg_0 \times Arg_1 \times \ldots \times Arg_m \times Res \rightarrow P_1$. Any statically or dynamically observable property can be included. However, all property functions must be evaluable before the call, e.g., properties defined on the *value* of the result are not admissible while properties defined on its *type* are.

The lookup function chooses the most appropriate algorithm implementation based on the context. It is a function from a domain of property types to the range of possible implementations $lookup : P_1 \times P_2 \times \ldots \times P_n \rightarrow Algo$. The function is implemented with the help of a dispatch table generalizing the dynamic dispatch of polymorphic calls in object-oriented programming languages. It is constructed based on profiling in the training phase, cf. Section 2.2. Finally, the selected algorithm implementation variant is invoked and delivers the algorithm's result $invoke : Algo \rightarrow Res$.

2.2 Training

The goal of the training phase is to identify the implementation variant that performs best for a certain context. A sample data generator $gen :\to Arg_0 \times Arg_1 \times \ldots \times Arg_m$ defines the call contexts profiled. We cannot generate data for *all* contexts. Therefore, we assume a function $sample : Arg_0 \times Arg_1 \times \ldots \times Arg_m \to Id$ that maps each call context to a profiled sample that represents it best.

The sample id is used as the index in our dispatch table. For each sample and each implementation variant, we calculate and compare the expected execution times. Hence, for each $Algo_{impl} \in Algo$, we expect a function for computing the execution times $time^{algo}_{impl} : Arg_0 \times Arg_1 \times \ldots \times Arg_m \times Res \to Time$. The time functions can be implemented as measurement functions, using mathematical models for the approximations, or a combination.

Training can now be described as iteratively generating profile data using gen, finding the corresponding sample number $sample(gen)$, measuring/approximating the corresponding execution times using $time^{algo}_{impl}(gen)$, and setting $lookup(gen)$ to the implementation $Algo_{impl} \in Algo$ with the minimum execution time.

Internal library calls may refer to and try to invoke a context that has not been trained yet and the time for this invocation is then difficult to estimate. For non-recursive implementations, the solution is straight-forward. We compute a conservative dependency graph over all library algorithms, where nodes are algorithms and edges potential usage. The implementation variants are then trained in topological order of their dependencies. For recursive algorithms, we generate sample data in an ordered way such that recursive calls always refer to call contexts that have been trained before. We generate call contexts for all the non-recursive base-cases first and then for the more complex recursive cases, iteratively in reverse recursion order.

2.3 Composition of Algorithms and Data Representations

Before each call to a library method, we select the best-fitting data representation implementation together with the best-fitting algorithm implementation. Each call triggers a dynamic selection, now in *three* instead of two steps: between the lookup of the best algorithm implementation and its actual invocation, a second lookup triggers data representation conversions if appropriate. Therefore, our library design needed to assume that all data representation implementation variants $Data_{impl} \in Data$ implement a converter $clone_{impl} : Data_{impl'} \to Data_{impl}$, which converts data from an arbitrary other $Data_{impl'}$ to the own representation implementation. Moreover, we assume a lookup function choosing the most appropriate data representation implementation for this argument based on the call contexts. Call contexts are defined by the property functions as before. Additionally, we assume special properties determining the current implementation of the arguments $data_1 : Arg_0 \to P_{n+1} \ldots data_m : Arg_m \to P_{n+m}$.

A lookup for the best representation implementation of argument i is a function from a domain of properties to the set of possible representation implementations $lookup^i_{data} : P_1 \times P_2 \times \ldots \times P_n \times P_{n+1} \ldots \times P_{n+m} \to Data$.

The training phase constructing the conversion tables is a straightforward generalization of the dispatch table generation: the sample generator *gen* needs to generate each original context for all possible data representation implementations. Measuring or approximating the corresponding execution times of $algo_{impl} \in Algo$ again uses $time^{algo}_{impl}(gen)$. However, it is preceded by all possible conversions of data representation implementations that have to be measured as well. If an algorithm implementation is not applicable on a certain data representation implementation, its time is defined as $time^{algo}_{impl} := \infty$. The best algorithm is stored in a *lookup* table. Additionally, the best conversion for each argument i is stored in a conversion table $lookup^i_{data}$.

3 Experiments

We conducted two experiments on matrix multiplication, one where we altered the algorithm used to perform matrix multiplication, and a second one where we additionally altered the data representation of the matrices.

The matrix data is captured in two vectors of vectors, representing the matrix in row- and column-major order. We selected between four different matrix multiplication algorithms: *Baseline*, *Inlined*, *Recursive*, and *Strassen*. *Baseline* is the naive $O(n^3)$ algorithm with each multiplication step implemented via a function call. *Inlined* is the same algorithm as *Baseline* but with all the functions inlined. *Recursive* applies a straight-forward recursive multiplication schema as defined in [2]. *Strassen* [14] uses a recursive schema similar to *Recursive* but recursively reduces a multiplication to 7 rather than 8 multiplications of submatrices, hence reducing the complexity to $\approx O(2^{2.81})$. *Recursive* and *Strassen* are only applicable to square matrices.

Each experiment is divided into two stages, training and execution. For training, we generate square matrices of sizes 1 to 256 in steps of 16. For each matrix size s, we generated matrices A and B with double precision values between 0 and 1, randomly and equally distributed. We then execute all the implementation variants $1024/s$ times for each problem size and implementation variant. The on-average fastest implementation variant is recorded for each problem size. During the execution stage, we measure the execution time for square matrices of size 1 to max. 1000 in steps of 10. The different sizes and step sizes are in order to avoid measuring the exact same data as we used to train. We invoked for a problem of size s the best the implementation variant for the largest $s' \leq s$ that we have trained before.

3.1 Dynamic Composition of Algorithms

The profile-guided versions of both *Recursive* and *Strassen* recursively invoke the profile-guided matrix multiplication via the abstract *Matrix Multiplication* interface which, in turn, looks up and invokes the best matrix multiplication algorithms implementation for the sub-matrix multiplications. The original versions use the *Recursive* and *Strassen* multiplication for recursive calls, respectively,

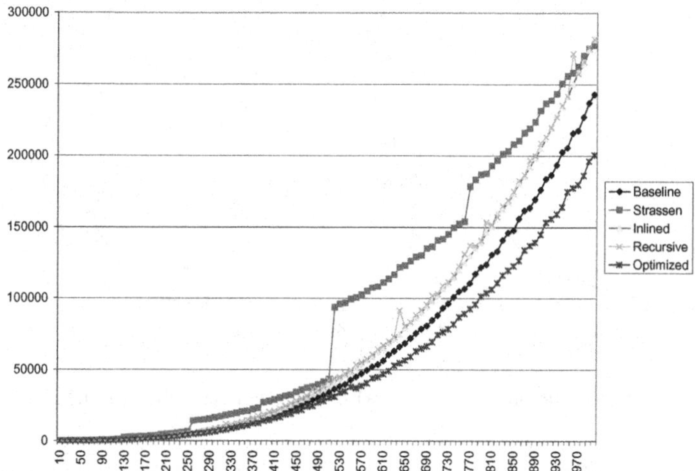

Fig. 1. Original vs. optimized matrix multiplication (times in ms)

if the sub-matrices are square and *Inlined*, otherwise. The measured execution times are averaged for each matrix size and each implementation variant. Figure 1 shows the measurement result.

The profile-guided (optimized) implementation variant starts outperforming the others on problems of size 256. Even for smaller problem sizes, it is comparable with the best of the original variants. When analyzing the lookup table, we observe that *Strassen* is selected for problems of sizes larger than 128. This might be surprising at the first glance since the original *Strassen* algorithm performs worst in almost all problems measured. However, the reason for originally being slow is the poor performance of *Strassen* on small problems. The profile-guided variant avoids this by automatically switching to the faster *Inlined* implementation for small problems. Therefore, the profile-guided variant is able to exploit the better asymptotic performance of *Strassen* already for medium size problems. Note that the derivatives of the original *Strassen* and the profile-guided variant using *Strassen* are almost identical.

3.2 Experiments Composing Algorithm and Data Representations

For testing the full concept, we needed some extension to the original implementation. First, we designed an alternative data representation for matrices. It is based on sparse vectors that store only non-*Null* elements. Converters between the two, the original dense and the new sparse implementation, are implemented in a straightforward way using the *set* and *get* iterators defined in the abstract data representation class. Second, we introduced two new properties *isDense* and *isDenseImpl*. The former predicate holds for matrices with more than 10% non-null entries, the latter predicate holds for matrices which are captured by the original (dense) matrix representation implementation. Third, we introduced a new algorithm variant *BaselineSparse* which tests *Null*-vectors and -elements

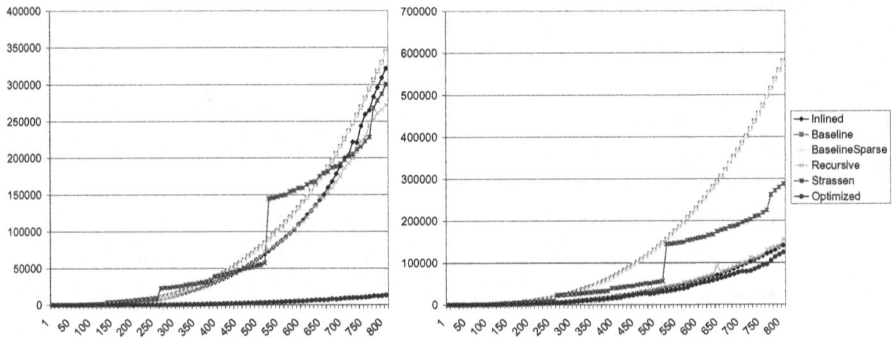

Fig. 2. Execution times (in *ms*) of scenarios (i) left and (ii) right

in the argument vectors and fields, respectively. It may then directly return the respective *Null*-results without further computation and, hence, do obviously less work for sparse matrices and vectors. These extensions, however, have an effect on the solution space that needs to be covered in training: for each problem size, we need to create a sparse and a dense matrix implementations for the arguments A and B and the result C, leading already to 8 scenarios. Additionally, each of A and B needs to be filled with values, sparsely or densely, which additionally quadrupled the number of scenarios.

Training was done on a profile-guided version using all 5 original algorithms, all 16 scenarios, testing all 4 conversion schemata. Execution time measurements executed the original and the profile-guided versions of matrix multiplication. Results for two representative scenarios – (i) sparse matrices, with matrix A in dense, B in sparse representation (left) and (ii) dense matrices, both in dense representation (right) – are shown in Figure 2. In the scenario (i), the *Optimized* version benefits from always selecting *BaselineSparse* after converting the first matrix to the sparse representation. The original *BaselineSparse* cannot keep up with the performance since matrix A is in the wrong representation. The same effect can be observed in all scenarios with sparse matrices involved. In the scenario (ii), the *Optimized* version benefits from selecting *Strassen* for medium-size and large problems and switching to *Inlined* for the smaller problems. Converting in this and the other dense matrix scenarios systematically leads to the same representations for both matrices.

4 Related Work

In object oriented library design, flexibility is a key property. From the start, the focus was on compile-time or load-time flexibility with parameterized types and dynamic libraries. More recent work, such as *Mixins* [13], *Policy-based design* [1], and *Aspect-oriented programming* [7] provide mechanisms that extends flexibility, even into run-time. These techniques are general and do not directly support profile-guided composition as described above, although they are still suitable as implementation techniques. Several predicate based dispatch methods exist, for instance JPred [11], which is an extension to Java that provides a general dynamic dispatch driven by predicates.

In high-performance computing, adaptive optimization has received increasing attention, e.g., for optimizing the cache behavior. Yu and Rauchwerger [15] apply it to self-optimizing reduction parallelization. They assess a machine profile in a training phase and use it for the selection of reduction algorithms during parallelization. Orthogonal to the selection of algorithms and data representation implementation, the expected best schedule and processor allocation for independent subtasks can be looked up at runtime in tables computed off-line, as we demonstrated in earlier work [3,6].

Automatic program specialization is a concern when the costs of genericity is sometimes unacceptable. For object-oriented languages, the work of Schultz *et al.* [12] demonstrates how advices from developer may be used to automatically specialize applications. The work most closely related to ours is that of Li *et al.* [8]. Using sorting algorithms, they implemented a library generator that also uses dynamic tuning to adapt the library to the target machine. A number of machine parameters, input size and the distribution of input data, are parameters to a machine learning algorithm that is trained to pick the best algorithm. Similar to our results, the best algorithm is always picked. However, data representation conversions are not considered.

5 Conclusion and Future Work

The work presented improves the design and reuse of libraries by automatically optimizing the algorithms and data representation implementations during the library's deployment. More specifically, in a training phase the best implementations are determined for sample data and stored in tables for algorithm implementations and data representation conversions. Under execution, the sample that comes closest to the actual call scenario is determined and the corresponding algorithm and conversions are executed. In contrast to earlier approaches to the design of flexible and efficient libraries, it clearly separates the roles of library and application designers. The library designer provides implementation variants, implementations for probing the properties of call scenarios that could be performance relevant, a profiling infrastructure including sample data generator interface and default implementation, and execution time measurement/approximation. The application designer selects the properties actually relevant in the application context and may add more appropriate sample data generator implementations. The optimization is then done automatically at deployment and run time.

Quite a few issues should be addressed before applying our approach to existing libraries like the JAVA class libraries and the .NET foundation classes. First, we need to extend the experimental evidence to cover more languages and problems. Second, finding the representative sample data has shown to be crucial for the success of our approach. One way to improve this is to use production runs and if needed adjust the selection tables, i.e., integrate profiling into the application execution. We are currently designing and implementing the needed infrastructure. Finally, we want to apply this integrated profiling to parallel programs, where the selection of the algorithm and the best schedule are matter of profile-guided optimizations.

References

1. Alexandrescu, A.: Modern C++ design: generic programming and design patterns applied. Addison-Wesley, Reading (2001)
2. Cormen, T.H., Leiserson, C.E., Rivest, R.L.: Introduction to Algorithms. MIT Press, Cambridge (2000)
3. Eriksson, M., Kessler, C., Chalabine, M.: Load balancing of irregular parallel divide-and-conquer algorithms in group-spmd programming environments. In: PASA 2006, 8th Workshop on Parallel Systems and Algorithms. Lecture Notes in Informatics (LNI), GI vol. P-81 (2006)
4. Frick, A., Goos, G., Neumann, R., Zimmermann, W.: Construction of robust class hierarchies. Software Practice and Experience 30(5), 481–543 (2000)
5. Gamma, E., Helm, R., Johnson, R., Vlissides, J.: Design Patterns – Elements of Reusable Object-Oriented Software. Addison-Wesley, Reading (1995)
6. Kessler, C., Löwe, W.: A framework for performance-aware composition of explicitly parallel components. In: Proc. ParCo 2007, Parallel Computing: Architectures, Algorithms and Applications, Jülich/Aachen, Germany, IOS Press, Amsterdam (2008)
7. Kiczales, G.: Aspect-oriented programming. ACM Comput. Surv. 28(4), 154 (1996)
8. Li, X., Garzarán, M.J., Padua, D.: A dynamically tuned sorting library. In: CGO 2004: Int. Symp. on Code Generation and Optimization, p. 111 (2004)
9. Löwe, W., Neumann, R., Trapp, M., Zimmermann, W.: Robust dynamic exchange of implementation aspects. In: TOOLS 29—Technology of Object-Oriented Languages and Systems, pp. 351–360. IEEE Computer Society Press, Los Alamitos (1999)
10. Mehlhorn, K., Näher, S.: Leda: a platform for combinatorial and geometric computing. Commun. ACM 38(1), 96–102 (1995)
11. Millstein, T.: Practical predicate dispatch. SIGPLAN Not. 39(10), 345–364 (2004)
12. Schultz, U., Lawall, J., Consel, C., Muller, G.: Towards automatic specialization of Java programs. In: Guerraoui, R. (ed.) ECOOP 1999. LNCS, vol. 1628, pp. 367–390. Springer, Heidelberg (1999)
13. Smaragdakis, Y., Batory, D.: Implementing layered designs with mixin layers. In: Jul, E. (ed.) ECOOP 1998. LNCS, vol. 1445, pp. 550–570. Springer, Heidelberg (1998)
14. Strassen, V.: Gaussian elimination is not optimal. Numerische Mathematik 14(3), 354–356 (1969)
15. Yu, H., Rauchwerger, L.: An adaptive algorithm selection framework for reduction parallelization. IEEE Transactions on Parallel and Distributed Systems PDS-17(10), 1084–1096 (2006)

Loose Compositions for Autonomic Systems

Luciano Baresi and Giordano Tamburrelli

Dipartimento di Elettronica e Informazione, Politecnico di Milano
Via Golgi 40 – 20133 Milano, Italy
{baresi|tamburrelli}@elet.polimi.it

Abstract. *Autonomic computing* is one of the most promising techniques for managing the complexity of modern software applications. It fosters the idea of systems able to autonomously detect anomalies and react accordingly. Supervision and actual business logic are intertwined and work together to supply the autonomic features.

The paper presents our ongoing work on loose compositions for autonomic systems and introduces the first ideas of a framework based on Java, aspect oriented programming, and rules. The paper also sketches a first prototype implementation, based on the DIET agent framework.

1 Introduction

Software systems composed of heterogeneous and changing elements are becoming quite common, and managing their complexity is one of the key challenges for the efficient release of modern software systems. Recently, *autonomic computing* ([5,4]) has been imposing as a promising approach to address all these issues. Autonomic systems can autonomously react to anomalies and self-adapt their behavior to keep themselves on track and offer the same (best) quality of service without any external (human) intervention. An autonomic system comprises a set of *autonomic elements* that both execute the business logic and oversee it. Managing and managed entities define a control loop where the autonomic element becomes aware of the current situation through monitoring, analyzes acquired data, plans a reaction (if needed), and finally executes it.

Our approach elaborates on the idea of autonomic element and proposes a general-purpose solution useful to develop flexible and decentralized autonomic applications. This holistic view blurs the border between the execution of the actual business logic and its supervision and exploits the idea of *composition* in two orthogonal ways. Autonomic elements are composed, to create an application, and further grouped, usually with a granularity finer than the one used above, for their decentralized and extrinsic supervision. In the former case, we use the term *federation*, to identify the (loose) cooperation among the elements that belong to the application. The logic used to select and federate components is application-specific: for example, we might be interested in linking all the agents running on the mobile devices of the clients of a shopping center. In the latter case, we exploit *clusters* as means to further organize these elements and we exploit used-defined metrics to create them. In this paper, we do not thoroughly

C. Pautasso and É. Tanter (Eds.): SC 2008, LNCS 4954, pp. 165–172, 2008.

discuss the first concept, but we concentrate on the use of clusters as basis for the extrinsic supervision of autonomic applications. Besides autonomous reactions, where each single component acts in isolation, clusters let users implement and customize higher-level supervision policies without imposing any centralized control.

Besides the conceptual model, we are also conceiving a general-purpose framework for autonomic applications implemented in Java. Our proposal exploits aspect-oriented programming (AOP [1]) both to retrieve significant data from the field and to alter the behavior of each single component transparently. AOP probes work directly on the byte code of the application. Nothing is directly hard-wired in the application code, but configuration directives define how to set the probes (and the actuators).

The rest of the paper is organized as follows. Section 2 briefly surveys some related proposals, Section 3 illustrates how our approach works and Section 4 presents an agent-based prototype used for smart advertising in big shopping centers. Section 5 concludes the paper.

2 Related Work

Proposals for autonomic systems have been both for specific applications, like GRID computing [2] or power management [16], and for general-purpose infrastructures [9,12]. Despite the latter proposals, we believe that general purpose solutions still need further attention to provide fully decentralized control of transparently cooperating elements.

Many of the existing autonomic frameworks propose a centralized structure with a single central controller that easily becomes the bottleneck and the single point of failure of the whole system. For example, Silva et al. [6] describe a stream processing infrastructure in which a central component is in charge of job orchestration, optimization, and resource management. Failures are dealt with by means of centralized and persistent check-pointing. Ruth et al. [15] propose another example in which a shared distributed infrastructure is formed by federating computing resources of multiple domains, but a single centralized component is in charge of reallocating the different tasks.

Since our research goal is that autonomic infrastructures must provide the *decentralized* supervision of components that can change frequently, the communication infrastructure among all these components becomes a key element. Chakravarti et al. [2] provide a similar example where an overlay network self-organizes the computation on a peer-to-peer network. Similarly, Seshasayee et al. [16] propose an overlay network composed of cooperating mobile devices to minimize power consumption.

The last characterizing element is the way extrinsic supervision [7] grabs significant data from application elements. A widely adopted solution wraps managed elements in components that expose a standardized management interface (e.g., [17]), but this approach forbids code-level monitoring, and requires that a proper wrapper be developed for each managed resource. Kernel level abstractions (e.g., [13]), on the other hand, do not require wrappers, but usually involve the development of kernel modules. This technique is useful to monitor low-level resources, like CPU utilization or network traffic, to guarantee a particular quality of service, but it does not facilitate fine-grained application-specific monitoring. Code injection [7] would provide required support, but it also imposes that monitored applications be modified, thus compromising their transparency. Finally, external monitoring [8] does not require that managed applications be modified, but it only supports limited monitoring capabilities (like wrapping techniques, but without a common management interface).

3 Proposed Approach

The main goal of our approach is to enforce autonomic behaviors on application's components through decentralized and transparent supervision. Since we want to be transparent and totally independent of the supervised system, we propose an aspect-oriented solution [1] as means to inject the autonomic features. Since we believe that supervision is a crosscutting concern over supervised elements, aspects allow us to factor out supervision and deal with it separately.

Each element can either distribute its data autonomously (i.e., *push* mode), or be queried periodically by the supervision (i.e., *pull* mode), but in both cases, special-purpose aspects govern the process and allow us to be application transparent (i.e., extrinsic) and support low level probing, down to instruction level. More precisely, *bindings*, expressed through the powerful JBoss AOP expression language ([1]), indicate particular instructions of the supervised software that act as hooks between supervised elements and supervision. When the execution reaches these bindings, we execute the corresponding aspects to collect significant data (called *contexts*) and trigger the execution of supervision policies.

As example, we can consider a system for smart advertising in big shopping centers. The autonomic application comprises a number of mobile devices, which can come and go along with the clients in the mall, and some big screens to display the advertisements. The application is "smart" since while customers move around, their mobile devices interact with the screens closer to them to communicate users' preferences and let them customize displayed advertisements on retrieved data. Each screen ranks the different requests and only shows the top scorers.

If we think of each single element in isolation, we could say that aspects are in charge of analyzing collected data and decide reactions autonomously. This way, we can only enforce autonomic behaviors on single components and thus we need a technique that correlates the different contexts to deal with multiple and distributed components (e.g, we want to monitor properties that involve multiple elements or properties that check data spread across components). Figure 1 sketches our solution and introduces the idea of *cluster*. For the sake of simplicity, components are split in *supervised elements*, which represent the application's components, and *supervisors*, which can be thought as dedicated components

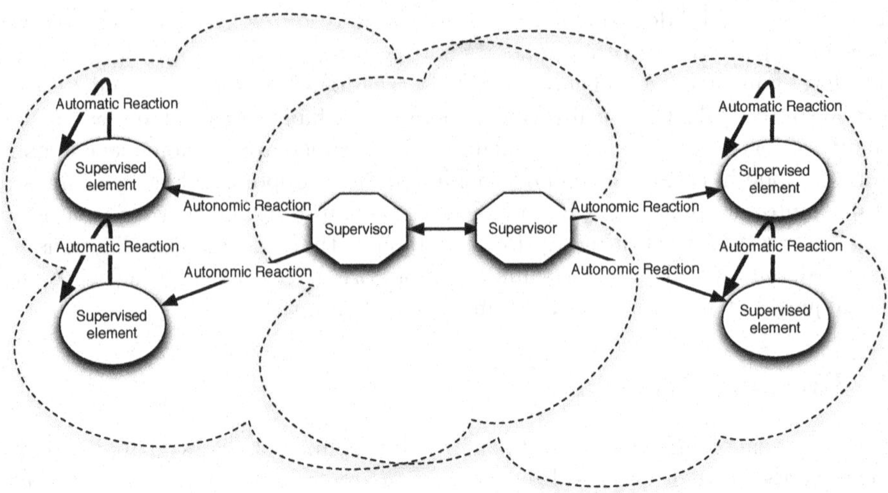

Fig. 1. Autonomic Framework

designed for aggregating and analyzing data collected from supervised entities. More precisely, supervisors are in charge of implementing system-wide autonomic features. It is important to notice that we do not want to consider the obvious solution where all the supervised elements send their data to a single controller that manages the whole system. This option would impose too heavy constraints and would also not leave room for possible changes in the topology of the application without requiring tedious re-configurations. In contrast, we want a fully decentralized and scalable autonomic architecture.

The first step of our solution consists in creating suitable *clusters* of supervised elements. The metrics used to create them is application specific (e.g., signal power in wireless networks). Our only constraint is that each cluster comprises (at least) one supervisor. Dedicated techniques, which are in charge of dynamically creating and maintaining clusters (e.g.,[11]), help us deal with systems whose set of components evolves at run-time. Each element is supposed to send its data (messages) to the supervisor. If we recall the example, software components installed on mobile devices represent supervised elements and a supervisor is associated with each area. At run-time, every cluster contains at least a screen, a supervisor, and some users (e.g., those that are close enough to the screen).

If we wanted to monitor the behavior of the different screens, local monitoring would not be enough. Even if the different mobile devices send users' preferences to the supervisor, it would only have a partial knowledge of the system, that is, it would only know the preferences of the users in its cluster, but it would not know the preferences of all the users in the area. This way, each supervisor only has a "partial" view of the application and thus it is not be able to take any system-wide decision. The solution is the adoption of clusters that are not fully disjoint, but the overlapping between two of them only comprises the supervisors of the two clusters (as in Figure 1). Each supervisor oversees the elements of its cluster, but it also becomes a supervised element of the other cluster. The key difference with respect to the other "plain" elements is that it provides the correlated information collected in its cluster. The obvious problems with this solution is that each supervisor must receive the information about all the other parts of the system, and it must receive it only once. Currently, we are experimenting with both a publish/subscribe middleware [3] and a dynamic overlay network [2,16] to implement efficient and effective solutions.

Finally, as for reaction planning, we adopt a rule-based approach [14] to state scope-wide solutions to react in case of anomalies detected through correlated data. Since each supervisor knows all the information needed to decide, its reactions are local to the elements in the cluster. While AOP techniques work locally, and only execute *automatic reactions*, rules take a wider perspective and allow the user to define more sophisticated and specialized reaction policies that are then communicated to the different components (in a cluster) through the aspects introduced so far. *Autonomic reactions* are thus plug-able fragments of code that define how the user wants to deal with retrieved contexts (i.e., the data about the execution). They are triggered by the AOP probes, as soon as the execution reaches the corresponding code binding, to analyze retrieved correlated data and provide proper solutions. External rules also allow for a neater modeling of the different aspects by fostering the separation between business and supervision logic. This modularity enables developers to write, deploy, modify, and manage their policies easily and seamlessly without any need for modifying production code and rebuilding the application. The two types of reactions also correspond to the two control loops embedded in the framework. Automatic reactions act like a low-level control loop, while a higher-level control loop, based on the autonomic reactions introduced so far, provides system-wide reasoning capabilities. If an automatic behavior is not able to recover from detected anomalies, it forwards the context to the supervisor, which analyses it and checks whether it triggers any autonomic reaction. A detailed description of the rule engine adopted in our framework can be found in [14].

In the end, it is important to notice how the loose composition of supervisors leads to a fully decentralized architecture in which every supervisor manages a cluster of supervised elements and assesses properties that involve the whole system without any centralized control. Moreover, the flexibility of our proposal also helps us conceive fault tolerant systems since supervisors can easily be backed up, injected in clusters, and promoted by means of special-purpose autonomic reactions.

4 Case Study

The proof of concept described in this section implements the aforementioned system for smart advertising. To keep things simple, user preferences are nothing but colors, and thus each screen is supposed to display the color with the highest number of requests (from its nearby customers). Figure 2 shows a basic simulated environment to fully control and visualize the key aspects of the case study.

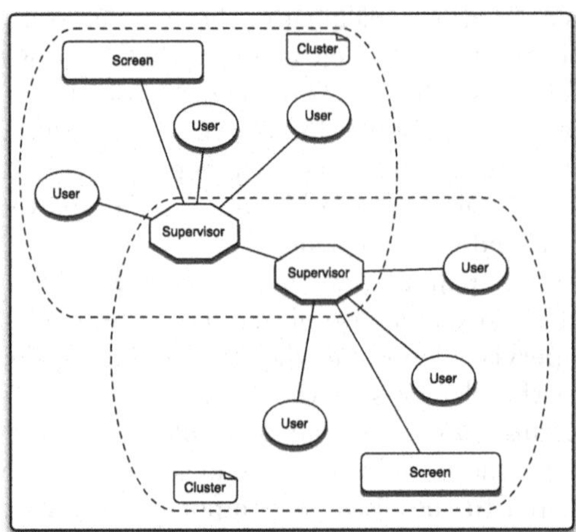

Fig. 2. Our simulated shopping center

Our prototype is implemented on top of the DIET (Decentralized Information Ecosystem Technologies [10]) agent framework, which is a middleware platform conceived for developing agent-based applications in Java. DIET supports the bottom-up and ecosystem-inspired design and development of scalable, adaptive, and robust systems by means of lightweight agents: the authors claim that we might have up to several hundreds thousands agents on a single machine.

Each DIET *agent* resides in an *environment* that enables the creation, destruction, and migration of agents and also the communication among them. On the other hand, a DIET *world* is a placeholder for environments. It manages functionality that can be shared by environments, such as agent migration. Usually, in a DIET application, there is one world per Java virtual machine and, inside it, we can create as many environments as we need. Agents can only communicate with other agents in the same environment through *connections*, that is, bi-directional communication channels between couples of agents. DIET agents exchange text messages and optionally plain Java objects. We can also have inter-environment communications, but in this case, we need to use dedicated agents.

In our example application, the areas of the mall are implemented through DIET environments, each containing some advertisement screens. Customers' devices run special-purpose agents, while each area hosts other agents to detect user preferences and display them on its screens by following a particular policy (e.g., the color of the majority). More specifically, at a given point, each environment contains as many *user agents* as the customers in the area, a *screen agent*, for each screen in the area, and a *supervisor agent* for each cluster.

Figure 2 shows a possible configuration of the system in which we only consider one environment, six users, two screens, and two supervisor agents. For the sake of simplicity, we assume display-related clusters and thus clients are group based on their proximity to the two screens. When a user enters the room, the clustering algorithm starts considering it and adds the agent to the most suitable cluster. Then the user agent sends an identification message to the supervisor. The message contains the user's identity along with his/her preferences (i.e., the requested color). At fixed intervals, each supervisor correlates received data, that is, it ranks the different colors and provides the screen agent with the color to be displayed on the screen. This activity also enables the supervisor to become another application agent for the other cluster and then it sends its data to the other supervisor.

We also decided to adopt a slightly different approach and use the supervisor to assess the correctness of displayed colors. The big screens are controlled by direct interactions among them and the users in the area, but now they send their data to the supervisor in the cluster as the other application elements (user agents). To study faulty behaviors, we decided to inject a failure in the screen agent that then communicates wrong data to the supervisor agent, and thus displayed colors do not match user preferences. This is enough to allow us to check whether the panels are fed with the right colors with respect to the supervised application. The autonomic reaction resets the screen as soon as a fault is detected.

5 Conclusions and Future Work

The paper presents our first ideas and results for the definition of an autonomic framework for Java-based distributed components based on loose compositions. The key concepts are the adoption of an *extrinsic* supervision approach, the dynamic composition of application elements through clustering techniques, and the use of aspect-oriented programming and rules to implement the typical model-analyze-plan-execute loop. The paper also sketches our first prototype implementation and a simple case study used to validate the proposal.

Our future work comprises further experiments to better understand the dynamic creation of clusters and to support the communication among the elements in each cluster. We also need to continue refining the idea of automatic and autonomic reactions and apply them to other more complex case studies. All these initiatives are aimed to the definition of a complete and sophisticated autonomic infrastructure based on extrinsic and decentralized supervision.

References

1. JBoss AOP, `http://labs.jboss.com/jbossaop/`
2. Chakravarti, A.J., Baumgartner, G., Lauria, M.: The organic grid: self-organizing computation on a peer-to-peer network. Systems, Man and Cybernetics, Part A, IEEE Transactions on 35(3), 373–384 (2005)
3. Cugola, G., Picco, G.P.: Reds: a reconfigurable dispatching system. In: SEM 2006: Proceedings of the 6th international workshop on Software engineering and middleware, pp. 9–16. ACM, New York (2006)

4. Ganek, A.G., Corbi, T.A.: The dawning of the autonomic computing era. IBM Systems Journal 42(1), 5–18 (2003)
5. Horn, P.: Autonomic Computing: IBMs Perspective on the State of Information Technology. IBM TJ Watson Labs, NY (October 15, 2001)
6. Jacques-Silva, G., Challenger, J., Degenaro, L., Giles, J., Wagle, R.: Towards autonomic fault recovery in system-s. In: Proceedings of the 4th IEEE International Conference on Autonomic Computing (2007)
7. Kaiser, G., Gross, P., Kc, G., Parekh, J., Valetto, G.: Columbia Univ. New York. An Approach to Autonomizing Legacy Systems. Defense Technical Information Center (2005)
8. Kaiser, G., Parekh, J., Gross, P., Valetto, G.: Kinesthetics eXtreme: an external infrastructure for monitoring distributed legacy systems. In: Autonomic Computing Workshop, 2003, pp. 22–30 (2003)
9. Koehler, J., Giblin, C., Gantenbein, D., Hauser, R.: On Autonomic Computing Architectures. Research Report (Computer Science) RZ, 3487 (2003)
10. Marrow, P.: The diet project: building a lightweight, decentralised and adaptable agent platform. AgentLink News 3(12), 3–6 (2003)
11. Di Nitto, E., Dubois, D.J., Mirandola, R.: Self-Aggregation Algorithms for Autonomic Systems. Bionetics (2007)
12. Parashar, M., Hariri, S.: Autonomic computing: An overview. In: Banâtre, J.-P., Fradet, P., Giavitto, J.-L., Michel, O. (eds.) UPP 2004. LNCS, vol. 3566, pp. 257–269. Springer, Heidelberg (2005)
13. Poellabauer, C., Abbasi, H., Schwan, K.: Cooperative run-time management of adaptive applications and distributed resources. In: Proceedings of the tenth ACM international conference on Multimedia, pp. 402–411 (2002)
14. JBoss Rules, `http://www.jboss.com/products/rules`
15. Ruth, P., Rhee, J., Xu, D., Kennell, R., Goasguen, S.: Autonomic Live Adaptation of Virtual Computational Environments in a Multi-Domain Infrastructure. In: Proc. IEEE ICAC, pp. 5–14 (2006)
16. Seshasayee, B., Nathuji, R., Schwan, K.: Energy-aware Mobile Service Overlays: Cooperative Dynamic Power Management in Distributed Mobile Systems. In: Proceedings of the IEEE International Conference on Autonomic Computing (ICAC) (2007)
17. WSDM Specification, `http://www.oasis-open.org/committees/`

Supporting Multidisciplinary Software Composition for Interactive Applications

Stéphane Chatty[1,2]

[1] ENAC
Laboratoire d'Informatique Interactive
31055 Toulouse, France
chatty@enac.fr
[2] IntuiLab
Les Triades A, rue Galilée
31672 Labège, France
chatty@intuilab.com

Abstract. Producing interactive applications is a multidisciplinary software composition activity. This, and the nature of user interface code, puts particular requirements on component composition frameworks. We describe a component model that relies on a hierarchical tree of heterogeneous elements communicating through events and data flows. This model allows to assemble, reuse and apply late binding techniques to components as diverse as data management, algorithms, interaction widgets, graphical objects, or speech recognition rules at all levels of granularity. We describe implementations of the model and example uses. Finally, we outline research directions for making the model more complete and compatible with mainstream software models.

1 Introduction

Graphic designers and usability experts are increasingly involved in the design of applications, especially when the user interface goes beyond traditional widgets. Until recently, they did it by producing specifications that programmers tried to follow. This process was not optimal: work was duplicated, mistakes or technical constraints altered the original design, and it forced a sequential workflow between actors. It also impeded the redesign of applications. If a medical imaging company acquired a solution for analysing images, wanted to merge it with their image capture solution, and had consistency problems between the two user interfaces, they had to reprogram major parts of the software.

An emerging alternative process is the multidisciplinary production of software [1]. Graphic designers produce the visual parts, interaction designers produce interactive behaviours, and programmers only produce the functional core (data management and algorithms) and the overall application structure. This reduces the global amount of work, eliminates programmer-induced mistakes as well as incompatibilities, and allows for concurrent engineering: all actors can work in parallel and assemble their work just before delivering.

C. Pautasso and É. Tanter (Eds.): SC 2008, LNCS 4954, pp. 173–189, 2008.

In this article we propose a component model to support this new process. The main contributions are:

- an analysis of how this process and the nature of interactive software call for a software composition model, applicable to all types of user interfaces and to the functional core at all granularities of code;
- the description of a hierarchical component model using events and data flows for communications among components, aimed at addressing the corresponding requirements.

Contrasting with most models that describe graphical interactive components, our model is aimed at describing all parts of an application, including non-visual interaction as well as the parts that do not belong to the user interface. We examplify the use of this model through several development scenarios, involving various degrees of interaction. Finally, we outline some research directions.

2 Motivation: Assembling Interactive Software

Interactive software is hard to develop [2]. This is in part because the user interface per se, which accounts for half of the size of interactive applications, obeys different principles than the other half. It has external control, deals with state rather than computation, and heavily uses references because its objects have multiple interdependencies. With imperative or functional languages, its object behaviours tend to be split across multiple functions. The architecture patterns used for interactive components even give them concurrent semantics [3].

But most of all, the way interactive software is designed and produced poses a software composition problem that must be addressed. If software composition is about assembling components that have not be planned and designed together, then building an interactive application is a continuous software composition activity: from the beginning, unplanned reorganisation is the rule rather than the exception. Moreover, it deals with elements produced by actors with varied backgrounds and methods at any level of granularity and any degree of locality.

2.1 Varied Stakeholders

Interactive software requires skills from usability experts, domain experts, users, programmers, interaction designers and graphical designers. Their contribution can be very concrete in the actual production of software, whether during the development or later during application 'revamping' or customisation:

- domain experts define sequences of user tasks (game levels, for instance);
- graphical designers define all the graphics and the geometrical layout;
- natural language grammar designers, sound designers or other specialists may also produce parts of the application;
- usability experts or interaction designers may define the fine behaviour of interactive components: should buttons highlight when one enters them from the side or only when pressing directly?

– users or support staff may redefine the layout or alternate input configurations to suit their special needs.

All of these are the owners of concerns that should legitimately form individual components. All have their own abstractions and tools to manipulate them, but in the end their productions must be assembled and run together.

2.2 Planning Issues

The above actors do not follow the traditional schedules of software development. As already mentioned, their tasks are best achieved in parallel. More, the design is iterative: because user needs are difficult to elicit, iterative processes based on prototyping and evaluation have been devised. The iterations may continue and important design decisions may be delayed while the rest of the software is being developed: from the beginning, the application is in an unplanned customisation phase. This creates difficulties in large projects such as air traffic control systems: one both has to delay interface design issues and choose an architecture very early, which often leads to architecture conflicts later in the project. Only a component model suiting all types of user interfaces would alleviate this problem.

Interactive software also has the classical issues of application redesign: graphics instead of text dialogue, post-WIMP[1], interfaces instead of widgets, or fusion of several applications under a unified interface. The adaptation to varying platforms (screen size, input devices) also requires a redesign or even a dynamic adaptation of the visual layout, the dialogue sequence, or even the interaction style (a button does not work the same with a mouse or a touch screen). This will culminate with the ubiquitous computing paradigm, when applications will discover their execution context at run time. In summary, software composition occurs at any time from initial development to run-time.

2.3 Component Granularity

The components that are assembled or interchanged can have very different size and complexity. At the largest scale is the integration of two applications into one: an email application and a Web browser, for instance. At a smaller scale, a given widget must sometimes be replaced: changing a classic rectangular menu in favour of a pie-shaped one that works better on tabletop user interfaces, for instance. In some cases the replacement is at an even smaller scale: switching from a mouse interface to a touch screen interface just requires to change a part of the internals of some interactors[2]. For interaction designers this is best seen as a change of sub-interactor sized components from their own library of components: in buttons for instance, replacing the behaviour that reacts only to clicks initiated on the graphical object ('mouse-oriented' behaviour) with one that allows to start beside then enter ('touch-screen-oriented' behaviour).

---

1 Interfaces that do not rely on the Windows-Icons-Mouse-Pointing paradigm.

2 Components that deal with a given interaction: a widget, a drag and drop sequence, a speech-enabled dialogue box.

Furthermore, these various granularities cannot be handled independently: one often has to replace a component by another of a very different size. Consider a desktop metaphor in which applications are shown as pages in a book. When turning the pages, you see an image on each page; but as soon as a page is flat, the image is replaced with the actual running application. As another example, when adding animation to user interfaces so that visual changes are not too sudden, one has to replace assignments of numerical values by whole animation sequences: instead of jumping to its position, the temperature dial of a cooler will make a continuous movement. And the target itself can be a constant, or can be obtained by activating a speech grammar rule, or through a 'wizard' application that helps the user make the choice.

2.4 Crosscutting Concerns

Not all changes are as local as the ones above. When 're-skinning' a user interface, designers only change the graphics but all the visual components in the application are modified. Many facets of user interfaces are "crosscutting concerns" in the sense of aspect-oriented programming: graphical style, geometrical layout, animation, drag and drop management, localisation, time constants, etc. Spaghetti of code is still the norm today in most reasonable-size interactive applications because of this. For instance, building drag and drop behaviour as a component rather than a black box or a series of code fragments is still a challenge.

3 Requirements on Component Models

The situation described above generates requirements on the component model used for organising applications. Some are not new and have been adressed individually in the past. But the new multidisciplinary processes and post-WIMP interaction exacerbate them and make it important to address them collectively.

Unified framework. Because of the planning issues described above, it is desirable to have a unique model for all components in an application, so as not to limit how and when components can be interchanged and connected. This applies to components in the user interface as well as the functional core: for instance, an animated object such as a scrollbar index can be connected to the mouse, to a clock, or to the file-loading component at different times. Post-WIMP interface designers rely heavily on this, whereas most user interface component models apply only to graphical interactive components, and to their sub-components as long as they are themselves graphical interactive components. This only covers very few composition scenarios, and forces programmers to use several software composition models in the same application.

Heterogeneity support. An interactive application is a heterogeneous system by itself. Not only do developers come from different backgrounds, not only do they manipulate very different entities, but their preferred computation models are also very different. Some interaction styles are best defined through state machines; others are easier with data flows. Graphics are often seen as pure declarative objects. Some dialogue sequences are purely linear (levels in a game, steps in a wizard) but concurrency is always present, if only to provide animated feedback. Gesture recognition and similar algorithms, like computations, are well described with functional programming, while input handling calls for reactive programming [5]. Within the proposed model, it must be possible to build components as different as graphical objects, computations, interactive behaviours or speech grammar rules, by taking any of these points of views.

Multiple granularities. Heterogeneity also exists in the granularity of components, as identified in the previous section. The model must therefore have a component concept that is the same at all scales, from basic instructions to whole applications, like does functional programming.

Modularity. Not all user interfaces are only graphical. Some have sound, speech recognition, or video capture. Some even change over time: an application can act as a voice server when you are away from the office and launch a graphical interface when you use your computer. It is important that the parts of the framework that manage these modalities are as modular as dynamic libraries are today, and that developers can choose to use them or not.

Behaviour checking. The model must provide support for checking component composition, because interactive software also has the issues of traditional software. It is particularly important to check the compatibility of component behaviours, and not only data types [6].

Declarativeness. Some stakeholders in the development use purely graphical tools. If they are to contribute efficiently, they must be allowed to modify applications without the help of programmers. Therefore the model must support a declarative style of composition, that is a style in which the existence of a given component at a given location fully determines its semantics.

External control flows. In user interfaces, what triggers an action is not a control flow from the main program but an external condition: user's action, clock signal, etc. Function calls do not properly support this because they require that the source of the control flow has information about the recipient and thus is developed after it. It usually is developped before: device drivers and interactive components predate applications. Function references and callbacks, or the use of late binding for that purpose are workarounds that sometimes induce programmers into mistakes [3]. Events are more useful than functions, especially with post-WIMP user interfaces.

Concurrency. Some interactive components require concurrent semantics, for instance when two users manipulate two menus on a tabletop interface. Concurrency also shows more subtly when two programmers subscribe two components to the same event without knowing about the other, and a third programmer combines their components and expects them to respect some sequencing properties. Not only does the model need to support concurrency, it also needs to provide ways of reasoning about it and expressing ordering constraints.

4 The I* Component Model

To address the above requirements we propose a hierarchical component model named I*, that combines features of computer graphics scene graphs, interactive software models, and component models. Successive versions of it have been implemented in the IntuiKit model-oriented programming framework and used in an industrial context since 2003. Its major features are its tree of elements, its event-based communication model, and its modular execution model.

4.1 The Element Tree

In the I* model, an application is a tree of *elements*. An element is made of:

- a set of named *properties*, that store its state;
- a set of named children elements;
- an interface that exports the names of certain children, properties and *events*, and manages internal operations on children element and properties.

Some elements, called atomic, are built using the host language and their internals are not accessible within the model. All others, called *components*, are built by assembling elements, creating properties and defining interfaces. The I* model consists of the description of elements and operations on them, of a set of atomic elements that describe control, and of their execution semantics.

Application structure. The tree of elements not only represents the architecture of the application, but also the logical structure of its interface. It provides a reference framework for all actors of the development. For instance, a classical image editing program is made of a palette component, a menu bar component, a drawing area component, and a few pop-up dialogue box components. The palette contains buttons, and so on recursively. All interactors are components, and their children are components (smaller interactors) or atomic elements.

Atomic elements. In most user interface models, interactors are atomic. Here, atomic elements are smaller and more heterogeneous: computations, graphical objects, speech rules, state machines, event notifications, property assignments. The model allows a mapping from object-oriented classes to atomic elements, so as to facilitate integration with the host language. To build an atomic element one takes a class and turns an instance of it into an element, selecting some class members as exported properties and some methods as exported children.

Graphical objects and graphical context objects (brushes, gradients, etc) are atomic elements. For instance, a rectangle is an element, and thus forms a legitimate application; running it actually displays a rectangle on the screen. The code below shows how this is done with the IntuiKit Perl programming interface:

```
my $r = new GUI::Rectangle ( -x => 0, -y => 0, -width => 100, -height => 100);
$r->run;
```

The same principle applies to other interaction media; for instance, the IntuiKit environment also implements elements that represent 3D sounds and speech grammar rules. One of the classical techniques for describing the behaviour of interactors is the use of finite state machines. These, as well as data-flow connections for continuous behaviours and algorithms that recognise gestures from trajectories, are also implemented as atomic elements.

Finally, an interactive application also contains computation code and application domain objects. These too are elements, and are currently most often implemented as atomic elements by application programmers.

Element aggregation. Components are built by assembling other elements. Sometimes mere juxtaposition is enough, for instance when building a multimodal dialogue box by assembling a rectangular frame, two buttons (Yes and No), and a speech grammar rule that recognises "yes" and "no". More usually, elements need to be interconnected so as to exchange events or values, for instance when coupling a writing zone, a gesture recognition element, and a text element that shows what has been recognised; we will later see how event and data-flow propagation are described through specialised atomic elements.

But in some cases the children elements are too fine grain to have a significant semantics as such, and must be combined tightly to produce a significant effect: the state of a state machine has a meaning only if it is also the state of a perceptible element. By extending the model to sub-interactor elements, we have lost the natural sharing of data between the two parts of an interactor. Using event communication would be a solution, but at the cost of a poorly justified memory overhead. To avoid it, a tight aggregation mechanism called property *merging* is proposed, and managed in the parent component's interface. The result is that a memory slot for one property only is used, and this property is accessible under different names from the children elements. Control propagation when the property changes occurs as a special case of data-flow.

For instance, here is how one would describe a button made of arbitrary graphics for each of its two states, with an element of type *Switch* that uses its *branch* property to choose which of its children is active at a given time:

```
$btn = new Component;
$sw = new Switch (-parent => $btn);
$on = load Element (-parent => $sw, -name => 'on', -file => 'on.svg');
$off = load Element (-parent => $sw, -name => 'off', -file => 'off.svg');
$fsm = load Element (-parent => $btn, -file => 'behaviour.xml');
$btn->merge (-names => [$fsm->state, $sw->branch]);
$b->run;
```

Because it allows to delay the association of graphics (or any other perceptive channel) and behaviour, merging is useful for managing heterogeneity in a group of developers. Once a convention has been established about the names of elements and their properties, a programmer can build a component in which he or she just names the children and specifies the merged properties, an interaction designer builds a state machine that describes how the user's input is managed, and a graphic designer builds a set of graphical objects; the final component is assembled in a compilation or linking phase, just prior to executing the program.

Information hiding. The names given to children elements and properties are visible to all children of a component, as well as the events defined by children. From this internal symbol table is built an external one, by deciding what names are visible; during that operation, renaming is also allowed. Note that merging is also a manipulation of symbol tables within the component's interface.

Name hiding is for classical software engineering purposes. Renaming is for interactive software architecture purposes. Interactive components are defined in terms of interaction concepts; names such as 'button', 'icon', 'click', 'press', or 'drag' are used. At some point, they need to be connected to the functional core that uses names such as 'file', 'application', 'launch', or 'ship', 'profile', 'match'. This connection implies two operations. First, one needs to match concepts; for instance, a ship is represented as an icon, a profile as a button, and the 'match' operation is associated to the 'press' event. Then, because the names are different, one needs to translate them. This is called functional core adaptation; in object-oriented frameworks, it is implemented with classes whose only role is to glue objects of incompatible types together. Here, renaming makes functional core adaptation a framework-level feature, optimised out at compile time.

Another peculiarity is that there are different publics to hide information from. Application programmers do not need to see the implementation details of a button, but designers who customise an application do need it; symmetrically they do not care about the external interface of the button. This is currently handled at the implementation level only: name hiding applies to all programming interfaces to the I* tree languages such as Perl, C++ or Java, and not to interfaces in languages for designers such as CSS.

4.2 Communication and Control

The prevalent execution model in user interfaces, and particularly post-WIMP user interfaces, is the reactive model. This model usually coexists with the procedural model brought by the programming language. To satisfy the uniform framework requirement, I* solely relies on event communication and a variant: data-flow communication.

Events. Some elements in the tree are able to emit events when certain conditions are met. A clock emits events at regular intervals, a graphical object emits events when it is clicked on with the mouse, a finite state machine when it changes state, an animation when it ends, a button when its state machine changes state. Functional core elements can also be sources: a plane emits an event when it changes altitude or position, a file when it changes size, and so on. Event subscriptions are represented as *Bindings*, that is atomic elements that associate actions to conditions. A Binding is defined with:

- a reference to a *source*, that is a property or an element that may emit events;
- an *event specification*, that is a source-specific expression that describes what events are selected;
- a reference to an *action*, that is an element that is executed when a matching event is emitted.

For instance, this creates a rectangle whenever a multitouch surface is touched:

```
my $table = find Element (-uri => 'input:/intuiface');
my $b = new Binding (-source => $table->pointers,
                     -spec => 'add',
                     -action => "GUI::Rectangle␣(-x␣=>␣%X,␣-y␣=>␣%Y)");
```

A finite state machine is an atomic element made of a set of bindings that are only active when the machine is in a given state. Atomic actions named Notification allow component builders to emit their own events. Others named Assignment set the values of properties. Callback functions in the host language can be encapsulated as actions named NativeCode.

The Binding elements make behaviour declarative: one creates a control flow just by adding the appropriate Binding. It also helps to create state-dependent behaviours, by making bindings or state machines active or not depending on a state, without having to introduce hierarchical state machines or Statecharts: hierarchy is represented by the I* tree.

Data-flow. Data-flow is a special case of event communication. Properties are event sources, and atomic elements called *Connectors* are Bindings defined from two properties: they trigger an implicit action that copies the value of the first property into the second when it changes. For instance with the following code a rectangle follows the finger on a touchscreen.

```
my $t = find Element (-uri =>  'input:/touchscreen');
my $r = new GUI::Rectangle (-width => 10, -height => 10);
my $xc = new Connector (-in => $t->X, -out => $r->x);
my $yc = new Connector (-in => $t->Y, -out => $r->y);
```

Atomic elements named *Watchers* are used within elements to bind actions to changes of their own properties. This allows to build data-flow bricks such as those described in [4] or [7], and produces the control flows associated to merging.

This definition of data-flow does not only provide a declarative way of building behaviours. It also allows to define a consistent scheduling for event and data-flow propagation, so that mixing them leads to predictable results. Implementations of I* include a scheduling algorithm based on properties, comparable to those used in synchronous programming.

5 Implementing Element Semantics

We have built two implementations of the I* model named IntuiKit Perl and IntuiKit C++. We now describe what semantics they give to elements and how their architecture helps fulfill the initial requirements.

5.1 A Model-Based Implementation

For each type of elements, an XML format has been defined. For instance, the SVG format is used for graphics. IntuiKit includes parsers for these formats, in addition to a programming interface for instantiating elements, cloning them, or creating components. Developers can thus build the application tree by loading XML files, instantiating elements from code, or both.

Using XML files has allowed to use IntuiKit in a research project as the final execution engine in a model transformation chain. It also helps manage the heterogeneity of actors and the planning issues: graphic designers use their own tools to build graphics and export them as SVG. Programmers or interaction designers can build the rest of the application in code or XML. Then one can choose to load the XML files at run time, thus delaying integration to the last minute, or to generate code from them. Using XML also allows to migrate application parts from one IntuiKit implementation to another. The typical intended use for this is to carry out iterative prototyping with the Perl implementation, then export the graphics, behaviours, and structure of the application tree in XML and reuse them in the final C++ development.

The manipulation of part of the tree as data files introduces preliminary phases in the execution of applications: the loading or instantiation of elements, then their linking, prior to executing the tree. So as to make the programming interfaces for instantiating elements compatible with element creation in graphical editors, instantiation has been defined along the lines of prototype-oriented languages: elements can be copied from others, then modified.

5.2 Modules and Rendering Engines

Following the construction of the tree, IntuiKit takes charge of executing ('running') it. The associated semantics is that each element represents an instruction for a part of the execution environment named a module: graphical objects are rendered by a graphical engine, speech grammar rules are managed by a speech engine, bindings, actions and other behaviour-oriented elements are executed by the core module. This addresses the modularity requirement: each module is in charge of a set of element types.

Each module defines an XML namespace and implements the associated parser, provides a programming interface for instantiating the elements it defines, and includes a rendering engine for them. Leaving aside user-defined modules that contain user-assembled components such as WIMP interactors (buttons, menus, dialogue boxes) or dials for cockpits, most modules introduce atomic elements. The core module provides the central concepts of the model and a few types of control elements: bindings, connectors, state machines. Other modules are used only when required: a GUI module for graphical objects and basic WIMP objects such as windows, mouse and cursors; an input module for atypical input devices; an animation module for animation trajectories; a speech recognition module for grammar rules. Such modules are implemented by reusing an existing rendering engine, either as a library or a server, and encapsulating its primitives into the execution methods of atomic elements.

Using modules provides support for the management of crosscutting concerns while preserving declarativeness: to enrich a component with a new media, one just needs to add a child element from the corresponding module. All other complexity is hidden in the module internals. Furthermore, modules interact nicely with the application architecture, creating a two-dimensional structure: one dimension is the set of modules, the other is the application tree that drives the rendering in all modules. In our view, this is the key for providing an clear architecture for multimodal applications.

We have encountered two types of rendering engines with that regard. Some, such as OpenGL, do not store the objects they render and need to be called periodically. In this case, the I* tree serves not only as the application structure but also as the basis for rendering: once the tree is run, the graphical module periodically traverses the tree, updates its rendering context or the engine's, and has graphical objects rendered by the engine as it encounters them. In other words, the restriction of the tree to containers and graphical elements has the semantics of a graphical scene graph. Other rendering engines do manage their own internal structure. In that case the tree is only traversed once to create this structure, and the engine is then notified of changes in the tree that concern it; the engine acts as a server, and one can interpret this as an extension of event communication to the rendering itself.

6 Example Applications

IntuiLab and their partners have used IntuiKit during five years for developing dozens of interactive applications as diverse as car dashboard and multimedia displays, air traffic control tools, geographical information systems on tabletops, multimodal information query systems or lotto kiosks. We describe here some example uses that demonstrate the robustness of the I* model.

6.1 Skinning a Visual Component

Figure 1 shows the tree structure of a component that was built for a car multimedia system. It has a static background, four tabs that represent four parts of an application, a Switch element, and a finite state machine. The transitions of the state machine are bound to events from a set of keys located near the steering wheel, and its state is merged with that of the Switch. Depending on the SVG file used for the graphical elements, the result looks as in Figure 2a or Figure 2b.

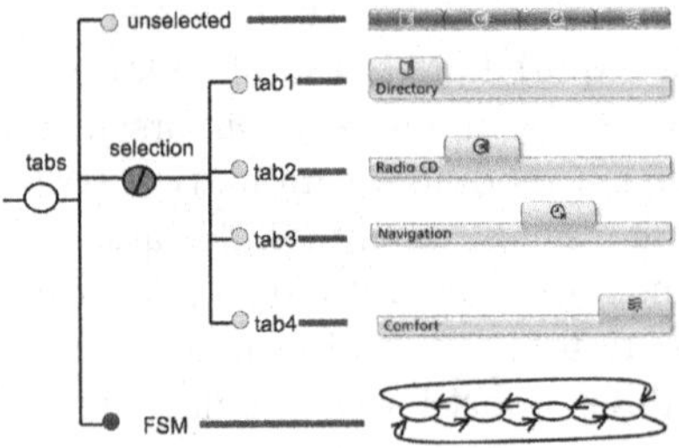

Fig. 1. An set of tabs for a car multimedia system

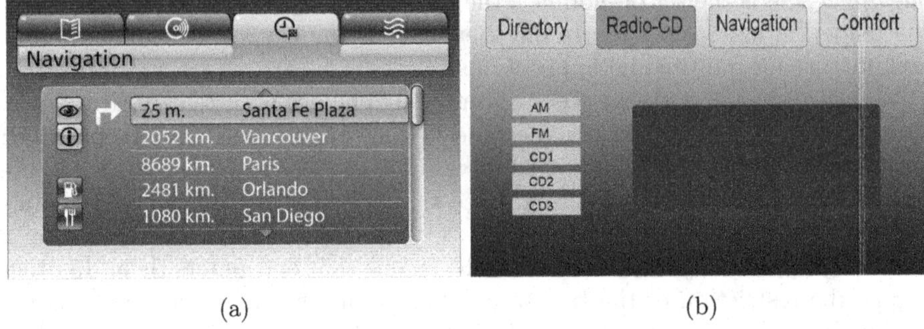

(a) (b)

Fig. 2. (a) With one graphics file. (b) and another.

6.2 Building a Multimodal Dialogue Box

The following code shows how one builds a simple multimodal Yes/No dialogue box from atomic elements: a rectangular frame; two rectangles and bindings on them that emit Y (resp. N) events when they are pressed on; a speech grammar; two bindings on the recognition of words by the grammar. For concision the parent component does not appear here, nor the arguments that create the elements within this parent.

```
my $r = new GUI::Rectangle (-x => 0, -y => 0, -width => 200, -height => 100);
my $y = new GUI::Rectangle (-x => 20, -y => 30, -width => 60, -height => 40);
new Binding (-source => $y, -spec => 'ButtonPress', -action => "notify('Y')");
my $n = new GUI::Rectangle (-x => 120, -y => 30, -width => 60, -height => 40);
new Binding (-source => $n, -spec => 'ButtonPress', -action => "notify('N')");
my $g = new Speech::Grammar (-grammar => 'yes-no');
new Binding (-source => $g, -spec => [command => 'yes'], -action => "notify('Y')");
new Binding (-source => $g, -spec => [command => 'no'], -action => "notify('N')");
```

The same events are emitted by this dialogue box whether the mouse or voice is used. The speech grammar, since it is a child element of the dialogue box, is only active when the box is active; the same holds for the rectangles and the bindings of course.

6.3 Application Design and Development

Figure 3 illustrates the use of IntuiKit in a phase of the multidisciplinary process described in the introduction of this article. The illustrated air traffic control project involved "virtual paper": objects that felt like paper strips through a combination of visual effects, animation and gesture recognition. A first phase of iterative design yielded a paper prototype that outlined the structure and the behaviour of the application. Designers and programmers used this prototype to define an I* tree and give names to elements to be produced by designers. Then each started to program, draw or otherwise build their elements and give them the appropriate names. For test purposes, someone in the group quickly produced very crude graphics, gave them the agreed names and saved them in a SVG file. This allowed programmers to test their work by loading these elements from the SVG file (left). When the final data management, behaviour, animation and graphical elements were ready, the programmers just had to put XML files delivered by designers at the right place, and test the application (right). This application later had several sets of graphics for different customers in Europe.

Measurements carried out on this case study (comparison with a project of similar size and complexity, by the same team, using a linear process) showed a reduction of project duration by about 50%, expenses by about 30%, and a dramatic decrease of coordination costs (estimated number of phone calls) [1].

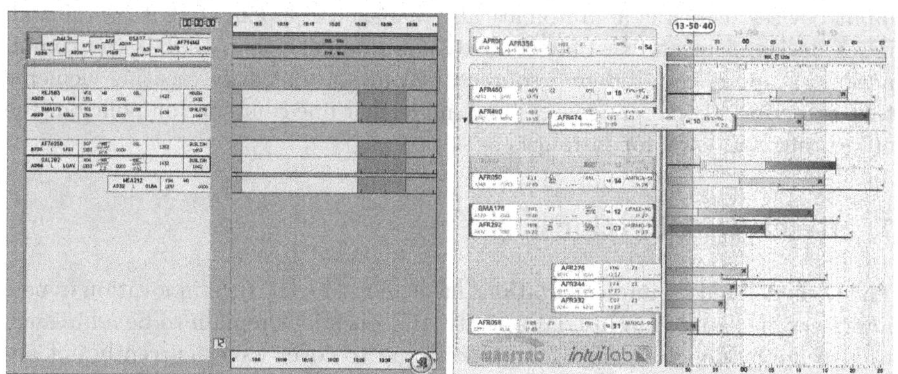

Fig. 3. ATC application before and after final integration

6.4 Transferring More Tasks to Designers

In the above example, graphic designers only produced graphics. However, some are willing to take more tasks from programmers, and particularly visual layout and its adaptation to size changes. We have designed artistic resizing [9], a technique where graphic designers provide examples of graphical objects at different sizes, and the system interpolates their appearance for any chosen size.

Implementing the artistic resizing algorithm with IntuiKit was a simple application of the I* model: we built a new atomic element that has properties `width` and `height`, implements the artistic resizing algorithm, is defined by passing it the examples as children elements, and then behaves as a single graphical element. This new element can then be placed in the tree wherever a resizable graphic element is desired, and its properties connected to the size of the available window. From then on, the graphical object adapts to the size of the window, respecting the designer's non-linear transformations.

6.5 Input Management

One of the future challenges for interactive software is that when building an application, developers will not have a precise idea of what input devices will be available at run time. We have been able to build an IntuiKit module to address this problem, by slightly extending the semantics of the I* model.

Input devices are event sources and hence candidate tree elements, but they are out of control of developers. It makes sense to decide that the application tree is just an element of a larger I* tree that contains the computer devices. Therefore, we just had to create a new element set and element discovery functions to allow programmers to test and use input devices [8]. Using a technique used for communicating dynamic data creation from the functional core to the user interface, the hot-plugging of devices is reported as an event by the set of input devices, which is an automatically managed component that contains all input device elements. In that context, multimodal fusion, that is the combination of inputs from different sources, becomes a matter of creating elements that subscribe to different sources and implement one combination policy or the other: time windows, for instance.

7 Research Directions

The I* model and its implementations have allowed us to turn innovation in user interfaces into a more industrial activity. But questions remain to be addressed, to give the model more solid foundations and to cover issues currently not addressed. First of all, the control structures described above are insufficient for building all of the functional core; this forces developers to build it as a set of atomic elements, and breaks the requirement for a uniform model. Similarly, one needs to devise a data-passing scheme that makes the implementation of data-flow elements as easy as functions in a functional framework, as well as a typing system for controlling bindings and connections. We may also need to propose a "service call" communication system on top of event communication, for the few cases where the caller is defined after the callee.

In another direction, defining a formal semantics for the I* tree and its communications would provide developers with an unmbiguous understanding of how their components behave, and help compare with more general frameworks. It could also serve as the basis for compiling components rather than just interpreting them: whereas during execution IntuiKit, even in Perl, compares favourably with all rich graphics frameworks, interpretation times are not satisfactory.

Finally, a strong similitude appears between elements and processes in reactive systems or other concurrent models, but the consequences of choosing a given semantics need to be explored. In particular, we must understand what level of control programmers and designers need over the sequencing of their actions, and how it fits in the available models of concurrency.

8 Related Work

Many composition scenarios and requirements have been studied by user interface software specialists. The proposed solutions either have been high level guidelines or patterns focused on a given requirement: for instance MVC or PAC [10] for separing the interface from the functional core; the use of active values (examplified recently by Cocoa's bindings) then data flows or one way constraints for describing user input, layout or animation [4,11]; hierarchies of visual components as in Self [12]; the Java source/listener and Qt signal/slot patterns for event communication. Most such patterns implement a reactive composition model on top of an existing function-oriented language (using inheritance, for instance), thus not addressing the uniform framework requirement. None of these have explored the heterogeneity requirement.

Recent products support the new development processes. Flash allows graphical designers to build complete applications; programmers can extend these using a dedicated language or even a mainstream language. Other solutions for Web applications, such as SVG+Javascript or Microsoft Silverlight, take a similar hybrid approach. However, such solutions are very specific to graphics, and do not propose a unified framework for complex applications: Flash has limited encapsulation features and the others fall in the hybrid model category.

Solutions for programming user interfaces have been proposed for nearly every programming paradigm: object-oriented programming of course, but also reactive programming [13], functional programming [5], etc. Many of these approaches, with the notable exception of reactive programming and the Smalltalk language [14], consist in providing patterns that extend or alter the semantics of the original framework to support interactive components.

With the advent of large heterogeneous systems [15], research on software architecture and software composition addresses requirements that are very similar to ours. The I* tree can be compared to the hierarchy of components in the Fractal framework [16]; component interfaces, including the experimental behaviour inspection features, and some aspects of internal control in I* components not described here can be compared to Fractal membranes. The main difference is probably that Fractal is service-oriented while I* is event-oriented. Aspect programming [17] also shares requirements with I*, particularly modularity (for handling cross-cutting concerns) and external control. One can interpret point-cuts and advices as the I* binding of actions to particular sources, with a particular event specification language. The main difference is that this event communication is the main control construction in I* whereas aspect programming uses it only for particular software engineering cases. I* can also be considered as an architecture description language, but one that would aim at describing the internal architecture of components as well, down to the level of instructions.

9 Conclusion

We have analysed in this article how the new multidisciplinary processes used for interactive software influence software architecture and composition. They create a need for a component model that unifies the heterogeneous concepts used by the various stakeholders, that combines with the more traditional requirements of user interface software. We have described the main features of the I* component model that addresses these issues. In particular, the ability to apply late binding techniques to heterogeneous components such as behaviours, graphical objects, speech rules or computations allows to implement concurrent development processes. One of the main challenges now is to compare our model with more mainstream results in software engineering. Understanding the links between interactive software and other heterogeneous systems may prove fertile, as well as comparing I* with formal models for describing concurrency. In the long term, our objective is to reconcile user interface design with software engineering theories, practices and tools.

Acknowledgements

This work was partly funded by the French government through the ITEA Emode project and by Agence Nationale de la Recherche through the Digitable and Istar projects. L. Bass, R. Kazman and S. Conversy provided useful advice on this article. The anonymous reviewers helped a lot to improve it.

References

1. Chatty, S., et al.: Revisiting visual interface programming: creating GUI tools for designers and programmers. In: Proc. of the ACM UIST, Addison-Wesley, Reading (2004)
2. Myers, B.A.: Why are human-computer interfaces difficult to design and implement? Technical Report CMU-CS-93-183, Carnegie Mellon University (1993)
3. Chatty, S.: Programs = data + algorithms + architecture. In: Proc. of the 2007 conference on Engineering Interactive Systems. LNCS, vol. 4940, Springer, Heidelberg (to appear, 2008)
4. Chatty, S.: Defining the behaviour of animated interfaces. In: Proceedings of the IFIP WG 2.7 working conference, pp. 95–109. North-Holland, Amsterdam (1992)
5. Elliott, C., Hudak, P.: Functional reactive animation. In: International Conference on Functional Programming (1997)
6. Accot, J., et al.: Formal transducers: models of devices and building bricks for the design of highly interactive systems. In: Proc. of DSVIS 1997, Springer, Heidelberg (1997)

7. Dragicevic, P., Fekete, J.D.: Support for input adaptability in the Icon toolkit. In: Proceedings of ICMI 2004, pp. 212–219. ACM Press, New York (2004)
8. Chatty, S., et al.: Multiple input support in a model-based interaction framework. In: Proceedings of Tabletop 2007, IEEE Computer Society Press, Los Alamitos (2007)
9. Dragicevic, P., et al.: Artistic resizing: A technique for rich scale-sensitive vector graphics. In: Proceedings of the ACM UIST (2005)
10. Coutaz, J.: PAC, an implementation model for dialog design. In: Proceedings of the Interact 1987 Conference, pp. 431–436. North-Holland, Amsterdam (1987)
11. Myers, B.: Separating application code from toolkits: Eliminating the spaghetti of callbacks. In: Proceedings of the ACM UIST (1991)
12. Smith, R.B., et al.: The Self-4.0 User Interface. In: OOPSLA 1995 conference proceedings, pp. 47–60 (1995)
13. Clement, D., Incerpi, J.: Programming the behavior of graphical objects using Esterel. In: Díaz, J., Orejas, F. (eds.) TAPSOFT 1989. LNCS, vol. 352, Springer, Heidelberg (1989)
14. Kay, A.C.: The early history of Smalltalk. ACM SIGPLAN (3), 69–75 (1993)
15. Hardebolle, C., et al.: A generic execution framework for models of computation. In: Proceedings of MOMPES 2007, pp. 45–54. IEEE Computer Society, Los Alamitos (2007)
16. Bruneton, E., et al.: An open component model and its support in Java. In: Crnković, I., Stafford, J.A., Schmidt, H.W., Wallnau, K. (eds.) CBSE 2004. LNCS, vol. 3054, Springer, Heidelberg (2004)
17. Kiczales, G.: Aspect-oriented programming. ACM Comp. Surveys 28(4es) (1996)

Compositional Modeling for Data-Centric Business Applications

Ethan K. Jackson and Wolfram Schulte

Microsoft Research,
One Microsoft Way, Redmond, WA
{ejackson,schulte}@microsoft.com

Abstract. Data-centric business applications comprise an important class of distributed systems that includes on-line stores, document management systems, and patient portals. However, their complexity makes it difficult to design and implement them. We address these issues from a model-driven perspective by developing a formal, compositional, and domain-specific set of abstractions for the specification and analysis of data-centric business applications. Our technique allows us to formally analyze the specified system at design time; in particular we can analyze whether the system is resilient to abnormal conditions, i.e. that key system invariants can always be re-established.

1 Introduction

Data-centric business applications comprise an important class of distributed systems that includes on-line stores, document management systems, and patient portals. However, many foundational issues make the design of correct business applications a non-trivial problem: Implementation technologies are diverse and problematic, e.g. the security of Web 2.0 applications is flawed [1]. Difficult non-functional requirements, such as privacy [2], are often overlooked. Anecdotally, even mature and well-tested distributed systems still fail under unexpected conditions [3].

A number of approaches have been suggested to address these issues: *Model-driven architecture* (MDA) [4] attempts to disentangle the implementation platform from the business logic, *enterprise patterns* [5] distill isolated kernels of programmer wisdom, and formal *work-flow models* [6] focus on arrangement and communication of processing tasks. Each approach addresses some aspect of the overall design problem, but no existing approach combines the specification of the business logic, its distributed implementation, and its formal analysis.

We address these issues from a model-driven perspective by developing a formal, compositional, and domain-specific set of abstractions for the specification and analysis of data-centric business applications. Our contributions are:

- We provide a new specification technique for modeling distributed and data-centric business applications. This is accomplished by the specification and composition of three models: A *data model* (Section 2) enumerates the essential

C. Pautasso and É. Tanter (Eds.): SC 2008, LNCS 4954, pp. 190–205, 2008.

data and data invariants of the system. An *operation model* (Section 3) characterizes the set of data manipulation operations. A *connectivity model* (Section 4) defines the agents of the system, the information flow between agents, and the bindings of data to agents, thereby generalizing data and operations over networks.
- We give these models a formal semantics based on term algebras and inference over terms using Horn logic extended with stratified negation [7]. With this framework we can characterize the unstable states, which are those distributed states that temporarily violate invariants of the data model.
- We show in Section 5 that for any system specified with BAM there exists a finite set of equivalence classes of unstable states of finite size. This allows the application of finite model checking to determine if a system is self-stabilizing; i.e. that a BAM system has adequate operations for reestablishing invariants.

We discuss related work in Section 6 and future work in Section 7.

1.1 Running Example: A Document Management System

The high-level requirements of data-centric applications are often straightforward. For example, the requirements for a document management system are:

1. Authorized users can view, create, and modify their documents, from a local *client*.
2. Authorized users can manage their documents, even if not connected to a *server*.
3. One or more *servers* synchronize with *clients* to record the latest versions of documents.

This example, while simple, still illustrates some important characteristics of data-centric business applications. First, the key data elements are readily apparent – e.g. servers contain *copies*. Second, data can be manipulated by some small set of (simple) operations – e.g. clients create documents. Third, heterogeneous agents act upon the data, and different agents have different capabilities – e.g. servers must synchronize with clients, while clients are free to modify the documents they own.

2 Data Model

BAM data models capture the data states of a business application using *metamodels* employing a notation similar to *UML class diagrams* [8]. Figure 1 shows a data model for our document management system. For example, the Document construct contains two pieces of information: The user who created it an its title. A Snapshot contains a set of DocumentCopy items. The consistency between Documents and DocumentCopies are specified with a set of formal invariants; these appear in the gray boxes on the right-hand side. (The invariants will be described in more detail later.)

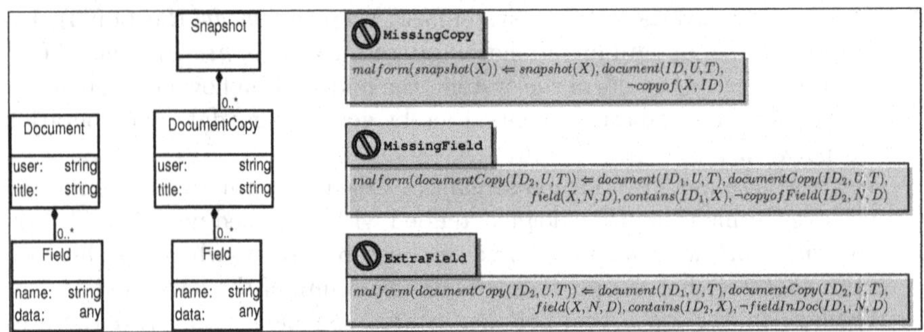

Fig. 1. Data model for document management system

Our terminology and formalization of metamodels and model transformations builds on previous work [9]. We briefly repeat necessary concepts below; for more details consult the reference.

Formally, a data model expresses a four-tuple $D = \langle \Upsilon, \Upsilon_C, \Sigma, C \rangle$ called a *domain*, where Υ is a finite signature representing the data constructs, Υ_C is a finite signature for representing derived properties, Σ is a set of values, and C is a set extended Horn axioms defined over $\Upsilon, \Upsilon_C, \Sigma$ for deriving properties. These axioms are used to capture data invariants. The set of all possible data states is the *powerset* of the *term algebra* over Υ generated by Σ. This is written $\mathcal{P}(\mathcal{T}_\Upsilon(\Sigma))$. A member $s \in \mathcal{P}(\mathcal{T}_\Upsilon(\Sigma))$ is a concrete instantiation of data, and describes the state of the management system at some time.

Returning to the example, Figure 2 shows a visualization for a particular state s. It contains two documents, entitled EmailToBob and ExpenseReport. The box labeled Snapshot contains several document copies, entitled EmailToBob and Payroll. Under the title of each document/copy is the user who created the document and the associated fields.

Table 1 shows the terms used to encode s, grouped by function symbol. For example, a document is represented by a term $document(ID, User, Title)$, where $document(\cdot,\cdot,\cdot)$ is ternary function symbol and $\{ID, User, Title\} \subset \Sigma$ are values for the unique ID of the document, the user who created the document, and the document's title. The Field, DocumentCopy, and Snapshot occurrences are encoded in a similar fashion. Containment of one occurrence within another is represented by the function symbol $contains(\cdot,\cdot)$, where a term $contains(ID_1, ID_2)$ denotes that the data with ID_1 contains the data with ID_2.

The data invariants are expressed using the help of a standard function symbol, $malform(\cdot)$. A data state s is *inconsistent*, violates invariants, if it is possible to derive any $malform(\cdot)$ terms.

For example, the axiom below explains that it is possible to derive a term of the form $malform(contains(ID_1, ID_2))$ if the state s has terms encoding the containment of a Document within a Snapshot.

$$malform(contains(ID_1, ID_2)) \Leftarrow contains(ID_1, ID_2), snapshot(ID_1), document(ID_2, U, N) \quad (1)$$

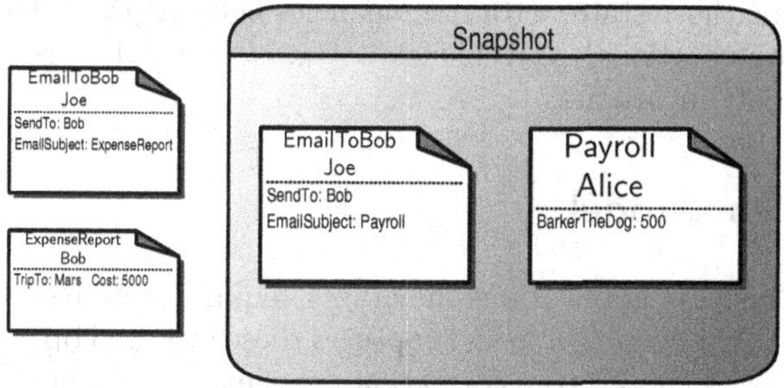

Fig. 2. An example state of a management system

Table 1. Abstraction of document management state as a set of terms

Signature	Terms
$document(\cdot,\cdot,\cdot)$	$document(1, \texttt{Joe}, \texttt{EmailToBob})$, $document(2, \texttt{Bob}, \texttt{ExpenseRep})$
$field(\cdot,\cdot,\cdot)$	$field(3, \texttt{SendTo}, \texttt{Bob})$, $field(4, \texttt{EmailSubject}, \texttt{ExpenseReport})$, $field(5, \texttt{TripTo}, \texttt{Mars})$, $field(6, \texttt{Cost}, 5000)$
$contains(\cdot,\cdot)$	$contains(1,3)$, $contains(1,4)$, $contains(2,5)$, $contains(2,6)$
$snapshot(\cdot)$	$snapshot(7)$
$documentCopy(\cdot,\cdot,\cdot)$	$documentCopy(8, \texttt{Joe}, \texttt{EmailToBob})$, $documentCopy(9, \texttt{Alice}, \texttt{Payroll})$
$field(\cdot,\cdot,\cdot)$	$field(10, \texttt{SendTo}, \texttt{Bob})$, $field(11, \texttt{EmailSubject}, \texttt{Payroll})$, $field(12, \texttt{BarkerTheGuardDog}, 100)$
$contains(\cdot,\cdot)$	$contains(7,8)$, $contains(7,9)$, $contains(8,10)$, $contains(8,11)$, $contains(9,12)$

Returning to the original data model, indeed we see that Documents cannot be contained in Snapshots. This is a simple invariant, but the data model can capture more complex invariants that are implied by the high-level requirements. These invariants a shown on the right-hand side of Figure 1. For example, we require that a Snapshot should contain a copy of any known Document. The invariant labeled MissingCopy expresses this

$$malform(snapshot(ID_1)) \Leftarrow snapshot(ID_1), document(ID_2, U, T), \neg copyof(ID_1, ID_2) \tag{2}$$

using the auxiliary axiom:

$$copyof(ID_1, ID_2) \Leftarrow snapshot(ID_1), document(ID_2, U, T), documentCopy(ID_3, U, T), contains(ID_1, ID_3) \tag{3}$$

Note that this expresses the synchronization between documents and copies in a data-centric manner, without explaining the protocols and services necessary to implement this synchronization. The remaining invariants, MissingField and

ExtraField, define those states with discrepancies between the fields of documents and copies. For notational convenience, let $models(D)$ denote the set of data states that satisfy invariants.

3 Operation Model

Data-centric business applications inevitably require some basic operations on data, and the BAM *operation model* captures these essential operations as *model transformations*. A model transformation changes the current data state s by adding new terms to s and/or deleting existing terms from s.

Formally, a model transformation $\lambda = (t^+_\lambda, t^-_\lambda)$ is comprised of two sets of Horn axioms. The axioms of t^+_λ derive the terms that should be added to s, and the axioms of t^-_λ derive the terms that should be removed. If the data state is s, then an operation λ changes the state to s_λ according to the state update equation:

$$s_\lambda = \left(s \cup [\![s]\!]^{t^+_\lambda} \right) - [\![s]\!]^{t^-_\lambda} \tag{4}$$

where $[\![\ ]\!]^t$ is the map that takes a set of terms s to the set of new terms derivable from s by axioms t.

3.1 Parameterless Operations

Figure 3.B shows a *parameterless* BAM operation, called CopyFields, that finds all the fields contained in a document that are not contained in its corresponding copy. This operation then adds these missing fields to the copy so that it is

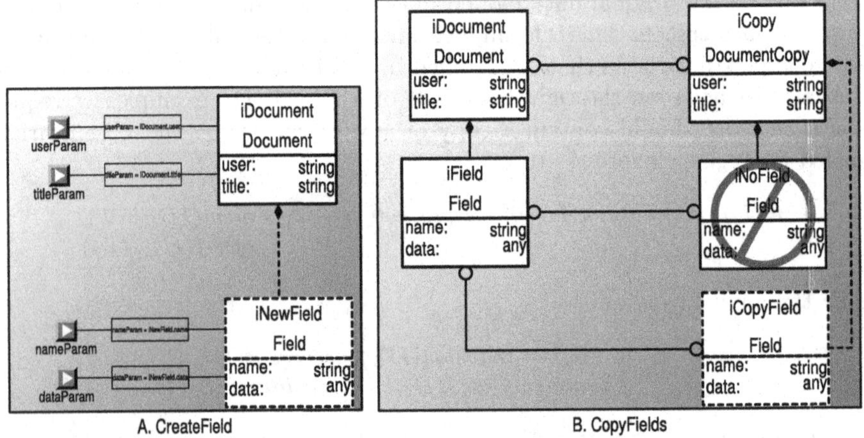

Fig. 3. Two BAM operations used by the document management system

consistent with the original document. Formally, the CopyFields operation has the following axioms in t^+_λ:

$$\begin{aligned} field(new(ID_3), N, D), contains(ID_2, new(ID_3)) \Leftarrow document(ID_1, U, T), \\ documentCopy(ID_2, U, T), field(ID_3, N, D), \\ contains(ID_1, ID_3), \neg copyofField(ID_2, ID_3) \end{aligned} \quad (5)$$

$$\begin{aligned} copyofField(ID_2, ID_3) \Leftarrow documentCopy(ID_2, U, T), field(ID_3, N, D), \\ contains(ID_2, ID_3) \end{aligned} \quad (6)$$

where $new(\cdot)$ creates new identifiers that are not currently in the state s.[1]

3.2 Parameterized Operations

Some operations must take input from the external environment. A user U may wish to create a new document with title T that does not exist in the current state. This issue can be addressed by parameterizing the transformation axioms of λ to create a family of concrete operations. A *parameterized transformation* $\lambda(p_1, p_2, \ldots, p_n)$ has n parameters and is concretized by assigning each $p_i = \sigma_i \in \Sigma$. The concrete transformation is a model transformation formed by replacing every occurrence of p_i with σ_i in the transformation axioms of $\lambda(p_1, \ldots, p_n)$.

The CreateField operation in Figure 3.A illustrates a parameterized operation. This operation has four parameters: p_u, p_t, p_n, p_d. The parameters p_u, p_t are used to find an existing document created by user p_u titled p_t. If such a document is found, then a new field named p_n with data p_d is created within this document. The parameterized axiom for CreateField is as follows:

$$field(new(ID_1), p_n, p_d), contains(ID_1, new(ID_1)) \Leftarrow document(ID_1, p_u, p_t), \quad (7)$$

For example, the operation CreateField(Bob,ExpenseReport,Taxi,50) adds a field to Bob's expense report indicating that he spent 50 dollars on a taxi.

4 Connectivity Model

The data and operation models specify the core functionality of data-centric business applications. The third BAM model, called the *connectivity model*, describes how data an operations interact across logical networks. The formal semantics of BAM uses this information to generalize the satisfaction of data invariants and calculation of state updates over arbitrary network topologies.

Formally, a connectivity model is a triple $G_{conn} = \langle A, F, \rho \rangle$ where A is the set of agent types, $F \subseteq A \times A$ is the information flow between agent types, and $\rho : A \to \mathcal{P}(\Upsilon)$ is a mapping from agent types to function symbols of the data model. The mapping ρ provides an access control mechanism, i.e. agents of type $a \in A$ can only access data of types $\rho(a)$. This access control respects

[1] Formally, $new(\cdot)$ is a state-dependent bijection $new : \Sigma \to \Sigma$ such that for each element σ appearing in s, $new(\sigma)$ is not in s.

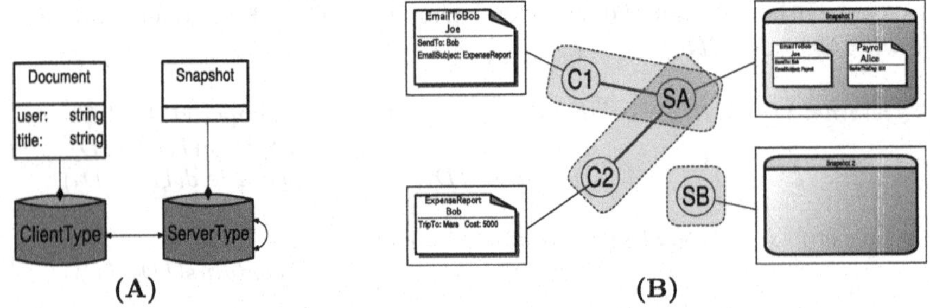

Fig. 4. (A) Connectivity model of document management system (B) Example of a composite state

containment relationships between data: If $f \in \rho(a)$ and occurrences of f can contain occurrences of g then $g \in \rho(a)$.

Figure 4.A shows the connectivity model for the document management system. There are two types of agents: ClientType and ServerType agents. Each agent has some data structures bound to it. For example, only ClientType agents contain Document items, while Snapshot items are only present in ServerType agents. The double-headed edges ($\blacktriangleleft\!\!\longrightarrow\!\!\blacktriangleright$) define which types of agents can communicate with each other, e.g. ClientType and ServerType agents can communicate. Notice that information flow must be explicitly defined, even for flow between agents of the same type. In this example information can pass between ServerType agents, but not ClientType agents. The connectivity model for the document management system is:

$$
\begin{aligned}
&A = \{ClientType, ServerType\},\\
&F = \{(ClientType, ServerType), (ServerType, ServerType), \ldots\}\\
&\rho(ClientType) = \big\{document(\cdot,\cdot,\cdot), field(\cdot,\cdot,\cdot), contains(\cdot,\cdot)\big\}\\
&\rho(ServerType) = \big\{snapshot(\cdot), documentCopy(\cdot,\cdot,\cdot), field(\cdot,\cdot,\cdot), contains(\cdot,\cdot)\big\}
\end{aligned}
$$

4.1 Composite States

Instead of viewing the system behaviors as a sequence of transitions through data states ($s_0 \rightarrow s_1 \rightarrow \ldots$), we can now view the system as transitioning through *composite states* ($\mathcal{C}_0 \rightarrow \mathcal{C}_1 \rightarrow \ldots$), which take into account the distributed state of the network.

Let D be a domain (as given by the data model) and G_{conn} be the connectivity model, then $\mathcal{C}(D, G_{conn})$ is a composite state parameterized by D, G_{conn}.

Definition 1. *A composite state* $\mathcal{C}(D, G_{conn}) = \langle V, E, type, \delta, \Lambda \rangle$ *is a quintuple where:*

1. *(V, E) is a finite undirected graph, where V is the set of agents and E is the information flow between agents. We call this the connectivity state.*
2. *$type : V \rightarrow A$ is a mapping from agents to agent types, denoting the type of each agent.*

3. *$\delta : V \rightarrow \mathcal{P}(\mathcal{T}_\Upsilon(\Sigma))$ is mapping from agents to data states. If $u \in V$ is an agent, then $\delta(u)$ is its local data state. We call δ the global data state.*
4. *Λ is the set of operations available from the current state; it is called the operation state.*

In order for a structure $\mathcal{C}$ to be a valid composite state it must respect the various models that parameterize it. First, the connectivity state must respect the connectivity model G_{conn}. This holds if the logical connectivity between agents respects the information flow:

$$\forall (v, u) \in E, \ (type(v), type(u)) \in F \tag{8}$$

Also, the local data state of each agent must respect the access control of the connectivity model:

$$\forall v \in V, \ \delta(v) \subset \mathcal{T}_{\rho(type(v))}(\Sigma) \tag{9}$$

In other words, the terms of the data state are a subset of a smaller term algebra created over the smaller signature $\rho(type(v))$. Finally, the operations of the *operation state* must defined over the signature Υ and alphabet Σ of the domain D.

Composite states have a preorder $\leq$ with respect to the data contained by the vertices. We say that $\mathcal{C}' \leq \mathcal{C}$ if the states have the same topology, but each vertex in $\mathcal{C}'$ contains the same or less data than the corresponding vertex in $\mathcal{C}$.

Definition 2. *Let $\leq$ be an ordering over composite states where $\mathcal{C}' \leq \mathcal{C}$ if:*

1. *$(V', E') \cong (V, E)$; the graphs are isomorphic as witnessed by π.*
2. *$type(\pi(v)) = type(v)$; the types are preserved between states.*
3. *$\delta(\pi(v)) \subseteq \delta(v)$; vertices in $\mathcal{C}'$ contain the same or less data.*

This ordering over composite states will become important in the latter sections.

4.2 Stability in Composite States

The invariants of the data model must also be extended to composite states. One solution might be to consider invariants over the union of the global data state $\bigcup_{v \in V} \delta(v)$. Figure 4.B shows a composite state for the document management system that illustrates why this approach fails. This state has two ServerAgent nodes SA, SB and two ClientAgent nodes C1, C2. Information flows between SA and C1, as well as between SA and C2. Attached to each vertex v is its data state $\delta(v)$. Consider server SB, which does not contain any copies of documents. If invariants were checked over the union of the data state, then SB would fail the requirement that snapshots contain copies of existing documents. However, no information can flow between the clients C1, C2 and SB; this should alleviate SB from the burden of satisfying this invariant. Information flow naturally induces a relaxation of the invariants. This suggests that invariants should be checked over the data models formed by connected components. However, this assumes a *transitive* flow of information that usually does not hold. For example, the two clients are not connected and will not be able to observe each others documents, even though they are transitively connected through the server.

We propose evaluating invariants over the *maximal cliques* of the connectivity state. These maximal cliques are the maximal subgraphs where information can flow between all agents in the subgraph.[2] A composite state $\mathcal{C}$ is *stable* if the data state formed by each maximal clique is consistent (i.e. satisfies the invariants):

$$\forall m \in \mathbf{maxcliques}(\mathcal{C}),\ \big(\bigcup_{v \in m} \delta(V)\big) \in models(D) \tag{10}$$

Figure 4.B shows the maximal cliques outlined in blue. Under this interpretation SB does not cause the state to be unstable. Mathematically, our maximal clique semantics partitions the network into symmetric subgraphs where information flow is universal within the subgraph. We shall see that this symmetry provides a powerful foundation for reasoning about distributed systems. Returning to Figure 4.B, notice that this state is still unstable because SA does not have a copy of the ExpenseReport document in client C2. (See Figure 2 for a larger view of the snapshot on server SA.) This situation can be rectified by applying an operation that copies new documents from the client to the server. However, this requires generalizing operations over arbitrary topologies, which we describe in the next section.

4.3 Operations over Composite States

Two issues must be addressed when operations are performed over arbitrary topologies. First, how many nodes in the network are involved in an operation? Second, how is distributed data state aggregated to form the input to an operation, and how are the effects of an operation propagated across nodes? To address these issues, we define the notion of an *information extent.*

The information extent of an operation λ, written **iext** λ, describes the data types it must access to operate. In particular, **iext** λ is a multiset of function symbols found in the transformation axioms.[3] The cardinality of a symbol f in **iext** λ determines the lower bound on the number of distinct network nodes that participate in the distributed operation.

For example, the operations of Figure 3 have information extent:

$$\begin{array}{l} \mathbf{iext}\ \mathsf{CreateField} = \{document(\cdot,\cdot,\cdot), field(\cdot,\cdot,\cdot)\} \\ \mathbf{iext}\ \mathsf{CopyFields} = \{document(\cdot,\cdot,\cdot), documentCopy(\cdot,\cdot,\cdot), field(\cdot,\cdot,\cdot)\} \end{array} \tag{11}$$

where each function symbol has cardinality 1.

---

[2] Formally, a clique is a set $m \subseteq V$ such that $\forall v, u \in m,\ (v, u) \in E$. The clique m is maximal if for every $w \in (V - m)$ then $m \cup \{w\}$ is not a clique.

[3] By a multiset, we mean a set X equipped with a function $\# : X \to \mathbb{N}$ assigning a positive non-zero cardinality to each element in X. We write $\#(f, X)$ to denote the cardinality of function symbol f in multiset X. Given two multisets X, Y, then $X \leq Y$ if $\forall f \in X,\ (f \in Y) \wedge (\#(f, X) \leq \#(f, Y))$.

A set of nodes V' in the network also has an information extent, which is the multiset of data types collectively accessible by those nodes. (The notation $\uplus$ denotes multiset union.)

$$\textbf{iext } V' = \biguplus_{v \in V'} \rho(type(v)) \tag{12}$$

A node n can execute operation λ, if there is some "reasonable" set of nodes V' such that $(\textbf{iext } \lambda) \leq (\textbf{iext } V')$. We calculate this set by growing a horizon from the node n out through the network until the information requirements are satisfied. This *information horizon* depends on the node n executing the operation, the operation λ, and the composite state $\mathcal{C}$:

$$\begin{aligned} ihr_0(n, \lambda, \mathcal{C}) &= \begin{cases} \{n\} & \text{if } (\textbf{iext } n) \cap (\textbf{iext } \lambda) \neq \emptyset \\ \emptyset & \text{otherwise} \end{cases} \\ ihr_{i+1}(n, \lambda, \mathcal{C}) &= \left\{ u \in N(ihr_i) \;\middle|\; \exists f \in (\textbf{iext } u) \begin{pmatrix} \#(f, \textbf{iext } ihr_i) < \\ \#(f, \textbf{iext } \lambda) \end{pmatrix} \right\} \\ ihr(n, \lambda, \mathcal{C}) &= ihr_\infty(n, \lambda, \mathcal{C}) \end{aligned}$$

where $N(ihr_i)$ denotes the neighbors of the set ihr_i in the connectivity graph. Effectively, the information horizon ihr is the least k such that $ihr_k = ihr_{k+1}$.

The information horizon has several important properties. First, every node in the information horizon must have access to some of the data types accessed by the operation. This prevents a node from calling operations that are not related to data on that node, effectively extending access control to operations. Second, the information horizon stops growing once all the nodes in the horizon satisfy the requirements of the operation. This limits the effects of the operation to a small horizon beyond n.

Figure 5 illustrates some information horizons generated by certain nodes in a composite state. The horizons in the left of the figure result from clients creating new documents. As one might expect, these operations are localized around the clients and do not involve any other nodes in the network. On the other hand, if a client wishes to reconcile documents with a server by calling the CopyFields operation, then this only involves the client and the server (center of the figure). However, if a server calls CopyFields it effects all the clients in its immediate

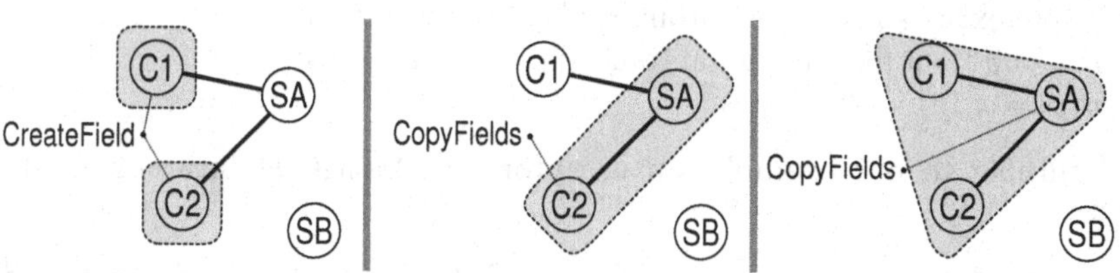

Fig. 5. Information horizons generated by various nodes and operations

horizon (right-hand side of the figure). All of these behaviors fall naturally from our characterization of the information horizon.

Once an information horizon has been determined, the nodes in the horizon must communicate their data state to aggregate data and calculate the result of an operation. Again, it may be both dangerous (from the security perspective) and inefficient (from the implementation perspective) to aggregate all of the data from all the nodes in the entire horizon. Instead, we reuse the approach from the previous section, and apply multiple instances of the operation over the maximal cliques of the information horizon. This limits communication to those nodes that are logically nearby and have explicit information paths. Let $\mathcal{C}[n,\lambda]$ denote the induced subgraph of $ihr(n,\lambda,\mathcal{C})$ and $\mathbf{maxcliques}(G,n) = \{m | m \in \mathbf{maxcliques}(G), n \in m\}$ be the set of all maximal cliques in a graph G containing a vertex n. For a maximal clique m, the aggregate data state formed by the nodes in the clique is $s(m) = \bigcup_{v \in m} \delta(m)$. Thus, an operation yields a set of state updates similar to Equation 4. For each vertex $v \in ihr(n,\lambda,\mathcal{C})$ the local data state changes to $\delta'(v)$ according to:

$$\delta'(v) = \bigcup_{m \in \mathbf{maxcliques}(\mathcal{C}[n,\lambda],v)} \left((\llbracket s(m) \rrbracket^{t^+_\lambda} \cup \delta(v)) - \llbracket s(m) \rrbracket^{t^-_\lambda} \right) \cap \mathcal{T}_{\mathbf{iext}\ v}(\Sigma) \quad (13)$$

This semantics dispatches a copy of λ to each maximal clique. The expression $(\llbracket s(m) \rrbracket^{t^+_\lambda} \cup \delta(v)) - \llbracket s(m) \rrbracket^{t^-_\lambda}$ denotes λ applied to a maximal clique m containing a vertex v. Finally, the results of the operations are projected against the data types that v is allowed to access: $(\ldots) \cap \mathcal{T}_{\mathbf{iext}\ v}(\Sigma)$.

5 Finitization

Distributed systems exhibit global behaviors that emerge from interacting local agents; predicting these global behaviors is key to validating correctness. In this section we show that the unstable states of the system can be understood in terms of a finite set of composite states. Understanding how instability occurs gives a basis for calculating if the operations are sufficient to correct these instabilities.

We introduce the notion of *acceptors* to represent the ways that invariants can be violated. Formally, an *acceptor* $\alpha = (p, n)$ is a pair such that p and n are sets of terms from some term algebra $\mathcal{T}_{\Upsilon}(\Sigma)$. The data state s is accepted by α (written $s \models \alpha$) if:

1. There exists some term automorphism π where $\pi(p) \subseteq s$.
2. If $n \neq \emptyset$ then for all term automorphisms π' it holds: $\pi(p) = \pi'(p) \Rightarrow \pi'(n) \nsubseteq s$

Returning to our example, an acceptor for MissingField invariant is shown below:

$$\begin{aligned} p &= \{document(7,2,3), documentCopy(1,2,3), field(8,9,10), contains(7,8)\} \\ n &= \{field(38,9,10), contains(1,38)\} \end{aligned} \quad (14)$$

The numerical arguments to the function symbols are just placeholder constants. Consider once again the data state s in Figure 2 where there exists a document called EmailToBob containing a field EmailSubject: ExpenseReport. There is a copy of this document, but the copy does not have a field matching this one. Thus, this state is accepted by the MissingField acceptor as witnessed by the following renaming function π:

$$\begin{array}{llll}\pi(1) \mapsto 8, & \pi(2) \mapsto \texttt{Joe}, & \pi(3) \mapsto \texttt{EmailToBob}, & \pi(7) \mapsto 1, \\ \pi(8) \mapsto 4, & \pi(9) \mapsto \texttt{EmailSubject}, & \pi(10) \mapsto \texttt{ExpenseReport} & \end{array} \quad (15)$$

The reader may confirm that $\pi(p) \subset s$ and that there is no renaming function π' that agrees with $\pi(p)$ and has $\pi'(n) \subseteq s$.

The set of acceptors I expresses the invariants as a set of *scenarios*. Each set of positive terms p from any acceptor $\alpha \in I$ describes one scenario of instability. In another words, if we take the data state s to be exactly equal to some p, then this state is unstable. By calculating the set of acceptors I from the invariants, we derive a special set of data states that characterize all the possible forms of instability. If some arbitrary state s' is unstable, then there must be an embedding of some p in s', and the scenarios causing s' to be unstable can be identified. Thus, the acceptors provide a finite description of the unstable data states; we now carry this result over to the more complex composite states. (Note that a term automorphism π (renaming) can be extended to composite states by renaming the data state $\delta(v)$ assigned to each vertex v.)

Composite states complicate analysis because the data state is distributed over the topology, and invariants are relaxed so that they hold over maximal cliques. Our first task is to show that every unstable composite state can be understood in terms of a finite set of scenarios, regardless of the size of the network. We begin by defining a relationship between composite states called a *folding*; this is similar to the familiar *graph homomorphism*:

Definition 3. *Given composite states $\mathcal{C}, \mathcal{C}'$, a folding morphism $\varphi : V \to V'$ assigns vertices of $\mathcal{C}$ to vertices of $\mathcal{C}'$ such that:*

1. *φ is onto.*
2. $\left[(u = w) \vee (u, w) \in E\right] \Leftrightarrow \left[\left(\varphi(u) = \varphi(w)\right) \vee \left(\varphi(u), \varphi(w)\right) \in E'\right]$
3. *φ is type-preserving: $type(u) = type'(\varphi(u))$*
4. *φ is data-preserving: $\delta'(u') = \bigcup_{\{u | u' = \varphi(u)\}} \delta(u)$.*

We say that $\mathcal{C}'$ is a folding of $\mathcal{C}$ if there exists a folding morphism from $\mathcal{C}$ to $\mathcal{C}'$. Foldings can be combined with the preorder $\leq$ to form a more general preorder $\preceq$ over composite states with varying topologies.

Definition 4. *Given composite states $\mathcal{C}', \mathcal{C}$ then $\mathcal{C}' \preceq \mathcal{C}$ if there exists a $\mathcal{C}''$ where $\mathcal{C}''$ is a folding of $\mathcal{C}$ and $\mathcal{C}' \leq \mathcal{C}''$.*

This ordering is essential to characterizing the types of instabilities that can occur.

In the general case invariants are evaluated against cliques, so we now turn our attention to complete graphs:

Lemma 1. *Let K_n be a composite state where the topology is a complete graph of size n. Furthermore, let K_m be any folding of K_n. In this case, $(s(K_n) \models I) \Leftrightarrow (s(K_m) \models I)$.*

This lemma explains that when the network topology of C is a complete graph, then the invariants that hold on C are preserved by folding. It it necessarily the case that any folding of a K_n yields a smaller complete graph of size $m \leq n$. This allows Lemma 1 to be repeatedly applied until no smaller m exists. From the definition of folding morphism, the smallest complete graph that is a folding of K_n must have at least as many vertices as their are types in the composite state K_n. The next lemma shows that this lower bound always exists.

Lemma 2. *Let K_n be a composite state with connectivity that is a complete graph. There exists a folding K_m where m is the number of types in K_n: $m = |\{type(u)|u \in V\}|$. There is no composite state C' with fewer vertices or fewer edges for which C' is a folding of K_n.*

Combining Lemmas 1 and 2 we conclude that if any complete graph fails an invariant (or is accepted by some $\alpha \in I$), then it can be folded into a minimum complete graph that also fails the invariant. Since these minimum complete graphs are determined only by the number of types in the system, they can be finitely enumerated.

Let $\emptyset \subset T \subseteq A$ be a set of agent types, then $K(T)$ denotes the set of all completely connected composite states with exactly one vertex for each type in T. Each $K(T)$ still contains an infinite number of states due to the data states. However, not all of these data states are important from the perspective of invariants. The only interesting composite states are those with aggregated data states $s(K_m) = p$ for some $\alpha \in I$. Let $K(T, s)$ be the set of all composite states K_m in $K(T)$ with aggregated data state $s(K_m) = s$:

Lemma 3. *Given a finite set of acceptors I and a finite set of agent types A, then the set I_K is finite.*

$$I_K = \bigcup_{T \subseteq A} \left\{ C \in K(T, p) \mid \exists (p, n) \in I \right\} \tag{16}$$

This set contains all completely connected composite states that are topologically minimal and have data states from some scenario in I. The number of acceptors $\alpha \in I$ is finite, each p is a finite set of data, and every minimal topology contains

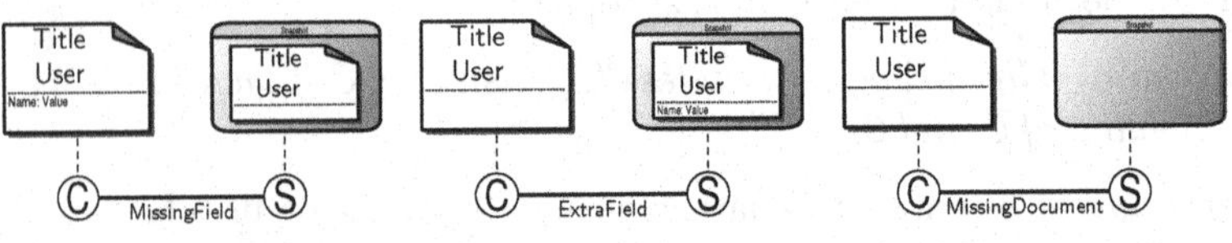

Fig. 6. Key unstable scenarios generated from BAM model of document management system

a finite number of nodes. Putting these together, there are only a finite number of ways that each p can be split across a fixed topology so I_K must contain a finite number of composite states.

In the general case of an arbitrary unstable composite state $\mathcal{C}$ there must be some maximal clique m where the data state $s(m)$ over the clique violates an invariant (Equation 10). This maximal clique is a completely connected composite state K_n and so it has a folding onto some $K_l \in K(T)$ where T is the set of types that appear in the clique. Furthermore, the data state $s(m)$ must embed some p from an acceptor; K_l also embeds this p as folding preserves data. Therefore, there is some scenario $i \in I_K$ and some term automorphism π (i.e. renaming of constants) such that $\pi(i) \preceq m$.

Theorem 1. *If $\mathcal{C}$ is an unstable composite state, then there exists a maximal clique m in $\mathcal{C}$ such that $\pi(i) \preceq m$ for some $i \in I_K$ and some renaming π.*

This result shows that I_K contains the fundamental ways that an arbitrary state can be unstable, and these can be calculated automatically from a BAM model.

Figure 6 shows the key scenarios generated from the BAM model of the document management system. The MissingField scenario occurs when a document has a field not found in its copy. Similarly, the ExtraField scenario occurs when a copy has a field not found in the original document. Finally, the MissingDocument scenario occurs when a snapshot does not have a copy of a document.

6 Related Works

This work uses the techniques of *model-based design* [10], which constructs complex systems through formal domain-specific abstractions and code synthesis techniques. Model-based design has been successfully applied to safety critical embedded systems [11] where behavioral properties must be guaranteed before deployment. Other successful applications of model-based design are security models [12] and patient portals [13].

Two key concepts in model-based design are *meta-modeling* [14] and *model transformations* [15], which create and relate domain specific abstractions. The semantics of model transformations has been extensively studied in the modeling community, where they are formalized as graph rewriting [16] systems, graph grammars [17], and production systems [15]. Like meta-modeling, model transformations are advantageous because they have a compact notation, formal foundation, and tool support. Model transformations are normally used for offline model synthesis; *model-driven architecture* (MDA) [18] and code synthesis [19] are two exemplars.

Modern business applications are now commonly implemented as *service-oriented architectures* (SOAs) deployed over the Web [20]. The composition of the different services has been studied in the context of work-flows, using formal techniques ranging from Petri-Nets [21] to Pi-Calculus [22].

7 Discussion and Conclusion

We presented BAM, a model-based framework for designing data-centric business applications. A system is described with three interrelated models: The data model provides an abstract characterization of the data states in which the system may find itself; high-level invariants added to the data model characterize which data states are problematic. The operation model provides an expressive framework for capturing the basic operations of the business applications. The connectivity model extends operations over arbitrary topologies while preserving the semantics of data access, information flow, and state-update. An analysis of these models yields a finite representation of the unstable states that the system might reach.

In future work, we intend to apply model checking [23] to the scenarios of I_K to determine if the operations are sufficient to correct the instabilities in the system. In fact, model checking derives the sequence of operations that evolve a system to a consistent state, and this can be used for protocol synthesis. The amount of model checking can be reduced by applying folding morphisms to the information horizons of the operations, which also produces a finite characterization of the distinct topologies touched by operations. Our final goals are **(1)** to decide if there exists a sequence of operations to stabilize any unstable system **(2)** to synthesize a protocol (sequence of operations) that stabilizes any unstable system. BAM makes this possible via a unique compositional language for specifying and analyzing this important class of systems. Finally, tools from model-based design make it possible to readily implement BAM.

References

1. Claessens, J., Preneel, B., Vandewalle, J.: A tangled world wide web of security issues. First Monday 7(3) (2002)
2. Barth, A., Datta, A., Mitchell, J.C., Nissenbaum, H.: Privacy and contextual integrity: Framework and applications. In: S&P, pp. 184–198 (2006)
3. Neumann, P.G.: System and network trustworthiness in perspective. In: ACM Conference on Computer and Communications Security, pp. 1–5 (2006)
4. Object Management Group: Mda guide version 1.0.1. Technical report (2003)
5. Fowler, M., Rice, D., Foemmel, M.: Patterns of Enterprise Application Architecture. Addison-Wesley, Reading (2002)
6. Aldred, L., van der Aalst, W.M.P., Dumas, M., ter Hofstede, A.H.M.: Communication abstractions for distributed business processes. In: Krogstie, J., Opdahl, A., Sindre, G. (eds.) CAiSE 2007. LNCS, vol. 4495, pp. 409–423. Springer, Heidelberg (2007)
7. Dantsin, E., Eiter, T., Gottlob, G., Voronkov, A.: Complexity and expressive power of logic programming. ACM Comput. Surv. 33(3), 374–425 (2001)
8. Object Management Group: Unified modeling language: Superstructure version 2.0, 3rd revised submission to omg rfp. Technical report (2003)
9. Jackson, E.K., Sztipanovits, J.: Towards a formal foundation for domain specific modeling languages. In: Proceedings of the Sixth ACM International Conference on Embedded Software (EMSOFT 2006), pp. 53–62 (October 2006)

10. Liu, X., Liu, J., Eker, J., Lee, E.A.: Heterogeneous Modeling and Design of Control Systems. pp. 105–122. IEEE Press and Wiley-Interscience (2003)
11. Berry, G., Kishinevsky, M., Singh, S.: System level design and verification using a synchronous language. In: ICCAD, pp. 433–440 (2003)
12. Jürjens, J., Shabalin, P.: Tools for secure systems development with uml. STTT 9(5–6), 527–544 (2007)
13. Masys, D., Baker, D., Butros, A., Cowles, K.E.: Giving patients access to their medical records via the internet: the pcasso experience. Journal of the American Medical Informatics Association 9(2), 181–191 (2002)
14. Karsai, G., Sztipanovits, J., Ledeczi, A., Bapty, T.: Model-integrated development of embedded software. Proceedings of the IEEE 91, 145–164 (2003)
15. Csertan, G., Huszerl, G., Majzik, I., Pap, Z., Pataricza, A., Varro, D.: Viatra: Visual automated transformations for formal verification and validation of uml models. In: 17th IEEE International Conference on Automated Software Engineering (September 2002)
16. Sprinkle, J., Agrawal, A., Levendovszky, T., Shi, F., Karsai, G.: Domain model translation using graph transformations. In: ECBS, pp. 159–167 (2003)
17. Königs, A., Schürr, A.: Multi-domain integration with mof and extended triple graph grammars. In: Language Engineering for Model-Driven Software Development (2004)
18. Bezivin, J., Gerbé, O.: Towards a precise definition of the omg/mda framework (2001)
19. Neema, S., Kalmar, Z., Shi, F., Vizhanyo, A., Karsai, G.: A visually-specified code generator for simulink/stateflow. In: VL/HCC, pp. 275–277 (2005)
20. Breu, R., Breu, M., Hafner, M., Nowak, A.: Web service engineering - advancing a new software engineering discipline. In: ICWE, pp. 8–18 (2005)
21. van der Aalst, W.M.P.: The Application of Petri Nets to Workflow Management. The Journal of Circuits, Systems and Computers 8, 21–66 (1998)
22. Lucchi, R., Mazzara, M.: A pi-calculus based semantics for ws-bpel. Journal of Logic and Algebraic Programming 70(1), 96–118 (2007)
23. Clarke, E.M., Grumberg, O., Long, D.E.: Model checking and abstraction. In: POPL, pp. 342–354 (1992)

A Composition-Based Approach to the Construction and Dynamic Reconfiguration of Wireless Sensor Network Applications

Dharini Balasubramaniam, Alan Dearle, and Ron Morrison

School of Computer Science, University of St Andrews,
St Andrews KY16 9SX, UK
{dharini,al,ron}@cs.st-andrews.ac.uk

Abstract. Wireless sensor network (WSN) applications are often characterised by close coupling between their software and hardware components, which may result in ad-hoc, platform-specific software, together with the loss of portability and evolvability. We introduce a fractal composition-based approach for constructing and dynamically reconfiguring WSN applications. The approach uses π-calculus semantics to unify the models of interaction for both software and hardware components, on both local and remote nodes. Applications are constructed by forming compositions of interacting components, and can be decomposed and reconfigured into different topologies. The advantages of the approach are that it reduces the complexity of WSN programming; results in portable and evolvable software; and allows changes to be managed during execution without having to take the system off-line. We present an outline of the approach, and illustrate it with an example specified in the Insense language.

Keywords: channel, component, composition, decomposition, dynamic evolution, reconfiguration, and wireless sensor network.

1 Introduction

A wireless sensor network (WSN) [1] consists of a number of typically small and resource constrained devices or nodes, which cooperate to achieve a common goal: customarily the generation, transmission and processing of data pertinent to the application domain. The nodes in a WSN comprise one or more sources that contain sensors to generate the required data, sinks that are the intended recipients of the data and, optionally, routing nodes that pass data from sources to sinks.

WSN applications are often characterised by close coupling between their software and hardware components. For example, the software may need to interact with the hardware in order to generate, receive or transmit data, or operations may need to be synchronised with a hardware clock. Without suitable software abstractions for the hardware components, the software becomes very specialised to the hardware being used. This characteristic, and the availability of limited resources on WSN nodes, have traditionally impacted on the development process, and resulted in ad-hoc, platform-specific software, characterised by a loss of portability and evolvability.

C. Pautasso and É. Tanter (Eds.): SC 2008, LNCS 4954, pp. 206–214, 2008.

We introduce an approach for constructing and dynamically reconfiguring WSN applications, based on fractal composition [2]. The approach uses communication semantics of the π-calculus [3] to unify the models of interaction for software and hardware components, on local and remote nodes. Applications are constructed by forming compositions of interacting components. Uniform models for composition and interaction of components enable applications to be decomposed and reconfigured during execution with minimal disturbance to unaffected parts.

The advantages of our approach are that it reduces the complexity of WSN programming through the use of uniform models for composition and interaction; results in portable and evolvable software; and allows changes in user requirements and operating environment to be managed during execution without having to take the system off-line. We present an outline of the approach, and illustrate it with an example specified in a language called Insense [4] developed for WSN programming.

2 A Sensor Network Example

A farmer wishes to measure average temperatures in different parts of a field. This information can be used, for example, to adjust the conditions under which a crop is grown. A WSN is to be used to obtain the required measurements. The requirements are that temperature sensors are distributed throughout the field, and the data from the sensors, averaged over short intervals, is sent to a sink.

For the purpose of this paper, we will assume that only the software needs to be constructed. Based on the positions for the temperature sensors indicated by the customer, the placement of hardware has been decided as shown in Fig 1.

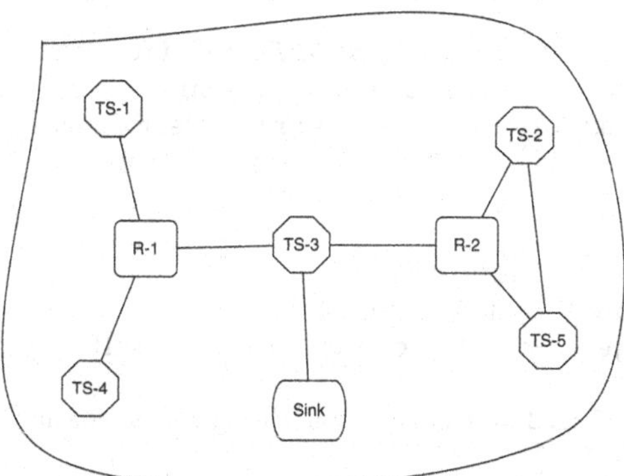

Fig. 1. The Required Placement of Nodes in Field and Possible Interactions among them

The octagonal nodes, TS-1 to TS-5, contain temperature sensors. The radio range of the nodes is such that, while TS-3 is able to communicate directly with the sink, the other sensor nodes cannot. Routing nodes R-1 and R-2 are introduced to solve this problem. They do not support any sensing capabilities but merely forward the data from sensor nodes towards the sink. Thus, TS-1 and TS-4 can route their data via R-1 and TS-3 to the sink. Similarly TS-2 and TS-5 can route their data via R-2 and TS-3.

The following sections of the paper show how a WSN application that executes on this topology may be constructed and evolved.

3 The Insense Language

We provide a brief overview of the Insense language in this section. Components are units of concurrent computation and form the building blocks of Insense applications. They interact with one another by communicating messages via typed channels. The communication semantics are based on the π-calculus. A component may present one or more interfaces, which list the channels available for communication with the component.

An instance of a component is created by invoking a constructor defined by the component. Each instance represents a thread of control and begins execution on creation. Systems are constructed by wiring instances together to enable interaction. The Insense code to wire two component instances is given in Fig 2 below.

```
type TempGaugeIF is interface(   in real input;
                                 in integer ticks;
                                 out real output )
component TempGauge presents TempGaugeIF {
   constructor() {}

   behaviour {
      receive tick from ticks
      receive temp from input
      send temp on output          }
}
type TempAveragerIF is interface( in real input;
                        out real output )
component TempAverager presents TempAveragerIF {
   // definition of TempAverager body
}

gauge = new TempGauge()
averager = new TempAverager()
connect gauge.output to averager.input
```

Fig. 2. Instantiation and Wiring of Components

The interface presented by the *TempGauge* component contains three channels: *input* to receive temperature values, a timer channel *ticks* to regulate the input and *output* to send the received temperature values. The behaviour of a component repeats itself indefinitely until stopped by itself or another component. In this case, the behaviour repeatedly receives a *tick* from *ticks*, receives a *temp* value from the *input* channel, and sends the value on the *output* channel.

TempAverager is a component that calculates the average of temperature values received via the *input* channel and sends it on the *output* channel.

The *new* operator instantiates the named component. In Fig 2, *gauge* and *averager* are instances of components. They begin to execute as soon as they are created. The *connect* statement wires the *output* channel of *gauge* to the *input* channel of *averager* to enable communication which is otherwise blocked. It is the wiring that forms the basis of composition.

4 Fractal Composition

Insense applications are constructed based on a fractal composition model. A component may connect instances of other components to produce a hierarchical composition. These instances may be instantiated within the component, or received by the component either as parameters to a constructor or via a channel. Instances created within a component are not visible outwith its behaviour. Components are self-contained and there is no shared state. Thus connection (wiring) is the sole mechanism for enabling both composition and interaction of components.

One of the novel features of our approach is its support for a uniform model of interaction between all components, namely communication via typed channels. This model applies to software and hardware components, on local and remote nodes. Communication with remote nodes is asynchronous while two software components on the same node communicate synchronously. Hardware components are non-blocking and thus communication with them will always succeed immediately.

In Insense, parts of hardware, such as the sensors on a node, may also be treated as components. Each hardware component exposes pre-defined channels, which are the only means of access to that component. Fig 3 shows how a channel for accessing the values captured by the temperature sensor may be created, and used in composition using the same mechanism as for channels from software components.

```
sensor_output = get_temp_sensor_channel()
connect gauge.input to sensor_output
```

Fig. 3. Wiring Hardware Components

A call to the pre-defined function *get_temp_sensor_channel* returns a channel of type *in real*. A *receive* operation on the channel returns the current value of the temperature sensor. This channel is then connected to the *input* channel of *gauge*.

Once the wiring is complete, the *gauge* can receive temperature readings from the sensor as though it was another software component. The underlying differences in interactions are handled by the language implementation. However, since a temperature value is always available, the *receive* operation will always proceed immediately, retrieving the current value in the sensor. Any synchronisation with other components is based on the *send* operation or added as an extra communication.

This uniform model of communication and composition contributes to both portability and evolvability of WSN applications.

5 Dynamic Evolution in the Compositional Model

Component-based development and uniform models of interaction and composition allow Insense applications to evolve during execution. A composition can be decomposed [5], and components can be added or replaced, and then recomposed again. In this section, we concentrate on changes taking place on the same node.

Evolution of a system may be triggered during execution as a result of changes in user requirements, or feedback from monitoring the system. Insense provides a *disconnect* clause to undo a composition created by the *connect* statement. Disconnecting a channel will remove any bindings made between that channel and any other channels.

We illustrate dynamic reconfiguration using a scenario from the example. We wish to change the behaviour of the averaging component so that it calculates the mode of the values rather than the arithmetic mean. Fig 4 below shows the replacement.

```
component TempModeAverager presents TempAveragerIF {
   //definition of new component body
}
// Instantiate the new averager component
new_averager = new TempModeAverager()
// Disconnect the original wiring
disconnect gauge.output
// Reconnect with the new averager instance
connect gauge.output to new_averager.input
```

Fig. 4. Reconfiguration with the *new_averager* Component

TempModeAverager is defined to calculate the mode of the values. The interface of the component has not changed. An instance of the new component, *new_averager*, is created. The connection between *gauge* and *averager* components is disconnected. After disconnection, these components will continue to execute until they reach their reduction limit, namely a communication via a disconnected channel. The *new_averager* instance is then wired to *gauge*, forming a new composition.

In the case of intra-node reconfiguration being considered in this section, this code must already exist on the relevant node, possibly as part of the main program. It may perform the initial configuration of components, and on receipt of a trigger for change, execute the code in Fig 4 to reconfigure the application.

6 Composition and Reconfiguration across the WSN

In a WSN, components on a node need to communicate with others on different nodes in order to send data from sources or sinks, or to evolve the overall application.

We have determined that the following set of additional facilities are required in order to enable interaction, composition and reconfiguration across a WSN:

- to discover all the top-level instances of components executing on a node;
- to iterate through all the channels in an interface;
- to expose the internal details of a component;
- to discover the application topology by following connections made to channels;
- to treat nodes as components; and,
- to find the set of neighbouring nodes (i.e. those within communication range).

These facilities do not assume a global name space, but rely on discovering software and hardware resources available on a node. Thus, they are mainly introspective.

Returning to our example, we assume the definition of an additional component called *TempRouter* to receive and pass on messages on router nodes. It repeatedly receives a value on the *input* channel and sends it on the *output* channel. Given the topology of the WSN in Fig 1, we would expect an instance each of *TempGauge*, and *TempAverager*, and a *sensor_output* channel to be present on every sensor node, and an instance of *TempRouter* to be available on every routing node as well as TS-3. These instances have to communicate across the nodes to deliver the data from sources to sink. For example, the *averager* on TS-2 must send its data to the *router* on R-2.

Our approach enables the required wiring by treating nodes as components. The channels from components that are available for inter-node communication are published by the application on each node. The set of these published channels on a node implicitly forms the interface for that node. Publication does not affect a channel's ability to communicate internally. Fig 5 below shows how the *input* and *output* channels of an instance of the *TempRouter* component are published.

```
router = new TempRouter()
publish router.input, router.output
```

Fig. 5. A *router* Instance with Published Channels

The next step in establishing communication is to identify the nodes with which interactions should take place. We will assume that the main program on each sensor node is designed to do this. A pre-defined function *getNeighbours* is provided to probe all nodes within communication range and gather their interfaces using an underlying mechanism similar to keep-alive messages. The identities of the nodes are tied to the interfaces returned by them. We introduce the *foreach* construct in Insense to iterate through a collection. Fig 6 shows how TS-2 may identify and bind to R-2.

```
foreach ( iface in getNeighbours() ) {
     project iface as matched onto  {
        TempRouterIF: {
             connect averager.output to matched.input }
        default: {}    }                  }
}
```

Fig. 6. Identification and Connection of a Remote Component

We wish to connect the *output* channel of *averager* on TS-2 to the *input* channel of *router* on R-2. Insense supports an environment type *env*, which is a collection of bindings. Interfaces, components and nodes can be treated as being of type *env* in addition to the results of pre-defined functions such as *getNeighbours*. The *foreach* construct iterates through an environment, with the control variable taking on the value of the next binding with each iteration. Thus, in Fig 6, the *iface* variable represents the interfaces of all neighbouring nodes. When an interface of the required type, *TempRouterIF*, is found, the connection can be made. In the case of TS-2, both R-2 and TS-5 are within communication range. However only the interface of R-2, exposed by its *router* instance, is of the required type. Connections are similarly made between the components on the other nodes to enable data to flow from the sensor nodes to the sink. The Insense interaction model entirely abstracts over the details of the radio, with the language implementation managing these details.

The interface of each node also has a standard channel of the type *in updater*, where type *updater* is defined as *interface(in env globalEnv)*. Each node is designed to receive a component, which, when connected as required, receives an environment with all the global instances of components. The connection is shown in Fig 7.

```
outEnv = new out env
receive updater on update_channel
connect updater.globalEnv to outEnv
send getGlobalEnv() on outEnv
```

Fig. 7. Receiving and Binding an *Updater* Component

The program on the receiving node defines an *outEnv* channel of type *out env*. When the *updater* component is received, it connects the *globalEnv* channel of the *updater* to *outEnv*. The result of a call to the pre-defined *getGlobalEnv* function, which returns an *env* with all the global bindings, is then sent on *outEnv*. Thus, the *updater* component discovers all the global components at the target node. The *updater* component to perform the reconfiguration shown in Fig 4 is defined as:

```
type UpdaterIF is interface( in env globalEnv )
component Updater presents UpdaterIF {
   constructor() {}
   behaviour {
      receive global on globalEnv
      use global with TempAveragerIF averager,
                      new_averager;
                      TempGaugeIF gauge in {
         disconnect gauge.output
         connect new_averager.input to gauge.output  }
      stop   }
}
```

Fig. 8. The Behaviour of an *Updater* Component

The *updater* receives a global environment *global* on its *globalEnv* channel. The *use* clause is used to project a binding of known name and type from an environment. In this case, the behaviour projects the original *averager*, the *new_averager* and the *gauge* instances from the global environment. Once it obtains handles to these values, it can perform the required decomposition and reconfiguration. Since the changes need only be carried out once, the behaviour contains a *stop* statement at the end, which ensures that the behaviour terminates after one iteration.

7 Conclusions, Implementation Status and Future Work

We have introduced a fractal composition-based approach for developing and reconfiguring wireless sensor network applications. Applications are constructed as hierarchical compositions of components. Elimination of implicit dependencies between components, and a uniform model of interaction for all components allow compositions to be decomposed and reconfigured at execution time with minimal disturbance to the rest of the system. The approach is illustrated using an example specified in the Insense language, developed for building WSN applications.

A prototype implementation of the Insense language has been built on top of the Contiki WSN operating system [6], and is being used as the basis for further implementation and evaluation of the compositional approach. The Insense compiler is written in Java and generates C source code.

The current implementation supports the concepts of components, instantiation, composition by connection (wiring), disconnection, and internal reconfiguration.

There are two avenues of further work in this area. The implementation of Insense is to be extended to include support for reflection, mobility of components between nodes, and the reconfiguration of components on remote nodes. We also intend to develop tools to support the compositional approach. For example, a graphical development tool for WSN applications, and an extended compiler to determine the worst-case space and time requirements of Insense programs are planned.

Another important aspect of future work is the evaluation of the approach and the Insense language in improving the portability and evolvability of WSN applications.

Acknowledgments. This work is supported by the EPSRC grant "Design, Implementation and Adaptation of Sensor Networks through Multi-dimensional Co-design" (EP/C014782/1).

References

1. Raghavendra, C.S., Sivalingam, K., Znati, T. (eds.): Wireless Sensor Networks. Kluwer Academic Publishers, Dordrecht (2004)
2. Bruneton, E., Coupaye, T., Stefani, J.B.: The Fractal Component Model. ObjectWeb, `http://fractal.objectweb.org/specification/index.html`
3. Milner, R.: Communicating and Mobile Systems: The π-calculus. Cambridge University Press, Cambridge (1999)

4. Dearle, A.: Insense Tutorial. University of St. Andrews Report, `http://dias.dcs.st-and.ac.uk/inSense/manual.pdf`
5. Warboys, B.C., Balasubramaniam, D., Greenwood, R.M., Kirby, G.N.C., Mayes, K., Morrison, R., Munro, D.S.: Collaboration and Composition: Issues for a Second Generation Process Language. In: Nierstrasz, O., Lemoine, M. (eds.) ESEC 1999 and ESEC-FSE 1999. LNCS, vol. 1687, pp. 75–91. Springer, Heidelberg (1999)
6. Dunkels, A., Gronvall, B., Voigt, T.: Contiki - A Lightweight and Flexible Operating System for Tiny Networked Sensors. In: First IEEE Workshop on Embedded Networked Sensors. Tampa (2004)

A Reflective Framework for Fine-Grained Adaptation of Aspect-Oriented Compositions

Paul Grace*, Bert Lagaisse, Eddy Truyen, and Wouter Joosen

Department of Computer Science, K.U. Leuven, Leuven, Belgium
p.grace@lancaster.ac.uk,
{Bert.Lagaisse,Eddy.Truyen,Wouter.Joosen}@cs.kuleuven.be

Abstract. Dynamic Aspect Oriented Programming (AOP) technologies typically provide coarse-grained mechanisms for adapting aspects that cross-cut a system deployment; i.e. whole aspect modules can be added and removed at runtime. However, in this paper we demonstrate that adaptation of the finer-grained elements of individual aspect modules is required in highly dynamic systems and applications. We present AspectOpenCOM, a principled, reflection-based component framework that provides a meta object protocol capable of fine-grained adaptation of deployed aspects. We then evaluate this solution by eliciting a set of requirements for dynamic fine-grained adaptation from a series of case studies, and illustrate how the framework successfully meets these criteria. We also investigate the performance gains of fine-grained adaptation versus a coarse-grained approach.

1 Introduction

Component frameworks must now support complex compositions of application components, including a broad range of services that deal with non-functional concerns. Aspect-component frameworks e.g. JAC [14], JBoss AOP [7], Spring [16], and Prose [15] have contributed to improving the modularization of such complex applications, by supporting an aspect-component model that offers aspect-oriented composition (AO composition) alongside traditional composition of provided and required interfaces. The core concept in AO composition is the aspect [5]: a first-class citizen that encapsulates one specific (often crosscutting) concern in a separate software module. An aspect defines *behaviour* and *composition logic* describing where and when this behaviour is executed. Aspect-component frameworks often separate aspect behaviour and composition logic, for the purpose of reusing aspect-behaviour across applications. Composition logic is specified declaratively, e.g. in the form of: *whenever event X in the application occurs, execute method behaviour Y of component Z.* For example, whenever a component operation is executed, execute the enforcement method of the authorization component. The search for expressive composition mechanisms is an ongoing track in the research community, yet the composition logic of a real world application remains complex and is subject to runtime changes. Therefore, there are increasing

* While on leave from Lancaster University, UK.

C. Pautasso and É. Tanter (Eds.): SC 2008, LNCS 4954, pp. 215–230, 2008.

requirements to adapt the composition logic at runtime, as exemplified by autonomic, self-repairing and self-optimising systems [8].

A recent advance in aspect-component frameworks is the ability to express dynamic AO compositions that weave and unweave aspects at runtime. For the purpose of this paper, we identify two styles of adaptation of dynamic AO compositions:

- *Coarse-grained adaptation.* An entire aspect (i.e. behaviour and composition logic) is added to or removed from the application.
- *Fine-grained adaptation.* The fine-grained elements that compose an aspect are reconfigured. For example, the composition logic is altered to change where the behaviour is executed. Similarly the aspect behaviour can be adapted.

However, state of the art dynamic AOP frameworks [14,16,15] typically only provide coarse-grained adaptation. In this paper, we present AspectOpenCOM[1] a component framework for fine-grained, runtime adaptation of aspects. AspectOpenCOM is an extension of the OpenCOM reflective component model [2]. A reflective system maintains a representation of itself that is causally connected to the underlying system, and provides a *meta object protocol (MOP)* with a set of methods to introspect and adapt this meta-representation [12]. AspectOpenCOM adds two features to OpenCOM: i) AO compositions, and ii) the *aspect MOP* which provides two key functions to the developer: *aspect introspection*, where the deployed aspects can be enumerated and inspected e.g. in terms of composition logic and behaviour descriptions; and *aspect adaptation*, whereby deployed aspects are adapted in-situ.

We evaluate AspectOpenCOM using a set of requirements elicited from a series of case studies and illustrate how the framework is used to meet these requirements compared against coarse-grained adaptations.We demonstrate that fine-grained adaptation has the following benefits over a coarse-grained approach:

- *Flexibility and robustness of adaptation.* The wider range of introspection and adaptation operations available in the fine-grained method provides more support for informing and performing complex adaptations.
- *Conflict resolution.* A well established problem of dynamic AO compositions is that the behaviour from separate aspects can conflict once deployed [5]. A fine-grained approach can resolve this by adapting behaviour at a location without recomposing multiple system-wide aspects.
- *Performance improvement.* An AO composition can cross-cut a large number of system modules; hence, coarse-grained adaptation can disrupt portions of the system unnecessarily and degrade the adaptation time, whereas targeted fine-grained adaptation only adapts the required elements improving performance.

The remainder of the paper is structured as follows. Section 2 provides a brief background on reflection and dynamic AOP technologies. Section 3 presents

[1] Available for download from `https://sourceforge.net/projects/gridkit/`

the series of case studies that require fine-grained aspect adaptation. Section 4 presents the concepts and implementation of the AspectOpenCOM component framework and the Aspect MOP, which is then evaluated in section 5. Section 6 provides analysis against related work, and finally section 7 draws concluding remarks and identifies areas of future research.

2 Background on AOP and Reflection

A key element in the specification of the aspect composition logic is the concept of a *pointcut* which is a description of a set of join points where aspects execute. *Join points* represent i) dynamic, runtime conditions that arise during program execution or ii) locations in the structure of the program code. The occurrence of such a condition or location can trigger the execution of aspect behaviour. *Advice* specifies what aspect behaviour should be executed and when the aspect behaviour should be executed (typically before, after or around the event) [9].

Pointcuts select join points by declaratively specifying the kind and context of join points. The *kind* of a join point refers to the type of instruction being executed. For example, two different kinds of join points are method call and field access. The *context* of joint points refers to additional information that can be made available to constrain the pointcut such as the method signature, the interface of the component and the component. Which kind of context and which available context that are supported by an aspect component framework, are defined by the framework's *join point model* [4].

Reflection is the capability of a system to reason about itself and act upon this information. For this purpose, a reflective system maintains a representation of itself that is causally connected to the underlying system that it describes [12]. Operations to introspect and make changes to the meta-representation are commonly referred to as the Meta Object Protocol (MOP). In component-based frameworks, two styles of reflection have emerged. Structural reflection is concerned with the underlying structure of objects or components i.e. it is possible to inspect interface information, and adapt software architecture topology. Behavioural reflection is concerned with activity in the underlying system, e.g. in terms of the sending and dispatching of invocations.

3 The Case for Fine-Grained Aspect Adaptation

To motivate fine-grained adaptation of aspects we consider the following reconfiguration rich use case scenario. A banking application has a façade-based architecture as seen in Figure 1; the façade *bankingservice* is a component which is accessed by remote clients; in this layered architecture the façade then interacts with entity components (e.g. *Account* and *BasicBanking*) at greater depths. We now illustrate scenarios involving tracing, security and caching aspects and elicit a set of requirements for fine-grained adaptation.

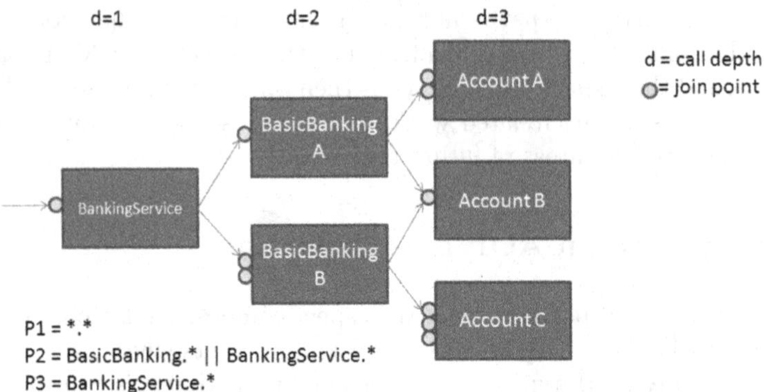

Fig. 1. Join point set adaptation

3.1 Join Point Set Adaptation

This use case illustrates the need for adaptation of the join point set of individual aspects. We show this in two cases: i) enforcing stricter security policy in the banking application, and 2) optimising resource usage while tracing the system.

Security policy enforcement. An authorization aspect is used in the banking application to check the current user's rights; this typically occurs (and must occur) at the façade component: *bankingservice*. However, a more severe enforcement of the authorization policy can apply in the case of suspicious behaviour (e.g. detected and triggered by an intrusion detection system). This dynamic detection of suspicious behaviour can be based on i) malformed incoming messages on the network, ii) a suspicious number of authentication attempts by the user (e.g. 3+), or iii) a suspicious (accumulative) amount in the financial transaction executed by the authenticated user. The more severe enforcement includes executing the authorization advice deeper in the control flow of the incoming messages: e.g. also at the Account and BasicBanking components (by **reconfiguring the join point set**).

Tracing. In the layered set of components as depicted in Figure 1 the application requires that a monitoring aspect applies a set of advices to create a trace of the call flow. Depending upon the load of the system, the call flow depth of the trace is dynamically adapted at runtime: at a high load detailed tracing can impact the system throughput, hence only the called operations on the façade (bankingservice) are traced (using pointcut P3). When the load is lower for the system, a deeper trace is created (e.g. pointcut P2 selects all join points up to a 2-layer depth, pointcut P1 selects all join points up to a depth of 3 layers. Hence, the scenario requires switching at runtime between these 3 pointcuts while maintaining the state of the aspect.

3.2 Aspect Behaviour Adaptation

Here we examine separate use cases that illustrate the need to adapt the advice deployments that form the behaviour of aspects. In the banking application, when the intrusion detection system is triggered an additional audit advice must be applied to all those operations in the control flow of the user's session to construct an irrefutable behavioural audit trail of the session. This trail is typically used as a security measure to detect fraud or tampering a posteriori. This is carried out **by adding a new audit advice to the existing security aspect**.

Alternative to the banking application, consider a traditional client-server system with no initial aspects woven into the system. However, when the mean execution time of client requests deteriorates beyond some predetermined threshold due to network latency, a cache aspect is woven into the system. This aspect intercepts client requests and checks a local cache to see whether the same request has already been issued. Later, when the system must operate in a secure mode, an authentication aspect is dynamically woven into the system; this consists of an advice that denies the client access to the server until they provide correct identification credentials. These two aspects execute at the same join point, and their order is critical for the correct operation of the system. If the cache advice is executed before the authentication advice, clients are able to get access to resources without authenticating themselves first. Hence, in order to determine if there is a conflict it must be possible for a third-party program to **inspect the current state of aspect compositions**; if there is a conflict the same program must **re-order the advices**.

3.3 Requirements

From the bold text in the previous scenarios we elicit four requirements; these must be met to fully support fine-grained adaptation of aspect compositions. We believe that these cover a broad range of requirements across scenarios, although this is not exhaustive and other requirements may emerge from alternative scenarios.

1. Dynamically adapt the pointcut expression to change the join points where an aspect is deployed.
2. Add advices to an already defined set of join points in an existing aspect. Also replace and remove advices.
3. Inspect information about current aspect deployments to provide information to third-party reconfiguration programs.
4. Dynamically reconfigure the order of advices at a join point.

4 The AspectOpenCOM Framework

In this section we discuss the AspectOpenCOM framework for supporting fine-grained aspect adaptation. We first introduce the underlying component and aspect composition mechanisms. Subsequently, we discuss the reflective meta-object protocol that allows third parties to adapt system aspects.

4.1 A Reflective Component Model

An overview of the AspectOpenCOM architecture for composing components and aspects is presented in Figure 2. Notably, reflection is at the core of this architecture, as we believe this technique is the most principled approach to dynamic adaptation; information is available about the current system state to inform both adaptation decisions and the verification of changes. We essentially extend the well-established OpenCOM component kernel [2] to include AO compositions. The key features of the original component composition model are as follows. *Components* are encapsulated units of functionality and deployment that interact with other components exclusively through interfaces and receptacles. *Interfaces* are expressed in terms of sets of operation signatures and associated datatypes. *Receptacles* are "required" interfaces that are used to make explicit the dependencies of a component on other components. *Bindings* are associations between a single interface and a single receptacle. The kernel provides an API to create new components and aspect components and the bindings between them. In Figure 2 there are two components bound by a receptacle and interface, and an aspect component bound to component's interface.

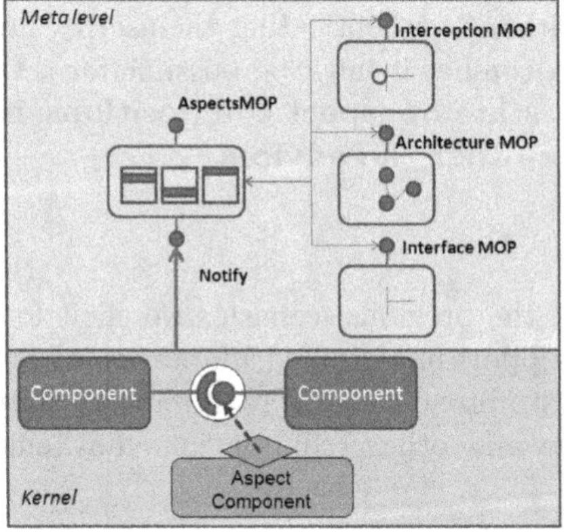

Fig. 2. The AspectOpenCOM Component Kernel Architecture

The kernel also maintains a set of four meta-object protocols each supporting the inspection and adaptation of a distinct system view. Changes made via these MOPs are reflected in the underlying compositions using a causal connection. We will show later how these MOPs can be combined to implement fine-grained aspect adaptation (i.e. we can re-use common reflection behaviour). The MOPs are briefly described as follows; we will examine the aspect MOP solely in this paper; for more information about the other three see [1].

- The *interface MOP* supports inspection of a component's provided and required interfaces. Typically, you can examine the operations available on these interfaces, and or dynamically invoke one of the operations.

- The *architecture MOP* accesses the software architecture of a component represented by a component graph; which is a meta-data description of components and bindings, where a binding maps between a required and provided interface in the same address space.
- The *interception MOP* enables the dynamic insertion of interceptors, which support the insertion of pre-, around and post- behaviour on to interfaces. The interceptors are executed before and after each operation invocation. Hence, the interception MOP provides similar behaviour to traditional aspect compositions, however interceptors are interface specific and do not support the deployment of system wide cross-cutting concerns; hence, it isn't suitable as a full aspect MOP, rather here it forms the underlying weaving mechanism (discussed later).
- The *aspect MOP* supports fine-grained introspection and adaptation of aspect compositions.

4.2 AO Compositions

In AspectOpenCOM, the kind of a join point is a method call on a component interface, either at the caller (on the receptacle) or the called side (on the interface). Table 1 describes the key elements of a pointcut expression that locates the join points; i.e. what kind, and a set of regular expressions to match to elements in the component graph. Further, advice behaviour is encapsulated in *aspect components*. Table 2 describes the elements of a created advice i.e. how it is executed (either before, after or around the original method call), and where that operation is hosted on an aspect component.

The runtime composition of aspects differs from a standard component to component binding (which is a direct reference from a receptacle to an interface). This binding infrastructure is illustrated in Figure 3. Each interface (execution join

Table 1. Elements of an AspectOpenCOM pointcut expression

Field	Description
PointcutType	Where applied: Call (receptacle) or Execution (Interface)
ComponentExpression	Regular expression for matching against component types
InterfaceExpression	Regular expression for matching against interface types
MethodExpression	Regular expression for matching against method signatures

Table 2. Elements of an AspectOpenCOM advice

Field	Description
AdviceRole	Before, After or Around advice
InstantiationScope	Singleton component per address space, per aspect, etc.
ComponentType	Type of advice component
Interface	Interface declaring advice operations
Method	Advice operation name

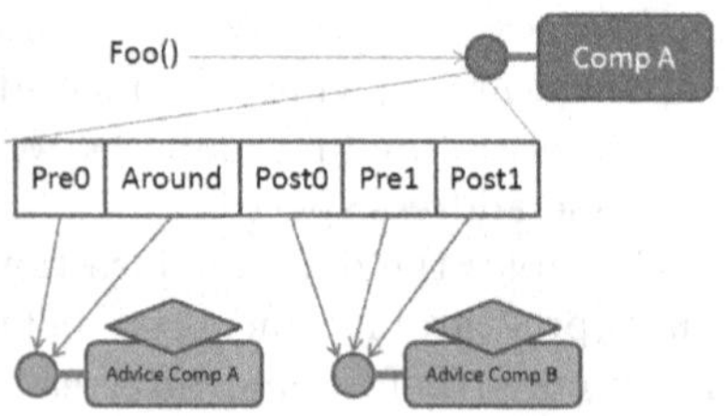

Fig. 3. Proxy-based advice execution chain

point) and receptacle (call join point) has a proxy that redirects the original call through a chain of advices. The call towards the original operation invokes pre and around advices in the order encountered (by redirecting to the corresponding advice component), ignoring post operations. After the call, the post and around advices are executed in the order encountered. Hence, in Figure 3 the order is: Pre0, Around (part before proceed), Pre1, Foo, Post1, Post0, Around (part after proceed).

4.3 Aspect Meta-Object Protocol

There are three parts to the aspect meta object protocol of AspectOpenCOM: i) the meta-representation of the deployed aspects, ii) the set of operations that act upon the meta-representation, and iii) the causal connection that ensures consistency between the base and meta-level.

The meta representation is illustrated in Figure 4; essentially the aspect MOP maintains two related data sets: one containing Aspect descriptions and one containing join point descriptions (i.e. locations in the component graph); these are related where an aspect is deployed at 0 or more join points, and a join point can have 0 or more aspects. The Aspect type is the description of the pointcut (described in table 1) related to a set of advices (whose attributes e.g. AdviceRole are discussed in table 2).

The **reflection operations** are also documented in Figure 4. The introspection operations are as follows. The *getAspectInfo* method returns the meta-data about a current aspect deployment; *enumerateAspects* lists all currently deployed aspects; *enumAdvices* lists the advices at either an individual join point or for a deployed aspect; *enumPoints* describes all the join points where an aspect is currently active at; finally, *AspectIntersect* takes two aspect deployments and calculates the set of join points where they are both active.

The dynamic adaptation operations are as follows. The *replacePointcut* method allows the developer to pass a new pointcut expression and the existing aspect behaviour will be moved from the prior join point set to the new join point set. Further, *addAdvice* adds new advice code to either an aspect composition or to an individual join point (*removeAdvice* the opposite); finally, *reorderAdvices* takes the new advice order for a join point location and adapts the behaviour accordingly. We also include coarse-grained adaptation with the

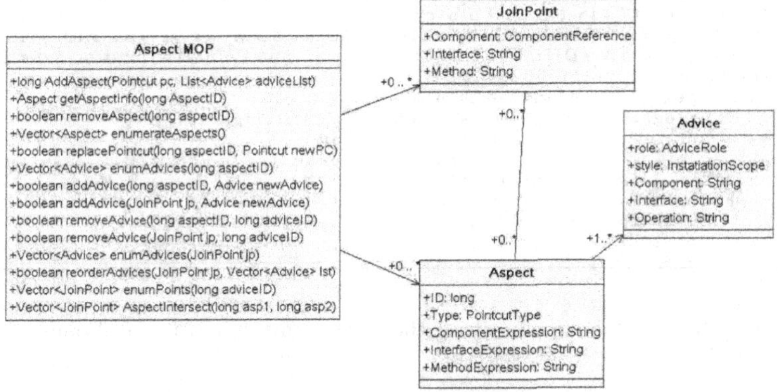

Fig. 4. The Aspect MOP

addAspect operation; this composes a new aspect into the running system and *removeAspect* removes it.

The **causal connection** is the key element of the aspect MOP implementation. Figure 2 illustrates this architecture. The Notify interface relationship between the kernel and the component implementing the MOP is a one-way notification mechanism that informs the meta-level of all base-level operations i.e. new component creations (including advice components), new binding compositions, component removals, etc. The MOP component then updates its meta-data to reflect the base level changes. It also ensures that Aspects are correctly applied, for example when new components are introduced whose join points match the composition logic of already deployed aspects then the meta-level automatically deploys these aspects to the newly introduced join points.

To perform the previously described introspection and adaptation operations, the aspect MOP interacts with the three additional reflective MOPs described earlier. For example, advice components can be created using the architectural MOP, composition of advices into the join point proxy chain is performed using the interception MOP, and join points can be discovered by introspecting the architecture, and interface MOPs. For brevity, we do not provide a complete description of how all fine-grained operations are performed; instead we examine the *replacePointcut* operation.

The pseudocode in Figure 5 illustrates the implementation of a reconfiguration of an aspect's pointcut description at runtime. The deployed aspect and new pointcut logic are passed as parameters to the *replacePointcut* meta operation. First the intersection of the two pointcuts is calculated to discover which join points will remain the same. Second, the difference between the original aspect's join point set and the intersection is calculated, and all of the aspect's advices are removed from these join points (n.b. the interception MOP is utilised for this behaviour). Finally, the intersection and new pointcut's join points is evaluated and all the aspect's advices are composed to this set.

```
ReplacePointcut(Aspect A, Pointcut B)
  List<Joinpoint> isect = AspectIntersect(A, new Aspect(B, null));
  List<Joinpoint> rDiff = JPSetDifference(enumPoints(A.pcut), isect);
    Foreach Joinpoint jp in rDiff
      Foreach Advice adv in A.adviceList
        Delegator del = InterceptionMOP.getDelegator(jp);
        del.removeOperation(adv.operation);
    List<Joinpoint> aDiff = JPSetDifference (enumPoints(B), intersect);
    Foreach Joinpoint jp in aDiff
      Foreach Advice adv in A.adviceList
        Delegator del = InterceptionMOP.getDelegator(jp);
        del.addOperation(adv.operation);
```

Fig. 5. Pseudocode describing the implementation of replacePointcut

5 The Benefits of Fine-Grained Adaptation

5.1 Meeting the Requirements of Fine-Grained Adaptation

We examine how AspectOpenCOM meets the requirements described in section 3 and show that the framework provides a robust, flexible method to better support the developer perform complex adaptations; we also compare this against implementations of the same adaptation behaviour using traditional coarse-grained weaving and unweaving of complete aspect modules. Further, we show how problems such as conflicting aspect deployments can be overcome in a fine-grained manner.

Requirement 1: Dynamically adapt the pointcut expression to change join points where an aspect is deployed. Figure 6 illustrates the simple 2 lines of code for performing the reconfiguration from pointcut P1 to P2 as illustrated in Figure 1; first the new pointcut description is defined (this is an execution type applied to interface join points, the second parameter is the component expression i.e. all *BasicBanking* and *BankingService* components, the final two parameters indicate any interface and method on these components. Subsequently, the *replacePointcut* operation is called. This is comparable to a coarse-grained approach where the entire aspect must first be removed, a new aspect module must be created, then this must be dynamically woven as the replacement. This performs unnecessary adaptation at join points whose behaviour does not change, and is more complex to manage due to multiple instances of the same aspect.

```
 Pointcut expr = new Pointcut(PointcutType.EXECUTION,
     "BasicBanking*||BankingService*", "*", "*");
aspectMOP.replacePointcut(traceAspect, expr);
```

Fig. 6. Java code for performing join point set adaptation

Requirement 2: Add advices to an already defined set of join points in an existing aspect. Figure 7 shows the code to create a new meta data description of the audit advice (described in the use case scenario) and then add this to the security aspect using the addAdvice MOP operation. Hence, the *auditOperation* hosted on the *IAudit* interface of the singleton *AuditComponen* is applied before execution of the operation. Note, if the advice component (*AuditComponent*) already exists it will be re-used, otherwise it will be created during the meta operation. As with the previous requirement, coarse-grained adaptation can mimic this behaviour by removing the complete existing aspect and replacing it with a new aspect that contains the additional advice. However, if multiple advices are deployed per aspect these will be unnecessarily adapted.

```
Advice audit = new Advice(AdviceRole.BEFORE, InstantiationScope.SINGLE,
     "AuditComponent", "IAudit","auditOperation");
aspectMOP.addAdvice(securityAspect, audit);
```

Fig. 7. Java code for adding an advice dynamically

Requirement 3: Inspect information about current aspect deployments to inform decisions. There are 5 introspection operations that allow the developer to fully discover the state of aspect configurations. Figure 8 shows how the *aspect-Intersect* operation is used to find where two conflicting aspects are deployed (in this case two aspects, one role-based access control the other credential based) and then deploy an advice at each resulting join point location using *addAdvice* to resolve this conflict (the resolve advice ensures authentic users are not denied by the conflicting access control method). Coarse-grained technologies typically provide only limited introspection capabilities that reflect the coarse-grained modules deployed, and as such do not support this behaviour.

```
Advice resolve = new Advice(AdviceRole.BEFORE, AdviceStyle.SINGLETON,
     "Resolver", "IResolve", "resolve");
Vector<JoinPoint> lstJP = aspectMOP.aspectIntersect(Role, Credential);
for(int i=0; i<lstJP.size();i++){
  aspectMOP.addAdvice(lstJP.get(i), resolve);
}
```

Fig. 8. Java code introspecting aspect behaviour

Requirement 4: Dynamically reconfigure the order of advices at a join point. Figure 9 illustrates how the security and cache conflict in section 3.2 can be resolved (note we assume only 2 aspects are deployed in this code). First we find the join point set of the security aspect, and calculate if the advices deployed here are in conflict; if so they are re-ordered. Coarse-grained adaptations do not have the fine-grained knowledge to re-order advices, one alternative is to remove all aspects and then add them in the correct order; again, this will perform unnecessary addition and removals of system elements.

```
Vector<JoinPoint> lstJP = aspectMOP.enumPoints(securityAspect);
Vector<Advice> correctOrder = new Vector<Advice>({security, cache});
for(int i=0; i<lstJP.size(); i++){
  Vector<Advice> adList = aspectMOP.enumAdvices(lstJP.get(i));
  If (after(security, cache, adList))
    aspectMOP.reorderAdvices(lstJP.get(i), correctOrder);
}
```

Fig. 9. Java code for reordering advices at a join point

5.2 Analysis of Fine-Grained Versus Coarse-Grained Adaptation

This demonstrates the flexibility of the AspectOpenCOM framework to robustly support a wide range of complex fine-grained adaptation requirements. We summarise in table 3 the differences in how the four requirements can be met using both fine and coarse-grained approaches. It can be seen that fine-grained fully meets all the requirements, and where both offer support fine-grained does so without performing unnecessary adaptations. Coarse-grained approaches partially meet the first two requirements, in that complete module adaptation mimics the behaviour, however, this performs unnecessary adaptation, has the potential to lose state (when advices are removed) and increases the time taken to perform reconfiguration. We illustrate these issues further in the next section.

Table 3. Meeting the adaptation requirements

Requirement	fine-grained	coarse-grained
1 join point set adaptation	YES	PARTIAL
2 aspect behaviour adaptation	YES	PARTIAL
3 deployment introspection	YES	NO
4 advice re-ordering	YES	NO

5.3 Investigating Performance Gains

We now investigate the performance benefits of fine-grained adaptation versus coarse-grained adaptation in terms of changing the join point set. For this we created an experimental application with a set of components and pointcuts as illustrated in Figure 10(a). Here there are two component types (A and B) with a set of 10 join points on each. P1 is the initial pointcut that activates all join points on component A (illustrated by the filled circles); we then reconfigure to poincut P2, which matches all methods starting with "b" on both components. Hence, we have a join point set size of 10 in both cases, where 5 join points remain the same and 5 new ones are activated (i.e. 50 % remains unchanged). In subsequent experiments, we change the percentage of join points that stay the same by increasing the "b" join points on component A and reducing them on B (90% = 9 on A and 1 on B, 20% = 2 on A and 8 on B etc.,). Finally, to test scalability we increase the join point set size from 10 upwards by deploying more instances of components A and B (e.g. 10 of A and 10 of B equals a join point

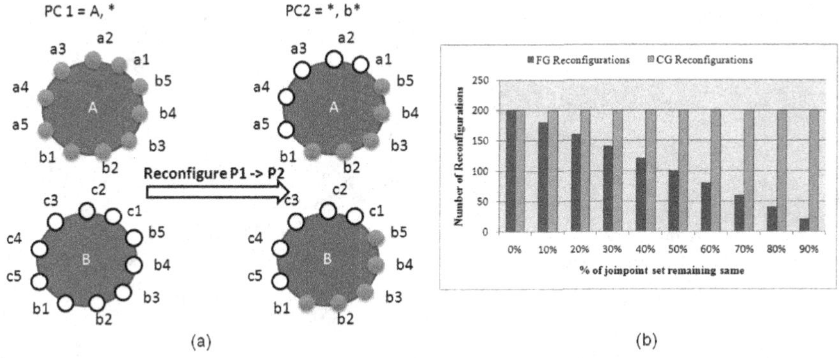

Fig. 10. (a) The application adaptation, (b) Unnecessary reconfigurations in coarse-grained adaptations

set size of 100). All experiments were executed in a single instance of a Java 1.5.0.10 virtual machine on a laptop with a 1.7 GHz Pentium 4 processor, 512 Mbyte of RAM and running Windows XP. For fine-grained adaptations (FG) we utilise the *replacePoincut* operation, for the coarse-grained approach (CG) we use the *removeAspect* followed by *addAspect* operations.

The first experiment illustrates the number of unnecessary reconfigurations undertaken by a coarse-grained approach. We created the application as described above with a join point set size of 100 and then traced the number of reconfigurations in terms of removing and adding advice behaviour. We did this for pointcut transformations between 0% of the set staying the same through to 90% of the set remaining unchanged. The results in Figure 10(b) indicate that in the worst case, where there are minimal changes to the join points, many unecessary adaptations are performed e.g. 180 at 90%.

Our second experiment illustrates the effect this has on the performance of the system in terms of the time taken to perform reconfigurations. For this, we timed the transformations from P1 to P2 for coarse-grained, and fine-grained with 0%, 30%, 60% and 90% of the join point remaining unchanged. Each of these five styles was measured with increasing join point set sizes from 10 up to 5000. Note, to discount anomolous results each measure was repeated 5 times with the median value being taken. Figure 11 illustrates the performance gains of the fine-grained approach. It can be first seen in Figure 11(a) that as the percentage of the join point set that stays unchanged increases then the adaptation takes considerably less time. Note, for 0% unchanged (which is equivalent to coarse-grained adaptation) the measurements are similar to the CG timings; this shows that the overhead of fine-grained reflection (e.g. calculating the changes) is not prohibitive even when all the join points must be changed. To demonstrate this further, Figure 11(b) shows the percentage performance increases of FG compared to the equivalent CG adaptation with much larger applications sizes; this illustrates the improvement is related to the change in the join point set (less

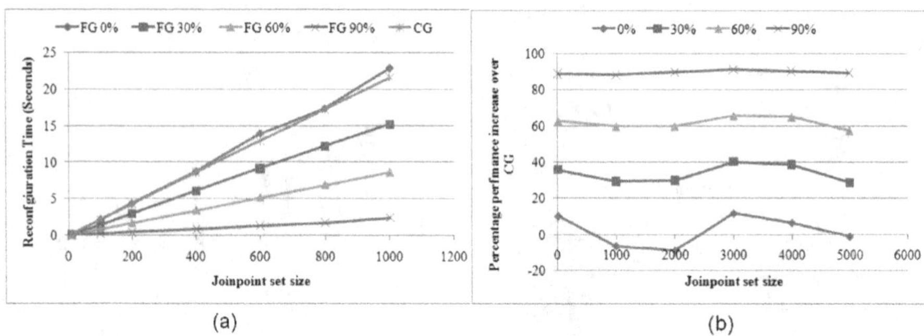

Fig. 11. Comparison of the performance of fine-grained and course-grained adaption (a) Time to Adapt, (b) % performance increase of FG over CG

change implies bigger performance gains), and that this effect is maintained as the system scales.

To conclude, we can see that the performance of adaptation is related to the number of unnecessary adaptations performed in a coarse-grained approach. Where elements of a join point set remain unchanged significant performance benefits can be realised using fine-grained adaptation.

6 Related Work

A number of dynamic AOP technologies have been developed; these typically vary in how aspects are weaved (e.g. efficient bytecode rewriting, dynamic proxies, etc.), when aspects are weaved (i.e. load-time or run-time), and where aspects are weaved (i.e. internal or external to the component module). JBoss dynamic AOP [7] weaves interceptor-based advices (i.e it relies on Java dynamic proxies) to Java-based components within an application server; notably, the component join points must be pre-prepared at compile-time for aspects to be applied at run-time, hence it may not be able to facilitate all unanticipated adaptations. Prose [15] uses JIT compiling techniques to weave advice implementation dynamically at join points of plain Java objects. The JAC framework [14] composes aspect-components to core Java-based components at run-time using byte-code rewriting; the framework also provides a set of reusable aspects, namely persistence, caching. Each of these technologies typically focus on coarse-grained composition of aspects. ByteSurgeon [3] is a bytecode manipulation framework supporting fine-grained computational reflection at runtime (as opposed to load-time), and offers an alternative implementation approach for our Aspect MOP.

However, some dynamic AOP solutions provide features for finer-grained adaptation as discussed in this paper; for example, PROSE contains operations to inspect some elements of the aspect composition, and also adapt advice behaviour. Similarly, JAC and JBoss can manipulate the advices deployed at join points. However, these have been added to the technologies via ad-hoc extensions, no solution currently provides a principled adaptation interface (cf reflection) with a complete set of fine-grained operations as advocated in this paper. Furthermore, none of these technologies supports join point set adaptations. In this respect, morphing aspects [6] is the closest to this concept; the join point shadow is morphed to apply only where required (reducing unnecessary checks to see if the aspect applies at the join point at a certain point in time). Our approach differs in that the morphing aspects are created at design time, and hence are not subject to third-party adaptations as available in a reflective approach.

Finally, the highly related nature of reflection and aspects (they are both meta-level technologies) means they are commonly combined. The Reflex AOP kernel [17] is a notable example of this; a partial reflection approach is developed that allows the meta-level to be tailored to particular requirements, in turn reducing the complexity of meta programming, and reducing resource usage; the kernel then utilises partial reflection for versatility, for example underpinning aspects from multiple languages. Alternatively, Kojarski et al. [10] explore the two-way relationship between aspects and reflection; they argue that AOP is another computational reflection mechanism, where a join point model reflects the program's behaviour and the advice provides the intercession capability. Further, they identify that AOP can be implemented atop reflection; pointcut descriptions rely on introspection information from structural MOPs, and advices rely on behavioural MOPs. Notably, they also identify that reflection can be implemented atop aspects i.e. using aspects to generate data provided by Java reflection (e.g. field introspection). Our approach differs from these related frameworks, in that we introduce an Aspect MOP with a richer set of fine-grained operations to support principled third-party adaptation of aspect compositions at run-time.

7 Concluding Remarks and Future Work

In this paper we have illustrated the need for fine-grained adaptation of aspect compositions. We have demonstrated scenarios where fine-grained adaptations are needed, and shown that significant performance gains can be attained compared against a coarse-grained approach. The AspectOpenCOM MOP was presented as a solution to meet the requirements for fine-grained adaptation, providing key operations to inspect all elements of aspects and adapt them e.g. changing the join point set, re-ordering advices and others. Notably, we advocated reflection as a key technology in underpinning the adaptation of deployed aspects.

In future work we plan to investigate the wider application of this technology. Distributed aspects are more likely to be affected by coarse-grained adaptations; this is because reconfigurations times are longer due to safety, security and verification mechanisms typically involving the shutting down (placing in a safe state) of remote components. Hence, unnecessary adaptations must be avoided. For this purpose, we will examine how to introduce fine-grained adaptations into distributed aspect composition technologies such as DyMAC [11] and AWED [13].

References

1. Blair, G., Coulson, G., et al.: The design and implementation of Open ORB 2. IEEE Distributed Systems Online 2(6) (September 2001)
2. Coulson, G., Blair, G., Grace, P., Joolia, A., Lee, K., Ueyama, J.: A component model for building systems software. In: IASTED Conference on Software Engineering and Applications (SEA 2004), Cambridge, MA, USA (November 2004)
3. Denker, M., Ducasse, S., Tanter, E.: Runtime Bytecode Transformation for Smalltalk. Journal of Computer Languages, Systems and Structures 32(2-3), 125–139 (2006)
4. Filman, R., Elrad, T., Clarke, S., Aksit, M.: Aspect-Oriented Software Development. Addison-Wesley, Reading (2004)
5. Greenwood, P., Blair, L.: Policies for an AOP based auto-adaptive framework. In: Proceedings of the NetObjectDays Conference, Erfurt, Germany (September 2005)
6. Hanenberg, S., Hirschfeld, R., Unland, R.: Morphing aspects: incompletely woven aspects and continuous weaving. In: AOSD 2004: Proceedings of the 3rd International Conference on Aspect-Oriented Software Development, pp. 46–55. ACM, New York, USA (2004)
7. JBoss. Jboss AOP. (last checked, October 2007), `http://labs.jboss.com/jbossaop`
8. Kephart, J.O., Chess, D.M.: The vision of autonomic computing. Computer 36(1), 41–50 (2003)
9. Kiczales, G., Hilsdale, E., Hugunin, J., Kersten, M., Palm, J., Griswold, W.: An overview of aspectj. In: Knudsen, J.L. (ed.) ECOOP 2001. LNCS, vol. 2072, pp. 327–353. Springer, Heidelberg (2001)
10. Kojarski, S., Lieberherr, K., Lorenz, D., Hirschfeld, R.: Aspectual reflection. In: AOSD 2003 Workshop on Software-engineering Properties of Languages for Aspect Technologies (2003)
11. Lagaisse, B., Joosen, W.: True and transparent distributed composition of aspect-components. In: Middleware 2006, pp. 42–61 (November 2006)
12. Maes, P.: Concepts and experiments in computational reflection. In: OOPSLA 1987: Conference proceedings on Object-oriented programming systems, languages and applications, Orlando, Florida, United States, pp. 147–155. ACM Press, New York (1987)
13. Navarro, L.B., Sudholt, M., Vanderperren, W., De Fraine, B., Suvée, D.: Explicitly distributed AOP using AWED. In: AOSD 2006: Proceedings of the 5th International Conference on Aspect-Oriented Software Development, pp. 51–62. ACM Press, New York, USA (2006)
14. Pawlak, R., Seinturier, L., Duchien, L., Florin, G., Legond-Aubry, F., Martelli, L.: JAC: an aspect-based distributed dynamic framework. Software Practice and Experience 34(12), 1119–1148 (2004)
15. Popovici, A., Gross, T., Alonso, G.: Dynamic weaving for aspect oriented programming. In: Proceedings of the 1st International Conference on Aspect-Oriented Software Development, pp. 141–147, Enschede, The Netherlands, April 2002 (2002)
16. SpringSource. Spring framework (last checked October 2007), `http://www.springframework.org`
17. Tanter, E.: From Metaobject Protocols to Versatile Kernels for Aspect-Oriented Programming. PhD thesis, University of Nantes and University of Chile (November 2004)

Composing Safely — A Type System for Aspects

Florian Kammüller and Henry Sudhof*

Technische Universität Berlin
Insititut für Softwaretechnik und Theoretische Informatik

Abstract. In this paper we present an approach towards safe software composition based on aspect-orientation. Aspects enable the systematic addition of code into existing programs but often they also introduce errors. In order to provide safe aspects for software composition we address the verification of the aspect-oriented language paradigm. We construct a basic calculus for aspects with types and prove formally type safety. More precisely, this paper presents the following contributions (a) a fully formalized type system for the Theory of Objects including the proof of type safety, (b) a theory of aspects based on the Theory of Objects including a type system for aspects, and (c) the definition of a notion of type safety for aspects including its proof. The entire theory and proofs are carried out in the theorem prover Isabelle/HOL.

1 Introduction

Aspect-orientation has enjoyed major attention for years and is supported by many major programming languages. There are, however, serious problems in the current implementations of aspect-oriented languages. In [13] we show how the lack of typing produces unforeseen runtime-errors. Jagadeesan et al. have more recently shown [11] that there are even contradictions in other seemingly simple situations. The described problem arises when using conform redefinition of functions in the base code, which causes a covariance issue at runtime.

But, even without considering inheritance, crashes can be produced. For instance, the predominant aspect-oriented language AspectJ still relies on partially untyped expressions, resulting in runtime failure. The program depicted in Figure 1 will compile without issue, but crash with a runtime error. This is obviously conflicting with the expected behaviour of well-typed programs. In fact, here, aspects are not typed at all. This essentially removes the ability to view aspects as compositional modules, as the aspect breaks the base code without any static hint that it might do so.

Automated formal analysis with proof assistants provides a strong support for the analysis of safety properties of programming languages [12]. Our approach to support the verification of systems consists of providing a fully formalized basis for aspect-oriented programming in Isabelle/HOL [10]. We construct a core calculus of objects and aspects with types in an object–oriented setting as an instance of the generic theorem prover Isabelle/HOL. The resulting framework serves to experiment with language features – like weaving functionality and pointcut

* This work was supported by the DFG project Ascot (grant Ja 379/18-1).

C. Pautasso and É. Tanter (Eds.): SC 2008, LNCS 4954, pp. 231–247, 2008.

```
public class Test {
  public Test test() {
    return this;
  }
}
```

```
public aspect asp {
  Object around() : call(* *.test(..)) {
    return "oops";
  }
}
```

Fig. 1. This code compiles using the current AspectJ compiler. It terminates with a `ClassCastException` whenever `test` is called.

selectors – and properties – like type safety and compositionality. At the same time, these experiments are on a firm basis. The results have mathematical precision and are mechanically verified. Moreover, we try to keep the formal model of the aspect calculus as constructive as possible. Thereby, we can extract executable protoypes for evaluators and type checkers from the Isabelle/HOL framework.

The basic idea of our calculus of aspects is similar to the theory of aspects [14] but we start from the Theory of Objects, unlike the former that is based on the λ-calculus. These models of aspects simply introduce labels in the base program. The labels represent so-called join-points, i.e. points at which advice might be woven in.[1] Given these labels, we can quite naturally define weaving. The idea is that advice is given as a function f that can be applied to a labelled term $l\langle t\rangle$, replacing the original term t bf $f(t)$. So, given an aspect as a pair $\langle L.f\rangle$ of pointcuts L and an advice f that shall be applied at all points specified by L, weaving can be simply constructed using function application, as illustrated in the following example, where weaving is represented as an infix downwards arrow $\Downarrow$ and functions and application using λ-calculus.

$$\langle L.\lambda\ x.\ e\rangle \Downarrow (v_1 + l_1\langle v_2\rangle) \stackrel{l_1 \in L}{\longrightarrow} v_1 + e[v_2/x]$$

Moreover, we can now attach types to join-points by typing labels. Then, a failure like the one illustrated in Figure 1 would be detected at compile-time.

A major difficulty for the definition of a simple and precise calculus for aspect-orientation is *obliviousness* — one of the major criteria of aspect-oriented programming languages according to the widely accepted definition of Filman and Friedman [8]. Obliviousness means that a programmer can adapt a base program by aspects while being oblivious of the exact details of this base program. This serves to guarantee maximal freedom and flexibility of adaptation. At first sight, our concept of placing labels from start into a base program seems to clash with this idea. There are several answers to this. In our view, even though complete obliviousness might seem an appealing idea, it cannot be achieved. At least, the programmer has to be aware that there are points in a program where it is already syntactically impossible to add an advice, for example, in the middle of a keyword. Conceptually, we consider our aspect labels as the set of all syntactically possible

[1] Representing pointcuts as sets of labels corresponds to the intuition that mathematically a predicate is equivalent to the set of all elements fulfilling that predicate. Thus the pointcut-selector predicate may as well be denoted by the set of all points that fulfill the predicate.

join-points of a program. That is, all possible points where an advice might be woven into the base program are marked by a label. Using this global assumption, we lose no generality. Ligatti et al. [14] take a different line of argument to justify labels. They construct a core calculus that serves as the target code for a high-level aspect-oriented language. This high-level language is oblivious while the core calculus is not. However, type preserving compilation between the two yields property preservation. De Moore et al. produce yet another justification of the label concept [3] by showing through practical solution that pointcut descriptors may be statically resolved into labels. Hence, they practically show that labels do not interfere with obliviousness.

The remainder of the paper is organized as follows. We begin in Section 3 with a short presentation of the Theory of Objects and its formalization in Isabelle/HOL [18]. Section 4 is dedicated to the type system and proof of type safety for the ς-calculus. In Section 5 we introduce our extension of this base calculus to a calculus for aspects introducing weaving functionality and a type system for aspects. We present the definition and proof of type safety for aspects. Finally, we conclude with a comparison to other approaches and an outlook to future work in Section 6. Before we start delving into the technical presentation we use Section 2 to provide a proper introduction to the relevant features of the theorem prover Isabelle/HOL, a brief introduction to the ς-calculus, and some basic techniques we had to provide for our aspect theory.

2 Preliminaries

2.1 Isabelle/HOL

Isabelle [15] is an interactive ML-based theorem prover. It was initially developed by Lawrence Paulson at the University of Cambridge and is today maintained there and at the TU Munich. Unlike many other interactive provers, Isabelle was written to serve as a framework for various logics, so-called object-logics. Today, mostly the object-logic for Higher-Order-Logic (HOL) and – on a smaller scale – the one for Zermelo-Fraenkel set theory are in widespread use. Isabelle has a meta-logic serving as a deductive framework for the embedded object-logics. This meta-logic is itself a fragment of HOL solely consisting of the universal quantifier and the implication. Isabelle features a powerful simplifier, and automated proof strategies; moreover, it is supported by the generic ProofGeneral user interface. For this paper, Isabelle/HOL [18] was used, e.g. Isabelle in its instantiation to HOL. In Isabelle/HOL automatic code generation is possible for constructive parts of a formalization, like datatypes and inductive definitions (see below), but also for constructive proofs.

The following meta-logical formula is an example illustrating the universal quantification with $\bigwedge$, higher order variables P and Q, and implication $\Longrightarrow$ of Isabelle's meta-logic (the square brackets $[\![]\!]$ act as a pseudo-conjunction).

$$\bigwedge \mathtt{P}\ \mathtt{Q}\ \mathtt{x}.\ [\![\ \mathtt{P}\ \mathtt{x};\ \mathtt{Q}\ \mathtt{x}\ ]\!] \Longrightarrow \mathtt{P}\ \mathtt{x}$$

The embedding of object-logics, like HOL, adds additional types, constants, and definitions gathered in a so-called *theory*. This extension of the meta-logic is performed according to a principle of *conservative* extension: new types and related constructors are defined on existing types; non-emtpiness of the new types must be proved; properties of new types are derived from their definition. Thereby, conservative extension guarantees soundness. Type definition for a restricted class of inductive types is more specifically supported by the *datatype* package in Isabelle/HOL. This feature resembles much an ML-style datatype definition. It is advisable to use this construction principle whenever possible for one's object-logic's specification because induction principles, distinction and exhaustion properties come along automatically with a structure defined as a datatype. In addition, functions over a datatype may be defined using primitive recursion which helps automated simplification in proofs and code generation from specifications. We will use the datatype feature, for example, to define the type of ς-terms in Section 3.1.

Isabelle/HOL features an additional inductive definition package enabling the definition of a minimal set of elements closed under given inductive rules. We will use inductive definition for the definitions of the type systems in Sections 4 and 5. A very generic parser enables application-specific definition of concrete syntax (so called mixfix syntax) making Isabelle formulae and proofs almost identical to pen-and-paper formalizations. We will point out the use of mixfix syntax in our formalization. In general, any Isabelle/HOL specific syntax that we will be using throughout the paper is going to be explained when we use it.

2.2 The ς-Calculus

In a *Theory of Objects*[1] Abadi and Cardelli developed the ς-family of calculi to formally study object-orientation. These calculi are widely accepted as conceptual equivalents of the λ-calculus for objects, since the objects can be directly used as a basic construct without having to be simulated through λ-expressions.

In the ς-calculi, an object is defined as a set of labelled methods. Each method is a ς-term in its own right and has a parameter *self*, in which the enclosing object is contained. There are three flavors of primitives from which to build such terms: *object definitions*, *method invocation* and *field update*, which are presented in Figure 2. Methods not using the self parameter are considered to be *fields*. There are various formalizations of the ς-calculus in interactive theorem provers, e.g. [7]. However, mechanizing aspects in Isabelle/HOL necessitates the following steps to accomodate the Theory of Objects.

Let $o \equiv [li = \varsigma(x_i)bi^{i \in 1..n}]$ (l_i distinct)
o is an object with method names l_i and methods $\varsigma(x_i)b_i$
$o.l_j \rightarrow b_j\{x_j \leftarrow o\}(j \in 1..n)$ selection / invocation
$o.l_j \Leftarrow \varsigma(y)b \rightarrow [l_j = \varsigma(y)b, l_i = \varsigma(xi)b_i^{i \in (1..n)-j}](j \in 1..n)$ update / override

Fig. 2. The primitive semantics of the ς-calculus as introduced in [2]

2.3 Finite Maps for Isabelle/HOL

For the definition of ς-terms it is necessary to first introduce a generic type of finite maps for the representation of objects. Defining a type of finite maps is a simple enough exercise, but defining it in a generic way is quite tricky.

We define a type constructor `fmap` for finite maps. For any finite type α and any β our type constructor enables now the definition of the new type $\alpha \rightharpoonup \beta$ of finite maps from elements of α to elements of β. Moreover, existing Isabelle/HOL machinery for (infinite) maps is reused so that we can construct new finite maps from old ones using the predefined notations, e.g. `f(x ↦y)` to update finite map `f` at point `x` with value `y`. We omit the technicalities of the Isabelle/HOL construction of `fmap` (see the web-page for full details).

We furthermore derive the necessary infrastructure to support the use of finite maps in proofs. We establish an induction scheme for finite types. Then using a representation of finite maps as finite sets of pairs that behave like functions, we derive the following induction scheme for the new generic type `fmap` from the induction scheme for finite sets by using a domain isomorphism between `fmap` and the set of pairs with function properties.

The type `label` is a concrete finite type defined to represent a type for field names of objects in the following definition of ς-terms.

```
⟦ P empty;
  ⋀ x (F::label ↦ dB) y . ⟦  P F; x ∉ dom F ⟧ ⟹ P (F(x ↦ y))
⟧  ⟹ P F
```

Fig. 3. The induction scheme on finite maps. If a predicate is true for the empty finite map and stays true when adding an element, it holds true for all finite maps.

2.4 Binding with de Bruijn Indices

It is a known difficult problem how to represent binders when formalizing programming languages for meta-theoretical reasoning [4]. One very recent way of dealing with this problem is provided by Nominal Techniques [19]. Here, basically an implicit factorization over concrete variable names, using a so called "support" representing all possible permutations of variables, enables to abstract from concrete names of variables. We have experimented with a recent implementation of a package for Nominal Techniques in Isabelle/HOL, but had to find out that neither recursive datatypes nor fancier constructs like our `fmap` are currently being supported. We decided to use the classical technique of de Bruijn indices. De Bruijn indices overcome the problem of concrete variable names, and thus α-conversion, by simply eliminating them. A variable is replaced by a natural number that represents the distance — in terms of nesting depth — of this variable to its binder. Thereby terms contain only numbers, no variable; α-conversion becomes obsolete. This is a considerable advantage as α-conversion is a difficult problem both from a practical point of view and for mechanical proofs. An example for illustrating the use of de Bruijn indices is given by the following simple λ-term.

$$\lambda x.\lambda y.(\lambda z.\, x\, z)y = Abs(Abs(Abs(Var\, 2)\$(Var\, 0))(Var\, 0))$$

Note that, different variables may be represented by the same number, e.g., z and x both are $Var\,0$. De Bruijn indices relieves one from having to deal with α-conversion: for example both $\lambda x.x$ and its α-equivalent $\lambda y.y$ are represented by $Abs(Var0)$. The disadvantage of de Bruijn indices is that substitution, normally used for the definition of application, is difficult to construct. A term has to be "lifted", that is, his "variables" have to be increased by one, when it moves into the scope of an abstraction in the process of substitution.

3 The Theory of Objects in Isabelle/HOL

3.1 Formalizing ς-Terms

The type `dB` of ς-terms in Isabelle/HOL is given by the following datatype declaration. Note, that there are two types of labels: `label` represents the method descriptors in an object while `Label` is the type of aspect labels. Both actual types are just type synonyms for `nat`, the type of natural numbers in Isabelle/HOL.

```
datatype dB =  Var nat
            |  Obj (label ⇀ dB) type
            |  Call dB label
            |  Upd dB label dB
            |  Asp Label dB     ("⟨ _ ⟩")
```

The constructor `Var` builds-up a new term `dB` from a `nat` representing the de Bruijn index of the variable. In the constructor `Obj` for objects we see now our `fmap` constructor being used: an object is recursively defined by a finite map from `label`, the predefined types of "field names", to arbitrary terms of type `dB`. The second argument of type `type` to the `dB`-constructor `Obj` is the Object's type. It will be formally introduced in Section 4. We insert the type with an object in order to render the typing relation unique (see Section 4). The cases `Call` and `Update` similarly represent, field selection and update of an object's field. The field constructor `Asp` enables the insertion of aspect labels into object terms. We do not assign any semantics to labels until we define weaving in Section 5. The annotation behind the constructor in quotation marks defines the mixfix syntax: we can use the notation `l⟨t⟩` as abbreviation for `Asp l t`.

Next, we need to define lifting and substitution in order to arrive at a reduction relation for our object-terms. These definitions are very technical, so we skip them here. For a full account see the Isabelle/HOL sources at the authors' web page [10]. The Isabelle/HOL mixfix syntax enables a definition of substitution for ς-terms as t[s/n] meaning *replace* n *by* s *in* t. We define a small step operational semantics by a relation $\to_\beta$ using an inductive definition.

```
inductive →β
intros
  beta: l ∈ dom f  f ⟹ Call (Obj f) l →β the(f l)[(Obj f)/0]
  upd : l ∈ dom f   ⟹ Upd (Obj f T) l a →β  Obj (f (l ↦ a) T)
  sel : s →β t ⟹ Call s l →β Call t l
  updL: s →β t ⟹ Upd s l u →β Upd t l u
  updR: s →β t ⟹ Upd u l s →β Upd u l t
  obj : ⟦ s →β t; l ∈ dom f ⟧
        ⟹ Obj (f (l ↦ s) T)  →β Obj (f (l ↦ t) T)
  asp : s →β t ⟹ l ⟨ s ⟩ →β l ⟨ t ⟩
```

The rules sel, updL, and updR merely encode that reduction can be performed in contexts. The others represent quite closely the original semantics of ς (cf. Figure 2). The substitution [(Obj f T)/0] in the rule beta replaces the self parameter for the outermost variable in the object's *lth* field f l. The operator the selects an α-element in an option datatype when it is defined, i.e. unequal to None. The cases upd and obj just replace inside objects. Additionally in some cases, the additional proviso l ∈ dom f assures that there is no call out of range of an object. The case asp enables, similar to the rules sel, updL, and updL, to evaluate in a labelled context. There is no other case for labels corresponding to the fact that no semantics is attached to labels until later.

This is the basic machinery for ς-terms in Isabelle/HOL with which we can represent any object term and evaluate it. The original notation used by Abadi and Cardelli (see Section 2.2) does not differ very much from our notation in Isabelle/HOL. The object $[l = \varsigma(x)x.l, n = \varsigma(x)x]$ is, for example, represented as Obj(∅(l ↦Call(Var 0) l)(n ↦(Var 0))) T for some suitable T where ∅ represents the empty map. It would be easy to add more syntactic sugar by defining additional mixfix syntax to achieve even closer resemblance.

The next important property to examine is determinacy of the evaluation.

3.2 Confluence

Confluence means that the reduction relation is deterministic. That is, whenever the reduction of an expression x of the language can return differing results y and z there are further reductions possible to a term u such that x and y can be further reduced to u. Formally, this property is based on the *diamond property* of a relation $\sim$.

```
diamond(∼) ≡df ∀ x y. x ∼ y ⟶ ∀ z. x ∼ z ⟶ ∃ u. y ∼ u ∧ z ∼ u
```

Confluence of a relation $\sim$ is defined as diamond($\sim^*$) where $*$ denotes the reflexive, transitive closure of a relation. We proved confluence of the reduction $\to_\beta$ in Isabelle/HOL.

Theorem 1 (Confluence of $\rightarrow_\beta$)

`diamond` $(\rightarrow_\beta^*)$

We were able to re-use the existing structure of the confluence proof from our earlier experiment [9], which used Nipkow's framework for the classical Church-Rosser proof as described by Barendregt in [5]. The classical trick already used in the application for the λ-calculus is to use a so-called *parallel reduction* $\rightarrow_\parallel$ for which the diamond property is true. Indeed, in general, the original reduction relation $\rightarrow_\beta$ does not verify `diamond` $\rightarrow_\beta$, and proving `diamond` $\rightarrow_\beta^*$ directly is very difficult. Thanks to the following theorem, we only have to show the inclusion of the parallel reduction relation in between the original reduction relation $\rightarrow_\beta$ and its transitive, reflexive closure.

$\llbracket$ `diamond` $\rightarrow_\parallel$; $\rightarrow_\beta \subseteq \rightarrow_\parallel$; $\rightarrow_\parallel \subseteq \rightarrow_\beta^*$ $\rrbracket \Longrightarrow$ `confluent` $\rightarrow_\beta$

Naturally, there were numerous adjustments to be made to the proofs in [9]. These were partly due to the – compared to plain lists – relative lack of prepared lemmas for finite maps. Especially the automatically generated induction schemas for datatypes using finite maps were not readily usable and had to be replaced by manually proved counterparts.

4 Type Safety for Objects

Generally, types in programming languages are a means to ensure statically as much soundness as possible. A type system defining types in an inductive style encodes therefore a decidable portion of the semantics of the language in question. Type safety entails that, whenever a program can be typed according to the type system, it fulfils the semantic property that is encoded in the type system. Classically, type systems encode the properties *progress* and *preservation* [20]. Progress describes the property that a well typed term is either a value or can be reduced further according to the evaluation relation. Preservation states that reduction does not change the type of a term, thereby ensuring that the evaluation does not endanger the semantic properties. When encoding a type system in Isabelle/HOL we implicitly prove the decidability of this type system by expressing the rules of the type system as rules of an inductive definition. This is a nice by-product of using a theorem prover.

The type system we define is derived from the original simple type system that Abadi and Cardelli presented in their work [2]. However, we could simplify it by omitting their "outcome" function which they use to describe definedness. Instead we use the explicitness readily available in our model: since finite maps are functions we can use the notion of "domain" to describe that a call is within the range of an object. Since the ς-calculus does not contain values, we consider that a value is reached whenever a term is an object even though inside the object further reduction might be possible. This is as much as we can get because in the ς-calculus non-terminating objects may well be defined. For example, the ς-term $[l = \varsigma(x)x.l]$ enters a non-terminating reduction, and — what is more important for safety – reproduces itself. Hence, there is generally no progress unless we refrain from evaluation inside objects — as we will prove shortly.

In the ς-calculus every term is an object. Hence, the following recursive Isabelle/HOL datatype defines the possible types.

```
datatype type =  Object (label ⇀ type)
```

To access the actual type at a given label we define the following projection.

```
(Object l)!n = the (l n)
```

The type system for ς-term is defined by an inductive typing relation. This relation `typing` is given as a set of triples containing the type environment, the term, and its type.

```
typing  :: (type list × dB  × type) set
```

We use Isabelle's mixfix possibilities to define the syntax `env ⊢ x : T` conveniently annotating that term `x` has type `T` in environment `env`, or, more formally, `(env,x,T) ∈ typing`. Type environments, like `env`, are defined such that they can be simply extended using a stack operator that we defined for this purpose. For example, `env⟨0:A⟩` denotes the environment `env` extended with the type assumption that the outermost variable has type `A`.

Now, the inductive definition for the typing relation consists of the following rules.

```
inductive typing
intros
  T_Var  : ⟦ x < length env; (env ! x) = T ⟧  ⟹ env ⊢ Var x : T
  T_Obj  : ⟦ dom b = dom B; ∀ l ∈ dom B. env⟨0:B⟩ ⊢ the(b l)  : B!l ⟧
                        ⟹ env ⊢ Obj b B :  B
  T_Call: ⟦ env ⊢ a : A; l ∈ dom A ⟧    ⟹ env ⊢ Call a l : A!l
  T_Upd  : ⟦ env ⊢ a : A; l ∈ dom A ; env⟨0:A⟩ ⊢ n : A!l ⟧
                        ⟹ env ⊢ Upd a l n : A
```

The variables `A` and `B` range over types. The variable `env` represents a type environment containing type assumptions for variables. A type environment is a mapping from variables to types, its extension by a new assumption of "`x` has type `A`" is annotated as `env⟨x:A⟩` (where `x` is a natural number in our de Bruijn representation). The operator `!` is used for selecting the nth element of a type environment. It is already provided in Isabelle/HOL for selecting the nth element of a list. Note, that we also use it in an overloaded fashion as the projection for object types. The rule `T_Var` accesses the type environment `env` to ensure variable types. The rule `T_Obj` describes how an object's type is derived from its constituents. An object of type `B` is formed from bodies `the(b l)` of types `B!l` that may use the self parameter fixed as `0` in the type environment. When a method `l` is invoked on an object `a` of type `A` the result `Call a l` has type `A!l` (`T_Call`). Similarly an update of a method may take place in a position `l` of an object that has the right body type under the assumption of the self parameter (`T_Upd`).

Given this type system we prove type safety first for the ς-calculus in Isabelle/HOL. We prove the following two theorems.

Theorem 2 (Progress)

$[\![$ `[] ⊢ t : A; ∄ c. t = Obj c` $]\!] \Longrightarrow$ `∃ t'. t` $\rightarrow_\beta$ `t'`

The second theorem is the preservation theorem, sometimes also called *subject reduction*.

Theorem 3 (Subject Reduction)

$[\![$ `env ⊢ t : A; t` $\rightarrow_\beta$ `t'` $]\!] \Longrightarrow$ `env ⊢ t' : A`

For the proofs of these Theorems, we could gather some initial inspiration from the type safety proof for the typed λ-calculus that has been performed by Nipkow [16]. Although the preservation theorem for the λ-calculus has a lot in common with our case, the progress theorem differs already in its formulation (for the simply typed λ-calculus strong normalization is proved which includes termination). Consequently the proof for progress is quite different in the two formalizations.

We were also able to show the uniqueness of the types.

Theorem 4 (Uniqueness)

$[\![$ `env ⊢ t : T; env ⊢ t : T'` $]\!] \Longrightarrow$ `T = T'`

This property would not hold true without the type annotation introduced in the initial datatype declaration. For example, the object $[l = \varsigma(x)x]$ would have types `Object (empty (l ↦ T))` *for any type* `T`, if we had not fixed the type inside the object. Accidentally, we would have introduced some kind of polymorphic functions.

5 Aspects, Weaving, and Types for Aspects

The ingredients of an aspect-oriented program are a base program written in an object-oriented language, and a set of aspects. The aspects consist of a selection of pointcuts and an advice that shall be applied at those points. The process of actually plugging in the advice at the specified pointcuts is called weaving. In this section we present these features in Isabelle/HOL for the ς-calculus together with a type system for aspects.

5.1 Aspects

An aspect can be simply defined as a selection of pointcuts and an advice. Since our model is in Higher Order Logic, where sets are isomorphic to predicates, we can assume that our selection of pointcuts is a set of labels. The advice is a ς-term with a free variable thereby mimicking a function over subexpressions of a ς-program marked by labels. Hence, in Isabelle/HOL aspects can be simply defined as follows.

```
datatype aspect = Aspect (Label list) dB    ("⟨ _._ ⟩")
```

The first element is the pointcut set and the second element the advice to be applied to all points matching the pointcut description, i.e. being member of this set. The mixfix syntax at the righthandside enables the annotation of an aspect as ⟨L.a⟩.

5.2 Weaving

Given a base program in the ς-calculus readily labelled with aspect labels and given some aspects, the weaving function now only has to step through the term while applying the aspect. We consider this approach to resemble static weaving, but given the functional nature of our calculus, we consider the result to be valid for dynamic approaches as well. Therefore, we define a function "weave", represented as ⇓, that takes a ς-program and an aspect and returns a ς-program. The second operator `weave_option` is an auxiliary function that is needed to "map" the weaving function over the finite maps representing objects.

```
weave :: [ dB, aspect ] ⇒ dB    ("⇓")
weave_option :: [ dB option, aspect ] ⇒ dB option ("⇓opt")
```

We define the weaving function for the simple case of applying one aspect to a program. The general case is later derived by repeated application. The definition of the simple case is given below in a mutual recursive definition defining the semantics of `weave` and `weave_option` by simple equations. In case of weaving an aspect onto a variable `Var n` the advice has no effect. The case `l⟨t⟩` is the interesting one because now the ς-term for aspects, `Asp`, is finally equipped with semantics. In case that the label is in the pointcut specified by the first component of the aspect, the aspect matches. Consequently, the advice part of the aspect `a` is applied to the current term `t`. Otherwise the aspect has no effect. The label is not eliminated during the weaving process to enable repeated weaving.

```
primrec
  (Var n) ⇓ ⟨L.a⟩ = Var n
  l ⟨ t ⟩ ⇓ ⟨L.a⟩ = if  l ∈ set(L) then l ⟨ a[(t ⇓ ⟨L.a⟩)/0] ⟩
                                    else l ⟨ t ⇓ ⟨L.a⟩ ⟩
```

The Isabelle/HOL projection `set` transforms a list (here, of labels) into the set of all elements contained in the list. Note, that the functional application of the advice `a` to the term `t` is realized using substitution for `0` using the same idea as in the rule `beta` of the reduction relation.

The next two equalities for `Call` and `Upd` simply define that the weave process is to be passed through to the corresponding sub-terms.

```
(Call s l) ⇓ A = Call (s ⇓ A) l
(Upd s l t) ⇓ A = Upd (s ⇓ A) l (t ⇓ A)
```

The primitive recursive equations defining the semantics for Obj is now the point where the recursion changes to the auxiliary operator weave_option. The auxiliary operator enables the pointwise definition of advice on the fields of the object by lifting the weaving function over the λ to argument position. In the defining equations for weave_option ($\Downarrow_{\text{opt}}$) we see the benefit gained by using the option type: we can explicitly use pattern matching to distinguish the case for unused field labels (None) and actual object fields matching out the field value with Some.

```
(Obj f T) ⇓ A = Obj (λ l. ((f l) ⇓opt A)) T
None ⇓opt A = None
(Some t) ⇓opt A = Some (t ⇓ A)
```

The generalization of the weaving function to lists of aspects is simply defined using the predefined functor foldl. This realizes the application of a function repeatedly to an argument taking second arguments from a list. This is exactly what we need: iterated application of weaving to a ς-term t using advice from a list of advice l.

```
Weave t l ≡df delabel(foldl (op ⇓) t l)
```

The function delabel is a simple recursive function that deletes all labels from the weaving result thereby producing a "label-free" ς-calculus term. This final step is necessary to arrive at an unambiguous term at the end of weaving. Otherwise we would have to consider equivalence classes of labelled terms.

5.3 Type System

We next present a type system for aspects. We have succeeded in designing this type system for aspects and proved type safety completely in the theorem prover Isabelle/HOL. Here, we introduce the major definitions and the proved theorems. The entire proof development in Isabelle/HOL is available on the authors' web-page [10].

The basic idea of the type system is that we attach types to aspect labels. Any advice that may be woven in at a particular point has to be conform to the type attached to this point's label. For type safety, we found an elegant way of proving that aspect weaving respects types. This general results grants to recover type safety for weaving from the previous type safety results for the typed ς-calculus (see Section 4). We extend this basic type system of our Isabelle/HOL formalization for objects of the ς-calculus. We use a second environment L – besides the basic type environment – to keep track of label types during the process of typing.

Compared to the rules dealing with the existing, pure, ς-constructors in the dB datatype (cf. Section 4) the only notable change is that the environments now are complemented by a label environment L. Hence, the new inductive relation typing has four parameters. The additional label environment L maps labels to types. It enforces that a given label has the same type at all occurrences.

For instance, the `Var` case features now an additional environment `L` of label types.

```
T_Var : ⟦ x < length env; (env ! x) = T ⟧ ⟹ env, L ⊢ Var x : T
```

Similarly, the other three rules are identical to the rules for the pure ς-calculus (see Section 4), except for the additional parameter `L` as the label type environment in all typing judgements.

Finally, we add one new rule for the typing of labels. It states that a label has the type assigned in the environment and that a labelled term's type has to be conform to the label type. Given a term `a` of type `A` we can insert a label `l` in front of `a` if we are in the same environment.

```
T_lab : ⟦ l!i = A; i < length L; env, L ⊢ a : A ⟧ ⟹ env, L ⊢ l⟨a⟩ : A
```

The introduction of the second parameter has little impact on the proofs presented in the previous section. These are all additions we made to the type system. Still, one decisive information for a meaningful static analysis is missing. We know how to type aspect labels now and we know how to type labelled programs. However, in aspect-orientation, the process of weaving plays a rôle in the semantics. So, we need to lift the typing to the weaving operation. Since we added weaving not as a term constructor of the actual term language of labelled ς-terms `dB`, the typing for the weaving function is not part of the type system seen above.

But, as we are in HOL weaving is a function of the meta-level, i.e. Isabelle/HOL, and we can introduce the well–formedness of weaving also at the meta-level. Therefore, our expressivity is not lessened. First, we define a predicate that ensures that a set of pointcuts and an advice are compatible.

```
wf_adv L ⟨L. a⟩ ≡df ∀ l ∈ set(L). ∃ A. L!l = A ∧ [] ⟨0: A⟩, L ⊢ a : A
```

This predicate enforces that there must be one environment (empty base-types and some appropriate label-types) such that all labels in the pointcut set of the aspect can be typed according to the advice. Note, that an advice is thereby constrained to have identical input and output type. Further loosening of this constraint towards some kind of conform subtyping here is future work (see Section 6.3).

Given this internal well-formedness of aspects, we can lift it up to define well-formedness between an aspect and a base program.

```
wf_at L t a ≡df ∃ T. wf_adv L a ∧ [], L ⊢ t: T
```

This predicate can again be lifted to sets of aspects.

```
wf L t A ≡df ∀ a ∈ set(A) . wf_at L t a
```

With all these preparations we are now able to identify a theorem that encodes the preservation of typing through weaving.

Theorem 5 (Weaving Preservation)

$\llbracket$ `wf L t A; [], L` $\vdash$ `t : T` $\rrbracket \Longrightarrow$ `[], L` $\vdash$ `t` $\Downarrow$ `A : T`

This theorem is the central theorem for type safety for aspects in our setting because the usual type safety theorems, progress and preservation, are simply implied by it.

Corollary 1 (Aspect Progress)

$\llbracket$ `wf L t A; [], L` $\vdash$ `t A: T;` $\nexists$ `c B. t` $\Downarrow$ `A = Obj c B` $\rrbracket$
$\Longrightarrow \exists$ `t'. t` $\Downarrow$ `A` $\rightarrow_\beta$ `t'`

Corollary 2 (Aspect Preservation)

$\llbracket$ `wf L t A; [], L` $\vdash$ `t : T ; t` $\Downarrow$ `A` $\rightarrow_\beta$ `t'` $\rrbracket \Longrightarrow$ `env, L` $\vdash$ `t' : T`

6 Conclusions

In this paper we have presented a formalization of our theory of aspects in the theorem prover Isabelle/HOL. It consists of the ς-calculus with an extension by so-called labels for the representation of join-points and definitions of weaving functions. We have proved the confluence and type-safety of the basic language of ς-objects and for the extension to aspects.

6.1 Related Work

There are some, partly still ongoing, strands of research concerning theoretical work for the support of aspects. The approach which is probably closest to ours is the work by Ligatti et al. [14]. We differ from their approach in that we use the ς-calculus as a basis, thus being object-oriented in the core-calculus, whereas they start from some λ-like functional language. Clifton and Leavens devised their MiniMao language [6] which is a typed aspect-oriented language based on a small imperative Java-subset. Another approach taken by Jagadeesan et al [11] concentrates on generics and uses a FeatherweightJava based calculus.

However, none of the above mentioned theoretical accounts provides a mechanization in a theorem prover or similar tool. We are not aware that there are any attempts to formalize a theory of aspects inside a theorem prover. In particular, in the field of language semantics and type systems we consider definitions and proofs sufficiently complex to render automated proofs an imperative condition for high quality developments.

6.2 Compositionality and Run-Time Weaving

An important question for aspects and their practical usability is the compositionality of weaving. A similar question is whether run-time weaving is possible. Figure 4 illustrates this question graphically: when does this diagram commute?

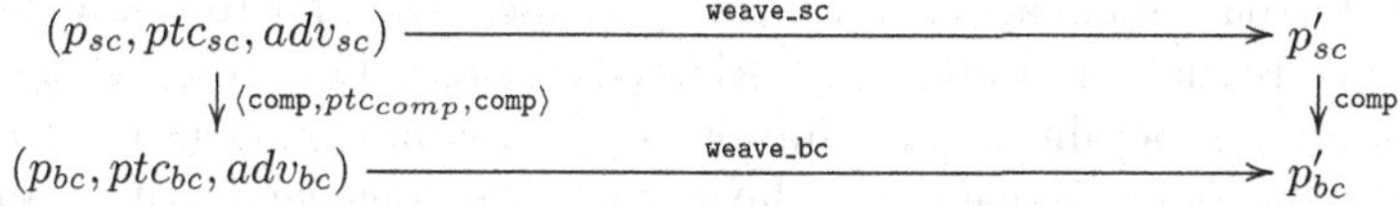

Fig. 4. Do compile-time and run-time weaving commute?

(index *sc* stands for source, *bc* for bytecode, *p* for program, and *ptc* and *adv* for pointcut and advice.)

An immediate success of our formalization is that we have made one step towards identifying the conditions for a precise analysis for this question. In the aspect-calculus that we have presented in this paper we can state the corresponding compositionality proposition as follows.

$$[\![\ \mathtt{t} \rightarrow_\beta \mathtt{t'};\ \mathtt{a} \rightarrow_\beta \mathtt{a'}\ ]\!] \Longrightarrow \mathtt{t} \Downarrow \langle\ \mathtt{L.\ a}\ \rangle \rightarrow_\beta \mathtt{t'} \Downarrow \langle\ \mathtt{L.a'}\ \rangle$$

Essentially the condition states that advice can be reduced prior to weaving without changing the semantics compared to reduction after weaving. Compilation is here replaced by interpretation because our calculus is functional.

6.3 Future Work

As we have seen in Section 5.3 the type system for aspects is constrained to have identical input and output types. We are considering the extension of our simple type system with sub-types. This would, in principle, give the means to relax the constraints on aspect types. However, neither a contravariant nor a covariant type refinement is possible for aspects in general: counterexamples may be constructed (see Jagadeesan et al. [11]).

As noted earlier (2.4), we have used the classical technique of DeBruijn indices to avoid α–conversion. Our experiments with the more elegant nominal approach [19] revealed that the datatype support is not yet sufficient for our purposes. We are in the process of evaluating the use of a locally–nameless solution [4].

6.4 Discussion

We did not embed weaving as a first-class function into our term language. This might at first sight seem odd, but we do not need to make weaving first-class. As we are in Higher Order Logic, we can reason about a meta-level function over ς-terms also in the object-logic. It has proved to be, on the contrary, an advantage to formalize weaving as a meta-logical HOL-function because we did succeed, in addition, to express its semantics using primitive recursion. The fact that weaving is a HOL-function implicitly grants us many useful properties – function properties combined with a primitive recursive definition save us a lot of explicit proof work because they are well supported in Isabelle/HOL.

One part of any aspect-oriented language is an object-oriented language for writing the base program and the advice. Therefore we chose the Theory of Objects by Abadi and Cardelli [1] as a basis for our mechanized theory of aspects.

Although this base language is fairly small, it does – similar to the λ-calculus – enable the construction of all object-oriented features. On the other hand, this choice preserves generality of our approach: we stay independent of any particular implementation language, say Java, when we consider features and their related properties. Certainly, it must be shown that a small core language like the ς-calculus and our extension to aspects are equivalent to realistic programming language. Therefore, we intend to follow the approach taken in [14], where a type-preserving compilation is finally added from a real-world aspect-oriented language to the core-calculus.

Apart from providing a theoretical calculus for aspect-orientation, that is moreover mechanically verified, we believe our work to contribute to the safe use of this paradigm for the adaptable systems of the future. Our formalisation is a tool to experiment with different language constructs using the mechanical proof support to verify gradually type-safety and other more advanced properties like non-interference. In addition, a formalization as constructive as ours enables extraction of executable programs.

References

1. Abadi, M., Cardelli, L.: A Theory of Objects. Springer, Heidelberg (1996)
2. Abadi, M., Cardelli, L.: A Theory of Primitive Objects. In: Hagiya, M., Mitchell, J.C. (eds.) TACS 1994. LNCS, vol. 789, Springer, Heidelberg (1994)
3. Avgustinov, P., et al.: Semantics of Static Pointcuts in Aspect. In: Principles of Programming Languages, POPL 2007, ACM Press, New York (2007)
4. Aydemir, B., Charguéraud, A., Pierce, B.C., Pollack, R., Weirich, S.: Engineering Formal Metatheory. In: Principles of Programming Languages, POPL 2008, ACM Press, New York (2008)
5. Barendregt, H.P.: The Lambda Calculus, its Syntax and Semantics, 2nd edn. North-Holland, Amsterdam (1984)
6. Clifton, C., Leavens, G.: Minimao: Investigating the semantics of proceed. In: Foundations of Aspect-Oriented Languages, FOAL 2005 (2005)
7. Ciaffaglione, A., Liquori, L., Miculan, M.: Reasoning about object-based calculi in (co)inductive type theory and the theory of contexts. Journal of Automated Reasoning 39, 1–47 (2007)
8. Filman, R., Friedman, D.: Aspect-Oriented Programming is Quantification and Obliviousness. In: Workshop on Advanced Separation of Concerns, OOPSLA 2000, October 2000, Minneapolis, USA (2000)
9. Henrio, L., Kammüller, F.: A Mechanized Model of the Theory of Objects. In: Bonsangue, M.M., Johnsen, E.B. (eds.) FMOODS 2007. LNCS, vol. 4468, Springer, Heidelberg (2007)
10. Jähnichen, S., Kammüller, F.: Ascot: Formal, mechanical foundation of aspect-oriented and collaboration-based languages. DFG (2006), Web-page at, `http://swt.cs.tu-berlin.de/~flokam/ascot/index.html`
11. Jagadeesan, R., Jeffrey, A., Riely, J.: Typed Parametric Polymorphism for Aspects. In [17], 267–296
12. Kammüller, F.: Interactive Theorem Proving in Software Engineering. Habilitationsschrift (habilitation thesis), Technische Universität Berlin (2006)

13. Kammüller, F., Vösgen, M.: Towards Type Safety of Aspect-Oriented Languages. In: Foundations of Aspect-Oriented Languages, FOAL 2006 (2006)
14. Ligatti, J., Walker, D., Zdancewic, S.: A type-theoretic interpretation of pointcuts and advice. In [17], pp. 240–266
15. Paulson, L.C.: Isabelle. LNCS, vol. 828. Springer, Heidelberg (1994)
16. Nipkow, T.: More Church Rosser Proofs. Journal of Automated Reasoning 26, 51–66 (2001)
17. Science of Computer Programming: Special Issue on Foundations of Aspect-Oriented Programming. vol. 63(3), Elsevier (2006)
18. Nipkow, T., Paulson, L.C., Wenzel, M.T.: Isabelle/HOL. LNCS, vol. 2283. Springer, Heidelberg (2002)
19. Urban, C., Tasson, C.: Nominal Techniques in Isabelle/HOL. In: Nieuwenhuis, R. (ed.) CADE 2005. LNCS (LNAI), vol. 3632, Springer, Heidelberg (2005)
20. Wright, A., Felleisen, M.: A Syntactic Approach to Type Soundness. Information and Computation 115, 38–94 (1994)

Practical Conflict Resolution for the Composition of Program Transformations

Andreas I. Schmied and Franz J. Hauck

Institute of Distributed Systems, Ulm University, Germany
{andreas.schmied,franz.hauck}@uni-ulm.de

Abstract. The composition of separate concerns is a cornerstone for the construction of complex software. By now, aspect-oriented techniques have been established as the *sine qua non* in several application areas. However, their abilities to cope with composition conflicts are mostly limited to the linear ordering of aspects. This paper describes a more general and practical approach for the resolution of composition conflicts as it is realised in our general-purpose transformation system *LLTS*.

Our system divides a composition into two phases. In the expansion phase separate transformations add concern code within their isolated copies of the base code. In the subsequent contraction phase the manipulations of the first phase are compared and merged wherever possible. A hinting mechanism guides the semi-automatic merging on three levels: Conflicts are detected using compatibility relations between operators, by reconciling annotations of complex transformation tasks, and based on semantic predicates of the base code language. Conflicts are reported to the user with a comprehensive explanation and can be resolved with manual by-case deviations from the original transformation code. As a result, conflicts can be remedied on a finer granularity, e.g., by revising only parts of a transformation in a certain context.

Keywords: Software Transformation, Transformation Language, Software Composition, Conflict Resolution.

1 Introduction

Complex software is commonly built from a large number of modularised software artefacts, which are to be composed by software engineering techniques. A large number of composition concepts have evolved and have been successfully put into practice with a plethora of technical implementations. Prominent representatives are the instrumentation of base code with code weaving, client migration and merging by correspondence, and interception/wrapping techniques [1]. These concepts provide convenient means to compose an application from several separated concerns. Also, a range of composition conflicts have been taken into consideration.

AspectJ [2], for instance, permits adding of more than one superclass only if they are in a common subtype hierarchy. Since aspects are a means for the separation of concerns, they are often designed independently of each other,

C. Pautasso and É. Tanter (Eds.): SC 2008, LNCS 4954, pp. 248–262, 2008.

or they are obtained from different third-party developers. Then, a superclass conflict can only be solved by introducing a static prioritisation from within auxiliary aspects. It is questionable whether this approach always reflects the meaning of the composition with respect to the intended application semantics. Another frequent source of conflicts are signature collisions among inter-type declarations. To avoid them with private introductions, the aspect source code must be available.

In general, incompatibilities between independently developed aspects are hard to solve. For simple conflict cases, the current technologies provide relatively simple mechanisms. On the one hand they are easy to understand and to apply, but on the other hand they fail for even slightly more difficult problems. For instance, a strict ordering of aspects may solve one part of a problem but raise another or even disrupt the intended semantics. In [3] the authors illustrate theses doubts concerning *independent extensibility* with the *door example*: A pair of methods *start* and *end* shall each get two *before-advices*, which are described in separate aspects. The first aspect needs to call *openTheDoor* and *closeTheDoor* before these methods. The second aspect needs to call *goInside* and *goOutside* before them. In any case, there is no proper ordering by priority that allows one to enter the room after opening the door and leaving it before closing the door. We will show that this composition can be solved with our approach.

The remainder of this paper is structured as follows: Sections 2 and 3 present a compact outline of our solution, the data model, and the *LLTS*[1] transformation language. We define the term *composition* in Section 4 and discuss a classification of conflicts, their detection and resolution strategies in Sections 4.1-4.3. Section 4.4 briefly reflects on the complexity of our approach and possible optimisations. After a discussion of related work in Section 5, we conclude with a summary of our current activities.

2 Solution Sketch

Owing to the insight that there is no general and perfect solution for composition conflicts, we propose a practical approach to handle conflicts and to create application-specific solutions.

We deal with composition issues from the perspective of our general-purpose code transformation system *LLTS*. Its data model is lean but powerful enough to represent arbitrary source code. In this paper, terms for code artefacts refer to Java since this is our primary application language. We follow the MDA [4] approach and name the analysed source code files of a base application a *model* that conforms to a *metamodel*. The model contains typed *elements*, which maintain named, directed *links* to each other and may carry a single primitive value. This generic structure of an attributed, directed graph, reflects both the syntactic structure of the input data as well as semantic relations between elements

[1] Low-Level Transformation System, pron. 'iltis, German for polecat.

(type graph, control flows, usage references). The metamodel is implemented as a pluggable part of the transformation system. It defines the parser for the input data, the pretty printer for the output, the element types, and the sorts of links. Routines that enforce the type system conformity and the syntactic and semantic rules of a language are also defined in the metamodel.

In *LLTS*, we express concerns as a combination of code fragments and transformation tasks. These procedure-like tasks use low-level operators — such as creating elements, managing links, changing the primitive value — to adapt the base code for the needs of a concern and integrate its code fragments at the appropriate locations.

The main idea for the composition of concerns is to divide a composition into two phases, namely an *expansion phase* and a subsequent *contraction phase*. Figure 1 illustrates the entire process, which can also be nested for a more detailed composition of sub-transformations.

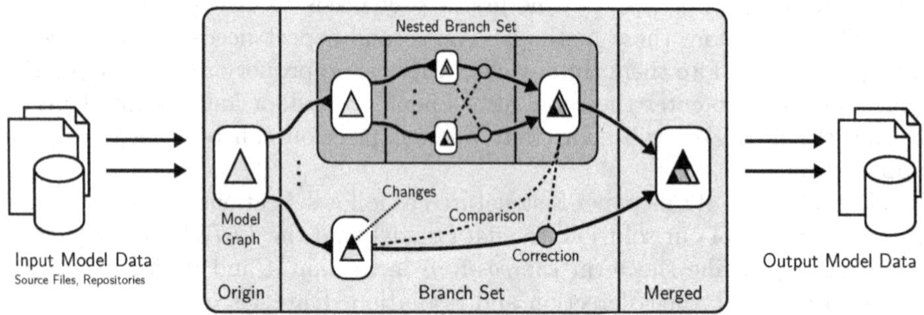

Fig. 1. Nested branch sets with comparison and correction

In the expansion phase each transformation manipulates an isolated copy of the base code, the so-called *branch* of the *origin model*. As every branch manages a single self-contained concern its transformation is considered to be conflict-free. The separation of the branches is accomplished by the data model of our system and uses an efficient copy-on-write mechanism: Data is principally read from the origin model, which is immutable during the expansion phase; only the parts to be transformed are copied to the branch. The contraction phase combines an automated conflict detection between branches with an incremental conflict resolution by the user. Conflicts are detected by comparing annotations that have to be defined by the transformation developer, and by inspecting possible incompatibilities at locations of multiple operator execution. In contrast to more abstracting techniques, such as aspect weaving or refactoring, we take advantage of a dual view on both low-level operators and higher-level tasks. The prior define primitive manipulations and the latter can be engaged to form abstract concepts, such as entire refactorings or weaving instructions.

The transformation engine produces a detailed conflict report, which has to be interpreted by the user. Based on the report, the user eliminates conflicts by enhancing the composition with corrective operators. This involves her domain knowledge about the concerns. Because this procedure may in general introduce new collisions, its termination cannot be guaranteed. The user needs to abort the comparison–correction cycle manually, if he reckons a lifelock or considers a composition unachievable. Eventually, if all branches are conflict-free then their manipulations are merged back as a composite transformation into the origin model. Our current merging algorithm implements a combination of *intensional* replay of the manipulating operators and the *extensional* copying of actual changes. The metamodel implementation oversees the composite transformation and reports a conflict should the model semantics be violated.

3 The *LLTS* Transformation Language

We use the *LLTS* language syntax throughout this paper to illustrate our approach. It is an imperative, dynamically-typed language that adopts a mix of XPath [5] and LISP [6] style for the purpose of being both concise and precise for multi-valued hierarchical expressions. The first item of a list determines whether the expression is grouping for precedence, a declaration (**task** X...), or an action, such as a call to a task (X ...) or an operator (**attach** ...). The navigation within the model is accomplished by dot-separated path expressions; elements are selected with predicates written in square brackets. An important consequence of path expressions is that every action is evaluated within a *context* element. For instance, *Class*[*name* ~matches~ "Bean$"].(AddInterface ⟨arguments⟩...) runs the task (AddInterface ...) for every class whose name ends on "Bean"; the context of this task is the respective class element.

The following example illustrates parts of the transformation of a simple Java model: An additional interface is being added to a set of existing classes using a task (AddInterface). The example uses expression labels of the form ⟨expr⟩=label.

```
(task main
  (load java "src={llts.home}/samples/src ...")      ; load a model with Java metamodel
  Package["samples.basic.java"]                                ; select a certain package
     .Class [name ~matches~ "Bean$"]                            ; therein a set of classes
     .(AddInterface "java.io.Serializable") )                 ; call the task for each class
(task AddInterface
  (context Class)                                     ; context declaration for runtime checks
  (argument @text=Iname)                                  ; one textual argument, label Iname
  (JavaLookup Iname)=Iface                             ; find the interface element, label Iface
  (assert Iface ~instanceof~ Interface                                 ; runtime type check...
    "argument must be an interface name")                        ; may abort with error message
  (if Implements.Type.target ~!contains~ Iface          ; if not already implementing Iface...
     Implements.(attach (JavaTyperef Iface)) ) )             ; add it to implements statement
```

Please note: We leave details, such as modularisation issues, model persistence, name disambiguation, and fully-qualified signatures, to the reader's imagination to improve the conciseness of the examples and to focus on the ideas of this paper. Please refer to our technical report [7] for further information.

4 Composition of Transformations

The *LLTS* system allows the modular composition of built-in and user-defined tasks as in regular procedural programming languages. Likewise, an author has to spend some reasonable effort and needs a fair knowledge of the transformation internals to orchestrate the enlisted operations towards a sensible result. The outcome is a self-contained transformation that is able to accomplish some well-defined task, such as integrating one concern into the base code.

However, our actual interest lies in the further composition of such self-contained transformation tasks. The crucial point is that these tasks could have been developed separately and for independent concerns. Their composition may happen within a completely different development environment. Hence, the exact composition scenario and the participating transformations are unknown in advance from the perspective of their original developers.

A composition is expressed in *LLTS* with the (**compose**) operator that enters the *expansion phase* by declaring at least two branches. Each branch stands for a self-contained transformation that integrates a certain concern independently into the base code. Each branch declaration contains a name and states a start-up task. This so-called *branch set* is optionally followed by conflict resolution statements (see below). Embedded into a task declaration, we form a composite task:

```
(task composite
  (compose
    (branch name1 task1)
    ...
    (branch nameN taskN)
))
```

The goal of a composition is to bring the modifications of the entire branch set into a valid execution sequence. Due to the independence of concerns, any order could be valid. In particular, it may not exactly be possible to find an order of whole branches, but to find an order of sub-tasks. In advance, an (**order** ⟨branchname⟩$^+$) declaration within (**compose**) imposes coarse restrictions for the later resolution of conflicts.

4.1 Conflict Classification

The composition of transformations may reveal several kinds of interference. On the positive side, some transformations may have common parts that could be reused, e.g. by creating scaffolding code only once. We will get back to this case in Section 4.4. For now, we distinguish three kinds of negative interference: namely, operator conflicts, task conflicts, and metamodel conflicts.

Operator conflicts are low-level conflicts, which carry a weak semantics due to the locality of their effect to single elements. They are useful for detecting disagreements about the links of an element or its primitive value. For instance, the (**clear**) operator, which detaches all elements from a link at one stroke, is conflicting with the (**attach**) operator at the same link. Two (**set**) operators conflict at the same element, because they are changing its primitive value. Also, attaching more elements at a certain link than allowed by its cardinality is considered a collision. This applies to the *parent* link inhibiting more than one element from being attached.

Task conflicts appear between complex transformation tasks. To enable their detection, the tasks must be prepared by the task author. We enrich tasks with (**conflict**) annotations that declare a *conflict class* and describe the scope of search for potential conflicts. For instance, our transformation library provides a number of AOP-like tasks, including (BeforeExec), which resembles AspectJ's *before execution advice*. This task can be applied to a *Method* context and declares the **samecontext** conflict class:

```
(task BeforeExec
  (context Method)                          ; required context element type
  (conflict samecontext)                    ; conflict class declaration
  ...
)
```

Thus, the task principally conflicts with any other (BeforeExec) executed at the same context element: It would not be decidable which of the tasks should be chosen as the very first to implement the *before all others* correctly. As a generalisation, the **task** conflict class relates a selection of different tasks. The following code fragments shows the conflict declaration between the refactoring (RenameClass) and the creational task (AddMethod) from our Java support library. In order to avoid new constructors being added with reference to the obsolete class name, adding a method with the same name as the (yet unchanged) class name is inhibited:

```
(task RenameClass
  (context Class)
  (conflict task AddMethod samecontext (argument name==@this.name) )
  ...
)
```

Other conflict classes involve a search among the sub-elements of the context or in the entire model. For instance, a task modifying the coordination strategy of a single method needs to rule out any other task modifying the **synchronized** modifier or **synchronized** statements within the method body. In the following code fragment, the task uses the **modification** conflict class to shield the modifier as well as any coordination block from foreign modification:

```
(task changeMethodCoordination
  (context Method)
  (conflict modification Modifier["synchronized"])
  (conflict modification [[transitive]].Synchronized.Arg)
  ...
)
```

However, this preparation is only possible in a precise manner for co-developed tasks; just as it is the case for a self-contained transformation library having the entire transformation code available.

Metamodel conflicts occur when the conditions of a metamodel are violated, e.g., when a method with the same signature is being added twice, or if an abstract type is used for an object creation statement. Metamodel conflicts have an exceptional position. They may already appear during an erroneous transformation within a branch, whereas operator and task conflicts only make sense during the contraction of branches.

4.2 Conflict Detection

We define per branch that a completely passed transformation be valid with respect to its own exclusive model view. The author of a transformation has to ensure this property by profiting from her domain knowledge and by writing sensible modifications. Before and after an element is being changed, the metamodel implementation performs pre-/postcondition checks. Normally, any violation of these conditions creates a metamodel conflict, which results in an immediate abort of the entire transformation. Yet, to allow extensive model changes with temporal inconsistencies, the checks can be postponed until a group of modifications reach a consistent state again. This process of verified low-level transformations is akin to the approach in [8].

All changes are tracked together with an execution record about their model context and the causing operators and tasks. This information is the basis for the following *contraction phase*. The contraction phase is an incremental process of repeated conflict detection and continuous conflict resolution. Conflicts are detected automatically by the system and are solved by intervention of the user.

The conflict detection mechanism runs in several stages. It begins with a pairwise comparison of all related branches of a branch set to reveal mutual conflicts. This part is illustrated in Figure 2, where the branches of an origin model are compared with each other.

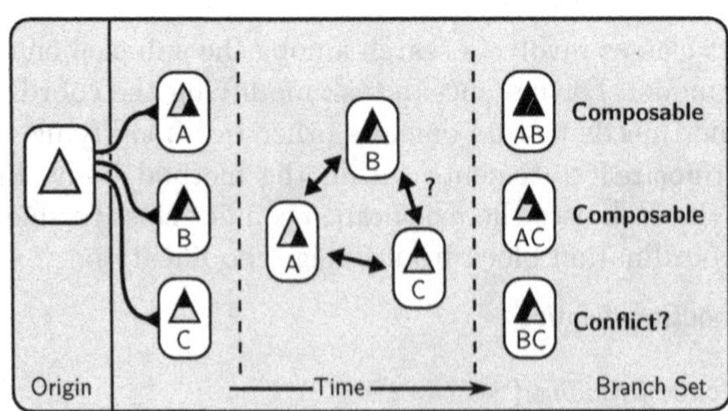

Fig. 2. Pairwise conflict detection between branches

In this so-called *intensional comparison*, we compare the tasks from the execution record of two branches at a time and report conflicts based on task annotations. Predefined (**order**) declarations between branches are taken into account to minimise order-related conflicts. After all conflicts could be eliminated by the user and a clean task comparison could be executed, the so-called *extensional comparison* follows. Now, the branches are compared at the operator level. In every branch every changed element is inspected whether the related element in any other branch has been changed, too. If so, the operators used for the overlapping manipulation are compared for operator conflicts. The summary of conflicts is again reported to the user for further measures.

The following example recalls the *door example* and shows the conflict detection. The task door_example initiates a composition in line 2, calling two tasks aspectDoor/Go in separate branches:

```
1 (task door_example
2   SomeClass.(compose
3     (branch A aspectDoor) (branch B aspectGo) ) )
```

Both tasks use the (BeforeExec) task to insert a call to an aspect method at the respective beginning of the base code methods. We use a helper task (CallMethod) to hide details of the metamodel in the example code:

```
4 (task aspectDoor
5   Method["start"].Body.(BeforeExec (CallMethod "openTheDoor") )
6   Method["end"]. Body.(BeforeExec (CallMethod "closeTheDoor") )
7 )
8
9 (task aspectGo
10   Method["start"].Body.(BeforeExec (CallMethod "goInside") )
11   Method["end"]. Body.(BeforeExec (CallMethod "goOutside") )
12 )
```

After a successful execution in the branches, the conflict detection proceeds using the fact that the (BeforeExec) task declares (**conflict samecontext**). Because the calls to (BeforeExec) in lines $5, 10$ refer to a context element *Body* of the same *Method*["start"], the pair will be reported to be conflicting. The same happens to lines $6, 11$ for the *Method*["end"].

4.3 Conflict Resolution

The conflict resolution has to be accomplished by the developer. Based on the conflict report the (**compose**) statement is being enhanced with corrective statements. The transformation engine unveils the cause of a conflict together with its element context and the task call history. Finding an appropriate correction requires understanding the effect of both involved transformations. To guide the user's decision a transformation developer should choose intention-carrying task names or should add (**intent**) annotations to his code with a textual description of its meaning. The benefit for the report is a narrative semantics which is gradually refined along the call history of a conflicting task. For the *door example* the following listing summarises the annotations for the branch tasks and the conflicting (BeforeExec) task. The above scattered listings have been combined for easier reference and are reduced to the *Method*["start"] case:

```
1 (task BeforeExec
2   (intent "code to be executed before any other code in a method body")
3   (context Method)
4   (conflict samecontext) ...)
5 (task aspectDoor
6   (intent "adds opening/closing of the door at the start/end methods")
7   Method["start"].Body.(BeforeExec (CallMethod "openTheDoor") ) ...)
8 (task aspectGo
9   (intent "adds entering/leaving through the door at the start/end methods")
10  Method["start"].Body.(BeforeExec (CallMethod "goInside") ) ...)
11 (task door_example
12  (intent "combines opening/closing a door with entering/leaving")
13  SomeClass.(compose
14    (branch A aspectDoor)
15    (branch B aspectGo)
16 ) )
```

The following listing shows parts of the corresponding conflict report in its plain textual representation; the line numbers have been adjusted to the combined listing:

```
Task Conflict at BeforeExec: samecontext
Branches: A, B
Context: SomeClass, Method "start", Body
Branch A:
  door_example: (line 11)
    combines opening/closing a door with entering/leaving
  aspectDoor: (line 5)
    adds opening/closing of the door at the start/end methods
  BeforeExec: (line 1)
    code to be executed before any other code in a method body
Branch B:
  door_example: (line 11)
    combines opening/closing a door with entering/leaving
  aspectGo: (line 8)
    adds entering/leaving through the door at the start/end methods
  BeforeExec: (line 11)
    code to be executed before any other code in a method body
```

Composition conflicts are solved by enhancing the (**compose**) statement with corrective statements. To solve the above problem, the user would use (**taskorder**) statements to rearrange the conflicting sub-tasks. As a side effect, the problem of the *door example* is solved: We now *goInside* after *openTheDoor*, but *goOutside* before *closeTheCoor*. This is not feasible to declare with simple prioritisation. Hence, we decided to use per-conflict corrections of the relevant parts inside a transformation:

```
SomeClass.(compose
  (branch A aspectDoor)
  (branch B aspectGo)
  (solve
    (conflict samecontext)
    (context Method["start"].Body)                    ; in context Method["start"].Body
    (taskorder A:BeforeExec B:BeforeExec) )            ; the order is first A, then B
  (solve
    (conflict samecontext)
    (context Method["end"].Body)                      ; in context Method["end"].Body
    (taskorder B:BeforeExec A:BeforeExec) )            ; the order is reversed
)
```

It is necessary for a robust resolution to identify conflicting locations more precisely, e.g., with the *LLTS* annotation mechanism (not shown here). This avoids ambiguities between multiple occurrences of similar, potentially conflicting tasks/operators, and relates a certain conflict with its specific resolution.

Apart from (**taskorder**), and (**oporder**) for operator conflicts, the user can choose among several correction operators, depending on the type of conflict. For example, (**ignore**) is used to wipe out false positives. Not every seeming conflict is a real one, or in the application context the composite effect is negligible or even appreciated. The (**eliminate**) operator suppresses the execution of parts of one branch. This is of use if the other conflicting branch would overwrite the changes of the first one or render them dispensable. For instance, modifications in a method that is deleted completely in the other branch may be superfluous in some applications. The user has to decide whether the elimination is without consequences for the composite semantics or not. As a last resort, one branch can be designated to be the *corrective branch* for a certain conflict. As a consequence, this enforces that the ordering of the corrective branch in relation to the conflicting ones be specified explicitly. We apply corrective branches in a *meta-transformation setting*: They are used to adjust the parametrisation of tasks in order to eliminate signature collisions.

4.4 Complexity and Optimisation

The amount of pairwise branch comparisons has quadratic growth in the size of the branch set. Currently a low (< 5) number of branches satisfies our needs, so this complexity is acceptable for the time being. The further development of our concept certainly has to take larger branch sets into consideration. The number of called tasks per branch and their amount of operator calls has a determining influence on the overall complexity of the process. The comparison of tasks is pairwise commutative, hence for t_{A}, t_{B} tasks per branch A, B we have $t_A \cdot t_B$ comparisons, which also has quadratic complexity. The comparison of operators is assumed to be linear in the number of operators, because only few of them have to be inspected at conflicting elements. Non-overlapping modifications of two models do not need to be compared anyway and the remaining operator conflicts will have been solved implicitly during task corrections.

However, the total number of comparisons can become quite large. We are currently investigating optimisation strategies to reduce the comparisons to a minimum. One approach is to execute branches concurrently and implement a fast-fail detector for both task and operator conflicts. This also gives us the opportunity to gain a speed-up by parallelism. Another approach for conflict reduction is to mark shareable transformation parts between branches. For instance, the creation of scaffolding code for the integration of AOP-like *around advice* can be designed to be reusable. We anticipate large shareable parts in our application domain of transformations for middleware-based source-code.

5 Related Work

A large part of the current work about transformation and composition is concerned with aspect weaving and the composition of refactorings. Often, a proposed formalism is taken as a foundation for an *a-priori reasoning* about sequential and non-deterministic composition, dependencies, conflicts, and resolution strategies. This is particularly appropriate for the well-defined nature of high-level aspects and refactorings.

In Condor [9] conditional transformations are used as a foundation for composite refactorings. A major contribution of their work is that a joint precondition of the composition can be derived automatically. Consequently, a composite refactoring is either proven in advance to be non-conflicting or it is not executed at all. This work has also been compared in [10] to AGG [11], which detects dependencies and so-called parallel conflicts by comparing the preconditions of critical pairs in graph transformations. Another explicitly graph-based model for composition conflicts has been shown in [12]. The base program itself, code introductions, and violation rules are represented as graph (matching) patterns. The transitions are labelled to express syntactic and semantic relationships as well as transformation-related information.

A first process-algebraic foundation for proving the correctness of aspect weaving algorithms is presented in [13]. In [14] composition operators build robust sequences of aspects by transferring control at certain crosscut events. Along with composition adapters, conflicts between aspects can be resolved by transformation, for instance, by ordering or partially ignoring interacting aspects. Their concept of composition adapters is closely related to our corrective approach. The Reflex AOP kernel [15] detects aspect interaction based on the reflection of links between cuts and actions as an abstraction of several AOP conceptions.

Reported conflicts must be resolved by the user grounded on pre-defined kernel operators, e.g., for ordering and nesting.

In contrast to the above group of related work, we use an *a-posteriori comparison* of branches on tasks and low-level operators. We consider this rather practical approach helpful for per-conflict resolution strategies that go well with the composition of independent, low-level transformations since they may have arbitrary side-effects. It should yet be profitable to investigate whether a more formal approach can be applied to our perspective on composition issues.

The concept of high-level conflict declarations, as it is adopted in our work, is reversed in [16]. Aspect integration contracts declare which interference is permitted and enhance the comprehensibility of aspect composition as a basis for later conflict analysis. In [17] this concept is adjusted to a more coarse-grained component model within an aspect-oriented middleware and uses contracts for conflicts, dependencies, and resolution. The CompAr language [18] allows the specification of the execution environment of aspects and their inter-aspect constraints as a concise, abstract aspect program. The CompAr compiler, which can be used as a supporting utility for other AOSD techniques, shows constraint violations for a composition of aspects in context with the relevant execution trace. The conflict detection for a combined sequence of operations per abstract resource is presented in [19]. Although on a higher abstraction level, this approach is comparable to a match of conflict declarations on the same context in our concept. The resolution of aspect dependencies on the knowledge of their algebraic properties is shown in [20]. Especially, pseudo-commutativity and the sandwiching technique shown in this paper has a relation to the correction of sub-tasks in our approach. Interactive support for the detection of conflicts is presented by [21]. Based on a dependency-graph analysis, interference criteria check for undefined advice precedence. A user interface presents appropriate conflict reports.

Although in a different context, object-oriented languages need to deal with composition issues, especially concerning multiple inheritance and mixin composition. The research community has produced solutions that share a lot with our approach of corrective operators. After a symmetric combination of Traits [22] a conflict due to identically named methods can be solved by redefinition, aliasing, and exclusion of these methods. To overcome the same problem, Eiffel allows the renaming of methods within the inheriting class [23].

6 Conclusion and Future Work

This paper presents a practical mechanism for the composition of program transformations that are based on low-level modification operators written in the *LLTS* transformation language. Its main contribution is to partition a composition into an expansion phase, in which transformations operate on separated model branches, and a contraction phase, wherein the transformation engine detects composition conflicts and merges the separate modifications, combined with user-defined corrections, back into the origin model.

We have shown several conflict classes that appear on different abstraction levels in the code. Task conflicts are detected based on user-defined annotations that describe several classes of incompatibilities between tasks in different contexts. Operator conflicts are raised by pairwise incompatibilities between operators. Finally, the metamodel implementation checks every modification in a branch for violations of its conditions, and the composite transformation for the overall model semantics. The user has to interpret a generated conflict report that is enriched with an execution record and a narrative semantics of the conflicting tasks. Based on this information the user enhances the composite task by adding corrective operators that directly influence each conflict. This process of automatic detection and manual correction has to be repeated until either all conflicts are solved or the user considers the composition unachievable.

For now, we aimed for the composition and conflict resolution for specific applications. As a next step, we consider the generalisation of compositions towards self-contained, reusable composite transformations. With a careful construction of resolutions using the right repertoire of corrective operators, it should be possible to incrementally improve composite transformations towards a decreasing probability of conflicts. We are currently investigating further conflict classes and are looking for means to increase the semi-automatism of our system. For instance, it is possible to aid the conflict resolution by finding tasks that render others dispensable. In this case the system may suggest the appropriate resolution strategy (**eliminate**). This is also an opportunity to optimise the system performance: The analysis of dispensable transformation parts can be deferred to decrease the number of comparisons. Furthermore, the resolution of order-related conflicts can be effectively aided by adding the anticipated solution strategy directly to the task declaration. This is a recognised strategy within several other approaches in our field and should be implementable for the *LLTS* engine with reasonable effort. For instance, a sound ordering of (AddMethod) and (RenameClass) for the same context could be pre-declared and suggested by the system in case of a conflict. We have developed an Eclipse-based debugger that allows to trace the internal behaviour in details. A tighter integration of the conflict resolution mechanism is currently being implemented, which promises a better comprehension of conflict reports.

Acknowledgements. We thank the reviewers for their constructive comments on our paper and the helpful hints towards a broader view on related work.

References

1. Elrad, T., Filman, R., Bader, A.: Editorial: Aspect-oriented programming (and following articles). In: Elrad, T., Filman, R., Bader, A. (eds.) Communications of the ACM, vol. 44(10) (2001)
2. Kiczales, G., Hilsdale, E., Hugunin, J., Kersten, M., Palm, J., Griswold, W.G.: An overview of AspectJ. In: Knudsen, J.L. (ed.) ECOOP 2001. LNCS, vol. 2072, pp. 327–355. Springer, Heidelberg (2001)

3. Ostermann, K., Kniesel, G.: Independent extensibility - an open challenge for aspectj and hyper/j. In: Lopes, C.V. (ed.) ECOOP 2000 Workshop on Aspects and Dimension of Concerns (2000)
4. Kleppe, A., Warmer, J., Bast, W.: MDA Explained. The model driven architecture: practice and promise. Addison-Wesley, Reading (2003)
5. W3C: XML Path Language (XPath) 2.0, `http://www.w3.org/TR/xpath20/`
6. Steele, G.: COMMON LISP: the language. Digital Press (1990), ISBN 1-55558-041-6
7. Schmied, A.I.: The LLTS Transformation Language. Technical Report TR-2007-1, Institute of Distributed Systems, Ulm University, Germany (online publication pending) (2007)
8. Heuzeroth, D., Aßmann, U., Trifu, M., Kuttruff, V.: The COMPOST, COMPASS, Inject/J and RECODER tool suite for invasive software composition: Invasive Composition with COMPASS aspect-oriented connectors. In: Lämmel, R., Saraiva, J., Visser, J. (eds.) GTTSE 2005. LNCS, vol. 4143, Springer, Heidelberg (2006)
9. Kniesel, G., Koch, H.: Static composition of refactorings. Sci. Comput. Program. 52(1-3), 9–51 (2004)
10. Mens, T., Kniesel, G., Runge, O.: Transformation dependency analysis - a comparison of two approaches. In: Rousseau, R., Urtado, C., Vauttier, S., (eds.) LMO, Hermès Lavoisier, pp. 167–184 (2006)
11. Taentzer, G.: AGG: A graph transformation environment for modeling and validation of software. In: Pfaltz, J.L., Nagl, M., Böhlen, B. (eds.) AGTIVE 2003. LNCS, vol. 3062, Springer, Heidelberg (2004)
12. Havinga, W., Nagy, I., Bergmans, L., Aksit, M.: A graph-based approach to modeling and detecting composition conflicts related to introductions. In: Barry, B.M., de Moor, O. (eds.) AOSD, pp. 85–95. ACM, New York (2007)
13. Andrews, J.H.: Process-algebraic foundations of aspect-oriented programming. In: Yonezawa, A., Matsuoka, S. (eds.) Reflection 2001. LNCS, vol. 2192, pp. 187–209. Springer, Heidelberg (2001)
14. Douence, R., Fradet, P., Südholt, M.: Composition, reuse and interaction analysis of stateful aspects. In: Murphy, G.C., Lieberherr, K.J. (eds.) AOSD, pp. 141–150. ACM, New York (2004)
15. Tanter, É.: Aspects of composition in the Reflex AOP kernel. In: Löwe, W., Südholt, M. (eds.) SC 2006. LNCS, vol. 4089, pp. 98–113. Springer, Heidelberg (2006)
16. Lagaisse, B., Joosen, W., De Win, B.: Managing semantic interference with aspect integration contracts. In: International Workshop on Software-Engineering Properties of Languages for Aspect Technologies (SPLAT), Lancaster, United Kingdom (2004)
17. Greenwood, P., Lagaisse, B., Sanen, F., Coulson, G., Rashid, A., Truyen, E., Joosen, W.: Interactions in AO middleware. In Proceedings of Workshop on Aspects, dependencies and Interactions at ECOOP 2007 (2007)
18. Pawlak, R., Duchien, L., Seinturier, L.: CompAr: Ensuring safe around advice composition. In: Steffen, M., Zavattaro, G. (eds.) FMOODS 2005. LNCS, vol. 3535, pp. 163–178. Springer, Heidelberg (2005)
19. Durr, P., Bergmans, L., Aksit, M.: Reasoning about semantic conflicts between aspects. In: Proceedings of ADI 2006 Aspect, Dependencies, and Interactions Workshop, held at ECOOP, Lancaster University (2006)

20. Apel, S., Liu, J.: On the notion of functional aspects in aspect-oriented refactoring. In: Proceedings of ADI 2006 Aspects, Dependencies, and Interactions Workshop, held at ECOOP, Lancaster University (2006)
21. Störzer, M., Sterr, R., Forster, F.: Detecting precedence-related advice interference. In: 21st IEEE International Conference on Automated Software Engineering (ASE 2006) (2006)
22. Ducasse, S., Nierstrasz, O., Schärli, N., Wuyts, R., Black, A.P.: Traits: A mechanism for fine-grained reuse. ACM Transactions on Programming Languages and Systems 28(2), 331–388 (2006)
23. Meyer, B.: Harnessing multiple inheritance. JOOP (Journal of Object-Oriented Programming) 1(4), 48–51 (1988)

Author Index

Lecture Notes in Computer Science

Sublibrary 2: Programming and Software Engineering

For information about Vols. 1–4290
please contact your bookseller or Springer

Vol. 4954: C. Pautasso, É. Tanter (Eds.), Software Composition. X, 263 pages. 2008.

Vol. 4906: M. Cebulla (Ed.), Object-Oriented Technology. VIII, 204 pages. 2008.

Vol. 4902: P. Hudak, D.S. Warren (Eds.), Practical Aspects of Declarative Languages. X, 333 pages. 2008.

Vol. 4899: K. Yorav (Ed.), Hardware and Software: Verification and Testing. XII, 267 pages. 2008.

Vol. 4888: F. Kordon, O. Sokolsky (Eds.), Composition of Embedded Systems. XII, 221 pages. 2007.

Vol. 4880: S. Overhage, C.A. Szyperski, R. Reussner, J.A. Stafford (Eds.), Software Architectures, Components, and Applications. X, 249 pages. 2008.

Vol. 4849: M. Winckler, H. Johnson, P. Palanque (Eds.), Task Models and Diagrams for User Interface Design. XIII, 299 pages. 2007.

Vol. 4839: O. Sokolsky, S. Taşıran (Eds.), Runtime Verification. VI, 215 pages. 2007.

Vol. 4834: R. Cerqueira, R.H. Campbell (Eds.), Middleware 2007. XIII, 451 pages. 2007.

Vol. 4829: M. Lumpe, W. Vanderperren (Eds.), Software Composition. VIII, 281 pages. 2007.

Vol. 4824: A. Paschke, Y. Biletskiy (Eds.), Advances in Rule Interchange and Applications. XIII, 243 pages. 2007.

Vol. 4807: Z. Shao (Ed.), Programming Languages and Systems. XI, 431 pages. 2007.

Vol. 4799: A. Holzinger (Ed.), HCI and Usability for Medicine and Health Care. XVI, 458 pages. 2007.

Vol. 4789: M. Butler, M.G. Hinchey, M.M. Larrondo-Petrie (Eds.), Formal Methods and Software Engineering. VIII, 387 pages. 2007.

Vol. 4767: F. Arbab, M. Sirjani (Eds.), International Symposium on Fundamentals of Software Engineering. XIII, 450 pages. 2007.

Vol. 4765: A. Moreira, J. Grundy (Eds.), Early Aspects: Current Challenges and Future Directions. X, 199 pages. 2007.

Vol. 4764: P. Abrahamsson, N. Baddoo, T. Margaria, R. Messnarz (Eds.), Software Process Improvement. XI, 225 pages. 2007.

Vol. 4762: K.S. Namjoshi, T. Yoneda, T. Higashino, Y. Okamura (Eds.), Automated Technology for Verification and Analysis. XIV, 566 pages. 2007.

Vol. 4758: F. Oquendo (Ed.), Software Architecture. XVI, 340 pages. 2007.

Vol. 4757: F. Cappello, T. Herault, J. Dongarra (Eds.), Recent Advances in Parallel Virtual Machine and Message Passing Interface. XVI, 396 pages. 2007.

Vol. 4753: E. Duval, R. Klamma, M. Wolpers (Eds.), Creating New Learning Experiences on a Global Scale. XII, 518 pages. 2007.

Vol. 4749: B.J. Krämer, K.-J. Lin, P. Narasimhan (Eds.), Service-Oriented Computing - ICSOC 2007. XIX, 629 pages. 2007.

Vol. 4748: K. Wolter (Ed.), Formal Methods and Stochastic Models for Performance Evaluation. X, 301 pages. 2007.

Vol. 4741: C. Bessière (Ed.), Principles and Practice of Constraint Programming - CP 2007. XV, 890 pages. 2007.

Vol. 4735: G. Engels, B. Opdyke, D.C. Schmidt, F. Weil (Eds.), Model Driven Engineering Languages and Systems. XV, 698 pages. 2007.

Vol. 4716: B. Meyer, M. Joseph (Eds.), Software Engineering Approaches for Offshore and Outsourced Development. X, 201 pages. 2007.

Vol. 4709: F.S. de Boer, M.M. Bonsangue, S. Graf, W.-P. de Roever (Eds.), Formal Methods for Components and Objects. VIII, 297 pages. 2007.

Vol. 4680: F. Saglietti, N. Oster (Eds.), Computer Safety, Reliability, and Security. XV, 548 pages. 2007.

Vol. 4670: V. Dahl, I. Niemelä (Eds.), Logic Programming. XII, 470 pages. 2007.

Vol. 4652: D. Georgakopoulos, N. Ritter, B. Benatallah, C. Zirpins, G. Feuerlicht, M. Schoenherr, H.R. Motahari-Nezhad (Eds.), Service-Oriented Computing ICSOC 2006. XVI, 201 pages. 2007.

Vol. 4640: A. Rashid, M. Aksit (Eds.), Transactions on Aspect-Oriented Software Development IV. IX, 191 pages. 2007.

Vol. 4634: H. Riis Nielson, G. Filé (Eds.), Static Analysis. XI, 469 pages. 2007.

Vol. 4620: A. Rashid, M. Aksit (Eds.), Transactions on Aspect-Oriented Software Development III. IX, 201 pages. 2007.

Vol. 4615: R. de Lemos, C. Gacek, A. Romanovsky (Eds.), Architecting Dependable Systems IV. XIV, 435 pages. 2007.

Vol. 4610: B. Xiao, L.T. Yang, J. Ma, C. Muller-Schloer, Y. Hua (Eds.), Autonomic and Trusted Computing. XVIII, 571 pages. 2007.

Vol. 4609: E. Ernst (Ed.), ECOOP 2007 – Object-Oriented Programming. XIII, 625 pages. 2007.

Vol. 4608: H.W. Schmidt, I. Crnković, G.T. Heineman, J.A. Stafford (Eds.), Component-Based Software Engineering. XII, 283 pages. 2007.

Vol. 4591: J. Davies, J. Gibbons (Eds.), Integrated Formal Methods. IX, 660 pages. 2007.

Vol. 4589: J. Münch, P. Abrahamsson (Eds.), Product-Focused Software Process Improvement. XII, 414 pages. 2007.

Vol. 4574: J. Derrick, J. Vain (Eds.), Formal Techniques for Networked and Distributed Systems – FORTE 2007. XI, 375 pages. 2007.

Vol. 4556: C. Stephanidis (Ed.), Universal Access in Human-Computer Interaction, Part III. XXII, 1020 pages. 2007.

Vol. 4555: C. Stephanidis (Ed.), Universal Access in Human-Computer Interaction, Part II. XXII, 1066 pages. 2007.

Vol. 4554: C. Stephanidis (Ed.), Universal Acess in Human Computer Interaction, Part I. XXII, 1054 pages. 2007.

Vol. 4553: J.A. Jacko (Ed.), Human-Computer Interaction, Part IV. XXIV, 1225 pages. 2007.

Vol. 4552: J.A. Jacko (Ed.), Human-Computer Interaction, Part III. XXI, 1038 pages. 2007.

Vol. 4551: J.A. Jacko (Ed.), Human-Computer Interaction, Part II. XXIII, 1253 pages. 2007.

Vol. 4550: J.A. Jacko (Ed.), Human-Computer Interaction, Part I. XXIII, 1240 pages. 2007.

Vol. 4542: P. Sawyer, B. Paech, P. Heymans (Eds.), Requirements Engineering: Foundation for Software Quality. IX, 384 pages. 2007.

Vol. 4536: G. Concas, E. Damiani, M. Scotto, G. Succi (Eds.), Agile Processes in Software Engineering and Extreme Programming. XV, 276 pages. 2007.

Vol. 4530: D.H. Akehurst, R. Vogel, R.F. Paige (Eds.), Model Driven Architecture - Foundations and Applications. X, 219 pages. 2007.

Vol. 4523: Y.-H. Lee, H.-N. Kim, J. Kim, Y.W. Park, L.T. Yang, S.W. Kim (Eds.), Embedded Software and Systems. XIX, 829 pages. 2007.

Vol. 4498: N. Abdennahder, F. Kordon (Eds.), Reliable Software Technologies - Ada-Europe 2007. XII, 247 pages. 2007.

Vol. 4486: M. Bernardo, J. Hillston (Eds.), Formal Methods for Performance Evaluation. VII, 469 pages. 2007.

Vol. 4470: Q. Wang, D. Pfahl, D.M. Raffo (Eds.), Software Process Dynamics and Agility. XI, 346 pages. 2007.

Vol. 4468: M.M. Bonsangue, E.B. Johnsen (Eds.), Formal Methods for Open Object-Based Distributed Systems. X, 317 pages. 2007.

Vol. 4467: A.L. Murphy, J. Vitek (Eds.), Coordination Models and Languages. X, 325 pages. 2007.

Vol. 4454: Y. Gurevich, B. Meyer (Eds.), Tests and Proofs. IX, 217 pages. 2007.

Vol. 4444: T. Reps, M. Sagiv, J. Bauer (Eds.), Program Analysis and Compilation, Theory and Practice. X, 361 pages. 2007.

Vol. 4440: B. Liblit, Cooperative Bug Isolation. XV, 101 pages. 2007.

Vol. 4408: R. Choren, A. Garcia, H. Giese, H.-f. Leung, C. Lucena, A. Romanovsky (Eds.), Software Engineering for Multi-Agent Systems V. XII, 233 pages. 2007.

Vol. 4406: W. De Meuter (Ed.), Advances in Smalltalk. VII, 157 pages. 2007.

Vol. 4405: L. Padgham, F. Zambonelli (Eds.), Agent-Oriented Software Engineering VII. XII, 225 pages. 2007.

Vol. 4401: N. Guelfi, D. Buchs (Eds.), Rapid Integration of Software Engineering Techniques. IX, 177 pages. 2007.

Vol. 4385: K. Coninx, K. Luyten, K.A. Schneider (Eds.), Task Models and Diagrams for Users Interface Design. XI, 355 pages. 2007.

Vol. 4383: E. Bin, A. Ziv, S. Ur (Eds.), Hardware and Software, Verification and Testing. XII, 235 pages. 2007.

Vol. 4379: M. Südholt, C. Consel (Eds.), Object-Oriented Technology. VIII, 157 pages. 2007.

Vol. 4364: T. Kühne (Ed.), Models in Software Engineering. XI, 332 pages. 2007.

Vol. 4355: J. Julliand, O. Kouchnarenko (Eds.), B 2007: Formal Specification and Development in B. XIII, 293 pages. 2006.

Vol. 4354: M. Hanus (Ed.), Practical Aspects of Declarative Languages. X, 335 pages. 2006.

Vol. 4350: M. Clavel, F. Durán, S. Eker, P. Lincoln, N. Martí-Oliet, J. Meseguer, C. Talcott, All About Maude - A High-Performance Logical Framework. XXII, 797 pages. 2007.

Vol. 4348: S. Tucker Taft, R.A. Duff, R.L. Brukardt, E. Plödereder, P. Leroy, Ada 2005 Reference Manual. XXII, 765 pages. 2006.

Vol. 4346: L. Brim, B.R. Haverkort, M. Leucker, J. van de Pol (Eds.), Formal Methods: Applications and Technology. X, 363 pages. 2007.

Vol. 4344: V. Gruhn, F. Oquendo (Eds.), Software Architecture. X, 245 pages. 2006.

Vol. 4340: R. Prodan, T. Fahringer, Grid Computing. XXIII, 317 pages. 2007.

Vol. 4336: V.R. Basili, H.D. Rombach, K. Schneider, B. Kitchenham, D. Pfahl, R.W. Selby (Eds.), Empirical Software Engineering Issues. XVII, 193 pages. 2007.

Vol. 4326: S. Göbel, R. Malkewitz, I. Iurgel (Eds.), Technologies for Interactive Digital Storytelling and Entertainment. X, 384 pages. 2006.

Vol. 4323: G. Doherty, A. Blandford (Eds.), Interactive Systems. XI, 269 pages. 2007.

Vol. 4322: F. Kordon, J. Sztipanovits (Eds.), Reliable Systems on Unreliable Networked Platforms. XIV, 317 pages. 2007.

Vol. 4309: P. Inverardi, M. Jazayeri (Eds.), Software Engineering Education in the Modern Age. VIII, 207 pages. 2006.

Vol. 4294: A. Dan, W. Lamersdorf (Eds.), Service-Oriented Computing – ICSOC 2006. XIX, 653 pages. 2006.